Linguistic Structure Prediction

Synthesis Lectures on Human Language Technologies

Editor
Graeme Hirst, *University of Toronto*

The series consists of 50- to 150-page monographs on topics relating to natural language processing, computational linguistics, information retrieval, and spoken language understanding. Emphasis is on important new techniques, on new applications, and on topics that combine two or more HLT subfields.

Linguistic Structure Prediction
Noah A. Smith
2011

Learning to Rank for Information Retrieval and Natural Language Processing
Hang Li
2011

Computational Modeling of Human Language Acquisition
Afra Alishahi
2010

Introduction to Arabic Natural Language Processing
Nizar Y. Habash
2010

Cross-Language Information Retrieval
Jian-Yun Nie
2010

Automated Grammatical Error Detection for Language Learners
Claudia Leacock, Martin Chodorow, Michael Gamon, and Joel Tetreault
2010

Data-Intensive Text Processing with MapReduce
Jimmy Lin and Chris Dyer
2010

Semantic Role Labeling
Martha Palmer, Daniel Gildea, and Nianwen Xue
2010

Spoken Dialogue Systems
Kristiina Jokinen and Michael McTear
2009

Introduction to Chinese Natural Language Processing
Kam-Fai Wong, Wenjie Li, Ruifeng Xu, and Zheng-sheng Zhang
2009

Introduction to Linguistic Annotation and Text Analytics
Graham Wilcock
2009

Dependency Parsing
Sandra Kübler, Ryan McDonald, and Joakim Nivre
2009

Statistical Language Models for Information Retrieval
ChengXiang Zhai
2008

Linguistic Structure Prediction

Noah A. Smith

ISBN: 978-3-031-01015-6 paperback
ISBN: 978-3-031-02143-5 ebook

DOI 10.1007/978-3-031-02143-5

A Publication in the Springer series
SYNTHESIS LECTURES ON HUMAN LANGUAGE TECHNOLOGIES

Lecture #13
Series Editor: Graeme Hirst, *University of Toronto*
Series ISSN
Synthesis Lectures on Human Language Technologies
Print 1947-4040 Electronic 1947-4059

Linguistic Structure Prediction

Noah A. Smith
Carnegie Mellon University

SYNTHESIS LECTURES ON HUMAN LANGUAGE TECHNOLOGIES #13

ABSTRACT

A major part of natural language processing now depends on the use of text data to build linguistic analyzers. We consider statistical, computational approaches to modeling linguistic structure. We seek to unify across many approaches and many kinds of linguistic structures. Assuming a basic understanding of natural language processing and/or machine learning, we seek to bridge the gap between the two fields. Approaches to decoding (i.e., carrying out linguistic structure prediction) and supervised and unsupervised learning of models that predict discrete structures as outputs are the focus. We also survey natural language processing problems to which these methods are being applied, and we address related topics in probabilistic inference, optimization, and experimental methodology.

KEYWORDS

natural language processing, computational linguistics, machine learning, decoding, supervised learning, unsupervised learning, structured prediction, probabilistic inference, statistical modeling

Contents

Preface

The title of this book is ambiguous. The intended reading involves structure of a linguistic nature (*linguistic structure*) that is to be predicted. This is the meaning implied by the disambiguated representation below:

$$[\,[\text{linguistic structure}\,]_{\text{noun phrase}}\ \text{prediction}\,]_{\text{noun phrase}}$$

By the noun phrase *linguistic structure*, we refer to symbolic representations of language posited by some theory of language. The representation above is a linguistic structure. The noun phrase *linguistic structure prediction* refers to automatic methods for annotating, analyzing, or disambiguating text.

The alternative reading of the title attaches the adjective *linguistic* to *prediction*, leaving it unclear what kind of structure is to be predicted, but suggesting that the method of prediction involves linguistics. The ambiguity in the title serves as a reminder that ambiguity is ubiquitous in human language, especially from the point of view of computer programs, and underlies much of the challenge of automatic natural language processing. The title is designed to evoke the three intellectual strands tied together in this volume.

Statistics: The word *prediction* suggests reasoning about something unknown or invisible. The techniques presented here aim to take electronic text data[1] as input and provide as output a hypothesized analysis of the text. Formulating this as a prediction problem leads naturally to the use of statistical models and methods that use past experience, or exposure to data, to make new predictions.

Computer science: The word *structure* evokes ideas about complexity and interconnectedness; in machine learning the term *structure prediction* (or *structured prediction*) is used to refer to prediction of a set of interrelated variables. Such problems arise in areas like computer vision (e.g., interpreting parts of a visual scene), computational biology (e.g., modeling how protein molecules fold), and, of course, speech and text processing. Here, we are interested in discrete structures that can be defined succinctly in mathematical terms and manipulated efficiently by computer programs.

Linguistics: The word *linguistic*, of course, refers to the fact that those discrete structures are stipulated by some theory of human languages. Linguistic structure prediction is perhaps most strongly associated with parsing sentences into syntactic structures as used in theories accounting for well-formedness of some conceivable sentences vis-à-vis others, but the techniques are

[1] Although we assume text to be a sequence of orthographic symbols, the methods here are also relevant when our starting point is even more raw, such as images of text written on a page or recordings of speech.

applicable at other levels of linguistic analysis as well: phonology, morphology, semantics, discourse, and so on. Linguistics as a field of inquiry is notable for the ways in which computational models have influenced theories.

In summary, then, this is a book about machine learning (ML), natural language processing (NLP), and computational linguistics (CL),[2] though it does not claim to cover any of them completely or in a balanced way. We aim for neither the union nor the intersection, but rather a useful and coherent selection of important and useful ideas that are best understood when synthesized.

HISTORICAL CONTEXT

Having parsed the title, we next attempt to explain the existence of this book.

In the past decade, NLP and ML have become increasingly interested in each other. The connection between the broader fields of linguistics and statistics is much older, going back to linguists like George Kingsley Zipf and Zellig Harris who emphasized the centrality of *data* in reasoning about the nature of language, and also to Claude Shannon and the information theorists of the post-World War II era who saw language processing problems like machine translation as problems of decryption that called for statistical reasoning (Weaver, 1949).

The trends of each field have recently deepened this connection substantially. In NLP, the rise in availability of enormous amounts of diverse, multilingual text data, due largely to the rise of the web, has opened the question of just how far data-driven approaches to text processing can go. In ML, advances in graphical models for probabilistic reasoning have permitted the exploration of learning problems with high-dimensional outputs far beyond the classical prediction problems addressed by regression and binary classification. Both fields have been enabled greatly by continued increases in the computational power of computers, of course.

Occasionally tension appears to arise between the field of linguistics and the use of data, particularly among NLP researchers. Linguistics-firsters have seen data-driven methods as "shallow" or, worse, unprincipled and ignorant of linguistic theory. Data-firsters have derided linguistics-based systems as "brittle" and labor-intensive, often questioning the helpfulness of representations that require heavy processing of the raw, "pure" data. Here we reject the linguistics-or-statistics choice as a false one that is based on uncharitably narrow views of what constitutes "data" and what constitutes "linguistics." The preponderance of evidence suggests that NLP works better when it uses data, and that ML works better when it takes into account domain knowledge. In NLP, "domain knowledge" often means linguistics. We take the view that linguistic knowledge is crucial in defining representations of NLP problems and efficient algorithms for handling those representations. Even when it is not acknowledged, it is implicit in NLP researchers' design decisions whenever we build

[2]We will use the term *NLP* throughout. Unfortunately there is no consensus on how this term should be defined. We use it here to refer to the class of computational problems of textual or linguistic analysis, generation, representation, or acquisition. This might include speech processing or text retrieval, though we do not address those here. Some researchers in the field distinguish between NLP and CL, using the former to emphasize engineering goals and the latter to emphasize the *human* language faculty and the use of computational models to understand the nature of language as a natural phenomenon. We do not take a position on whether NLP and CL are the same.

software that handles text. We do not claim that linguistic processing by machines should resemble linguistic processing by humans, but rather that scientific theories about linguistic data—the by-product of human linguistic behavior—offer useful insights for automatic linguistic processing. Of course, linguists do not generally keep NLP in mind as they do their work, so not all of linguistics should be expected to be useful.

Meanwhile, statistics and machine learning offer elegant, declarative formalisms and effective algorithms for transforming raw text data into forms that can support useful, text-related applications. While the abstractions of ML are attractive and show promise for general solutions that can be used in many fields, these abstractions cannot be applied to language problems in ignorance, and so in this book we keep NLP in mind as we explore these abstractions.[3]

WHAT TO EXPECT

This volume aims to bridge the gap between NLP and ML. We begin in chapter 1 by arguing that many central problems in NLP can be viewed as problems of structure prediction (i.e., reasoning about many interdependent events). We hope to demystify some of the core assumptions of NLP for ML researchers, explaining certain conventions and tradeoffs. In chapter 2, we turn to decoding: algorithmic frameworks for making predictions about the linguistic structure of an input. Decoding algorithms often shape the way NLP researchers think about their problems, and understanding the connections among algorithms may lead to more freedom in designing solutions. In chapters 3 and 4, we aim to provide a survey of current ML techniques suitable for linguistic structures. The goal is a unified treatment that reveals the similarities and connections among the many modern approaches to statistical NLP. Despite the complex history leading up to this set of techniques, they are, in many cases, quite similar to each other, though the differences are important to understand if one is to meaningfully use and extend them. Chapter 5 considers important inference problems that arise in NLP, beyond decoding, and the appendices consider topics of practical or historical interest.

The book assumes a basic understanding of probability and statistics, and of algorithms and data structures. The reader will be better prepared if she has taken an introductory course in ML and/or NLP, or read an introductory textbook for either (e.g., Bishop, 2006, for ML, Jurafsky and Martin, 2008, for NLP, and Manning and Schütze, 1999 for statistical NLP). The book was written with three kinds of readers in mind: graduate students, NLP researchers wanting to better understand ML, and ML researchers wanting to better understand NLP. Basic familiarity with NLP and ML is assumed, though probably only one or the other suffices.

WHAT NOT TO EXPECT

Linguists will find nothing here about specific linguistic theories, and perhaps too much about shallow and syntactic models of language. This is simply because so much remains to be done in the

[3]Given the accessibility of NLP problems, we suspect the book may be useful for researchers seeking to use ML for structured problems in other domains, as well. We all do know at least a little about language.

development of learnable, "deep" linguistic models. We hope this book will shed some light on how that development can take place and inspire more linguists to consider how interesting linguistic effects can be described in modern computational frameworks (e.g., feature-based statistical models) and then implemented through the use of appropriate algorithms. Further, we invite the challenge to find cases where the current framework is truly insufficient to model linguistic phenomena of interest, and note that methods that use "incomplete data" may provide a principled starting point for anyone who is unsatisfied with what is visible in data alone.

ML researchers may already be familiar with many of the modeling techniques in chapters 3 and 4, and may wonder why these models' application to language is any different. The short answer is to consider chapter 2 and note the challenges of doing inference efficiently in the presence of features that try to capture linguistic phenomena. Neither the imagination of linguists nor the nature of text data can be confined to the classical formalisms of machine learning.

Engineers may be annoyed at the level of abstraction; very few algorithms are presented for direct implementation. We often deliberately use declarative problem statements rather than procedural algorithms. This is partly for pedagogical reasons, and partly because this book is written primarily for researchers, not developers. In a similar vein, researchers in machine translation, an application of NLP that has become increasingly important and increasingly engineering-focused, may question the relevance of this book for their problems. To date, the cross-fertilization between translation research and other NLP research has been tremendous. Examples from translation are occasionally mentioned, but we do not believe the problem of translation should be treated in a fundamentally different way from other linguistic structure prediction problems. Source-language input and target-language output sentences are both linguistic structures. We hope that the material here will be useful to translation researchers seeking to better exploit ML.

A major topic that this book does not address directly is the scalability of learning algorithms. At this writing, this is an area of intense activity. Our view is that "scaling up" should not require a fundamental change in representations or the choice of learning algorithms, but rather innovation of new methods of approximation. Hence approximations that permit us to efficiently exploit very large datasets or large computer clusters should be considered orthogonal to the kinds of models we seek to learn, with the possible benefit of allowing more powerful models to be built. Often, large amounts of data are found to improve the performance of simpler models and learning approaches, relative to more complex ones that appear superior in smaller-data settings. Since very large amounts of data are not available for all languages, domains, and tasks, well-founded ML and structured NLP are still worthwhile research investments. In short, it is quite possible that scalability concerns will lead to a paradigm change in ML and NLP, but at this writing, we are unsure.

Computational linguists who work on natural language generation may be frustrated by the emphasis on analysis problems (e.g., parsing and sequence models). At a high level of abstraction, analysis and generation are inverses: analysis predicts linguistic structure from surface text (itself a sequential structure), and generation predicts surface text from linguistic structure (or, in some cases, other text). It is perhaps desirable to characterize natural language structure in such a way that the solutions to analysis and generation can be described as inverse operations (e.g., as with finite-state transducers). It remains to be seen whether linguistic structure prediction is a viable approach to generation.

ROAD MAP

The material here roughly corresponds to an advanced graduate course taught at Carnegie Mellon University in 2006–2009, though largely reordered. There are five main chapters and four appendices:

- Chapter 1 is a survey of many examples of linguistic structures that have been considered as outputs to be predicted from text.
- Chapter 2 presents the linear modeling framework and discusses a wide range of algorithmic techniques for predicting structures with linear models, known as "decoding."
- Chapter 3 discusses learning to predict structures from training data consisting of input-output pairs. This is known as supervised learning.
- Chapter 4 turns to learning when the training data are inputs only (no outputs), or otherwise incomplete. We consider unsupervised and hidden variable learning. (Semisupervised learning is not covered.)
- Chapter 5 discusses statistical reasoning algorithms other than decoding, many of which are used as subroutines in the learning techniques of chapters 3 and 4.

The first two appendices discuss some loose ends of practical interest:

- Numerical optimization algorithms (A) and
- Experimentation methods (B).

The remaining appendices are of mainly historical interest:

- A discussion of "maximum entropy" and its connection to linear models (C) and
- A discussion of locally normalized conditional models (D).

Acknowledgments

The development of this book was supported in part by the National Science Foundation through grants IIS-0915187 and CAREER IIS-1054319.

This book is the outcome of my interactions with many people. I thank first those who have taken the "Language and Statistics II" course (11-762) at Carnegie Mellon University in 2006–2009. This monograph reflects much of the dialogue in those lectures. I thank ARK members and alumni: Desai Chen, Shay Cohen, Dipanjan Das, Chris Dyer, Philip Gianfortoni, Kevin Gimpel, Michael Heilman, André Martins, Zack McCord, Daniel Mills, Behrang Mohit, Brendan O'Connor, Naomi Saphra, Nathan Schneider, Cari Sisson, Dan Tasse, Matthew Thompson, Mengqiu Wang, Tae Yano, and Dani Yogatama. I have learned at least as much from you about how to tell this story as you did about the story, and I hope this artifact will serve as a useful reference in your future work.

The project that became this monograph started as a tutorial at the 26th International Conference on Machine Learning in Montréal, June 2009. Thanks to Jen Neville for suggesting the tutorial and the audience for questions and conversations. Thanks to Graeme Hirst for convincing me to expand the tutorial into this volume and for his patience and advice during the writing. Thanks to Mike Morgan and C.L. Tondo for their encouragement, patience, and gentle introduction to the world of book publishing.

The way of thinking presented in this monograph is my own, but it is largely owed to the intellectual influences of Fred Jelinek (a giant now sorely missed) and to having worked closely with Jason Eisner and David Smith. They no doubt would have done it differently, but I hope they'd rather have this monograph than none at all.

This monograph was also shaped by (often subtly, sometimes radically) alternative ways of thinking, and for exposure to many of those over the years, I thank Pedro Aguiar, Jason Baldridge, Alan Black, David Blei, Jamie Callan, Jaime Carbonell, Eugene Charniak (thanks especially for Charniak, 1993), William Cohen, Michael Collins, Hal Daumé, Jacob Eisenstein, Mário Figueiredo, Sharon Goldwater, Carlos Guestrin, Rebecca Hwa, Mark Johnson, Sanjeev Khudanpur, Gary King, Dan Klein, John Lafferty, Alon Lavie, Lori Levin, Chris Manning, Dan Melamed, Tom Mitchell, Ray Mooney, Kemal Oflazer, Miles Osborne, Fernando Pereira, Philip Resnik, Roni Rosenfeld, Dan Roth, Bryan Routledge, Mark Steedman, Stephan Vogel, Bonnie Webber, Jan Wiebe, Eric Xing, and David Yarowsky. I thank Phil Blunsom, Shay Cohen, Chris Dyer, Jacob Eisenstein, Jenny Finkel, Kevin Gimpel, Michael Heilman, Adam Lopez, André Martins, Brendan O'Connor, Nathan Schneider, David Smith, and the anonymous reviewers for comments on drafts. All errors are, of course, solely the responsibility of the author.

And thanks to Karen Thickman for her patience and support; she only reminded me once that I swore, after finishing my thesis, that I'd never do anything like that again.

This volume is dedicated (i) to the memory of my father, Wayne Smith (1943–2010), to whom I owe more than can be expressed in words, and who would have loved to have seen this project completed, (ii) in honor of Julie Brahmer, the physician whose work extended by a precious 20% the time I was able to share with him, and (iii) in honor of my sister, Maria Smith, who is wise and gentle beyond her years and inspires me to believe that Dad is still with us.

Noah A. Smith
Pittsburgh
May 2011

CHAPTER 1

Representations and Linguistic Data

Among the various problems in computing that involve text—such as text retrieval from user queries or text mining—NLP problems are those that appear to fail when we view a piece of text as a "bag of words." In its simplest form, a bag of words model represents a piece of text by a histogram, or a mapping of words in the language to their frequencies in the document. Formally, let $\Sigma = \{\sigma_1, \ldots, \sigma_V\}$ be the vocabulary of V words in the language. A piece of text $\boldsymbol{x}$ may be understood as a vector $\mathbf{v} = \langle v_1, v_2, \ldots, v_V \rangle$, such that v_i is the frequency of the ith vocabulary word in the document. In our notation,

$$v_j = \mathit{freq}(\sigma_j; \boldsymbol{x}) \tag{1.1}$$

This representation, and ones derived from it, have been extremely successful in text retrieval (Manning et al., 2008).

NLP research can often be distinguished from text retrieval and mining in its focus on *structural* representations of text, or of the language the text is written in. This might include modeling deeper properties of the words in the bag, or their relationships to each other, or both. The assumption is that the linguistic structure of the text must be analyzed, inferred, or, in our terminology, *predicted*, for correct interpretation and action by a program. The bag of words is merely the simplest example of structure, one that can be deduced almost immediately upon observing a piece of (English) text.[1]

Many alternative representations are harder to obtain. Considerable NLP research has been devoted to the transformation of a piece of text into a desired representation. This chapter surveys examples of such representations. Each can be understood as a class of discrete structures that have been developed in linguistics or NLP for the purpose of describing and explaining aspects of the phenomenon of human language. In later chapters, we will mostly abstract away from the specific types of structure to be predicted, adopting a general methodology.

The different kinds of representations are organized roughly by increasing depth of linguistic analysis:

- sequence prediction (section 1.1),

[1] At this writing, NLP has focused largely on prediction problems alone, separate from any particular application, taking the view that the same modular linguistic structure predictors can be used within a wide range of applications. There is considerable dissent across the field about which kinds of predictors are useful in which applications, or might be someday. We will sidestep those debates, taking it for granted that *some* linguistic structure predictors are useful, and arguing that a general understanding will aid the development of additional ones.

- sequence segmentation (section 1.2),
- sequence labeling (section 1.3), and
- syntax (section 1.4).

In sections 1.5–1.10, we briefly discuss deeper levels of analysis that correspond more closely to the meaning of a piece of text. These are not the focus of the models introduced throughout this book, but considerable current research is applying linguistic structure prediction methods to them as well. We also discuss linguistic types as a kind of linguistic structure to be predicted (section 1.11).

Our coverage is not exhaustive; we seek to provide pointers into relevant parts of the literature, but do not attempt a full review. In particular, we do not address problems of natural language generation, in which meaningful, fluent text is the desired *output*. New linguistic structure representations are being proposed at a steady rate, and we provide some discussion about why this is the case.

1.1 SEQUENTIAL PREDICTION

We begin by noting the inherent sequential structure of a piece of text; a sentence or document is a sequence of words or characters. Let Σ denote a discrete, finite set of symbols. Σ^* denotes the set of all *sequences* of symbols. Suppose we observe the sequence $\boldsymbol{x} = \langle x_1, x_2, \ldots, x_{t-1} \rangle$, with each $x_i \in \Sigma$. Can we predict the *next* symbol, x_t?

Although modern NLP rarely studies sequential prediction directly (an exception is language modeling for noisy text input devices; see, for example, Goodman et al., 2002; Rashid and Smith, 2008), it is an important idea to understand because it underlies a very important modeling tool: the **language model**.

A language model defines a probability distribution over the next symbol given the symbols that precede it (referred to as the "history"). The simplest is a "unigram" model, which defines the probability of the next symbol to be insensitive to the history; each word in a document, for example, is drawn from a multinomial distribution over Σ. To account for the probability of *not* generating the next word (i.e., of reaching the end of the document), some probability is allocated for a special stop symbol, which we denote $\bigcirc$. If we wish to calculate the probability of the *whole* sequence $\boldsymbol{x} = \langle x_1, x_2, \ldots, x_n \rangle$ (where $n > 0$ is the arbitrary length of the sequence), we multiply together the probabilities of the independent (and identically distributed) events that produced the sequence, one per x_i. We use π_σ to denote the probability of choosing symbol $\sigma \in \Sigma$. The full set of probabilities is $\boldsymbol{\pi} = \{\pi_\sigma\}_{\sigma \in \Sigma \cup \{\bigcirc\}}$. We use the function form $p_{\boldsymbol{\pi}} : \Sigma^* \rightarrow \mathbb{R}_{\geq 0}$ to denote the probability distribution over sequences given the distribution defined by $\boldsymbol{\pi}$:

$$p_{\boldsymbol{\pi}}(\boldsymbol{x}) = \left(\prod_{i=1}^{n} \pi_{x_i} \right) \times \pi_{\bigcirc} \tag{1.2}$$

If we let $\mathit{freq}(\sigma; \boldsymbol{x})$ denote the number of times that symbol $\sigma \in \Sigma$ occurs in the sequence $\boldsymbol{x}$,

$$\mathit{freq}(\sigma; \boldsymbol{x}) = \Big| \{ i \in \{1, 2, \ldots, n\} \mid x_i = \sigma \} \Big| \tag{1.3}$$

then an expression equivalent to equation 1.2, but based on the unique symbol types, is given by:

$$p_{\boldsymbol{\pi}}(\boldsymbol{x}) = \left(\prod_{\sigma \in \Sigma} (\pi_\sigma)^{freq(\sigma;\boldsymbol{x})} \right) \times \pi_{\circledcirc} \tag{1.4}$$

The unigram model views the text as an unordered bag of words. The probability assigned to a sequence $\boldsymbol{x}$ only depends on the frequencies of symbols in $\boldsymbol{x}$, not on the order in which those symbols occur. Apart from its static knowledge about which words occur more or less often, the unigram model does not use any historical or contextual information (e.g., recent words or position in the sentence) to predict the next word.

More generally, $(m + 1)$-gram models[2] are a class of language models that use a finite amount of history—the previous m words—to predict the next word. Let X_i be a random variable over the ith word in a sequence. At time step t, the history corresponds to the observable outcomes of random variables $\langle X_1, X_2, \ldots, X_{t-1} \rangle$. These outcomes are denoted by $\langle x_1, x_2, \ldots, x_{t-1} \rangle$. We seek to predict the value of the random variable X_t. In this notation, the $(m + 1)$-gram model defines the conditional probability:

$$\begin{aligned} &\overbrace{p(X_t = \sigma \mid X_1 = x_1, X_2 = x_2, \ldots, X_{t-1} = x_{t-1})}^{\text{probability of next symbol given entire history}} \\ &= \underbrace{p(X_t = \sigma \mid X_{t-m} = x_{t-m}, X_{t-m+1} = x_{t-m+1}, \ldots, X_{t-1} = x_{t-1})}_{\text{probability of next symbol given only the past } m \text{ symbols}} \end{aligned} \tag{1.5}$$

That is, the tth symbol depends only on the m symbols immediately preceding it. The unigram model is the case where $m = 0$.[3]

Note that we've said nothing about how this probability model might go about making a prediction of what the next symbol will be. (The reader may have some intuition that such a prediction might involve considering symbols whose probability given the history is relatively high.) The reason is that language models are usually not used on their own for making predictions. They usually serve a role as *components* in applications like translation and speech recognition. Although no linguistic structure prediction problem is solved by the mere application of language models, it is important to note that the $(m + 1)$-gram model *does* imply a linguistic representation, namely that a piece of text is a bag of (overlapping and therefore statistically interdependent) $(m + 1)$-grams, each in $\Sigma^{(m+1)}$.

We have also not discussed the provenance of the values $\boldsymbol{\pi}$ that score different candidates for the next word. We will return to that matter—learning the model—in chapter 3, in a more general setting. See chapters 4, 8, 10, and 13–15 of Jelinek (1997) for more about language models based on words.

[2]These are traditionally called "n-gram models."

[3]Note that when $m > 0$, the probabilities $\boldsymbol{\pi}$ must now be understood as *conditional* probabilities of a word given a history; we might denote by $\pi_{\sigma,\sigma'}$ the probability of σ' given that the previous symbol is σ (a bigram probability, used when $m = 1$). In general, there is one π for every m-gram consisting of an $(m - 1)$-symbol history and a candidate for the next symbol.

1.2 SEQUENCE SEGMENTATION

Segmentation is the problem of breaking a sequence into contiguous parts called segments. More formally, if the input is $\boldsymbol{x} = \langle x_1, \ldots, x_n \rangle$, then a segmentation can be written as

$$\left\langle \langle x_1, \ldots, x_{y_1} \rangle, \langle x_{y_1+1}, \ldots, x_{y_1+y_2} \rangle, \ldots, \langle x_{1+\sum_{i=1}^{m-2} y_i}, \ldots, x_{\sum_{i=1}^{m-1} y_i} \rangle, \langle x_{1+\sum_{i=1}^{m-1} y_i}, \ldots, x_n \rangle \right\rangle$$

where the structure $\boldsymbol{y} = \langle y_1, \ldots, y_m \rangle$ corresponds to the segment lengths, in order, and $\sum_{i=1}^{m} y_i = n$. The number of segments, here denoted m, is not generally assumed to be known in advance.

Word segmentation considers a piece of text as a sequence of characters (i.e., Σ is the character set), and aims to break the text into words. In English, whitespace is a strong clue for word boundaries, but it is neither necessary nor sufficient. For example, in some situations, we might wish to treat *New York* as a single word, or *Montréal, Québec* as three words (not two): *Montréal* followed by , followed by *Québec*. For languages like English, this is often called **tokenization** and is more a matter of convention than a serious research problem. For languages like Chinese, which does not separate words with whitespace, the problem is considerably more difficult. Many standards exist for Chinese word segmentation, and it is unclear which is best for any application (Sproat and Emerson, 2003). In languages with rich agglutinative morphology, such as Turkish, more aggressive tokenization (rather than simply using whitespace) may be appropriate, and may require sophisticated models for unraveling the morphological structure of words (see section 1.3.1). As with many NLP problems, native speakers, including experts, may not agree on conventions for splitting words into tokens. Segmentation problems also arise in modeling lexical acquisition from unsegmented streams, simulating child language acquisition (Goldwater et al., 2006a).

Sentence segmentation involves breaking a tokenized document into sentences (i.e., here Σ is the tokenized word vocabulary). Punctuation usually provides the strongest clues for sentence segmentation; in English, if punctuation has been tokenized separately from real words, then the period symbol . is likely to occur at positions x_{y_i}, though it is neither a necessary nor a sufficient condition for the end of a sentence (e.g., it occurs after abbreviations mid-sentence, and some sentences end in *?* or *!*). Sentence segmentation is generally seen as a solved problem for English text that follows standard punctuation conventions (see, for example, Reynar and Ratnaparkhi, 1997), though it is more difficult for casual, unedited, or unconventional text.

Segmentation can also be used to model larger segments of documents, such as objective and subjective regions (Pang and Lee, 2004) or topically coherent parts (Eisenstein and Barzilay, 2008, Hearst, 1994).

Notice that segmentation might be a preprocessing step before constructing a language model (section 1.1). Very often linguistic predictors are combined sequentially in a "pipeline," so that the output of one serves as the input to another. This modularity is advantageous from a research and development perspective, but it can lead to the propagation of errors from one module to the next.

If we build a language model on poorly segmented text, for instance, its predictive performance will suffer.[4]

1.3 WORD CLASSES AND SEQUENCE LABELING

A simple observation about words in text is that they are sparsely distributed, usually in power-law or "Zipfian" distributions. For this reason, data sparseness—the situation where a huge number of events are possible, but most are very rare in a given sample—is a recurring theme in NLP, and one way to mitigate it is to map words to a more abstract and smaller set of symbols. Fortunately, this is also an old idea in linguistics.

Stemming and **lemmatization** are simple solutions to this problem where each word is mapped to a simpler vocabulary. These are typically solved using simple rule-based systems. Stemming usually involves deleting certain suffixes known to serve as grammatical markers (e.g., *s* and *es* mark the plural form of most English nouns). Lemmatization involves mapping words in a lexicon of inflected forms to canonical stems (e.g., *gave*, *given*, and *give* map to *give*). Some information is lost in these transformations; for example, the semantically distinct words *organ* and *organization* both map to *organ* in the Porter (1980) stemmer. For many applications (notably, document retrieval), the reduction in data sparseness may make up for the conflation of semantically unrelated words. Usually (at least for English), stemming and lemmatization are implemented using deterministic rules, not the kinds of structure-predicting models we will consider.

Syntactic word categories, also known as **parts of speech** (POS), are a common choice for abstracting away from raw words. Part of speech sets range from coarse ("noun," "verb," etc.) to very fine-grained (e.g., "singular common noun" for *cat*, "plural proper noun" for *Americans*, and "third person singular present-tense verb that can take a sentential argument" for *knows*). Formally, let Λ be a finite set of part of speech tags such that $|\Lambda| \ll |\Sigma|$; the task of **part of speech tagging** maps (for any $n > 0$), $\Sigma^n \rightarrow \Lambda^n$. If $\boldsymbol{x} = \langle x_1, \ldots, x_n \rangle$ is an input sequence of words, then $\boldsymbol{y} = \langle y_1, \ldots, y_n \rangle$ denotes a sequence in Λ^n, where each y_i is the POS for x_i.

POS tagging involves mapping words to their tags *in context*. The distinction between a **token** (a linguistic element in context, such as an utterance manifested at some point in time) and a **type** (an abstract linguistic form that is, perhaps, reused in many utterances) is important to grasp. The mapping of vocabulary items (types) in Σ to their POS tags is quite different, and in many cases may require a mapping into subsets of Λ, due to ambiguity.

To take an example, the word *bills* can be a noun (plural of *bill*, a statement of charges, among other meanings) or a verb (third person present form of *bill*, to send a statement of charges). The word *broke* can be a verb (the past tense of *break*) or an adjective (referring to a state of having no money). These facts render the following sentence at least four-ways ambiguous (as far as part of speech structure):[5]

[4]Some recent research has sought to combine multiple predictors into a single joint predictor; see Cohen and Smith (2007), Finkel and Manning (2009), Finkel et al. (2006).

[5]Note that we have tokenized the sentence, splitting punctuation, and indexed each token.

After$_1$ paying$_2$ the$_3$ medical$_4$ bills$_5$,$_6$ Frances$_7$ was$_8$ nearly$_9$ broke$_{10}$.$_{11}$

It is possible to build part of speech taggers that assign tags to each word x_i independently of the tags assigned to others. The majority of taggers, however, consider the full sequence $\boldsymbol{y}$, predicting the whole sequence "all at once," because the syntactic categories of nearby words can help to disambiguate a word. In the example above, *bills*$_5$ is easily disambiguated as a noun if we know that the preceding word is an adjective, since nouns are far more likely than verbs to follow adjectives. Similarly, *broke*$_{10}$ is an adjective, signaled by the fact that the clause it appears in has a verb (*was*$_8$).

Decisions about adjacent (or, more generally, nearby) words are, then, interdependent; words and POS tags near an ambiguous word are important, especially for handling unknown words. For example, in

After$_1$ biweffing$_2$ the$_3$ kergool$_4$,$_5$ Frances$_6$ was$_7$ nearly$_8$ mallunt$_9$.$_{10}$

it is expected that native speakers will interpret *biweffing*$_2$ as a verb (because of its *ing* ending and its context between a temporal preposition and a determiner), *kergool*$_4$ as a noun (because of its position after a determiner), and *mallunt*$_9$ as an adjective or past participle (because of its position after an adverb).[6]

At this writing, POS tagging performance, as measured on English newstext, has converged to per-word-error rates below three percent of tokens (Toutanova et al., 2003). POS tagging of text in most other domains and languages remains an open challenge (Blitzer et al., 2006, Gimpel et al., 2011).

It is important to note that the set of POS tags (here, Λ) is a choice made by the developer of the POS tagger. There are a few conventions for English, with the number of tags ranging from fewer than twenty coarse tags to more than a hundred. POS tags sometimes incorporate much more detailed information about word structure and grammatical type, encoding a rich combinatorial structure (e.g., "supertagging" as in Bangalore and Joshi, 1999, or the morphologically-enhanced tags of the Prague Dependency Treebank for Czech, Böhmová et al., 2003). The difficulty of the POS tagging task depends on the POS tag conventions, of course, and the choice of a tag set should depend on the language and what the tagged text will be used for.

1.3.1 MORPHOLOGICAL DISAMBIGUATION

A more difficult problem that arises for languages with rich word-formation systems is **morphological disambiguation**. In languages like Turkish, German, and Arabic, many words are formed by concatenating smaller, meaning-bearing units called *morphemes*. English shows this effect very slightly (e.g., the word *morphemes* consists of the stem *morpheme* and the plural-marking suffix *s*; *slightly* consists of the stem *slight* and the derivational suffix *ly* that makes the word an adverb). In

[6] Readers who find this Lewis Carroll-inspired example unrealistically whimsical are invited to consider scientific literature in a field in which they lack training, or policy documents from the United States federal government, or Twitter messages written by teenagers.

some languages, words can break into many meaningful parts (or, conversely, we say that words can be formed by combining morphemes in many different ways, often with a combinatorial explosion of possible surface words to be found in text). Further, there are often sound changes at the boundaries of morphemes, which may be visible in the spellings of the words (e.g., deletion or insertion of characters), or there may be spelling changes that have nothing to do with sound changes. For example, in English, *happy* and *ness* usually concatenate into *happiness*, not *happyness*.

The need for morphological disambiguation is more clear when we consider languages like Turkish, which has very rich morphological structure (see figure 1.1 for an example due to Eryiğit et al., 2008). Turkish phenomena include derivational and inflectional affixes, case endings, and vowel harmony, all of which combine to complicate the mapping from a surface string to its disambiguated sequence of morphemes.

In the word *öğrencilerin*, there are three morphemes. The first, *öğrenci*, translates to *student*, while the suffixes *ler* and *in* make the word plural and possessive, respectively. When we consider the explosion of morphological variants of each word in Turkish, it becomes clear that a massive vocabulary is conceivable, only a small fraction of which will be observed in a finite sample of text. Splitting words into smaller parts will be important for overcoming the data sparseness problem.

Segmenting a piece of text into morphemes is essentially the same as word segmentation, except that the units desired happen to be shorter in length and possibly more difficult to separate (whitespace may not be as reliable). The most challenging part is often segmenting words into morphemes, recovering canonical forms of the morphemes (e.g., "undoing" spelling changes at morpheme boundaries) and tagging the morphemes with POS or other information to make them less ambiguous. Because different languages have different morphological properties and because different linguistic annotation efforts have chosen different conventions, there is no universal convention for representing morphological analyses.

Research on computational models of morphology has focused much more extensively on the representation of a language's morphological lexicon, or mapping between valid surface words and their analyses at the level of types rather than tokens in context. Implemented models of morphology based on finite-state machines have received considerable attention and can be licensed for many languages (Beesley and Kartunnen, 2003). Such models of the lexicon do not perform disambiguation of ambiguous words in context; they only provide a set of possible analyses for a word *type* (e.g., one $\sigma \in \Sigma$).

We note again the interaction among different levels of linguistic structure. Predicting a word token's morphological structure relies on having first identified the word (section 1.2). "Deeper" linguistic structure predictors, in turn, tend to assume that the text has been preprocessed into well-behaved, less-ambiguous units (lemmas or morphemes, perhaps with POS tags).

1.3.2 CHUNKING

Sentences and words are not the only substrings of text that are "interesting." **Chunking** is the problem of finding important phrases (subsequences of words, usually contiguous in English), usually

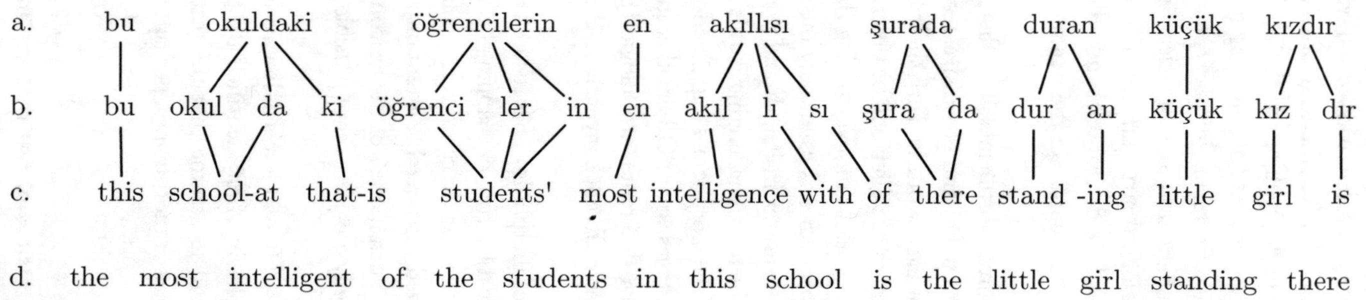

Figure 1.1: This figure shows (a) a sentence in Turkish, (b) its words segmented into morphemes, (c) English glosses for the morphemes, and (d) a more readable translation. The example is due to Eryiğit et al. (2008).

noun phrases.[7] Chunking is also known as **shallow parsing**. Base noun phrase chunking, for example, involves finding substrings corresponding to noun phrases that do not include smaller noun phrases. **Named entity recognition** involves finding substrings that refer to people (e.g., *Barack Obama*), organizations (e.g., *Carnegie Mellon University*), geopolitical entities (e.g., *United States*), locations (e.g., *Pittsburgh*), and other real-world entities that have names. These tasks involve jointly finding the relevant substrings and labeling them; they can be understood as predicting a structure that consists of a segmentation and a labeling of the segments. They are central to applications involving **information extraction**, where text is used to populate structured databases. For an overview of information extraction, see the tutorial by Cohen (2004).

A common encoding, IOB tagging (sometimes also called BIO tagging) involves tagging a sequence of words $\boldsymbol{x}$ with tags in $\{\mathsf{O}\} \cup (\{\mathsf{B}, \mathsf{I}\} \times \Lambda)$ where $\Lambda = \{\ell_1, \ldots, \ell_L\}$ is the set of substring labels. Labeling a word "O" means the word is outside any chunk. Labeling a word "(B, ℓ)" marks it as the beginning of a ℓ chunk ($\ell \in \Lambda$) and (I, ℓ) marks it as inside a ℓ chunk.[8] The use of IOB encodings is so widespread that predictors for chunking are almost always assumed to be sequence labeling models. Note that chunking can also be understood as a kind of segmentation, where different segments are assigned different labels.

We will make use of a running example of named entity recognition with the IOB encoding in chapter 2.

1.4 SYNTAX

Parsers take the idea of "interesting substrings" in text to the extreme, seeking to label every syntactically coherent substring. In chunking, substrings of interest may not overlap; parsers find and label substrings of interest that are related to each other compositionally or recursively.[9]

A **phrase-structure** or **constituent** parse is an analysis of the syntax of a sentence. For a sentence $\boldsymbol{x} = \langle x_1, \ldots, x_n \rangle$, a phrase-structure parse consists of a set of phrases, denoted $\langle \ell, i, j \rangle$ where $\ell \in \Lambda$ is a syntactic category label, and i and j are the indices of the first and last words in a phrase ($1 \leq i \leq j \leq n$). The *yield* of $\langle \ell, i, j \rangle$ is defined to be $\langle x_i, \ldots, x_j \rangle$. The Penn Treebank (Marcus et al., 1993) is the best-known dataset of syntactically annotated text; it is annotated with phrase-structure trees that are labeled with classic linguistic categories. The trees also include some additional elements of structure; an illustration is shown in figure 1.2. Treebanks are also available in a variety of other languages.

[7] A noun phrase, informally, is a sequence of words that refer to a person, place, or thing. In the previous sentence, the noun phrases are: *A noun phrase*; *a sequence of words that refer to a person, place, or thing*; *words*; *a person*; *place*; and *thing*. Note that noun phrases can contain other noun phrases.

[8] Different labels are used for "beginning" and "inside" so that, for example, two adjacent ℓ chunks are labeled differently (e.g., $\langle(\mathsf{B}, \ell), (\mathsf{I}, \ell), (\mathsf{B}, \ell), (\mathsf{I}, \ell), (\mathsf{I}, \ell)\rangle$) from one single five-word ℓ chunk. Variations on IOB tagging may include additional tag to mark the final word in a chunk, or the only word in a single-word chunk.

[9] In some research communities, *parsing* refers to *any* analysis of the kinds discussed in this chapter. At times, we have tried to use the term with this broader meaning (i.e., *parsing* refers to any kind of linguistic structure prediction), and found that it results in confusion within the NLP community, which associates the term strongly with syntactic processing. We therefore adopt *linguistic structure prediction* for the general case and *parsing* for the specific one.

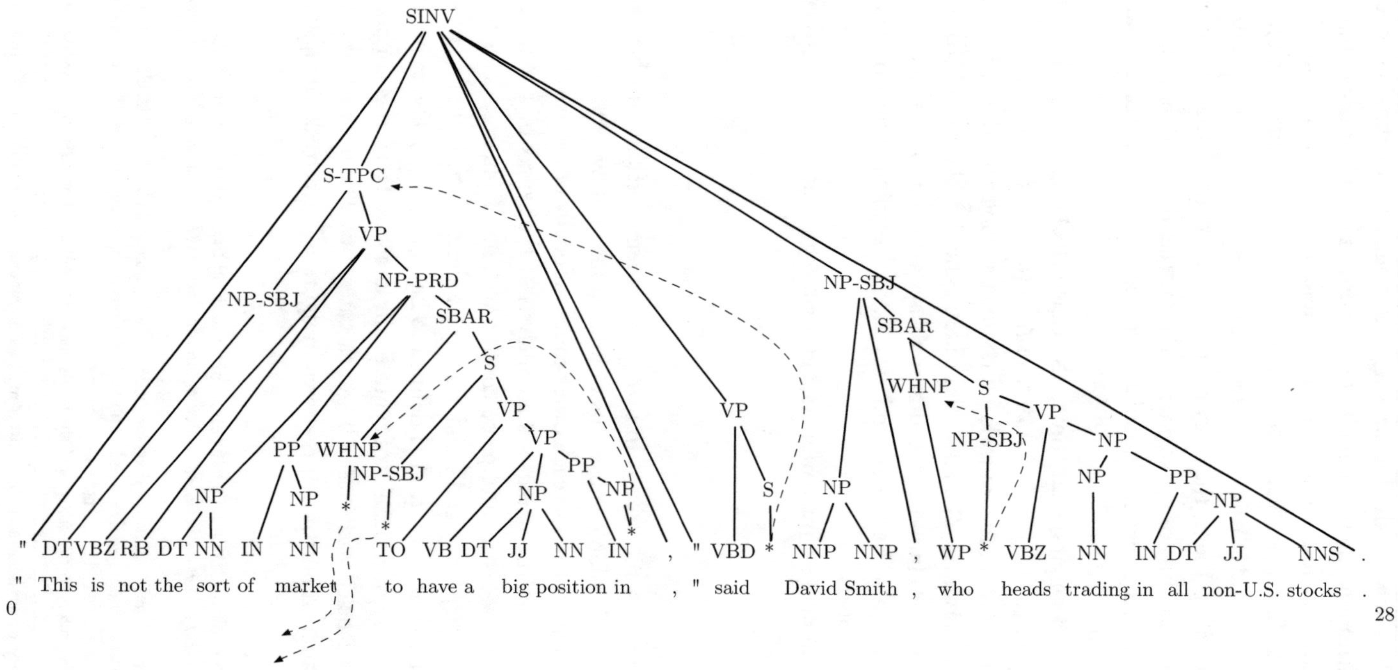

Figure 1.2: A graphical representation of a parse from the Penn Treebank (Marcus et al., 1993). The $*$ symbol indicates an empty category, and dashed lines show the phrases with which empty categories are co-indexed (two of them are not co-indexed). There are 30 phrases in this parse, not counting the one-word phrases labeled by parts of speech. They include ⟨SINV, 1, 28⟩, ⟨S-TPC, 2, 14⟩, ⟨NP-SBJ, 18, 27⟩, five phrases of width zero corresponding to empty categories, and 22 others.

Phrase-structure parses are very often constrained to correspond to the derivations of **context-free grammars** (CFGs). In such a derivation, each phrase that is longer than one word is made of a sequence of non-overlapping "child" phrases or words, such that the children "cover" the yield of the parent phrase. Hence a CFG with nonterminals Λ and terminals Σ can be used to define the set of possible parses of sentences. There do exist alternative syntactic analyses that do not obey this property, making use of *discontinuous* constituents (see, e.g., Johnson, 1985); this phenomenon is more frequent, or more preferred, in some languages compared to others. Most of the top-performing phrase-structure parsers for English make use of CFGs, though they are not always described explicitly as CFGs in the classical sense (Charniak, 2000, Collins, 2003, Klein and Manning, 2003, Petrov and Klein, 2008).

Another syntactic analysis widely used in NLP is **dependency parsing**. A dependency parse is a directed tree where the words in $\boldsymbol{x}$ are vertices. Edges correspond to syntactic relations and may be labeled with a vocabulary Λ of relation types. One word is the root of the tree, and each other word each has a single in-bound edge from its syntactic parent. In **nonprojective** parsing,[10] any tree is allowed; in **projective** parsing, the trees are constrained so that all the words between any parent x_i and child x_j are descendents (reachable from) x_i. Projective dependency parsing can also be represented as context-free parsing with a grammar whose nonterminals are annotated with words. English structures are predominantly projective; an example is shown in figure 1.3.

Phrase structures and dependency relationships can be united in a single framework through the use of **lexicalized** grammars. In a lexicalized context-free grammar, each phrase is annotated with a head word from its yield. The children of a nonterminal correspond to phrases headed by dependents of the head word; the lexicalized CFG's rules therefore model the syntactic relationship between a word and its dependents as well as nesting structure of phrases. One popular representation, Stanford typed dependencies, is closely linked to both phrase-structure and dependency syntax (de Marneffe and Manning, 2008).

There are a wide variety of syntactic formalisms for natural language parsing. Some of them are based on linguistic theories that seek to account for phenomena not elegantly captured by context-free grammars, and indeed lead to context-sensitive grammars. Most of these representations involve, to varying extents, notions of constituents and dependencies among words or consituents. A tremendous body of literature explores algorithms for parsing with different formalisms. Many of these have been implemented and tested within the structure prediction framework we consider here (Carreras et al., 2008, Clark and Curran, 2004, Riezler et al., 2000).

1.5 SEMANTICS

A long-standing question in computational linguistics is the representation of meaning. Unlike programming languages, natural languages can be used to talk about anything in the world, making broad-coverage meaning interpretation a serious challenge. There have been many attempts to computationally model the relationship between text and the world.

[10]This name is misleading; while more awkward, "not necessarily projective" parsing is a more accurate name.

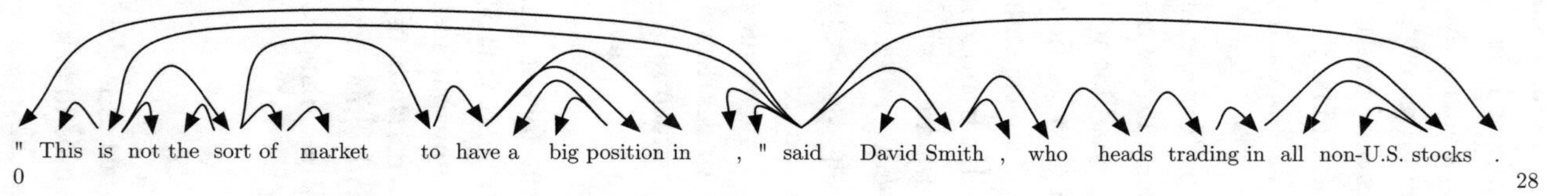

Figure 1.3: A dependency tree, constructed from the tree in figure 1.2 by application of "head rules" from Collins (1999), deletion of empty categories, and merging of nodes. In this figure, the edges are not labeled (to preserve clarity), but dependency labels are commonly used to differentiate different types of arguments and modifiers.

The major division is the question of whether semantic models should aim to fully capture the truth-conditional semantics of a piece of text, possibly restricted to a focused domain, or to capture elements of meaning robustly, with broad coverage, without necessarily representing all aspects of meaning. The former approach tends to use **logic** to represent meaning (Montague, 1973), often variations on the first-order predicate calculus. Carpenter (1998) gives a thorough treatment that maps linguistic phenomena in English to logical expressions. In data-driven research, such logical representations have been considered in focused domains such as geographical database queries (Zelle and Mooney, 1996), robot command languages (Ge and Mooney, 2005), and travel reservation systems (Mooney, 1997). The discrete structures to be predicted in this approach are logical expressions. For example, consider this sentence from the ATIS corpus (Dahl et al., 1994):

List flights to Boston on Friday night .

The logical form might be represented as:

$$\lambda x.\text{flight}(x) \wedge \text{to}(x, \text{Boston}) \wedge \exists t.\text{departs}(x, t) \wedge \text{friday}(t) \wedge \text{night}(t)$$

Syntactic structures (e.g., phrase-structure trees) are usually important in transforming sentences into logical forms (Wong and Mooney, 2007, Zettlemoyer and Collins, 2005)—again, we see how different levels of linguistic analysis interact. Transforming natural language sentences into logical expressions is often called **semantic parsing**, although the term is sometimes used more broadly to refer to other structured semantic analyses. Recent work has sought to use extrinsic signals to drive semantic parsing (Clarke et al., 2010, Liang et al., 2011).

The second approach is more shallow. This work tends to focus more on meanings of *words*. These approaches have been applied to broader domains (often newstext). One strand of research has studied **word sense disambiguation**, in which word tokens are mapped to less ambiguous forms. For example, consider a token of the word *heads*. Even after disambiguating its part of speech—suppose it is a verb—*heads* has a variety of possible meanings:

1. travels towards a destination;
2. travels in front (e.g., of a procession), or directs the course;
3. is in charge (e.g., of a project);
4. is the leading or first member (e.g., of a class or a list);
5. takes its rise (e.g., said of a river);
6. forms a head (e.g., said of wheat);
7. removes the head of (e.g., fish)

The above senses are taken from WordNet (Fellbaum, 1998),[11] with some modification. In the running example of figure 1.2, *heads* takes the third of these senses.

[11] `http://wordnetweb.princeton.edu`

Word sense disambiguation was one of the NLP problems in which statistical methods were pioneered (Yarowsky, 1992). In most settings, some encoding of prior knowledge of the set of possible meanings for each ambiguous word must be provided; e.g., in Yarowsky's work, a thesaurus was the starting point. More recently, WordNet (Fellbaum, 1998) and other lexical resources have been used. Word sense disambiguation, like part of speech disambiguation, is sometimes treated as a whole-sequence disambiguation problem. For example, Ciaramita and Altun (2006) built a tagger of coarse word senses into 41 "supersense" categories corresponding to groups of WordNet synonym sets.

Considerable research has considered **semantic role labeling**, in which a word token (usually a verb) is seen as evoking a predicate, and the arguments of the predicate are identified in its context and labeled. In the example of figure 1.2, there are three predicates $have_{10}$, $said_{17}$, and $heads_{22}$. Each one has a set of semantic roles, illustrated in figure 1.4.

The PropBank dataset (Palmer et al., 2005) is widely used to build and evaluate semantic role-labeling models (Carreras and Màrquez, 2004, Carreras and Màrquez, 2005). FrameNet (Baker et al., 1998) is a lexicon that maps words to abstract "frames," which are unambiguous semantic units that have associated named "frame elements" or roles; frame-semantic parsing involves mapping word tokens to the frames they evoke and labeling the words and phrases in context that fill the frames' roles (Das et al., 2010, Gildea and Jurafsky, 2002, Johansson and Nugues, 2007). Predicting semantic role structure typically assumes input that has already been syntactically analyzed (section 1.4).

1.6 COREFERENCE RESOLUTION

A key problem in computationally representing and interpreting text is grounding in real-world "entities" like specific people, groups, organizations, places, and events. Pieces of the text can be linked to pieces of the world. **Coreference resolution** is one part of this problem. Given a text where entity mentions have been identified (e.g., through named entity recognition and perhaps noun phrase chunking; see section 1.3.2), coreference resolution is the problem of determining which mentions refer to the same real-world entity. In some cases, this requires us to identify the entity in a list or ontology; more frequently, only the grouping of mentions that corefer is required. Coreference resolution must deal with the fact that many minor variations on names and titles can be used to refer to the same individual (e.g., *Barack Obama*, *Obama*, *Barack H. Obama*, *President Obama*, *Mr. Obama*, *the President*, *the U.S. President*, *the American leader*, etc.; at present, none of these corefers with *Mrs. Obama*). Another important sub-problem, often studied on its own, is resolving anaphoric pronouns like *he*, *she*, *it*, *they*, *himself*, and *themselves*.

Coreference resolution can be understood as a predicting a partition structure over the set of mentions in a document (or set of documents); those mentions that co-refer should be grouped together. Transitivity—the property that, if mentions m_1 and m_2 co-refer and mentions m_2 and m_3 co-refer, then m_1 and m_3 must co-refer—is desired, but they can make the prediction problem computationally expensive. Data-driven approaches to coreference resolution date back at least to Bagga and Baldwin (1998) and Ng and Cardie (2002); more recent work ties coreference resolution

predicate	arguments
have ("own, possess" sense)	... "This is not the sort of market to * **have** a big position in * ," said David Smith ...
	owner *possession*
say	"This is not the sort ... position in * ," **said** * David Smith , who heads ... stocks .
	utterance *sayer*
head ("lead" sense)	... said * David Smith , who **heads** trading in all non-U.S. stocks .
	leader *organization*

Figure 1.4: The semantic roles in the sentence from figure 1.2, taken from Proposition Bank (Palmer et al., 2005). Empty categories are marked with *.

to machine learning formalisms that allow the integration of a wide range of different types of clues (Culotta et al., 2007, Haghighi and Klein, 2009, Poon and Domingos, 2008).

An example illustrating some of the challenges of coreference resolution is shown in figure 1.5. Coreference resolution is also an important part of information extraction, where the aim is to convert unstructured text into structured databases. If such a database is to support more complex reasoning, all relational information about the same entity should be linked through some common identifier. In the example of figure 1.5, a failure to link expressions 1 and 3 might lead to a failure to recognize that Singh is a prime minister.

> $[$The prime ministers of India and Pakistan$]_1$ will meet on Thursday at a regional summit in Bhutan, $[$the Indian foreign ministry$]_2$ has said. $[$Manmohan Singh$]_3$ and $[$Yousuf Raza Gilani$]_4$ have arrived in Bhutan for the two-day gathering of South Asian countries. $[$The Indian official$]_5$ said that $[$the two leaders$]_6$ will meet on the sidelines of the summit. $[$He$]_7$ gave no indication as to how long the talks would last or what would be on the agenda.

Figure 1.5: An example of text with expressions referring to people marked in brackets. The coreference structure, not shown, partitions these seven expressions as follows: $\{1, 6\}$; $\{5, 7\}$. It is possible that expression 2 should be grouped with 5 and 7, and further that some relationship exists between 3 and $\{1, 6\}$ and also between 4 and $\{1, 6\}$, since $\{1, 6\}$ refers to the pair of people referred to individually by 3 and 4.

1.7 SENTIMENT ANALYSIS

In the past ten years or so, NLP methods have been used to infer the subjective nature of a piece of text, often the author's attitude toward a particular subject; this is known as a sentiment analysis (Pang et al., 2002, Turney, 2002). Structured approaches have been applied to modeling sentiment at different levels from the sentence to phrases to the document (Choi and Cardie, 2008, McDonald et al., 2007, Pang and Lee, 2004, Wilson et al., 2005), and also to model opinion source (Choi et al., 2005) and "flow" of sentiment (Mao and Lebanon, 2009). At this writing, sentiment analysis is an extremely active area of research; for an overview, see Pang and Lee (2008).

1.8 DISCOURSE

Discourse analysis includes the prediction of structures spanning multiple sentences, explaining how sentences or propositions in a document relate to each other. Although attention from the machine learning community has been less intense than in syntactic analysis, a wide range of structures have been modeled, and there exist annotated corpora like the RST Discourse Treebank (Carlson et al., 2003), the Discourse Graphbank (Wolf and Gibson, 2005), and the Penn Discourse

Treebank (Prasad et al., 2008). We refer the reader to the tutorial by Webber et al. (2010) for an overview. Problems discussed earlier, especially coreference resolution and document segmentation, are related to discourse, and their solutions may interact with other kinds of discourse processing.

1.9 ALIGNMENT

A widely studied relation that may hold between pieces of text is **translational equivalence**, i.e., pieces of text that are in two different languages having the same meaning. Automatic translation (usually called **machine translation**) is one of the oldest applications of computer science, and it has seen a huge surge in interest in the 2000s with the rise of statistical models, increased computing power, and—most importantly—the availability of data in the form of documents paired with their high-quality human-produced translations, known as **parallel corpora.**[12]

Sentence alignment is the problem of identifying sentences that are translations of each other. In real parallel text, some portion of the data often have correspondences that are not one-to-one; additional material may exist in one document or the other, or the translator may use more or fewer sentences in the translation than were in the original text. This problem is not widely studied at present; most datasets available for research are pre-aligned using longstanding techniques such as that of Gale and Church (1993).

More widely studied has been the problem of **word alignment** (Brown et al., 1990): given two sentences in translation $\boldsymbol{x} \in \Sigma^*$ and $\boldsymbol{x}' \in \Lambda^*$ (where Σ and Λ are the vocabularies of two languages), identify the correspondences between word tokens that, in the context of the two sentences, have the same meaning. Most generally, a correspondence $\boldsymbol{y} \in 2^{\{1,2,\ldots,|\boldsymbol{x}|\}\times\{1,2,\ldots,|\boldsymbol{x}'|\}}$ is a relation between the word tokens in $\boldsymbol{x}$ and the word tokens in $\boldsymbol{x}'$. An example is shown in figure 1.6.

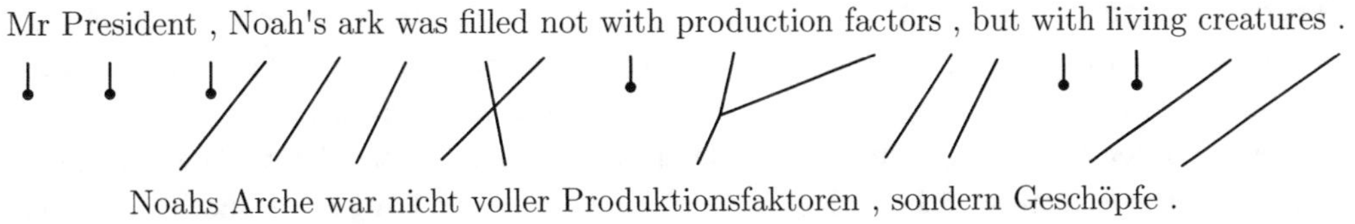

Mr President , Noah's ark was filled not with production factors , but with living creatures .
Noahs Arche war nicht voller Produktionsfaktoren , sondern Geschöpfe .

Figure 1.6: Two sentences, one in English and one in German, with a graphical depiction of their word alignment. Note that 6 of the 17 English tokens do not align to any German word; one German word, *Produktionsfaktoren*, aligns to two English words, and the alignment is not monotonic (there are crossing links). For a more complicated example, consider aligning figure 1.1(a) with 1.1(d).

Going beyond words, alignments can be modeled at higher levels, such as between chunks (often called *phrase alignment*) and between syntactic structures (phrases in trees, dependencies, or even subtrees). Integrated models of the alignment and segmentation or hierarchical structure

[12]These are the natural by-product of bilingual or multilingual organizations like the United Nations, the governments of Canada and Hong Kong, and certain news agencies.

on one side or the other, either for the purpose of translation (Chiang, 2005, Yamada and Knight, 2001), or for the purpose of inferring structure in one language through parallel corpora, is an active area of research (Burkett and Klein, 2008, Hwa et al., 2005, Smith and Smith, 2004, Snyder et al., 2008, Wu, 1997, Yarowsky and Ngai, 2001). Alignment models are also appropriate below the word level, for modeling morphological patterns (Dreyer and Eisner, 2009) and lexical changes over time (Bouchard-Côté et al., 2007).

1.10 TEXT-TO-TEXT TRANSFORMATIONS

Of course, translation itself is a structure prediction problem: given a sentence $\boldsymbol{x}$ in one language, the predictor must choose its translation $\boldsymbol{y}$ in the other language; the sequence $\boldsymbol{y}$ is a structure. This view has been espoused by Liang et al. (2006) and Gimpel and Smith (2009) and continues to be, at a high level, a reasonable description of how machine translation works. We will not discuss translation here; Koehn (2009) provides a detailed and current survey. Text-to-text, translation-like problems involving only a single language include paraphrase generation (Barzilay and Lee, 2003), question generation (Heilman and Smith, 2010), and sentence compression (Knight and Marcu, 2002, McDonald, 2006).

1.11 TYPES

Finally, we briefly mention that structured prediction problems also appear when we aim to model the structure in the language itself, not just the text data that are samples of the language. An important distinction in NLP is that between *tokens* and *types*. This is best illustrated with respect to words: an instance of the word *university* in a corpus is a token, and all such instances are of the same type (*university*). We can talk about types and tokens of words, morphemes, sentences, categories, or any other unit. So far, we have argued that many linguistic analysis problems can be seen as structure prediction problems, and we have been discussing predictions about *tokens*.

Certain aspects of language are also best described in terms of *types*. For example, when we talk about forming the past tense of the verb *go* in English, we are not talking about specific instances of the verb; any specific instance will either be in the past tense or not. We are talking about properties of the verb type, what linguists call its lexical properties. Models of morphology very often tend to focus on types, for the simple reason that text corpora tend to be very imbalanced and sparse when it comes to the many morphological forms of a word.

There are other types of lexicon construction that might be seen as structure prediction. We refer to research efforts that have adopted this view, not necessarily the canonical references for these problems. These include

- **translation dictionaries** for two or more languages (Haghighi et al., 2008);
- **transliteration** rules for importing words from one language into another (Knight and Graehl, 1998);

- pairs of words that are **cognates** (having the same historical linguistic derivation; Kondrak, 2000);
- lexicons of words and phrases indicative of **perspective**, for use in sentiment analysis (Hardisty et al., 2010, Riloff and Wiebe, 2003); and
- **lexical ontologies** that relate the meanings (senses) of words to each other, including synonyms, antonyms, part-whole relationships, and generalizations (hypernymy), and also relationships among entities (Snow et al., 2006).

These are important problems in NLP. An unanswered question is how statistical reasoning can be used when we encounter questions about *types*. Statistical learning algorithms make assumptions about the data they model, most commonly that the data are drawn independently from the same distribution. In structure prediction, we break that independence assumption, often by enlarging our notion of what a single datum is (e.g., sentences rather than words) and making an independence assumption at a "higher" level, across larger pieces of text (say, sentences rather than words, or documents rather than sentences). Linguistic types arise as part of a natural process of language evolution and adaptation to new realities in the world. It seems appropriate to view a *language* as a single structured object, yet this is challenging; we do not have complete, uncontestedly accurate information about any single language, and it is not clear the extent to which generalizations can be made across languages. Further, there are only a few thousand languages in the world,[13] only some of which have available data. Factors like dialect variation, domain, and genre make it difficult to argue for a specific categorization scheme. Hence, as elsewhere in NLP, stronger, approximating independence assumptions must be made.

1.12 WHY LINGUISTIC STRUCTURE IS A MOVING TARGET

In NLP, tasks tend to change frequently. We infer several reasons for this restlessness.

Theories of language are always evolving. Linguistics is a research enterprise like any other, and new theories and ideas are to be expected. Occasionally, these catch on in computational research and make their way into NLP. In the early 2000s, for example, frame semantics gained interest as a candidate for representing sentence meanings robustly (Gildea and Jurafsky, 2002).

Data are always changing. In the hard sciences, data come from measurements of natural phenomena. NLP data do, as well, but the phenomena are social and behavioral: people produce language to talk about the ongoing events occurring in the world each day. Changes in the world often lead to sudden availability of new text resources that serve as datasets. For example, if a news agency opts to report bilingually, a new stream of parallel text is born. Often, the creation of a new dataset by NLP researchers results in increased or renewed interest in a particular problem; in 2006 and 2007, the Conference on Computational Natural Language Learning sponsored shared tasks on dependency parsing, making datasets available in many languages in a single format (Buchholz and Marsi, 2006,

[13]The exact count varies depending on the definition, which is usually based on political and cultural rather than technical criteria.

Nivre et al., 2007). Dependency parsing has enjoyed considerable attention since; similar trends can be noted following earlier CoNLL shared tasks. Another example is the rise in open social media platforms, which have led to text data from previously ignored populations of authors.

The development of a new algorithm or programming technique, or its adaptation to structured problems, can make a "hard" problem seem more feasible by opening up new approaches. For example, Gibbs sampling in Markov random fields for sequence analysis led to the use of many new features in problems like named entity recognition (Finkel et al., 2005). Another example is the MapReduce framework for cluster computing on large numbers of commodity machines (Dean and Ghemawat, 2008), which has permitted much larger amounts of data to be used in training language models, in turn, giving large improvements in applications like machine translation (Brants et al., 2007); see Lin and Dyer (2010) for an overview of its use in NLP.

The introduction of a new automatic evaluation technique often leads to a surge in research interest. The Bleu score for measuring translation quality, introduced by Papineni et al. (2002), provided an inexpensive way to estimate how well a system translated sentences, against reference translations, without human evaluations of system output. This led to a resurgence in machine translation, now seen as one of the main commercial applications of NLP.

1.13 CONCLUSION

We have briefly surveyed some examples of linguistic structure prediction. None of the kinds of structure presented here are trivial to predict (at least all of the time), because of the pervasive problem of ambiguity. In short, linguistic structure prediction equates to resolving ambiguity of kinds that humans may not even notice.

Many of these kinds of linguistic structure have become popularized in NLP only in the last few years, and we expect new representations to continue to arise in the future, due to new sources of data, new algorithmic capabilities, and new ideas about evaluation.

To avoid bewilderment in a field where the central problems are always in flux and under debate, we propose the linguistic structure prediction framework as an abstraction that breaks a problem down into a few key steps:

1. Formally define the inputs and outputs. This chapter has sketched some examples.

2. Identify a scoring function over input-output pairs, and an algorithm that can find the maximum-scoring output given an input. Defining the function requires an understanding of the phenomena that serve as clues to the relationship between the input and the output, as well as the phenomena that make prediction challenging. Chapter 2 presents many kinds of algorithms, which we unify under the abstraction of *decoding*.

3. Determine what data can be used to learn to predict outputs from inputs, and apply a learning algorithm to tune the parameters of the scoring function. Ideally, input-output pairs are available and in large numbers, but often they are not. Chapter 3 discusses techniques for the case

where input-output pairs *are* available, and chapter 4 discusses techniques for the case where they are not.

4. Evaluate the model on an objective criterion measured on unseen test data. Some issues related to evaluation are discussed in appendix B.

CHAPTER 2

Decoding: Making Predictions

This chapter presents algorithmic techniques for decoding with linear models. We begin with some definitions, then discuss several views of decoding that are useful for understanding decoding algorithms. We present important methods for exactly solving decoding problems. We briefly discuss some approximate techniques, as they are becoming increasingly important for rich NLP models.

2.1 DEFINITIONS

As in chapter 1, we consider the problem of predicting a linguistic structure from an input $\boldsymbol{x}$. We use $\mathcal{X}$ to denote the set of all possible inputs, and $\mathcal{Y}$ to denote the set of all possible outputs. For a given $\boldsymbol{x} \in \mathcal{X}$, it is usually the case that only a subset of $\mathcal{Y}$ should be considered well-formed; for example, if $\boldsymbol{x}$ is a sequence to be labeled, then only the labelings in $\mathcal{Y}$ that have the same length as $\boldsymbol{x}$ should be considered well-formed labelings for $\boldsymbol{x}$. In some cases, we will use "$\mathcal{Y}_{\boldsymbol{x}}$" to emphasize this filtering of ill-formed outputs. In structure prediction problems, $\mathcal{Y}$ is assumed to be too large to enumerate exhaustively. It is typical that $|\mathcal{Y}_{\boldsymbol{x}}|$ is exponential in the size of $\boldsymbol{x}$.

The problem of **decoding** is to find the best $\boldsymbol{y} \in \mathcal{Y}$, given $\boldsymbol{x} \in \mathcal{X}$. This operation has many names in different literatures, but we have chosen "decoding" to avoid drawing a strong association with a particular type of algorithm or prediction problem. The decoding metaphor comes from information theory, is often attributed to Fred Jelinek, and is commonly used in automatic speech recognition and machine translation. Here we use it more broadly. In this view, $\boldsymbol{y}$ is a "message," and $\boldsymbol{x}$ is an encryption of $\boldsymbol{y}$. We seek to recover the original message, which in natural language processing is usually some underlying, less ambiguous linguistic structure.

In order to define a notion of "best," we require a scoring function that maps each $\boldsymbol{y} \in \mathcal{Y}$ onto $\mathbb{R}$-valued scores, or, more precisely, a scoring function that considers the input $\boldsymbol{x}$ as well. Our formulation of the scoring function here will continue to be used throughout the book. Let $score : \mathcal{X} \times \mathcal{Y} \rightarrow \mathbb{R}$. The simplest such function, and one that is used very widely, is defined in two steps. First, the space of input-output pairs $\mathcal{X} \times \mathcal{Y}$ is mapped to a d-dimensional $\mathbb{R}$ space through a **feature vector function, g**:

$$\mathbf{g}(\boldsymbol{x}, \boldsymbol{y}) = \begin{bmatrix} g_1(\boldsymbol{x}, \boldsymbol{y}) \\ g_2(\boldsymbol{x}, \boldsymbol{y}) \\ \vdots \\ g_d(\boldsymbol{x}, \boldsymbol{y}) \end{bmatrix} \tag{2.1}$$

Each $g_j(\boldsymbol{x}, \boldsymbol{y})$, called a feature function, maps pairs in $\mathcal{X} \times \mathcal{Y}$ to real values. In modern research, it is not unusual for d to be in the range of 10^6 or 10^7, or even greater. The next step defines the score as a linear combination of the feature vector components.

$$score(\boldsymbol{x}, \boldsymbol{y}) = \mathbf{w}^\top \mathbf{g}(\boldsymbol{x}, \boldsymbol{y}) = \sum_{j=1}^{d} w_j g_j(\boldsymbol{x}, \boldsymbol{y}) \tag{2.2}$$

Given the linear score, the decoding problem, then, requires solving

$$\boldsymbol{y}^* = \operatorname*{argmax}_{\boldsymbol{y} \in \mathcal{Y}_{\boldsymbol{x}}} \mathbf{w}^\top \mathbf{g}(\boldsymbol{x}, \boldsymbol{y}) \tag{2.3}$$

While other scoring functions are easily conceived, the vast majority of NLP models, including many probabilistic models not often described this way, can be understood in the linear decoding framework.

As an example, consider the prediction task of finding named entities in the sentence (given here in tokenized form):

> Britain sent warships across the English Channel Monday to rescue Britons stranded by Eyjafjallajökull 's volcanic ash cloud .

In the correct analysis of this sentence, there are at most five named entities: the geopolitical entity *Britain* ($\langle x_1 \rangle$), the location *English Channel* ($\langle x_6, x_7 \rangle$), the temporal expression *Monday* ($\langle x_8 \rangle$), the group *Britons* ($\langle x_{11} \rangle$), and the location *Eyjafjallajökull* ($\langle x_{14} \rangle$).

In the IOB tagging representation, and assuming that we collapse all named entity types to a single class,[1] two analyses are shown in figure 2.1. The first analysis, $\boldsymbol{y}$, is correct, and the second, $\boldsymbol{y}'$, incorrectly labels *Britain* as O, or "outside" any named entity mention. Figure 2.2 shows some of the feature functions a typical scoring function might include and their values on $\langle \boldsymbol{x}, \boldsymbol{y} \rangle$ and $\langle \boldsymbol{x}, \boldsymbol{y}' \rangle$. Note that features specific to the word *Eyjafjallajökull* are unlikely to be included in the model,[2] so shape and prefix features will help to generalize from other long, capitalized words. Note that each of the features listed in figure 2.2 considers only one element of the label sequence at a time; this need not be the case in general. For example, we might wish to include a feature noting that the bigram *English Channel* is labeled B I.

2.2 FIVE VIEWS OF DECODING

We have chosen the linear scoring function as our starting point because it serves as a substrate for most current linguistic structure prediction methods. It is, unfortunately, a very low-level representation of the problem. It is not especially helpful for designing practical decoding *algorithms* that solve

[1]In many schemes, four classes are used: person, location, organization, and "miscellaneous." Others are sometimes introduced, such as geopolitical entity and temporal expression. Here we use just one class, to keep things simple.

[2]Why not? If the features are manually crafted, it is unlikely that the developer will have heard of this particular volcano. If the features are derived from training data (see chapter 3), features specific to this word will only be included if the word is in the training data.

		1	2	3	4	5	6	7	8	9	10
$\boldsymbol{x}$	=	Britain	sent	warships	across	the	English	Channel	Monday	to	rescue
$\boldsymbol{y}$	=	B	O	O	O	O	B	I	B	O	O
$\boldsymbol{y}'$	=	O	O	O	O	O	B	I	B	O	O

11	12	13	14	15	16	17	18	19	20
Britons	stranded	by	Eyjafjallajökull	's	volcanic	ash	cloud	.	
B	O	O	B	O	O	O	O	O	O
B	O	O	B	O	O	O	O	O	O

Figure 2.1: Named entity analysis, represented by IOB tags. $\boldsymbol{y}$ is the correct analysis, and $\boldsymbol{y}'$ is an alternative, incorrect analysis.

feature function $g : \mathcal{X} \times \mathcal{Y} \rightarrow \mathbb{R}$		$g(\boldsymbol{x}, \boldsymbol{y})$	$g(\boldsymbol{x}, \boldsymbol{y}')$
bias:	count of i s.t. $y_i = \mathsf{B}$	5	4
	count of i s.t. $y_i = \mathsf{I}$	1	1
	count of i s.t. $y_i = \mathsf{O}$	14	15
lexical:	count of i s.t. $x_i = \textit{Britain}$ and $y_i = \mathsf{B}$	1	0
	count of i s.t. $x_i = \textit{Britain}$ and $y_i = \mathsf{I}$	0	0
	count of i s.t. $x_i = \textit{Britain}$ and $y_i = \mathsf{O}$	0	1
downcased:	count of i s.t. $lc(x_i) = \textit{britain}$ and $y_i = \mathsf{B}$	1	0
	count of i s.t. $lc(x_i) = \textit{britain}$ and $y_i = \mathsf{I}$	0	0
	count of i s.t. $lc(x_i) = \textit{britain}$ and $y_i = \mathsf{O}$	0	1
	count of i s.t. $lc(x_i) = \textit{sent}$ and $y_i = \mathsf{O}$	1	1
	count of i s.t. $lc(x_i) = \textit{warships}$ and $y_i = \mathsf{O}$	1	1
shape:	count of i s.t. $shape(x_i) = \textit{Aaaaaaa}$ and $y_i = \mathsf{B}$	3	2
	count of i s.t. $shape(x_i) = \textit{Aaaaaaa}$ and $y_i = \mathsf{I}$	1	1
	count of i s.t. $shape(x_i) = \textit{Aaaaaaa}$ and $y_i = \mathsf{O}$	0	1
prefix:	count of i s.t. $pre_1(x_i) = B$ and $y_i = \mathsf{B}$	2	1
	count of i s.t. $pre_1(x_i) = B$ and $y_i = \mathsf{I}$	0	0
	count of i s.t. $pre_1(x_i) = B$ and $y_i = \mathsf{O}$	0	1
	count of i s.t. $pre_1(x_i) = s$ and $y_i = \mathsf{O}$	2	2
	count of i s.t. $shape(pre_1(x_i)) = A$ and $y_i = \mathsf{B}$	5	4
	count of i s.t. $shape(pre_1(x_i)) = A$ and $y_i = \mathsf{I}$	1	1
	count of i s.t. $shape(pre_1(x_i)) = A$ and $y_i = \mathsf{O}$	0	1
	$\left[\!\left[shape(pre_1(x_1)) = A \wedge y_1 = \mathsf{B} \right]\!\right]_{\mathcal{K}}$	1	0
	$\left[\!\left[shape(pre_1(x_1)) = A \wedge y_1 = \mathsf{O} \right]\!\right]_{\mathcal{K}}$	0	1
gazetteer:	count of i s.t. x_i is in the gazetteer and $y_i = \mathsf{B}$	2	1
	count of i s.t. x_i is in the gazetteer and $y_i = \mathsf{I}$	0	0
	count of i s.t. x_i is in the gazetteer and $y_i = \mathsf{O}$	0	1
	count of i s.t. $x_i = \textit{sent}$ and $y_i = \mathsf{O}$	1	1

Figure 2.2: Feature functions commonly used in named entity recognition and their values on the running example and an incorrect output (see figure 2.1). Only some features are shown; there are many more that could be nonzero for some $\boldsymbol{y}'' \in \mathcal{Y}_{\boldsymbol{x}}$. lc is the lower-casing function on strings. pre_1 returns the first character of a string (e.g., $pre_1(\textit{Smith}) = S$). $shape$ maps each capital letter to A and each lower-case letter to a (e.g., $shape(\textit{Smith}) = \textit{Aaaaa}$). A gazetteer is a list of words or phrases known to refer to named entities; in this example, only *Britain* and *English* are in the gazetteer.

view	output $y \in \mathcal{Y}_x$	$\mathcal{Y}_x$	part π
graphical model (section 2.2.1)	variable assignment	valid assignments	clique
polytope (section 2.2.2)	vertex	polytope	dimension
grammar (section 2.2.3)	derivation	derivation forest	rule
hypergraph (section 2.2.4)	hyperpath	all hyperpaths	source vertex
logic program (section 2.2.5)	proof (value)	all proofs	weighted axiom

Figure 2.3: Five views of linguistic structure prediction. Decoding means finding the best output $\boldsymbol{y} \in \mathcal{Y}_{\boldsymbol{x}}$ (given input $\boldsymbol{x}$), defined by (i) a mapping of "parts" $\boldsymbol{\pi}$ to $\mathbb{R}$ and (ii) a combination of the parts of $\boldsymbol{y}$ into a single score to be maximized. None of these views encompasses *all* decoding techniques.

equation 2.3. We next present five views of linguistic structure prediction that interpret the linear model in different ways (see figure 2.3). We emphasize that these views are not equally expressive. Which view is most suitable for a given problem is a matter of personal taste as well as the research questions being asked. Some views are more helpful in certain learning settings, or if certain types of new features are to be introduced, or under different accuracy-runtime tradeoffs.

An important recurring theme is how the set $\mathcal{Y}_{\boldsymbol{x}}$, the feasible set of outputs for $\boldsymbol{x}$, is represented, which interacts with the scoring function and has a strong effect on decoding.

2.2.1 PROBABILISTIC GRAPHICAL MODELS

Graphical models are a formalism widely used in statistical machine learning. Let $\boldsymbol{X} = \langle X_1, \ldots, X_n \rangle$ and $\boldsymbol{Y} = \langle Y_1, \ldots, Y_m \rangle$ be two sets of random variables, with each X_i (or Y_i) taking values in $\mathcal{X}_i$ (or $\mathcal{Y}_i$). (For NLP problems, $\mathcal{X}_i$ and $\mathcal{Y}_i$ are usually discrete.) The original input space $\mathcal{X}$ is now interpreted as $\mathcal{X}_1 \times \cdots \times \mathcal{X}_n$, and the output space $\mathcal{Y} = \mathcal{Y}_1 \times \cdots \times \mathcal{Y}_m$.[3] Probabilistic graphical models define probability distributions over collections of random variables such as

$$p(X_1 = x_1, \ldots, X_n = x_n, Y_1 = y_1, \ldots, Y_m = y_m) \tag{2.4}$$

We will use $\boldsymbol{V} = \{V_i\}_{i=1}^{n+m}$ to denote the union of the random variables in $\boldsymbol{X}$ and $\boldsymbol{Y}$.[4]

The key idea is to represent the family of the probability distribution using a graph. Each random variable corresponds to a vertex in the graph. (We will overload notation and use V_i to denote both a random variable and its vertex.) Edges, roughly speaking, correspond to direct statistical dependencies between two random variables. The precise interpretation of the edges differs, depending on whether we work in the **directed** graphical modeling framework (known as **Bayesian networks**)

[3] Note that there is likely to be more than one way to map $\mathcal{X}$ into a product of simpler discrete spaces $\{\mathcal{X}_i\}_{i=1}^{n}$, and the same holds for $\mathcal{Y}$.

[4] In some representations, $\boldsymbol{X}$ is not treated as a collection of random variables, but rather collapsed into the scoring function since the value of $\boldsymbol{X}$ is observed. In others, $\boldsymbol{X}$ is included. Hence, we use an abstract representation in terms of variables $\boldsymbol{V}$.

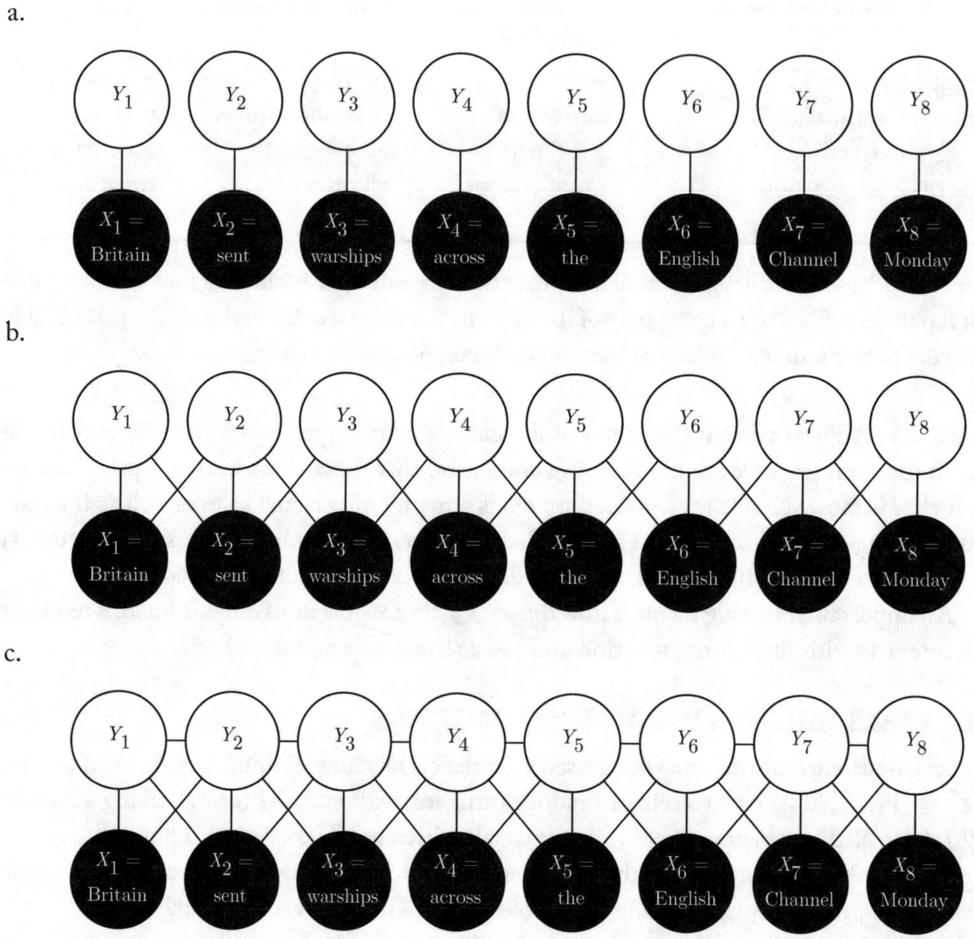

Figure 2.4: Three different undirected graphical models for labeling the sequence *Britain sent warships across the English Channel Monday*. Each word corresponds to an input random variable X_i; these variables' values are observed and so the vertices are filled. Each word's label corresponds to an output random variable Y_i ranging over, for example, {B, I, O} for named entity recognition. In (a), each word's label depends only on the word. In (b), each word's label is conditionally independent of all the others, given the word and its predecessor and successor words. In (c), the labels are interdependent, and it is possible to disprefer long named entities and to forbid subsequences like "OI" (which is meaningless in the IOB representation).

or the **undirected** graphical modeling framework (known as **Markov networks** or **Markov random fields**, MRFs). We focus on undirected graphical models here.[5] In this case, the (undirected) edges of the graph correspond to a set of conditional independence statements. Letting $\boldsymbol{V}_{obs} \subseteq \boldsymbol{V}$ denote the set of random variables whose values are observed, two variables V_i and V_j, both in $\boldsymbol{V} \setminus \boldsymbol{V}_{obs}$, are conditionally independent given $\boldsymbol{V}_{obs}$ if there is no path between them consisting only of unobserved nodes. Hence, two random variables are conditionally independent given all other nodes if and only if they do not share an edge.

MRFs assign probabilities as in equation 2.4 based on the **cliques** on the graph. A clique is a subset of vertices that are all connected to each other. Let $\mathcal{C}$ denote the set of cliques in the graph; each $C \in \mathcal{C}$ corresponds to a subset of vertices $\boldsymbol{V}$.[6] In the example of figure 2.4:

- In (a), there are eight cliques, each consisting of two aligned vertices (e.g., $\{Y_2, X_2\}$).
- In (b), there are an additional 14 cliques, each containing two vertices (e.g., $\{Y_2, X_3\}$ is a clique).
- In (c), those same 8 + 14 = 22 two-vertex cliques are present, but there are also 14 three-vertex cliques (e.g., $\{Y_1, Y_2, X_1\}$).

Let "$i \in C$" mean that variable V_i is in clique C, and let $\mathcal{V}_C$ denote the set of all possible assignments of values to the variables $\{V_i\}_{i \in C}$. (A guide to notation is provided in figure 2.5.) Let $\Pi_C : \mathcal{V} \to \mathcal{V}_C$ denote a projection from complete assignments of $\boldsymbol{V}$ to the assignments of the variables in C. It is useful to think of each clique as corresponding to a random variable; clique C is a random variable that takes values in $\mathcal{V}_C$. We denote this random variable $\Pi_C(\boldsymbol{V})$, overloading notation in a convenient way. Note that two cliques that share a variable V_i are not independent.

A MRF then defines the probability that $\boldsymbol{V} = \boldsymbol{v} = \langle v_1, \ldots, v_{m+n} \rangle$ by a product of **factor potentials**, or positive $\mathbb{R}$-valued functions, one per clique, $\phi_C : \mathcal{V}_C \to \mathbb{R}_{\geq 0}$. The formula is:

$$p(\boldsymbol{V} = \boldsymbol{v}) = \frac{1}{z} \prod_{C \in \mathcal{C}} \phi_C \left(\Pi_C(\boldsymbol{v})\right) \tag{2.5}$$

where z is a normalization constant chosen to ensure that

$$\sum_{\boldsymbol{v} \in \mathcal{V}} p(\boldsymbol{V} = \boldsymbol{v}) = 1 \tag{2.6}$$

To be precise,

$$z = \sum_{\boldsymbol{v}' \in \mathcal{V}} \prod_{C \in \mathcal{C}} \phi_C \left(\Pi_C(\boldsymbol{v}')\right) \tag{2.7}$$

[5] Bayesian networks may be a more natural representation for some NLP problems, but general methods for decoding are, we believe, easier to understand in the undirected case.

[6] For structure prediction problems, the number of cliques will depend on the input $\boldsymbol{x}$, just as the number of variables in $\boldsymbol{Y}$ and hence $\boldsymbol{V}$ may depend on $\boldsymbol{x}$.

While there are many ways to define the clique potentials, the most common is to let them be exponentiated linear functions:

$$\phi_C(\Pi_C(\boldsymbol{v})) = \exp\left(\mathbf{w}^\top \mathbf{f}(\Pi_C(\boldsymbol{v}))\right) \tag{2.8}$$

The MRF is then known as a **log-linear model**,[7] and some algebraic manipulation leads to

$$\log p(\boldsymbol{V} = \boldsymbol{v}) \;=\; \underbrace{\mathbf{w}^\top \left(\sum_{C \in \mathcal{C}} \mathbf{f}(\Pi_C(\boldsymbol{v}))\right)}_{\mathbf{g}(\boldsymbol{v})} - \log z \tag{2.9}$$

where $\mathbf{g}$ is the "global" feature function obtained by summing the feature functions at all the cliques. In the running example, the features g in figure 2.2 can all be rewritten as sums of local features f that factor based on the cliques in any of the three graphical models of figure 2.4, including the simplest case in (a).[8]

Note that we can think of $g_j(\boldsymbol{V})$ as a random variable; it is a deterministic function from assignments of $\boldsymbol{V}$ (which are random) to $\mathbb{R}$.

random variable	possible values (cardinality)	notes
$\boldsymbol{X}$	$\mathcal{X}$	structured input
$\boldsymbol{Y}$	$\mathcal{Y}_{\boldsymbol{x}}$ (exponential in input size)	structured output
$\boldsymbol{V}$	$\mathcal{V}$ (exponential in input size)	combined $\boldsymbol{X}$ and $\boldsymbol{Y}$
X_i	$\mathcal{X}_i$ (small)	atomic part of $\boldsymbol{X}$
Y_i	$\mathcal{Y}_i$ (small)	atomic part of $\boldsymbol{Y}$
V_i	$\mathcal{V}_i$ (small)	atomic part of $\boldsymbol{V}$
$\Pi_C(\boldsymbol{V})$	$\mathcal{V}_C$ (exponential in clique size)	assignment for clique C
$g_j(\boldsymbol{V})$	$\mathbb{R}$	jth global feature
$\mathbf{g}(\boldsymbol{V})$	$\mathbb{R}^d$	global feature vector
$f_j(\Pi_C(\boldsymbol{V}))$	$\mathbb{R}$	jth local feature of clique C
$\mathbf{f}(\Pi_C(\boldsymbol{V}))$	$\mathbb{R}^d$	local feature vector of clique C
$\phi_C(\Pi_C(\boldsymbol{V}))$	$\mathbb{R}_{\geq 0}$	factor potential ($= \exp(\mathbf{w}^\top \mathbf{f}(\Pi_C(\boldsymbol{V})))$) for clique C

Figure 2.5: Guide to notation in section 2.2.1.

[7]We will return to log-linear models at length in chapter 3. For now, the simple explanation of the term is that *logarithm* of the clique potential value (or of the probability) corresponds to a *linear* function of the feature vector representation.

[8]Of course, some features do not factor into a given model's cliques. For example, a feature counting the number of occurrences of the label trigram O O O is not local to the cliques in any of these models. A feature on label bigrams, e.g., one that counts occurrences of B I, is possible in (c) but not (a) or (b). Given the model, a feature that doesn't factor is called "non-local."

Graphical models are usually defined with a fixed set of variables given $\boldsymbol{x}$ and (at least in NLP) with a fixed structure. Given the values of $\boldsymbol{X}$, many linguistic structure problems can be represented with a graphical model where m (the number of Y variables) is known and polynomial-sized, and the structure is fixed. The representation is not always the most natural, as the number of variables or edges may be very large. For other linguistic structure problems (e.g., context-free parsing with unary and ϵ productions), the number of variables is not fixed, and the graphical model view is less helpful.

Structure prediction amounts to **maximum *a posteriori*** (MAP) inference, or finding the $\boldsymbol{y}$ that is most probable under the posterior distribution given that $\boldsymbol{X} = \boldsymbol{x}$. In general, finding the MAP assignment for a graphical model is an NP-hard problem (Shimony, 1994). In some cases, it can be done efficiently; specifically, these correspond to representations with smaller numbers of cliques, smaller cliques, and without cycles. These conditions correspond exactly to features that "stay local," i.e., features that do not depend simultaneously on many disparate parts of the structure random variable $\boldsymbol{Y}$.[9]

There are many generic techniques for exact and approximate inference in graphical models, though they are not usually applied directly to NLP models. (A complete discussion of algorithms for graphical models is out of scope; see Koller and Friedman, 2009.) Instead, methods based on the other four "views" are used in most cases, though it is helpful to remember that those "specialized" methods can often be interpreted as inference in graphical models. Graphical models are, then, perhaps most useful as a language for designing and explaining models in NLP, not as an out-of-the-box solution for decoding algorithms. Recently, Markov logic networks have gained interest in NLP; a Markov logic network is a set of weighted first-order clauses that, given a set of constants, defines a Markov network (Domingos and Lowd, 2009).

2.2.2 POLYTOPES

A geometric view of the linear structure prediction problem is also possible. Here, each $\boldsymbol{y} \in \mathcal{Y}_{\boldsymbol{x}}$ will correspond to the vertex of a polytope in a high-dimensional space. In this view, decoding will mean optimizing a linear scoring function over the polytope, thereby selecting the vertex corresponding to the best $\boldsymbol{y}$. (An important fact from the theory of linear optimization is that, if the optimum of a linear function over a polytope is finite-valued, then it is achieved at a vertex; Bertsimas and Tsitsiklis, 1997, Theorem 2.8.)

Let us assume again that the score of an output $\boldsymbol{y}$ given input $\boldsymbol{x}$ is defined by feature functions that break down into "parts" (analogous to the "cliques" in the graphical model). Here we make explicit use of $\boldsymbol{x}$ and $\boldsymbol{y}$ (rather than $\boldsymbol{v}$). Let $\#parts(\boldsymbol{x})$ denote the number of parts of $\mathcal{Y}_{\boldsymbol{x}}$ (analogous to $|\mathcal{C}|$ in the graphical model) and index parts by integers. (A guide to notation is provided in figure 2.6.) A value $\boldsymbol{y} \in \mathcal{Y}_{\boldsymbol{x}}$ can be defined by its $\#parts(\boldsymbol{x})$ parts; we now introduce notation to refer to those parts (each of which can be understood as a random variable, although that view is deemphasized here)

[9] If $\boldsymbol{X}$ and $\boldsymbol{Y}$ are the only random variables, then MAP inference is equivalent to finding the "most propable explanation" (MPE). For a discussion of the difference between MAP and MPE, see section 4.2.1.

and the values they can take. The set of values that the ith part can take is $\mathcal{R}_i = \{\boldsymbol{\pi}_{i,1}, \ldots, \boldsymbol{\pi}_{i,|\mathcal{R}_i|}\}$; i.e., we assume a fixed (arbitrary) ordering of values. Let $\Pi_i : \mathcal{X} \times \mathcal{Y} \to \mathcal{R}_i \times \{i\}$ map a complete structure $\langle \boldsymbol{x}, \boldsymbol{y} \rangle$ to its ith part (analogous to Π_C for cliques in graphical models) and the index i.[10] Then the feature vector function $\mathbf{f} : \bigcup_{i=1}^{\#parts(\boldsymbol{x})} (\mathcal{R}_i \times \{i\}) \to \mathbb{R}^d$ maps indexed parts to their local feature vectors. Then:

$$score(\boldsymbol{x}, \boldsymbol{y}) = \mathbf{w}^\top \mathbf{g}(\boldsymbol{x}, \boldsymbol{y}) = \sum_{i=1}^{\#parts(\boldsymbol{x})} \mathbf{w}^\top \mathbf{f}(\Pi_i(\boldsymbol{x}, \boldsymbol{y})) = \mathbf{w}^\top \mathbf{g}(\boldsymbol{x}, \boldsymbol{y}) \tag{2.10}$$

As before, we let the global feature vector $\mathbf{g}(\boldsymbol{x}, \boldsymbol{y}) = \sum_{i=1}^{\#parts(\boldsymbol{x})} \mathbf{f}(\Pi_i(\boldsymbol{x}, \boldsymbol{y}))$.

Returning to our running example of finding named entities (figure 2.1), we consider two different ways of breaking the $\boldsymbol{y} \in \mathcal{Y}_{\boldsymbol{x}}$ into parts, corresponding to figure 2.4(b–c). In the first, each y_i is a part, so $\#parts(\boldsymbol{x}) = 20$. The ith part can take values in $\mathcal{R}_i = \{\mathsf{B}, \mathsf{I}, \mathsf{O}\}$. Each feature g_j is defined as a sum of local part features f_j; the features in figure 2.2 provide examples. Suppose we wish to include features that consider pairs of adjacent labels for words, corresponding to the probabilistic graphical model in figure 2.4(c). In this case, we let each pair $\langle y_i, y_{i+1} \rangle$ be a part that can take values in $\mathcal{R}_i = \{\mathsf{BB}, \mathsf{BI}, \mathsf{BO}, \mathsf{IB}, \mathsf{II}, \mathsf{IO}, \mathsf{OB}, \mathsf{OO}\}$.[11] This second representation introduces some complexity, since the assignments to two adjacent parts (e.g., $\langle y_1, y_2 \rangle$ and $\langle y_2, y_3 \rangle$) should agree. We will refer to this example as we continue.

Consider (for a particular $i \in \{1, \ldots, \#parts(\boldsymbol{x})\}$ and $\boldsymbol{y} \in \mathcal{Y}_{\boldsymbol{x}}$) the value of $\Pi_i(\boldsymbol{x}, \boldsymbol{y})$; it can take any value in the finite set $\mathcal{R}_i$, augmented with the index i. We can represent the choice of values in $\mathcal{R}_i$ as a binary vector $\mathbf{z}_i \in \{0, 1\}^{|\mathcal{R}_i|}$ such that

$$\forall k \in \{1, \ldots, |\mathcal{R}_i|\}, \qquad z_{i,k} = \begin{cases} 1 & \text{if } \Pi_i(\boldsymbol{x}, \boldsymbol{y}) = \boldsymbol{\pi}_{i,k} \\ 0 & \text{otherwise} \end{cases} \tag{2.11}$$

Note that this $|\mathcal{R}_i|$-length vector for the ith part is not necessarily the most efficent encoding possible for $\mathcal{Y}_{\boldsymbol{x}}$, but it is still linear in $\#parts(\boldsymbol{x})$.

By concatenating together the $\mathbf{z}_i$ for all $i \in \{1, \ldots, \#parts(\boldsymbol{x})\}$, we have

$$\mathbf{z} = \langle \mathbf{z}_1, \mathbf{z}_2, \ldots, \mathbf{z}_{\#parts(\boldsymbol{x})} \rangle \tag{2.12}$$

which serves as a binary-vector representation of the whole structure $\boldsymbol{y}$. Every value $\boldsymbol{y} \in \mathcal{Y}_{\boldsymbol{x}}$ can be so mapped into $\{0, 1\}^{N_{\boldsymbol{x}}}$, where $N_{\boldsymbol{x}} = \sum_{i=1}^{\#parts(\boldsymbol{x})} |\mathcal{R}_i|$. We let $\boldsymbol{\zeta} : \mathcal{Y}_{\boldsymbol{x}} \to \{0, 1\}^{N_{\boldsymbol{x}}}$ denote the function that performs that mapping, defined as in equations 2.11–2.12. Assuming a relatively small number of parts, each with a relatively small number of possible values, the length of this vector will be manageable. In our running named entity example, there are $O(n)$ parts if n is the length of $\boldsymbol{x}$, and the number of possible values for each part is 3 or 8, depending on whether the parts consider one word's label or two. Each $\boldsymbol{y} \in \mathcal{Y}_{\boldsymbol{x}}$ will have a concise representation as a fixed-length

[10]This extra bit of machinery allows the features to depend not only on the properties of the part but also its index.

[11]Note that "OI" must be forbidden in a model that can capture the fact that named entities must start with a "B."

binary vector. (Recall again that the length of this vector may differ for different *inputs* $\boldsymbol{x} \in \mathcal{X}$ since each $\boldsymbol{x}$ corresponds to a different $\mathcal{Y}_{\boldsymbol{x}}$ and different parts.) Not every point in $\{0, 1\}^{N_{\boldsymbol{x}}}$ necessarily corresponds to a valid $\boldsymbol{y} \in \mathcal{Y}_{\boldsymbol{x}}$. In our named entity example with two-label parts, it is possible to label $\langle y_1, y_2 \rangle$ with BO and simultaneously label $\langle y_2, y_3 \rangle$ as II. Let

$$\mathcal{Z}_{\boldsymbol{x}} = \left\{ \mathbf{z} \in \{0, 1\}^{N_{\boldsymbol{x}}} \mid \exists \boldsymbol{y} \in \mathcal{Y}_{\boldsymbol{x}}, \boldsymbol{\zeta}(\boldsymbol{y}) = \mathbf{z} \right\} \tag{2.13}$$

$\mathcal{Z}_{\boldsymbol{x}}$ is the range of the function $\boldsymbol{\zeta}$. Geometrically, it can be understood as a set of points in $\mathbb{R}^{N_{\boldsymbol{x}}}$, each a vertex of the $N_{\boldsymbol{x}}$-dimensional unit cube. The size of $\mathcal{Z}_{\boldsymbol{x}}$ is bounded by $\prod_{i=1}^{\#parts(\boldsymbol{x})} |\mathcal{R}_i| = O(2^{\#parts(\boldsymbol{x})})$. In general, not every vertex of the cube ($\{0, 1\}^{N_{\boldsymbol{x}}}$) is in $\mathcal{Z}_{\boldsymbol{x}}$, since not every vertex encodes a valid $\boldsymbol{y} \in \mathcal{Y}_{\boldsymbol{x}}$.

object	possible values	notes
$\boldsymbol{x}$	$\mathcal{X}$	structured input
$\boldsymbol{y}$	$\mathcal{Y}_{\boldsymbol{x}}$	structured output
$\#parts(\boldsymbol{x})$	$\{1, \ldots\}$	number of parts of $\mathcal{Y}_{\boldsymbol{x}}$
$\Pi_i(\boldsymbol{x}, \boldsymbol{y})$	$\mathcal{R}_i = \{\boldsymbol{\pi}_{i,1}, \ldots, \boldsymbol{\pi}_{i,\|\mathcal{R}_i\|}\}$	value of the ith part of $\boldsymbol{y}$
$z_{i,k}$	$\{0, 1\}$	does part i take its kth possible value?
$\mathbf{z}_i$	$\{0, 1\}^{\|\mathcal{R}_i\|}$	concatenation of $\{z_{i,k}\}_{k=1}^{\|\mathcal{R}_i\|}$
$N_{\boldsymbol{x}}$	$\{1, \ldots\}$	total number of part values, $\sum_{i=1}^{\#parts(\boldsymbol{x})} \|\mathcal{R}_i\|$
$\mathbf{z}$	$\{0, 1\}^{N_{\boldsymbol{x}}}$	concatenation of $\{\mathbf{z}_i\}_{i=1}^{\#parts(\boldsymbol{x})}$
$\mathcal{Z}_{\boldsymbol{x}}$	$2^{\{0,1\}^{N_{\boldsymbol{x}}}}$	attainable values of $\mathbf{z}$ (see equation 2.13)
$\boldsymbol{\zeta}(\boldsymbol{y})$	$\mathcal{Z}_{\boldsymbol{x}} \subseteq \{0, 1\}^{N_{\boldsymbol{x}}}$	vector representation of $\boldsymbol{y}$

Figure 2.6: Guide to notation in section 2.2.2.

Recall that $\mathbf{f}$ is the local feature function that maps parts in each $\mathcal{R}_i$ to d-dimensional feature vectors. We next define a $d \times N_{\boldsymbol{x}}$ matrix, $\mathbf{F}_{\boldsymbol{x}}$, that encodes all of the $\mathbf{f}$ values of all parts $\boldsymbol{\pi} \in \mathcal{R}$. Let the portion of the matrix corresponding to the ith part be defined by:

$$\mathbf{F}_{\boldsymbol{x},i} = \begin{bmatrix} f_1(\boldsymbol{\pi}_{i,1}, i) & f_1(\boldsymbol{\pi}_{i,2}, i) & \cdots & f_1(\boldsymbol{\pi}_{i,|\mathcal{R}_i|}, i) \\ f_2(\boldsymbol{\pi}_{i,1}, i) & f_2(\boldsymbol{\pi}_{i,2}, i) & \cdots & f_2(\boldsymbol{\pi}_{i,|\mathcal{R}_i|}, i) \\ \vdots & \vdots & \ddots & \vdots \\ f_d(\boldsymbol{\pi}_{i,1}, i) & f_d(\boldsymbol{\pi}_{i,2}, i) & \cdots & f_d(\boldsymbol{\pi}_{i,|\mathcal{R}_i|}, i) \end{bmatrix} \tag{2.14}$$

Note that if a feature only applies to some parts, and feature j does not apply to part i, then the jth row of $\mathbf{F}_{\boldsymbol{x},i}$ will be all zeros. The complete matrix is

$$\mathbf{F}_{\boldsymbol{x}} = \left[\mathbf{F}_{\boldsymbol{x},1} \mid \mathbf{F}_{\boldsymbol{x},2} \mid \cdots \mid \mathbf{F}_{\boldsymbol{x},\#parts(\boldsymbol{x})} \right] \tag{2.15}$$

Decoding then becomes:

$$\boldsymbol{\zeta}^{-1}\left(\operatorname*{argmax}_{\mathbf{z}\in\mathcal{Z}_{\boldsymbol{x}}} \mathbf{w}^\top \mathbf{F}_{\boldsymbol{x}}\mathbf{z}\right) = \operatorname*{argmax}_{\boldsymbol{y}\in\mathcal{Y}_{\boldsymbol{x}}} \mathbf{w}^\top \mathbf{g}(\boldsymbol{x}, \boldsymbol{y}) \tag{2.16}$$

where we assume it is efficient to take the inverse of $\boldsymbol{\zeta}$ to recover $\boldsymbol{y} \in \mathcal{Y}_{\boldsymbol{x}}$. That is, rather than searching in $\mathcal{Y}_{\boldsymbol{x}}$ to find the best output, we can search for a binary vector in $\mathcal{Z}_{\boldsymbol{x}}$. This binary vector can be converted back into a valid output structure.

Crucially, note that the function inside the maximization operator is linear in $\mathbf{z}$. This would not be the case if our scoring function were not linear in the feature functions. Meanwhile, the feasible space is a set of discrete integral points $\mathcal{Z}_{\boldsymbol{x}}$. These properties make the maximization problem an **integer linear program** (ILP). This general problem representation, as used in machine learning, is discussed in more depth by Wainwright et al. (2003) and Taskar et al. (2004a); we give a brief overview.

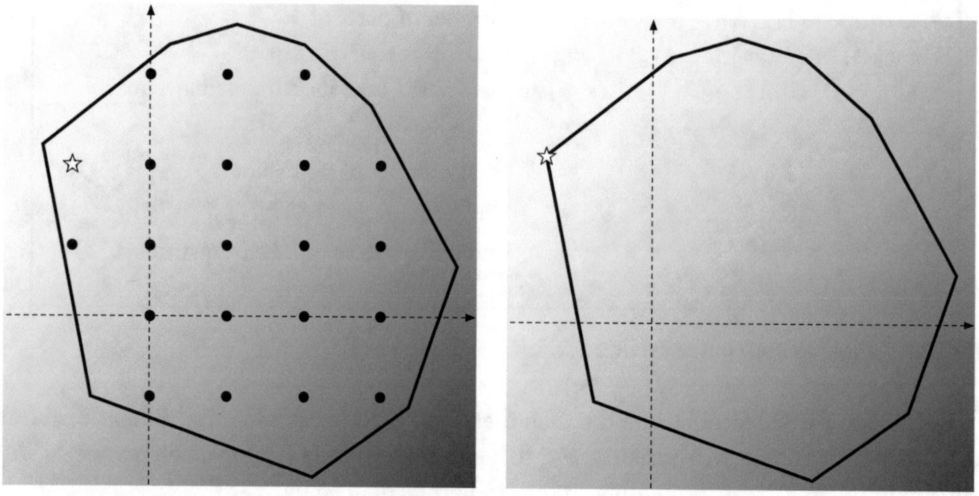

Figure 2.7: On the left, a representation of an integer linear program. The polytope is the region bounded within the heavy black lines. The shading shows the cost function (lighter is lower cost). Each feasible solution is an integer point within the polytope, marked with a star (the solution to the ILP) or a dot. On the right, the linear program relaxation of the problem on the left. Here there is no integer constraint, and the solution (marked with a star) is at a vertex of the polytope. The problem on the left is NP-hard in general, while the problem on the right can be solved in polynomial time.

Linear Programming

To understand ILP, it is helpful to understand a simpler problem, **linear programming**. Linear programming (without the word *integer* as a modifier) refers to problems of the following form:[12]

$$\begin{aligned} \max_{\mathbf{z}\in\mathbb{R}^n} \quad & \mathbf{c}^\top \mathbf{z} \\ \text{such that} \quad & \mathbf{A}\mathbf{z} \leq \mathbf{b} \end{aligned} \tag{2.17}$$

where vectors $\mathbf{c}, \mathbf{b} \in \mathbb{R}^n$ and matrix $\mathbf{A} \in \mathbb{R}^{m\times n}$ define the problem. Each row of the matrix $\mathbf{A}$, $\mathbf{A}_{j,*} \in \mathbb{R}^n$, can be understood as a single linear constraint on $\mathbf{z}$:

$$\left(\mathbf{A}_{j,*}\right)\mathbf{z} \leq b_j \tag{2.18}$$

Note that linear equality constraints can be encoded this way by mapping, for instance, $\mathbf{v}^\top\mathbf{z} = b$, to two linear inequality constraints

$$\begin{aligned} \mathbf{v}^\top\mathbf{z} & \leq b \\ -\mathbf{v}^\top\mathbf{z} & \leq -b \end{aligned}$$

Geometrically we can understand $\mathbf{A}$ and $\mathbf{b}$ as specifying a convex polytope that contains all feasible solutions to the problem. $\mathbf{c}$ defines a cost function that is linear in the solution $\mathbf{z}$. Linear programming can be solved efficiently in polynomial time and space using interior point methods (Karmarkar, 1984), and well-designed software packages are available for this purpose (e.g., CPLEX). An important result is that the solution of a linear program, if it is finite-valued, will always be one of the vertices of the polytope. See appendix A for further discussion of optimization.

Integer Linear Programming

Integer linear programming adds further constraints that the components of $\mathbf{z}$ be integers:

$$\begin{aligned} \max_{\mathbf{z}\in\mathbb{R}^n} \quad & \mathbf{c}^\top \mathbf{z} \\ \text{such that} \quad & \mathbf{A}\mathbf{z} \leq \mathbf{b} \\ & \mathbf{z} \in \mathbb{Z}^n \end{aligned} \tag{2.19}$$

Solving an ILP is, in general, NP-hard, though implementations exist which are sufficiently fast for practical use on some problems. These often proceed by *relaxing* the ILP by removing the integer constraints, then solving the linear program without those constraints. An illustration is shown in figure 2.7. The solution to the relaxed problem will lie at one of the vertices of the convex polytope defined by $\mathbf{A}\mathbf{z} \leq \mathbf{b}$. If this solution is integral, then the ILP is solved.[13] If the polytope has vertices that are not integers, and one of them is found when solving the linear program, we call the

[12]It is more standard to give the general form as a *minimization* problem, but it makes no difference as one can always be converted to the other. Maximization arises more frequently in NLP.

[13]In some cases, it is possible to prove that the solution *will* be integral, based on the structure of the problem.

solution non-integral or "fractional," and we must resort to a more expensive search for the optimal solution or use an approximate method such as rounding.

A more general technique, often used when the number of constraints (m) is unmanageably large, is to first relax the ILP by removing some or all constraints. The relaxed ILP is solved, and then checked for violation of the excluded constraints. Constraints it violates are then added to the ILP, and the more constrained version is then solved. The process repeats until the optimizing solution also satisfies all constraints.

Apart from the computational challenge of *solving* the ILP, it is not always straightforward to efficiently represent the space $\mathcal{Z}_{\boldsymbol{x}}$ in a declarative fashion. To represent the problem as an ILP, in other words, we must write a set of linear equations and linear inequalities that constrain $\mathbf{z}$ to be within $\mathcal{Z}_{\boldsymbol{x}}$, the feasible set. This is quite different from defining the function $\boldsymbol{\zeta}$ that maps $\mathcal{Y}_{\boldsymbol{x}} \rightarrow \mathcal{Z}_{\boldsymbol{x}}$; we must now give a set of declarative constraints that define the whole of $\mathcal{Z}_{\boldsymbol{x}}$. It is not always clear that such an encoding will be compact.

Returning briefly to our running example of named entity labeling with two-label parts, it *is* straightforward to write constraints to make sure each part agrees with its neighbors. Consider the ith part, corresponding to $\langle y_i, y_{i+1} \rangle$. This part corresponds to eight elements of the vector $\mathbf{z}$:

$$\langle z_{i,\mathsf{BB}}, z_{i,\mathsf{BI}}, z_{i,\mathsf{BO}}, z_{i,\mathsf{IB}}, z_{i,\mathsf{II}}, z_{i,\mathsf{IO}}, z_{i,\mathsf{OB}}, z_{i,\mathsf{OO}} \rangle$$

First, we must constrain that only one of these values is equal to one. Taken together with the integer constraints, that $\mathbf{z} \in \{0, 1\}^{N_{\boldsymbol{x}}}$, the following (for each part i) ensures that only one value for the part is selected:

$$z_{i,\mathsf{BB}} + z_{i,\mathsf{BI}} + z_{i,\mathsf{BO}} + z_{i,\mathsf{IB}} + z_{i,\mathsf{II}} + z_{i,\mathsf{IO}} + z_{i,\mathsf{OB}} + z_{i,\mathsf{OO}} = 1 \tag{2.20}$$

Note that the above is a linear equation in $\mathbf{z}$. Next, we must ensure that the ith part and the $(i + 1)$th part agree:

$$\begin{aligned} z_{i,\mathsf{BB}} + z_{i,\mathsf{IB}} + z_{i,\mathsf{OB}} &= z_{i+1,\mathsf{BB}} + z_{i+1,\mathsf{BI}} + z_{i+1,\mathsf{BO}} \\ z_{i,\mathsf{BI}} + z_{i,\mathsf{II}} &= z_{i+1,\mathsf{IB}} + z_{i+1,\mathsf{II}} + z_{i+1,\mathsf{IO}} \\ z_{i,\mathsf{BO}} + z_{i,\mathsf{IO}} + z_{i,\mathsf{OO}} &= z_{i+1,\mathsf{OB}} + z_{i+1,\mathsf{OO}} \end{aligned} \tag{2.21}$$

Note again that the above are linear equations. Instantiating them for all i will guarantee that each adjacent pair of parts is consistent, so that the entire vector $\mathbf{z}$ corresponds to a well-formed $\boldsymbol{y} \in \mathcal{Y}_{\boldsymbol{x}}$.

ILP is an extremely powerful technique; any linear decoding problem can be represented this way, although a very large number of constraints may be required to define $\mathcal{Z}$ in the "$\mathbf{Az} \leq \mathbf{b}$" formulation. There is, however, little practical advantage to representing a problem as an ILP if there are faster, more specialized algorithms. The ILP representation can be useful for analysis and when integrating decoding into training algorithms, but by and large it should be seen as either a "first resort" for prototyping (if it is easy to represent $\mathcal{Z}$, getting a prototype decoder working based on ILP may be useful for exploring an idea) or a "last resort" when techniques like those discussed below, based on dynamic programming and graph algorithms, are insufficient. The chief advantage of ILP is that adding non-local structure to a model, either features that depend on many "parts" of $\boldsymbol{y}$ or constraints defining $\mathcal{Y}_{\boldsymbol{x}}$, is straightforward if the number of features or constraints is manageable.

Examples of NLP problems framed as integer linear programs include sequence labeling (Roth and Yih, 2004), dependency parsing (Martins et al., 2009, Riedel and Clarke, 2006), semantic role labeling (Punyakanok et al., 2004), translation (Germann et al., 2001), sentence compression (Clarke and Lapata, 2006), coreference resolution (Denis and Baldridge, 2007), and many others.

2.2.3 PARSING WITH GRAMMARS

In the third view of decoding, $\boldsymbol{x}$ is a string of symbols from some alphabet Σ, and prediction is viewed as choosing the maximum-scoring derivation from a **grammar**. Given a grammar G, we use $\mathcal{D}(G)$ to denote the set of (complete) derivations of the grammar and $\mathcal{L}(G)$ to denote the set of strings in the grammar's language. A string is in $\mathcal{L}(G)$ if and only if there exists some derivation in $\mathcal{D}(G)$ whose yield is the string.

The literature on grammar formalisms is, of course, vast. Here we will not adopt a particular grammar formalism. Instead, we will simply say that a grammar consists of a set of rules, each corresponding to a derivation step that is possible to take under particular conditions (encoded in the rule). Regular and context-free grammars are the most frequently used in practical NLP, so we briefly define them in their weighted form, but emphasize that the ideas here are not restricted to those classes. Among the various unifying frameworks for grammars are linear context-free rewriting systems (Vijay-Shanker et al., 1987) and multiple context-free grammars (Kasami et al., 1987).

Regular Grammars A regular grammar consists of a set of states or nonterminals $\mathcal{S}$, one of which is designated the initial state $S_{\Rightarrow}$, a vocabulary Σ, and a set of rules $\mathcal{R}$ of one of the two forms:

$$S \rightarrow x S' \tag{2.22}$$
$$S \rightarrow \epsilon \tag{2.23}$$

where $S, S' \in \mathcal{S}$ and $x \in \Sigma$; ϵ denotes the empty string. Regular grammars can be easily compiled into **finite-state automata** that recognize whether any string in Σ^* is in the language of the grammar. We can attach a real-valued weight to each rule, giving us a weighted regular grammar. Let $\omega : \mathcal{R} \rightarrow \mathbb{R}$ be the function that assigns weights to rules.

Context-Free Grammars A context-free grammar consists of a set of states or nonterminals $\mathcal{N}$, one of which is designated the start state $N_{\Rightarrow}$, a vocabulary Σ, and a set of rules $\mathcal{R}$ of the form:

$$N \rightarrow \alpha \tag{2.24}$$

where $N \in \mathcal{N}$ and $\alpha \in (\mathcal{N} \cup \Sigma)^*$. Although context-free grammars are parseable using pushdown automata, and some parsing algorithms in NLP are based on stacks, it is more common to build decoders based on efficient dynamic programming algorithms, as we will see. As in the case of regular grammars, we can attach a real-valued weight to each rule, giving us a weighted CFG. Let $\omega : \mathcal{R} \rightarrow \mathbb{R}$ be the function that assigns weights to rules.

From here on, when we use the term *grammar*, unless otherwise noted, we do not assume any particular grammar formalism. Suppose we are given a weighted grammar G. Let $\boldsymbol{x}$ denote a string in Σ^* and let

$$\mathcal{Y}_{\boldsymbol{x}} = \{\boldsymbol{y} \in \mathcal{D}(G) \mid \mathit{yield}(\boldsymbol{y}) = \boldsymbol{x}\} \tag{2.25}$$

We define the score of a derivation $\boldsymbol{y}$ to be the sum of rule-weights for all rules used in the derivation. If a rule is used more than once, its weight is included once per use; let $\mathit{freq}(\boldsymbol{\pi}; \boldsymbol{y})$ denote the number of times rule $\boldsymbol{\pi} \in \mathcal{R}$ is used in derivation $\boldsymbol{y}$. Then

$$\mathit{score}(\boldsymbol{x}, \boldsymbol{y}) = \sum_{\boldsymbol{\pi} \in \mathcal{R}} \mathit{freq}(\boldsymbol{\pi}; \boldsymbol{y})\omega(\boldsymbol{\pi}) \tag{2.26}$$

This score is a linear function of the rule frequencies. If we index the features and weights in our linear model by $\boldsymbol{\pi} \in \mathcal{R}$ and let

$$g_{\boldsymbol{\pi}}(\boldsymbol{x}, \boldsymbol{y}) = \mathit{freq}(\boldsymbol{\pi}; \boldsymbol{y}) \tag{2.27}$$

$$w_{\boldsymbol{\pi}} = \omega(\boldsymbol{\pi}) \tag{2.28}$$

then we have a linear score of the form in equation 2.3. Therefore, our derivation-scoring model is an instance of decoding with a linear scoring model. If we have algorithms for finding the maximum-scoring derivation of $\boldsymbol{x}$ under a weighted grammar, then we can decode. As we will see in section 2.3, symbolic parsing algorithms for recognition are not difficult to adapt for efficient decoding.

In figure 2.8, we define a grammar with seven nonterminals and $13 + 3|\Sigma|$ rules (for a given vocabulary Σ). This grammar is capable of generating any string in Σ^*; unlike grammars in traditional computer science and linguistics, it does not distinguish between grammatical and ungrammatical strings. Instead, it serves to succinctly encode all of the valid output structures, $\mathcal{Y}_{\boldsymbol{x}}$, that are possible for a given string $\boldsymbol{x}$. There is a bijection between derivations of $\boldsymbol{x} \in \Sigma^*$ under the grammar and valid IOB labelings for $\boldsymbol{x}$.

By assigning weights to each of the grammar rules $\boldsymbol{\pi} \in \mathcal{R}$, we can score the derivations and hence the labelings. In the simplest form, this model lets us score sequence labelings based on the frequencies of two-label subsequences, through rules like $R_B \rightarrow I R_I$ (corresponding to BI) and $R_O \rightarrow O R_O$ (corresponding to OO), and frequencies of individual word-label pairs, through rules like $B \rightarrow \mathit{the}$ (corresponding to *the* being at the beginning of an entity mention). In a more complex scoring model, the weights might be assigned based on more fine-grained features that are shared across rules.

The grammar as shown is context-free, although it defines a regular language and there exists a regular grammar that accomplishes the same encoding. The regular grammar will be far less concise (with many more states than this grammar has nonterminals), but it might lead to a more efficient decoding algorithm.

$$
\begin{array}{lllllllllllll}
N_{\Rightarrow} & \rightarrow & B\ R_B & R_B & \rightarrow & B\ R_B & R_I & \rightarrow & B\ R_B & R_O & \rightarrow & B\ R_B \\
N_{\Rightarrow} & \rightarrow & O\ R_O & R_B & \rightarrow & O\ R_O & R_I & \rightarrow & O\ R_O & R_O & \rightarrow & O\ R_O \\
 & & & R_B & \rightarrow & I\ R_I & R_I & \rightarrow & I\ R_I & & & \\
 & & & R_B & \rightarrow & \epsilon & R_I & \rightarrow & \epsilon & R_O & \rightarrow & \epsilon \\
\\
\forall x \in \Sigma, & & & B & \rightarrow & x & I & \rightarrow & x & O & \rightarrow & x
\end{array}
$$

Figure 2.8: A context-free grammar corresponding to the named entity labeling example task. Given a string $\boldsymbol{x} \in \Sigma^*$, each $\boldsymbol{y} \in \mathcal{D}(G)$ whose yield is $\boldsymbol{x}$ corresponds to a unique, valid labeling of the sequence with IOB symbols, and each valid labeling corresponds to a unique derivation. ϵ denotes the empty string.

2.2.4 GRAPHS AND HYPERGRAPHS

The fourth view of structure prediction is that it corresponds to choosing a path (or hyperpath) through a graph (or hypergraph). We will consider the graph case first, then the hypergraph case.

Given an input $\boldsymbol{x} \in \mathcal{X}$, we define a graph.[14] Let G be a graph with vertices $\mathcal{V}$ and directed edges (arcs) $\mathcal{A} \subseteq \mathcal{V}^2$. We denote by $\langle v, v' \rangle$ an arc from $v \in \mathcal{V}$ to $v' \in \mathcal{V}$. Let $\omega : \mathcal{A} \rightarrow \mathbb{R}$ assign weights to the arcs. A **path** can be defined two ways:

- A path is a sequence in $\mathcal{A}^*$ such that, for any consecutive pair of arcs in the path $\langle v, v' \rangle$ and $\langle v'', v''' \rangle$, $v' = v''$.
- A path is a sequence in $\mathcal{V}^*$ such that, for any consecutive pair of vertices in the path v and v', $\langle v, v' \rangle \in \mathcal{A}$.

In general, the arcs or vertices in a path need not be unique; i.e., cycles are allowed. Note that we can think of a path as a subgraph (i.e., a subset of $\mathcal{V}$ and a subset of $\mathcal{A}$), unless it contains cycles, in which case the subgraph does not fully specify the path.

Many structure prediction problems can be understood as choosing a path through a graph from a designated initial vertex $v_i \in \mathcal{V}$ to a designated final vertex $v_f \in \mathcal{V}$. To take one example, a word lattice is a graph whose edges are augmented with words. Each path through such a lattice corresponds to an output sequence, which may be a candidate translation or transcription for the input sequence (a sentence in another language, or a speech signal, respectively). To decode, we seek to find the maximum-scoring path. If we take the view that a path is a sequence of edges, then let $\boldsymbol{y} = \langle y_1, \ldots, y_n \rangle$ denote the path, each $y_i \in \mathcal{A}$. Then we can write the score of the path as:

$$
\mathit{score}(\boldsymbol{x}, \boldsymbol{y}) = \sum_{i=1}^{n} \omega(y_i) = \sum_{a \in \mathcal{A}} \omega(a)\mathit{freq}(a; \boldsymbol{y}) \tag{2.29}
$$

[14] It is important not to confuse this graph with the probabilistic graphical *model* of section 2.2.1.

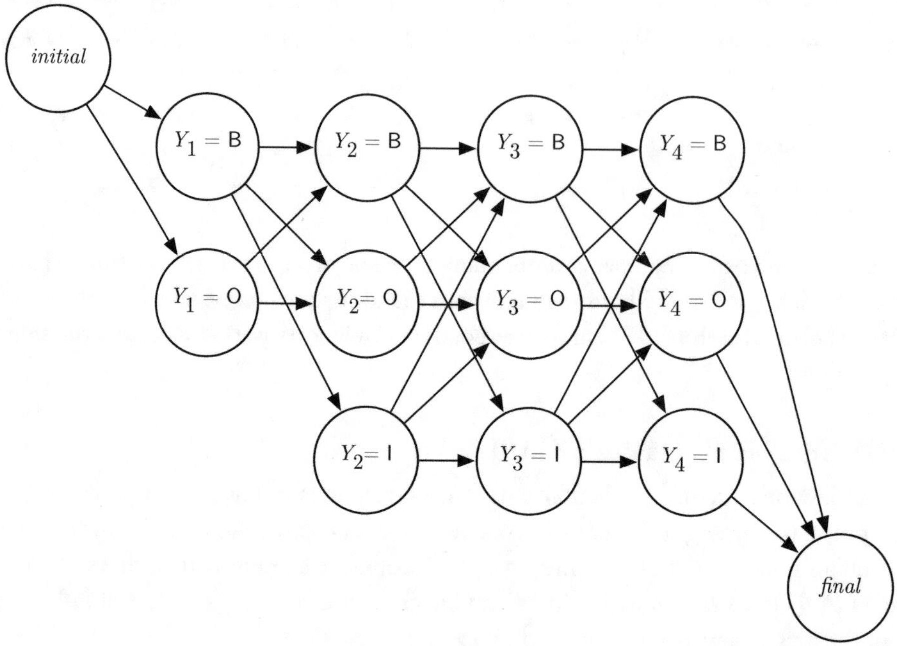

Figure 2.9: A graph corresponding to the named entity labeling task for a sequence of four words. Note that transitions from O nodes directly to I nodes are not possible.

where *freq*$(a; \boldsymbol{y})$ returns the number of times the path $\boldsymbol{y}$ crosses arc $a \in \mathcal{A}$. ($\boldsymbol{x}$, the input, defines the structure of the graph, but it is not explicitly mentioned in the definition of the scoring function.) Finding a best path can mean finding a maximum-scoring path, or a minimum-scoring path, depending on the semantics of the weight function ω.

Figure 2.9 shows a graph corresponding to the named entity sequence labeling problem, using IOB tags. There is a bijection between paths from the vertex marked *initial* to the vertex marked *final* and valid sequence labelings of a four-word sequence. The weight on each arc would be defined in terms of the IOB tags on its source and target vertices, as well as the words in the specific sequence $\boldsymbol{x}$ to be labeled.

The problems of finding a path and finding a maximum-scoring path are well-studied in computer science (Dijkstra, 1959, *inter alia*), of course, though specialized algorithms are often helpful when the graph's structure is known to have certain properties.

A more general version of the graph reachability problem arises when we consider a **hypergraph** instead of a graph. In a hypergraph, the arcs are replaced by **hyperarcs**. A hyperarc connects a *set* of source vertices to a *set* of target vertices, so that the set of hyperarcs $\mathcal{A} \subseteq 2^{\mathcal{V}} \times 2^{\mathcal{V}}$. For our purposes, hyperarcs will have only one target vertex, so that $\mathcal{A} \subseteq 2^{\mathcal{V}} \times \mathcal{V}$.[15] Two kinds of paths are possible in hypergraphs. A **simple path** is a sequence of vertices such that, for any consecutive pair v and v', there is some hyperarc $\langle \bar{\mathcal{V}}, v' \rangle$ such that $v \in \bar{\mathcal{V}}$. A **hyperpath** from initial vertex $v_i \in \mathcal{V}$ to final vertex $v_f \in \mathcal{V}$ is a set of vertices $\mathcal{V}' \subseteq \mathcal{V}$ and a partially ordered bag[16] of hyperarcs from $\mathcal{A}$, each involving only vertices from $\mathcal{V}'$. A hyperpath is connected in the following sense: for every $v' \in \mathcal{V}' \setminus \{v_f\}$, the hyperpath includes a simple path from v' to the final vertex v_f. If a hyperarc is included in the hyperpath, all of its source vertices and its target vertex must be in $\mathcal{V}'$. The partial ordering is such that, apart from v, every vertex in $\mathcal{V}$ must be some hyperarc's target vertex before it is any hyperarc's source vertex. Note that a single hyperpath may be understood as having many different initial vertices, but only one final vertex. An example of a hypergraph is shown in figure 2.10.

In *graph* reachability and best path problems we designate one initial vertex v_i and seek a path to a designated final vertex v_f. Best *hyperpath* problems usually involve a *set* of initial vertices $\mathcal{V}_i \subset \mathcal{V}$, any subset of which may be sources in the hyperpath to v_f; no other vertices in $\mathcal{V} \setminus \mathcal{V}_i$ may be sources. In a weighted hypergraph, each hyperarc is assigned a weight through a function $\omega : \mathcal{A} \to \mathbb{R}$. If we let $\boldsymbol{y}$ denote a hyperpath and let $\mathit{freq}(a; \boldsymbol{y})$ denote the number of times hyperarc $a \in \mathcal{A}$ is crossed in $\boldsymbol{y}$, then equation 2.29 serves to define the score of $\boldsymbol{y}$.

Note that not every structure prediction problem has a natural, concise representation as a graph or as a hypergraph. (For instance, dependency parsing with arbitrary nonprojective structures, as discussed in section 1.4, has not yet been demonstrated to map well into this framework.) Further, while many NLP problems can be represented as best hyperpath problems with $|\mathcal{V}|$ and $|\mathcal{A}|$ polynomial in the size of the input $\boldsymbol{x}$, the size of the hypergraph is often extremely large, and it may not be desirable to explicitly represent the whole hypergraph.

Another formalism that relates hypergraph problems to a polytope-like representation that also generalizes graphical models is **case-factor diagrams** (McAllester et al., 2004).

2.2.5 WEIGHTED LOGIC PROGRAMS

Logic programming refers to a declarative system of **inference rules**.[17] Starting with a set of **axioms**, usually represented as "terms" or typed tuples, the inference rules can be applied to deductively prove **theorems** (also represented as terms). Each inference rule gives a template for a theorem (called the **consequent**) that follows from a set of theorems and/or axioms (called **antecedents**). In classical logic programming, axioms and theorems are associated with **truth values**.

If we let *Proofs*(t) denote the set of proofs of theorem t and *Axioms*$(\boldsymbol{y})$ denote the bag of axioms used in proof $\boldsymbol{y}$,[18] then a theorem t is true if and only if at least one proof in *Proofs*(t) is

[15] Klein and Manning (2001) call these "B-arcs."

[16] A bag is a set with possible duplicate elements; we define the hyperpath as a bag to permit cycles, though in practice, most NLP problems do not make use of cyclic hypergraphs.

[17] For a brief history, see Kowalski (1988). For a more thorough treatment, see Lloyd (1987).

[18] Note that an axiom may be used more than once in a proof, so *Axioms*$(\boldsymbol{y})$ is in general a bat, not a set. In the example in figure 2.15, the axioms for the costs of various edits can be reused many times.

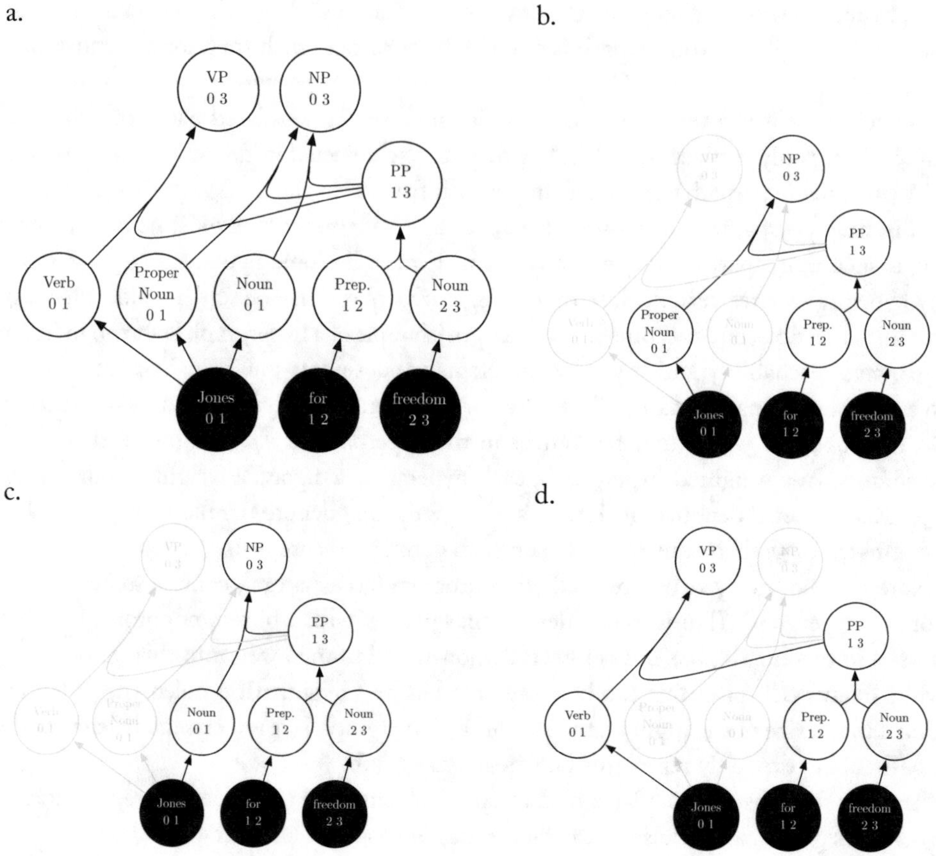

Figure 2.10: Decoding the structure of *Jones for freedom*: a hypergraph with 11 vertices and 9 hyperarcs (a). One hyperpath (b) to the node labeled "NP 0 3" corresponds to a parse that could be a political slogan (similar to *Dean for democracy*). Another (c) to the same node correponds to a noun phrase that could be paraphrased as *compulsive desire for freedom*. The single hyperpath to the node labeled "VP 0 3" (d) corresponds to a verb phrase, which might be embedded in the sentence, *Forced to work on his thesis, the sun streaming in the window, Mike began to jones for freedom.*

valid, i.e., *all* of its axioms are true:

$$Value(\mathsf{t}) = \bigvee_{y \in Proofs(\mathsf{t})} \bigwedge_{\mathsf{a} \in Axioms(y)} Value(\mathsf{a}) \tag{2.30}$$

where *Value* maps theorems and axioms to their (truth) values. A logic program is usually specified in terms of recursive inference rules. A classic example is a logic program for deducing genealogical relationships. Suppose we have axioms of the form parent(*John*, *Wayne*) (meaning John is a parent of Wayne) and $\mathsf{parent}(Mary, Susan)$ (meaning Mary is a parent of Susan). The following inference rules can be used to define the "ancestor" relationship.

$$\forall A, C, \qquad \mathsf{ancestor}(A, C) = \mathsf{parent}(A, C) \vee \bigvee_{B} \mathsf{ancestor}(A, B) \wedge \mathsf{parent}(B, C) \tag{2.31}$$

Proving that A is C's ancestor may depend on proving that A is B's ancestor first. Inference rules are usually written as a set of conjunctive rules, e.g.,

$$\begin{array}{lrcl} \forall A, C, & \mathsf{ancestor}(A, C) & \Leftarrow & \mathsf{parent}(A, C) \\ \forall A, C, & \mathsf{ancestor}(A, C) & \Leftarrow & \bigvee_{B} \mathsf{ancestor}(A, B) \wedge \mathsf{parent}(B, C) \end{array}$$

where the disjunctive operator across proofs from different rules is implied.

More generally, we can associate scores with proofs by letting axioms and theorems take values other than true and false. This is called a **weighted logic program**. If $\mathcal{A}$ is the set of all axioms, then $\omega : \mathcal{A} \rightarrow \mathbb{R}$ denotes a weighting function. There is an even more general formulation, in which the scores and weights take values in a **semiring**; we will return to semiring-weighted logic programming in section 2.3.3.

The connection to decoding is as follows. We use the input $\boldsymbol{x}$ to define a set of axioms $\mathcal{A}$ and a set of inference rules. These are usually general to the decoding problem, and the axioms are usually a mix of general and example-specific. Each output $\boldsymbol{y} \in \mathcal{Y}_{\boldsymbol{x}}$ corresponds to a proof of a designated "goal" theorem denoted goal. A proof $\boldsymbol{y}$'s score is given by

$$score(\boldsymbol{x}, \boldsymbol{y}) = \sum_{\mathsf{a} \in Axioms(\boldsymbol{y})} \omega(\mathsf{a}) = \sum_{\mathsf{a} \in \mathcal{A}} \omega(\mathsf{a}) freq(\mathsf{a}; \boldsymbol{y}) \tag{2.32}$$

where $freq(\mathsf{a}; \boldsymbol{y})$ is the number of times axiom a is used in proof $\boldsymbol{y}$. Decoding equates to finding the maximum-weighted proof $\boldsymbol{y} \in \mathcal{Y}_{\boldsymbol{x}}$, or the "best" way to prove the theorem goal.

For our named entity IOB tagging example, the inference rules and axioms might be instantiated as in figure 2.11. The figure only shows the axioms and the inference rules. Augmenting the axioms with meaningful weights and interpreting the program as seeking the maximum-weighted proof of goal leads to a view of decoding as solving the weighted logic program.

The connection among the weighted logic program view, the hypergraph view (section 2.2.4), and the parsing view (section 2.2.3) is quite strong. The three have equivalent expressive power; Nederhof (2003), describes, for example, how a logic program can be understood as a grammar. Each of these three views can help to give an interpretation to **dynamic programming**, which underlies the majority (but not all) of NLP decoding problems. We turn next to dynamic programming, drawing on each of these views when it is helpful. A key point to remember, which is often missed, is that all three views are computational ways of understanding a low-level problem of maximizing equation 2.3.

$$
\begin{array}{rl}
& \text{label-bigram}(\text{"B"}, \text{"B"}) \\
& \text{label-bigram}(\text{"B"}, \text{"I"}) \\
& \text{label-bigram}(\text{"B"}, \text{"O"}) \\
& \text{label-bigram}(\text{"I"}, \text{"B"}) \\
& \text{label-bigram}(\text{"I"}, \text{"I"}) \\
& \text{label-bigram}(\text{"I"}, \text{"O"}) \\
& \text{label-bigram}(\text{"O"}, \text{"B"}) \\
& \text{label-bigram}(\text{"O"}, \text{"O"}) \\
\forall x \in \Sigma, & \text{labeled-word}(x, \text{"B"}) \\
\forall x \in \Sigma, & \text{labeled-word}(x, \text{"I"}) \\
\forall x \in \Sigma, & \text{labeled-word}(x, \text{"O"})
\end{array}
$$

$$
\begin{aligned}
\forall \ell \in \Lambda, \ \mathsf{v}(\ell, 1) &= \text{labeled-word}(x_1, \ell) \\
\forall \ell \in \Lambda, \ \mathsf{v}(\ell, i) &= \bigvee_{\ell' \in \Lambda} \mathsf{v}(\ell', i-1) \wedge \text{label-bigram}(\ell', \ell) \wedge \text{labeled-word}(x_i, \ell) \\
\text{goal} &= \bigvee_{\ell \in \Lambda} \mathsf{v}(\ell, n)
\end{aligned}
$$

Figure 2.11: The running IOB tagging example as a logic program. n is the length of the input sequence $\boldsymbol{x} = \langle x_1, \ldots, x_n \rangle$. Λ denotes the set of labels {"B", "I", "O"}. The label-bigram axioms encode legitimate bigrams of labels (OI is not included). The labeled-word axioms encode legitimate labels for each word in the vocabulary Σ. Assigning weights to these axioms and interpreting the logic program as a *weighted* logic program leads to bijection between proofs (with values) and valid outputs in $\mathcal{Y}_{\boldsymbol{x}}$ (with scores).

2.3 DYNAMIC PROGRAMMING

"**Dynamic programming**" is a confusing term that originated in the operations research community in the 1940s; the word *programming* in this context refers not to computer programming but to optimization. Making things even more confusing, dynamic programming is today used not only for optimization problems, but for counting and probabilistic inference.[19]

Dynamic programming is best understood not as a specific algorithm or class of algorithms, but rather as a problem representation that suggests an efficient solution using one of a few basic tabling techniques. We will use the term **DP** to refer to a "dynamic program," hopefully avoiding some of the potential confusion in the name. DPs are an elegant way to represent decoding problems with two key properties:

[19]The topic of decoding algorithms based on dynamic programming is potentially extremely broad, drawing on research in graph algorithms, speech recognition, probabilistic artificial intelligence (especially in graphical models), context-free parsing algorithms, and formal languages and automata. This section aims to introduce the key ideas rather than exhaustively connect all of the literature. The five views from section 2.2 will be helpful to keep in mind.

Optimal substructure: The desired decoding solution $\boldsymbol{y}^*$ that optimizes equation 2.3 must involve optimal solutions to subproblems that strongly resemble the main problem. This property is usually recursive: each subproblem breaks further into smaller subproblems.

Overlapping subproblems: The total number of subproblems that need to be solved is small (typically, polynomial in the size of the input), and each is potentially reused many times in solving the main problem.

Taken together, these properties suggest a solution strategy in which we solve each subproblem at most once (and therefore in an appropriate order), combining the solutions as we go until we have solved the main problem.

Of the five views in section 2.2, four have these properties under appropriate conditions. They are:

- graphical models (section 2.2.1) where the underlying graph is acyclic;
- parsing (section 2.2.3)—the derivation score factors into rule weights, and subproblems are partial parses;
- hypergraphs or graphs (section 2.2.4)—the hyperpath (path) score factors into hyperarc (arc) weights, and subproblems are hyperpaths (paths) to intermediate vertices; and
- weighted logic programs (section 2.2.5)—the proof score factors into axiom weights, and subproblems are proofs of intermediate theorems.

By contrast, the polytope view does not in general reveal optimal substructure or overlapping subproblems.

We will focus mainly on the parsing, hypergraph, and weighted logic program views, switching among them for convenience. The graphical models view is especially useful when we turn to learning (chapters 3 and 4). For further reading on dynamic programming, we recommend Huang (2008).

2.3.1 SHORTEST OR MINIMUM-COST PATH

The simplest example of a DP is the problem of finding the minimum-cost path through a weighted directed graph (see an example in figure 2.12). As in section 2.2.4, let G consist of a set $\mathcal{V}$ of vertices, a set $\mathcal{A}$ of arcs, and a mapping of edges to weights (now interpreted as costs) $\omega : \mathcal{A} \to \mathbb{R}_{\geq 0}$ or equivalently as $\omega : \mathcal{V} \times \mathcal{V} \to \mathbb{R}_{\geq 0}$, with $\omega(v, v') = \infty$ if no edge exists between v and v'. (In structure prediction problems, G is defined using the input $\boldsymbol{x} \in \mathcal{X}$.) We designate an initial vertex $v_i \in \mathcal{V}$ and a final vertex $v_f \in \mathcal{V}$. We seek a sequence of edges that form a path from v_i to v_f; we seek the path with the minimum total cost. To see the minimum-cost path problem as a decoding problem, index **g** and **w** by arcs, and let, for all $a \in \mathcal{A}$:[20]

$$g_a(\boldsymbol{x}, \boldsymbol{y}) = \begin{cases} -1 & \text{if } a \text{ is crossed by the path } \boldsymbol{y} \\ 0 & \text{otherwise} \end{cases} \tag{2.33}$$

$$w_a = \omega(a) \tag{2.34}$$

The minimum-cost path corresponds, then, to $\operatorname{argmax}_{\boldsymbol{y} \in \mathcal{Y}_{\boldsymbol{x}}} \mathbf{w}^\top \mathbf{g}(\boldsymbol{x}, \boldsymbol{y})$.

The minimum-cost path problem has optimal substructure. If a path $\boldsymbol{y}$ is optimal, then the path from v_i to any intermediate vertex v on the path must also be optimal, and so must the path from v to v_f. We can therefore think of the subproblems as finding minimum-cost path to each $v \in \mathcal{V}$, starting from v_i.

The minimum-cost path problem also has overlapping subproblems. Intuitively, the minimum-cost path from v_i to any vertex $v \in \mathcal{V}$ is required for finding the minimum-cost path from v_i to vertices that are reachable from v, especially those that can only be reached from v_i by paths passing through v.

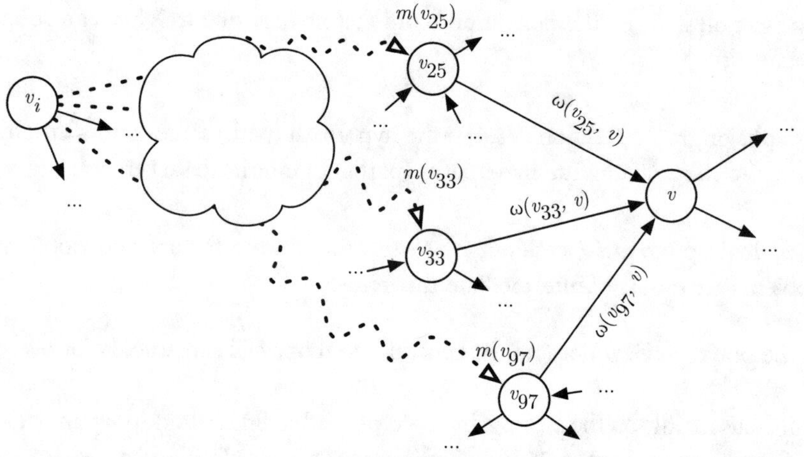

Figure 2.12: An example of the calculation performed to find in the DP equations for the minimum-cost path, equation 2.35. Here we consider the best path from v_i to v, which depends only on the best paths to v_{25}, v_{33}, and v_{97}, the vertices with edges going into v. Best paths are denoted as heavy, dashed lines. The local decision does not depend on any other properties of the graph than the scores of the best paths into v_{25}, v_{33}, and v_{97} and the scores of the edges from those vertices to v. We compare $m(v_{25}) + \omega(v_{25}, v)$, $m(v_{33}) + \omega(v_{33}, v)$, and $m(v_{97}) + \omega(v_{97}, v)$ to decide the best path to v.

[20] We can safely assume the best path would never cross the same edge more than once, since doing so would imply that the path has cycles, which cannot improve the total cost of the path. Therefore, the number of times an arc $a \in \mathcal{A}$ is crossed is either 0 or 1.

The DP equations (sometimes called Bellman equations) are a set of necessary conditions for solving a DP. For the minimum-cost path problem, these can be stated as follows, letting C^* denote the cost of the minimum cost path from v_i to v_f. We use the function $m : \mathcal{V} \to \mathbb{R}$ to denote the cost of the best path from v_i to each vertex.

$$\begin{aligned} m(v_i) &= 0 \\ \forall v \in \mathcal{V} \setminus \{v_i\}, \quad m(v) &= \min_{a \in \mathcal{A}: a = \langle v', v \rangle} m(v') + \omega(a) \\ C^* &= m(v_f) \end{aligned} \tag{2.35}$$

An illustration is shown in figure 2.12. It is important to remember that the above equations do not tell us *how* to calculate the minimum cost. Further, even if we solved the equations for the functional m, we would not have recovered the minimum-cost path. For that, we need to keep track of the argmin for each v, which we can do with a set of recursive equations that run in parallel to the DP equations 2.35:

$$\begin{aligned} \text{þ}(v_i) &= \langle\rangle \\ \forall v \in \mathcal{V} \setminus \{v_i\}, \quad \text{þ}(v) &= \text{þ}\left(\operatorname*{argmin}_{v' \in \mathcal{V}: a = \langle v', v \rangle \in \mathcal{A}} m(v') + \omega(a) \right) \smile \langle v \rangle \\ \boldsymbol{y}^* &= \text{þ}(v_f) \end{aligned} \tag{2.36}$$

We use $\text{þ}(v)$ to denote the sequence in $\mathcal{A}^*$ that is the best path from v_i to v, and we use $\smile$ to denote sequence concatenation. In implementation the best path need not be stored explicitly; we need only the incoming arc to v in the best path leading to v, $\operatorname{argmin}_{a \in \mathcal{A}: a = \langle v', v \rangle} m(v') + \omega(a)$. The entire path can be recovered by recursively looking up the predecessor until v_i is reached.

The minimum-cost path problem is suitable for representation as a DP because the cost total cost of a path breaks down into the sum of costs on the edges in the path:

$$\mathit{score}(\boldsymbol{x}, \boldsymbol{y}) = \mathbf{w}^\top \mathbf{g}(\boldsymbol{x}, \boldsymbol{y}) = \sum_{a \in \mathcal{A}} w_a g_a(\boldsymbol{x}, \boldsymbol{y}) \tag{2.37}$$

This "local factoring" of the path cost into edge costs is necessary for the optimal substructure property. By way of contrast, consider a path-scoring function that incurs the sum of the included edges' costs, plus an additional cost of C if the path fails to pass through every vertex once.[21] The cost of a path now depends on a property of the *entire* path. Optimal substructure does not hold; consider figure 2.13. The minimum-cost total path is either $v_i \to v_2 \to v_3 \to v_f$, with cost 3, or $v_i \to v_3 \to v_f$, with cost $2 + C$ (since it is not Hamiltonian). For $C > 1$, the minimum-cost path to v_3, which fails to include v_2, is not used in the minimum-cost path to v_f. This example is trivial, but for large graphs the factoring property is crucial for tractability.

[21] Paths that pass through every vertex once are known as Hamiltonian paths. If all edge costs are 0, this problem corresponds to the NP-complete problem of deciding whether a Hamiltonian path exists (Karp, 1972).

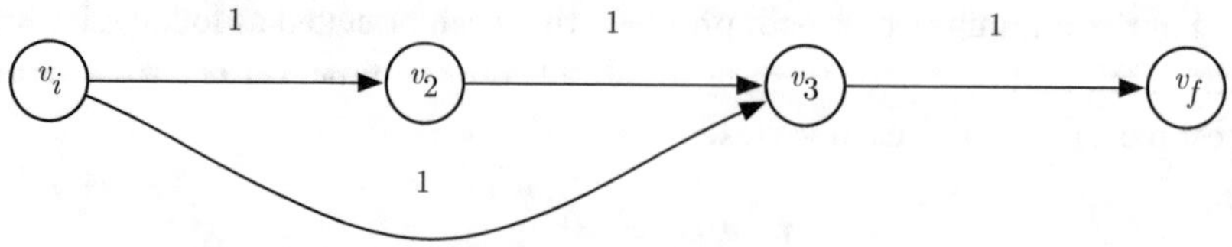

Figure 2.13: A graph used to illustrate a path cost that does not factor locally. See text.

A possible point of confusion arises when we notice that most of the classic DPs are presented as clever, efficient algorithms (with polynomial runtime and space) that solve combinatorial optimization problems over exponentially large spaces. It is important to remember that a set of DP equations need not imply polynomial runtime or space requirements.

Indeed, returning to the example, it is certainly possible to write DP equations such that the cost of non-Hamiltonian paths is taken into account, and doing so may even be helpful for the purposes of designing algorithms that approximately or exactly solve the problem. This is a seldom-mentioned advantage of the DP framework: even when the runtime of solving the equations can be exponential in the worst case, the DP equations provide a concise problem statement, and may also be used to find smaller exponential runtime algorithms through hypothesis recombination, or efficient approximations even when optimal substructure does not actually hold.

2.3.2 SEMIRINGS

Equations 2.35 and 2.36 have similar structure and appear redundant. We could rewrite them to work more closely in parallel by coupling the computations:

$$\begin{aligned}
\langle m(v_i), \flat(v_i)\rangle &= \langle 0, \langle\rangle\rangle \qquad (2.38)\\
\forall v \in \mathcal{V} \setminus \{v_i\}, \quad \langle m(v), \flat(v)\rangle &= \Bigg\langle \min_{a \in \mathcal{A}: a = \langle v', v\rangle} m(v') + \omega(a),\\
&\qquad \flat\left(\operatorname*{argmin}_{v' \in \mathcal{V}: a = \langle v', v\rangle \in \mathcal{A}} m(v) + \omega(a)\right) \smile \langle v\rangle \Bigg\rangle\\
\langle C^*, \boldsymbol{y}^*\rangle &= \langle m(v_f), \flat(v_f)\rangle
\end{aligned}$$

Equation 2.35 is more succinct than equations 2.36 and 2.38. A useful tool for abstracting from the details of the calculations is to use **semiring** notation, an idea proposed by Goodman (1999) and also explored extensively in work by researchers at AT&T for the finite-state/path setting (Mohri, 2002). We first state the path DP in semiring notation, then give a formal definition of semirings.

$$
\begin{aligned}
& \mathsf{m}(v_i) &=& \ \mathbf{1} \\
\forall v \in \mathcal{V} \setminus \{v_i\}, \quad & \mathsf{m}(v) &=& \bigoplus_{a \in \mathcal{A}: a = \langle v', v \rangle} \mathsf{m}(v') \otimes \omega(a) \\
& \mathsf{goal} &=& \ \mathsf{m}(v_f)
\end{aligned}
\tag{2.39}
$$

A semiring is defined by a tuple $\langle \mathcal{K}, \oplus, \otimes, \mathbf{0}, \mathbf{1} \rangle$.[22] $\mathcal{K}$ is a set of values; for costs it is $\mathbb{R}_{\geq 0}$. $\oplus$ is an associative, commutative aggregation operator and $\otimes$ is an associative combination operator that distributes over $\oplus$. The $\oplus$ identity is $\mathbf{0} \in \mathcal{K}$ and the $\otimes$ identity is $\mathbf{1} \in \mathcal{K}$. Formally, for all $\mathsf{u}, \mathsf{v}, \mathsf{w} \in \mathcal{K}$:

$$
\begin{aligned}
(\mathsf{u} \oplus \mathsf{v}) \oplus \mathsf{w} &= \mathsf{u} \oplus (\mathsf{v} \oplus \mathsf{w}) && \text{i.e., } \oplus \text{ is associative} \\
\mathsf{u} \oplus \mathsf{v} &= \mathsf{v} \oplus \mathsf{u} && \text{i.e., } \oplus \text{ is commutative} \\
\mathsf{u} \oplus \mathbf{0} &= \mathsf{u} && \text{i.e., } \oplus \text{ identity is } \mathbf{0} \\
(\mathsf{u} \otimes \mathsf{v}) \otimes \mathsf{w} &= \mathsf{u} \otimes (\mathsf{v} \otimes \mathsf{w}) && \text{i.e., } \otimes \text{ is associative} \\
\mathsf{u} \otimes (\mathsf{v} \oplus \mathsf{w}) &= (\mathsf{u} \otimes \mathsf{v}) \oplus (\mathsf{u} \otimes \mathsf{w}) && \text{i.e., } \otimes \text{ distributes over } \oplus \\
\mathsf{u} \otimes \mathbf{1} &= \mathsf{u} && \text{i.e., } \otimes \text{ identity is } \mathbf{1}
\end{aligned}
$$

Semirings are a concept from abstract algebra (Rosenfeld, 1968).

The advantage of writing the DP in semiring notation is that many related problems now appear identical. For example, the problems of **graph reachability** and **path sum** are represented by equations 2.39, using, respectively, the BOOLEAN and REAL semirings. Algorithms discussed in later chapters in many cases correspond to decoding algorithms with alternate semirings. Some useful semirings are shown in figure 2.14. Showing that equation 2.38 also corrsponds to a semiring is left as an exercise.

Figure 2.15 shows a generic semiring representation for DP equations corresponding to a family of string-pair calculations that include the Levenshtein (1965) distance between two strings $\boldsymbol{s} = \langle s_1, \ldots, s_n \rangle$ and $\boldsymbol{s}' = \langle s'_1, \ldots, s'_m \rangle$. For the traditional Levenshtein distance, the COST semiring is used.

The similarity between this problem and equations 2.39 suggests that Levenshtein distance can be reduced to a minimum-cost path problem by creating, for $0 \leq i \leq n$ and $0 \leq j \leq m$, a vertex $\mathsf{d}(i, j)$ corresponding to the i-length prefix of $\boldsymbol{s}$ and the j-length prefix of $\boldsymbol{s}'$. $\mathsf{d}(i, j)$ has up to three incoming edges, from $\mathsf{d}(i-1, j-1)$, $\mathsf{d}(i, j-1)$, and $\mathsf{d}(i-1, j)$, whose costs correspond to substitution, insertion, and deletion costs. Zero-cost edges are added from $\mathsf{d}(i-1, j-1)$ to $\mathsf{d}(i, j)$ whenever $s_i = s'_j$.

Of course, *solving* the Levenshtein edit distance by reducing it to a minimum-cost path problem is not likely to be efficient, since there is considerable structure present in the edit distance problem that gets ignored in the general minimum-cost path problem. We point out the connection merely to suggest that a wider class of problems exists, with different instances having their own special structure that may be exploited in implementation. Another example is the sequence labeling case illustrated in figure 2.9, which has a sequential structure that can be exploited.

[22]We use the sans serif typeface to indicate objects whose values fall in a semiring.

name	$\mathcal{K}$	$u \oplus v$	$u \otimes v$	**0**	**1**
BOOLEAN	$\{0, 1\}$	$u \vee v$	$u \wedge v$	false	true
COST	$\mathbb{R}_{\geq 0} \cup \{\infty\}$	$\min(u, v)$	$u + v$	∞	0
TROPICAL	$\mathbb{R} \cup \{-\infty\}$	$\max(u, v)$	$u + v$	$-\infty$	0
ALL-PROOFS	$2^{\mathcal{L}}$	$u \cup v$	$\bigcup_{u \in u, v \in v} u \smile v$	$\emptyset$	$\{\epsilon\}$
REAL	$\mathbb{R}_{\geq 0}$	$u + v$	$u \times v$	0	1
LOG-REAL	$\mathbb{R} \cup \{-\infty, +\infty\}$	$\log(e^u + e^v)$	$u + v$	$-\infty$	0

Figure 2.14: Important semirings. The first three are of primary concern here; the others will be useful later. See Goodman (1999) for more semirings and a more thorough discussion of ALL-PROOFS. We use $\mathcal{L}$ to denote a proof language; in the case of best path problems, we might let $\mathcal{L} = \mathcal{A}^*$, corresponding to equations 2.36. $\smile$ denotes concatentation.

$$
\begin{aligned}
\mathsf{d}(0,0) &= \mathbf{1} \\
\forall \langle i, j \rangle \in \mathbb{N}^2 \setminus \{\langle 0, 0 \rangle\}, \quad \mathsf{d}(i, j) &= \bigoplus \begin{cases} \mathsf{d}(i-1, j-1) \otimes \left\{ s_i = s'_j \right\}_{\mathcal{K}} & \text{match} \\ \mathsf{d}(i-1, j-1) \otimes \underline{\mathsf{subcost}} & \text{substitution} \\ \mathsf{d}(i, j-1) \otimes \underline{\mathsf{inscost}} & \text{insertion} \\ \mathsf{d}(i-1, j) \otimes \underline{\mathsf{delcost}} & \text{deletion} \end{cases} \\
\mathsf{D}^* &= \mathsf{d}(n, m)
\end{aligned}
$$

Figure 2.15: A DP for string transduction; with the COST semiring and $\underline{\mathsf{subcost}} = \underline{\mathsf{inscost}} = \underline{\mathsf{delcost}} = 1$, it gives necessary conditions for calculating the Levenshtein (1965) distance D^* between strings $\boldsymbol{s} = \langle s_1, \ldots, s_n \rangle$ and $\boldsymbol{s}' = \langle s'_1, \ldots, s'_m \rangle$. We use $\{e\}_{\mathcal{K}}$ to denote (semiring) **1** if e is true and (semiring) **0** if it is false. The DP can be generalized to maintain the minimum cost monotonic alignment, analogous to equations 2.36. Transposition edits can be permitted by including "$\mathsf{d}(i-2, j-2) \otimes \left\{ s_i = s_{j-1} \wedge s_{i-1} = s_j \right\}_{\mathcal{K}} \otimes \underline{\mathsf{transpcost}}$" inside the $\oplus$ operator.

Note the use of the notation $\{e\}_{\mathcal{K}}$ to map a logical expression e into the semiring. More generally, we will use $\{e\}_{\mathcal{K}}$ to map any expression into the semiring, clarifying when necessary how that interpretation is defined.

2.3.3 DP AS LOGICAL DEDUCTION

The generic formulation of string transduction calculations in figure 2.15 suggests a view of a DP as a weighted logic program. Here we introduce **semiring-weighted logic programs**, building on section 2.2.5. The central idea is that we can separate out the structure of a logic program (axioms, theorems, proofs) from the values (weights, scores).

In classic logic programming, values are always true or false (1 or 0). A theorem t is true if and only if one of its proofs is valued, i.e., *all* of the proof's axioms are true:

$$\mathsf{t} = \bigvee_{y \in \mathit{Proofs}(\mathsf{t})} \bigwedge_{\mathsf{a} \in \mathit{Axioms}(y)} \mathsf{a} \tag{2.40}$$

We describe such programs as being instantiated in the BOOLEAN semiring. (In figure 2.15 the BOOLEAN semiring is uninteresting, as it only determines whether two strings may be aligned at all via match, substitution, insertion, and deletion operations, regardless of the cost. The trivial solution is to set all d terms to value **1**, "true," if the substitution, insertion, and deletion costs are "true.") The BOOLEAN semiring is useful if we care only whether a proof (output structure) *exists*. For decoding, we seek the *optimal* proof.

When we use a particular semiring, axioms, theorems, and proofs all take values in the semiring. Solving a logic program equates to finding the semiring value of one or more theorems. The following relationship holds:

$$\mathsf{t} = \bigoplus_{p \in \mathit{Proofs}(\mathsf{t})} \bigotimes_{\mathsf{u} \in \mathit{Axioms}(p)} \mathsf{u} \tag{2.41}$$

This is simply a more general case of equation 2.40.

In figure 2.15, the axioms are <u>subcost</u>, <u>inscost</u>, and <u>delcost</u>, each of which is underlined in our notation to remind us that these are axioms provided before execution. The theorems in figure 2.15 are the d terms. Each $\left\{s_i = s'_j\right\}_{\mathcal{K}}$ expression can also be encoded using a theorem $\mathsf{match}(i, j)$ derived from axioms that encode the strings:

$$\mathsf{match}(i, j) = \bigoplus_{s \in \Sigma} \underline{\mathsf{s}(s, i)} \otimes \underline{\mathsf{s'}(s, j)} \tag{2.42}$$

Replacing $\left\{s_i = s'_j\right\}_{\mathcal{K}}$ with $\mathsf{match}(i, j)$ and adding the inference rule in equation 2.42 to figure 2.15 gets us most of the way to a well-formed logic program. To complete the conversion, we must include axioms to encode the strings $\boldsymbol{s} = \langle s_1, \ldots, s_n \rangle$ and $\boldsymbol{s}' = \langle s'_1, \ldots, s'_m \rangle$. We let $\mathsf{s}(s_i, i)$ represent the fact that the ith symbol in the string $\boldsymbol{s}$ is s_i, $\mathsf{s'}(s_j, j)$ represent the fact that the jth symbol in $\boldsymbol{s}'$ is s'_j, $\mathsf{slen}(n)$ represent the fact that the length of $\boldsymbol{s}$ is n, and $\mathsf{s'len}(m)$ represent the fact that the length of $\boldsymbol{s}'$ is m. All of these axioms are assigned value (semiring) **1**:

$$\begin{array}{rclrcl}
\underline{\mathsf{s}(s_1, 1)} & = & \mathbf{1} & \underline{\mathsf{s'}(s'_1, 1)} & = & \mathbf{1} \\
\vdots & \vdots & \vdots & \vdots & & \vdots \\
\underline{\mathsf{s}(s_n, n)} & = & \mathbf{1} & \underline{\mathsf{s'}(s'_m, m)} & = & \mathbf{1} \\
\underline{\mathsf{slen}(n)} & = & \mathbf{1} & \underline{\mathsf{s'len}(m)} & = & \mathbf{1}
\end{array}$$

Notice that we retain the semiring-general notation (the string-encoding axioms have value **1**, not 1). Since the logic program has access only to axioms, not to external values like n and m, we must also replace the inference rule "$\mathsf{D}^* = \mathsf{d}(n, m)$" with

$$\mathsf{D}^* = \bigoplus_{i,j \in \mathbb{N}} \mathsf{d}(i, j) \otimes \underline{\mathsf{slen}(i)} \otimes \underline{\mathsf{s'len}(j)}$$

While this generalization of logic programming suggests the use of theorem-proving techniques to solve DP equations, e.g., as implemented in Prolog-style declarative programming languages, it is important to recognize the difference between declarative view of the DP equations as a semiring-weighted logic program and the procedures we might use to *solve* the equations, addressed in section 2.3.4.

While symbolic parsing as deduction is an idea dating to the 1980s (Pereira and Shieber, 1987, Pereira and Warren, 1983), the notation we use for DPs was put forward by Sikkel (1993) and Shieber et al. (1995), particularly focusing on context-free parsing. A major emphasis of that research was to show the connections among different parsing algorithms, with the claim that the deductive framework made these disparate algorithms easier to compare and contrast.

The generalization to arbitrary semirings is due to Goodman (1999). Our notation borrows heavily from the Dyna language (Eisner et al., 2004, 2005), though we prefer to use more concise mathematical expressions where it is convenient, rather than strict Dyna notation (e.g., $\{s_i = s_j\}_{\mathbb{K}}$ rather than equation 2.42).

Sequence Labeling

Dynamic programming is highly suitable for sequence labeling problems. We now turn to more general treatments of problems like our running IOB tagging example. Letting $\boldsymbol{x} = \langle x_1, \ldots, x_n \rangle$, each $x_i \in \Sigma$ denote the input, and $\boldsymbol{y} = \langle y_1, \ldots, y_n \rangle$, each $y_i \in \Lambda$ denote an output labeling, we require, for now, the feature vector function $\mathbf{g}$ to factor as follows:

$$\mathbf{w}^\top \mathbf{g}(\boldsymbol{x}, \boldsymbol{y}) = \mathbf{w}^\top \left(\sum_{i=1}^{n+1} \mathbf{f}(\boldsymbol{x}, y_{i-1}, y_i, i) \right) = \sum_{i=1}^{n+1} \mathbf{w}^\top \mathbf{f}(\boldsymbol{x}, y_{i-1}, y_i, i) \tag{2.43}$$

(We interpret y_0 and y_{n+1} as special "before" and "after" symbols, respectively, denoted ➯ and ◉, equivalently assuming that the length of $\boldsymbol{y}$ is equal to the length of $\boldsymbol{x}$.) In sections 3.3.3 and 3.5.2 we will interpret this factored form in terms of independence assumptions among a collection of random variables $\langle Y_1, \ldots, Y_n \rangle$, and we show that it generalizes the **Viterbi** algorithm (Viterbi, 1967). For now it suffices to say that the optimal substructure requirement is satisfied if we use only feature functions that factor into adjacent label pairs y_{i-1} and y_i. Under this assumption, we may solve the decoding problem (equation 2.3) using the DP equations in figure 2.16.

A major advantage of the semiring DP equations is that they let us easily conduct asymptotic runtime and memory analyses of the programs (McAllester, 2002), under the assumption that we have an efficient solver (see section 2.3.4). An upper bound on memory requirements is given by

$$\forall \ell \in \Lambda, \quad \mathsf{v}(\ell, 1) = \left\{\mathbf{w}^\top \mathbf{f}(\boldsymbol{x}, ⧁, \ell, 1)\right\}_{\mathcal{K}} \tag{2.44}$$

$$\forall \ell \in \Lambda, i \in \{2, \ldots, n\}, \quad \mathsf{v}(\ell, i) = \bigoplus_{\ell' \in \Lambda} \mathsf{v}(\ell', i-1) \otimes \left\{\mathbf{w}^\top \mathbf{f}(\boldsymbol{x}, \ell', \ell, i)\right\}_{\mathcal{K}} \tag{2.45}$$

$$\mathsf{goal} = \bigoplus_{\ell \in \Lambda} \mathsf{v}(\ell, n) \otimes \left\{\mathbf{w}^\top \mathbf{f}(\boldsymbol{x}, \ell, ⬤, n+1)\right\}_{\mathcal{K}} \tag{2.46}$$

Figure 2.16: Sequence labeling DP suitable when $\boldsymbol{x} = \langle x_1, \ldots, x_n \rangle$ and $\mathbf{g}(\boldsymbol{x}, \boldsymbol{y}) = \sum_{i=1}^{n+1} \mathbf{f}(\boldsymbol{x}, y_{i-1}, y_i, i)$. For decoding, use the TROPICAL semiring with a solver that recovers the best proof. $\{e\}_{\mathcal{K}}$ denotes the value of e as interpreted in the semiring; in the TROPICAL semiring, $\{e\}_{\mathcal{K}} = e$.

counting the number of theorems and axioms that could be instantiated. For figure 2.16, this amounts to:

- $|\Lambda|^2(n+1)$ axioms of the form $\left\{\mathbf{w}^\top \mathbf{f}(\boldsymbol{x}, \ell', \ell, i)\right\}_{\mathcal{K}}$ and
- $|\Lambda| n$ theorems of the form $\mathsf{v}(\ell, i)$.

Hence, the memory required is quadratic in $|\Lambda|$ (the number of atomic labels) and linear in n (the length of the sequence).[23]

Asymptotic runtime is calculated by counting the number of instantiations of each inference rule, multiplying each by the number of possible values for variables scoped by $\oplus$ operators:

- $|\Lambda|$ instantiations of equation 2.44;
- $|\Lambda|(n-1)$ instantiations of equation 2.45, with $|\Lambda|$ values bound by the $\oplus$ operator, giving $|\Lambda|^2(n-1)$;
- 1 instantiation of equation 2.46, with $|\Lambda|$ values bound by the $\oplus$ operator, giving $|\Lambda|$.

The asymptotic runtime for figure 2.16, then, is $O(|\Lambda|^2 n)$. This does not take into account the time required for calculating the $\left\{\mathbf{w}^\top \mathbf{f}(\boldsymbol{x}, \ell, \ell', i)\right\}_{\mathcal{K}}$ terms, which is $O(|\Lambda|^2 nd)$ if there are d features.

Another major advantage of the DP equations is that we can often derive one algorithm from another. Consider these less-stringent factoring assumptions:

$$\mathbf{w}^\top \mathbf{g}(\boldsymbol{x}, \boldsymbol{y}) = \mathbf{w}^\top \left(\sum_{i=1}^{n+1} \mathbf{f}(\boldsymbol{x}, y_{i-2}, y_{i-1}, y_i, i) \right) = \sum_{i=1}^{n+1} \mathbf{w}^\top \mathbf{f}(\boldsymbol{x}, y_{i-2}, y_{i-1}, y_i, i) \tag{2.47}$$

[23]The reader may notice that considerable improvements can be obtained. We need not store all of the $\left\{\mathbf{w}^\top \mathbf{f}(\boldsymbol{x}, \ell, \ell', i)\right\}_{\mathcal{K}}$ and v theorems during the entire process of solving the DP equations; it may be possible to discard some results. It is left as an exercise to show how the space requirement can be reduced to $O(|\Lambda|)$ without depending on n, for the TROPICAL semiring.

(Assume that $y_{-1} = y_0 = ⬗$.) This lets features consider up to three adjacent symbols in $\boldsymbol{y}$, instead of two, as in equation 2.43. Figure 2.17 gives DP equations. Note that relaxing the factoring assumptions comes at a cost in runtime and space.

$$
\begin{aligned}
\forall \ell \in \Lambda, \quad \mathsf{v}(⬗, \ell, 1) &= \left\{\mathbf{w}^\top \mathbf{f}(\boldsymbol{x}, ⬗, ⬗, \ell, 1)\right\}_{\mathcal{K}} \\
\forall \ell', \ell \in \Lambda, i \in \{2, \ldots, n\}, \quad \mathsf{v}(\ell', \ell, i) &= \bigoplus_{\ell'' \in \Lambda \cup \{⬗\}} \mathsf{v}(\ell'', \ell', i-1) \otimes \left\{\mathbf{w}^\top \mathbf{f}(\boldsymbol{x}, \ell'', \ell', \ell, i)\right\}_{\mathcal{K}} \\
\mathsf{goal} &= \bigoplus_{\ell' \in \Lambda \cup \{⬗\}, \ell \in \Lambda} \mathsf{v}(\ell', \ell, n) \otimes \left\{\mathbf{w}^\top \mathbf{f}(\boldsymbol{x}, \ell', \ell, ●, n+1)\right\}_{\mathcal{K}}
\end{aligned}
$$

Figure 2.17: Sequence labeling DP suitable when $\mathbf{g}(\boldsymbol{x}, \boldsymbol{y}) = \sum_{i=1}^{n+1} \mathbf{f}(\boldsymbol{x}, y_{i-2}, y_{i-1}, y_i, i)$. Compare with figure 2.16.

"Branching" Proofs and Hypergraphs

So far we have introduced DP equations and connected them closely to finding a best path through a graph, using the language of weighted logic programming to explain and analyze the equations. Not all DPs reduce to path problems. An example of one that does not is the CKY algorithm for deciding whether a string is in the context-free language of a given context-free grammar in Chomsky normal form. The classic CKY algorithm (Cocke and Schwartz, 1970, Kasami, 1965, Younger, 1967) corresponds to the Boolean semiring variant of a more general DP.[24] In the Boolean semiring, it is helpful to think of the DP as a set of necessary conditions for $\boldsymbol{x}$ being in the context-free language of the grammar. The general program is shown in figure 2.18.

The property that makes this DP not reducible to a minimum-cost path problem is that, for $k > i + 1$, theorems of the form $\mathsf{c}(N, i, k)$ can depend on the $\otimes$-product of *two* other c terms, not just one. More generally, in the language of logic programming, a DP where some theorem's value depends directly (in a single inference rule) on the $\otimes$-product of *two* theorems' values (rather than just one theorem and perhaps some axioms) cannot be reduced to reasoning about paths in graphs.

Klein and Manning (2001) described the connection between context-free parsing algorithms and hypergraphs. The hypergraph view of the DP is as follows. If we converted figure 2.18 into a semiring-weighted logic program,[25] we could construct a hypergraph in which each theorem corresponds to its own vertex. Each application of an inference rule corresponds to a semiring-weighted hyperarc, with the antecedents comprising the source and the consequent the target. A proof of a theorem corresponds to a hyperpath from a subset of axioms to the theorem's vertex. The

[24] The probabilistic CKY algorithm (Baker, 1979) corresponds to the REAL semiring variant.

[25] This would be accomplished by replacing $\{N \rightarrow x_i\}_{\mathcal{K}}$ with $\bigoplus_{w \in \Sigma} \underline{\mathsf{x}(w, i)} \otimes \underline{\mathsf{unary}(N, w)}$, $\{N \rightarrow N'N''\}_{\mathcal{K}}$ with $\underline{\mathsf{binary}(N, N', N'')}$ and introducing appropriate grammar- and string-encoding axioms.

$$\begin{aligned}
\forall N \in \mathcal{N}, 1 \leq i \leq n, \quad \mathsf{c}(N, i-1, i) &= \{N \rightarrow x_i\}_{\mathcal{K}} && (2.48)\\
\forall N \in \mathcal{N}, 0 \leq i < k \leq n, \quad \mathsf{c}(N, i, k) &= \bigoplus_{N', N'' \in \mathcal{N}, j: i<j<k} \mathsf{c}(N', i, j) && (2.49)\\
&\quad \otimes \mathsf{c}(N'', j, k)\\
&\quad \otimes \{N \rightarrow N'N''\}_{\mathcal{K}}\\
\mathsf{goal} &= \mathsf{c}(S, 0, n) && (2.50)
\end{aligned}$$

Figure 2.18: CKY as a DP. Let $\langle \mathcal{N}, \Sigma, S, \mathcal{R} \rangle$ denote the CFG in Chomsky normal form, and let $\boldsymbol{x} = \langle x_1, \ldots, x_n \rangle$, each $x_i \in \Sigma$, denote the string. $\{r\}_{\mathcal{K}}$ maps the CFG production rule r to its semiring value, which in the BOOLEAN semiring is 1 if and only if $r \in \mathcal{R}$.

axioms can be understood alternately as source vertices or as weights on the hyperarcs. We seek the semiring-sum over proofs of the goal theorem.

The special case where the proof is a graph arises when every theorem depends on at most one other theorem, and we treat axioms as assigners of weights to arcs, not as vertices.

Side Conditions

An important element of the deductive framework that we have not discussed is **side conditions**. We extend our notation slightly to define, for a term c,

$$\mathsf{side}(\mathsf{c}) = \begin{cases} \mathbf{1} & \text{if } \mathsf{c} \neq \mathbf{0} \\ \mathbf{0} & \text{otherwise} \end{cases} \quad (2.51)$$

Figure 2.19 shows the DP equations for a semiring-general version of the Earley (1970) algorithm that uses a side condition to avoid unnecessary extra work. Note that the Earley algorithm involves an inference rule with two theorem antecedents, and therefore is a hyperpath (rather than path) problem.

2.3.4 SOLVING DPS

When dynamic programming is taught in courses on algorithms, the key insight is often the use of a one- or two-dimensional array data structure, with each cell corresponding to an intermediate result (in our jargon, the value of a subproblem, theorem, or hyperpath to an intermediate vertex). The recursive DP equations tell us how to calculate each cell's value using the previous cells' values, and we proceed in a carefully chosen order. We discuss the tabular approach first, then turn to an alternative based on search.

$$
\begin{array}{rcll}
\mathsf{need}(S,0) & = & \mathbf{1} & \\
\mathsf{need}(N,j) & = & \displaystyle\bigoplus_{(N'\to N\alpha)\in\mathcal{R},i:0\le i\le j} \mathsf{c}(N'/N\alpha,i,j) & \\
\mathsf{c}(N/\alpha,i,i) & = & \{N\to\alpha\}_{\mathcal{K}} \otimes \mathsf{side}\,(\mathsf{need}(N,i)) & \text{“predict”} \\
\mathsf{c}(N/\alpha,i,k) & = & \mathsf{c}(N/x_k\alpha,i,k-1) & \text{“scan”} \\
 & & \displaystyle\bigoplus_{N'\in\mathcal{N},j} \mathsf{c}(N/N'\alpha,i,j)\otimes\mathsf{c}(N'/\epsilon,j,k) & \text{“complete”} \\
\mathsf{goal} & = & \mathsf{c}(S/\epsilon,0,n) &
\end{array}
\tag{2.52}
$$

Figure 2.19: The Earley algorithm as a DP. Let $\langle\mathcal{N},\Sigma,S,\mathcal{R}\rangle$ denote the CFG, and let $\boldsymbol{x}=\langle x_1,\ldots,x_n\rangle$, each $x_i\in\Sigma$, denote the string. $\forall$-quantifiers are omitted for clarity. $\{r\}_{\mathcal{K}}$ maps the CFG production rule r to its semiring value, which in the BOOLEAN semiring is 1 if and only if $r\in\mathcal{R}$. α is used to denote an arbitrary sequence of terminals and/or nonterminals, and ϵ the empty sequence. $\mathsf{side}\,(\cdot)$ is as defined in equation 2.51. The need theorems calculate all of the nonterminals that might span any phrase starting after the jth word. "N/α" can be interpreted as a generalization of context-free nonterminals denoting "N that will be complete once the sequence α is found to the right." The inference rules for building c theorems correspond directly to the traditional "predict," "scan," and "complete" operators used to define the Earley algorithm procedurally.

Solving DPs with Tables

The key to the classic "table" or "memoization" solution of a DP is to identify an ordering of the theorems to be proved, such that each theorem comes *after* all theorems it depends on. We call such an ordering *felicitous*.[26] For DPs that correspond to directed graphs (not the more general case of hypergraphs), a felicitous ordering is provided by a topological sort on the vertices in the graph. The hypergraph case is similar, with a suitably generalized definition of the topological sort.[27] In logic programming research, a felicitous ordering is called a "stratification."

Felicitous orderings are readily apparent for some of the examples of DPs so far:

- For the string transduction DP in figure 2.15, $\mathsf{d}(i,j)$ can be calculated only after $\mathsf{d}(i-1,j-1)$, $\mathsf{d}(i,j-1)$, and $\mathsf{d}(i-1,j)$. The table and felicitous orderings are shown in figure 2.20.
- For the sequence labeling DP in figure 2.16, $\mathsf{v}(\ell,i)$ can be calculated only after $\mathsf{v}(\ell',i-1)$, for all $\ell'\in\Lambda$. The table and felicitous orderings are shown in figure 2.21.
- For the CKY algorithm in figure 2.18, $\mathsf{c}(N,i,k)$ can be calculated only after all $\mathsf{c}(N',j,j')$ such that $i\le j<j'\le k$. The table (often called the "chart" or "triangle") is shown in figure 2.22.

[26] Goodman (1999) describes an assignment of theorems to a sequence of ordered "buckets." Our notion of felicitous orderings is essentially the same: an assignment of theorems to buckets implies a felicitous ordering, as long as there are no "looping buckets."

[27] I.e., the vertices must be ordered so that, for all v and v' in the set of vertices, if there exists any hyperpath from v to v', then v must strictly precede v'.

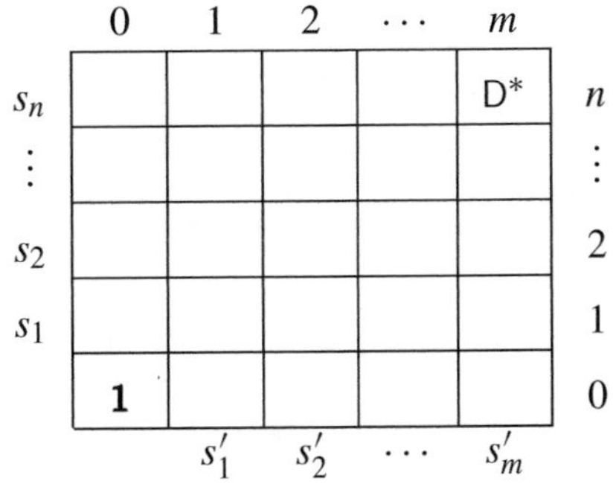

Figure 2.20: The table for solving the string transduction DP in figure 2.15. Three felicitous orderings, all starting from the bottom left cell, are: diagonal-wise (all $\mathsf{d}(i, j)$ such that $i + j = k$, for $k = 0, 1, 2, \ldots$), column-wise (for $j = 0$ to m do for $i = 0$ to n do ...), and row-wise (for $i = 0$ to n do for $j = 0$ to m do ...). The value of D^* will be in the top right cell (n, m).

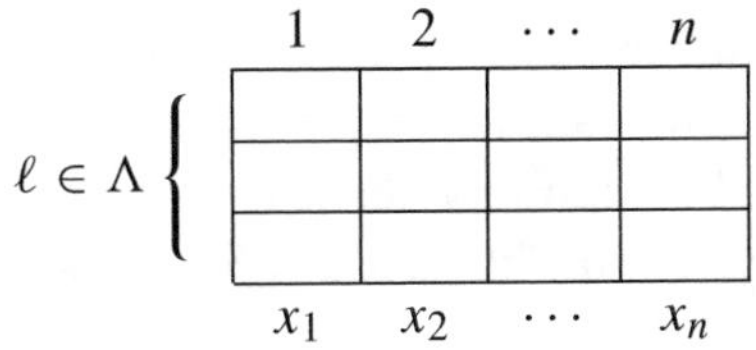

Figure 2.21: The table for solving the sequence labeling DP in figure 2.16. A felicitous ordering proceeds column-wise, starting at the left. The value of goal is calculated using the right-most column.

Given a felicitous ordering of theorems, the tabular approach is efficient and easy to implement. Unfortunately, it has two requirements that are not met by all DPs in all semirings.

The first is that we must be able to identify a felicitous ordering; this will be impossible if the hypergraph has cycles. For example, consider augmenting CKY to permit unary rules of the form $N \to N'$, with N and $N' \in \mathcal{N}$. Equation 2.49 can be altered to permit the construction of $\mathsf{c}(N, i, k)$ from $\mathsf{c}(N', i, k)$ as follows:

$$\begin{aligned} \mathsf{c}(N, i, k) \;=\; & \left(\bigoplus_{N', N'' \in \mathcal{N}, j : i < j < k} \mathsf{c}(N', i, j) \otimes \mathsf{c}(N'', j, k) \otimes \{N \to N' N''\}_{\mathcal{K}} \right) \\ & \oplus \left(\bigoplus_{N' \in \mathcal{N}} \mathsf{c}(N', i, k) \otimes \{N \to N'\}_{\mathcal{K}} \right) \end{aligned} \tag{2.53}$$

It should be clear that any unary cycles (the simplest of which results from any rule $N \to N$) will create problems for ordering the theorems. In the simplest case, if $N \to N$, then for any i and k, $\mathsf{c}(N, i, k)$ depends on itself. Calculating $\mathsf{c}(N, i, k)$ in this case leads to an infinite $\oplus$-summation. DP cycles do not arise frequently in NLP models; Goodman (1999) provides solutions for a few

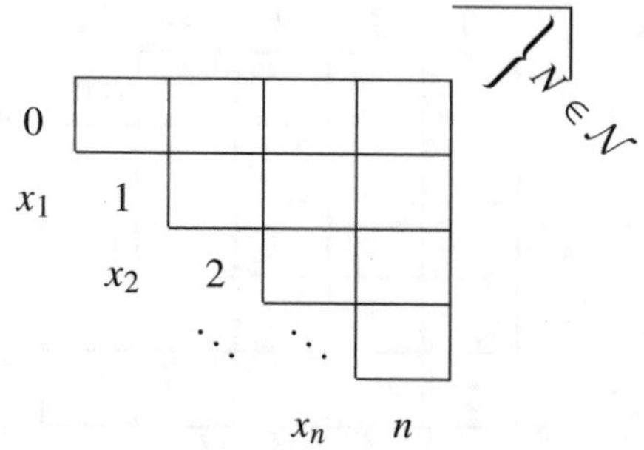

Figure 2.22: A slice of the table for solving the CKY DP in figure 2.18. Each nonterminal $N \in \mathcal{N}$ corresponds to its own $n \times n$ half-grid. A felicitous ordering proceeds diagonal-wise, building narrower $\mathsf{c}(N, i, j)$ theorems with smaller $j - i$ before wider ones with larger $j - i$. The value of goal will be in the top right cell of the slice corresponding to the start symbol $S \in \mathcal{N}$.

different semirings, the most difficult of which are hypergraph problems with the REAL semiring, handled using an iterative approximation technique subsumed by the agenda approach discussed below. For some kinds of cycles, linear solvers can be used to solve for the theorem values involved in the cycle (Stolcke, 1995). Cycles notwithstanding, felicitous theorem orderings are not always apparent.

The second limitation of the tabular method is that it forces us to exhaustively calculate the value of every provable theorem before finding the value of goal. This may involve wasted effort, since some theorems may not be used in any proof of goal; or, to use the language of hypergraphs, we may be able to avoid doing work for vertices that do not lie on any hyperpath to goal.

Solving DPs by Search

In the context of decoding, TROPICAL semiring DPs are the most relevant. The hypergraph view of decoding is helpful here. The goal is to find the maximum-scoring hyperpath, where the hypergraph is defined using a set of equations. A very natural solution is to think of this as a **search** for the best hyperpath to goal. This view has several advantages:

- The recursive DP equations suggest very natural search operators for proposing extensions at any point during the search: proceed outward, from already-reached vertices, to those that can be reached from them. (In the logic program view, this is equivalent to proceeding *deductively*, from already-proved axioms and theorems to the theorems they can be used to prove.)

- Approximate search, in which a high-scoring but not necessarily optimal hyperpath is found, may allow us to trade optimality for faster runtime. Intuitively, sacrificing guarantees of an optimal solution, or allowing the possibility of **search error**, implies that we are willing to let accuracy decrease. Note, however, that our models are seldom "perfect," and we should not conflate optimality of the decoder's output with accurate prediction. There have even been situations were search error led to accuracy gains.

- Generic search methods, which classically view the state space as a graph, may be used for graph problems and adapted for hypergraph problems.

Shieber et al. (1995) suggested the use of an agenda to keep track of updates to values of theorems, for the BOOLEAN semiring. For the TROPICAL and COST semirings, Nederhof (2003) shows how Knuth's generalization of Dijkstra's algorithm (Knuth, 1977) suggests a generic agenda-based solver. Eisner et al. (2005) provide a semiring-general agenda-based algorithm for solving arbitrary semiring-weighted logic programs (see algorithm 1).

For efficiency, the choice of a priority function (*Pri* in algorithm 1) is crucial. Assuming the TROPICAL semiring (which is, again, the one most strongly associated with decoding), we would like to process each axiom or theorem exactly once. A bad priority function might lead us to process a theorem too soon, before all of its possible antecedents have been assigned *their* correct values. This is analogous to solving a DP with a table and an ordering that is not felicitous. In such a situation, the agenda algorithm is still *correct* (if it is run until the agenda is empty as in algorithm 1), but it may be highly *inefficient*, returning to each theorem many times.

If we process a theorem t before its antecedents have converged, we will have to return to it later on, when its antecedents' values change and spawn updates for t. Making things even worse, t may have spawned updates to other theorems that it helps to prove, and they will all have to be updated whenever t changes. It is not hard to imagine a priority function that goes "deep" into the graph,[28] assigning values to many theorems, but assigning values that are premature.

If a felicitous ordering is known, it can be used to define *Pri*. For example, in figure 2.15, $Pri(\mathsf{d}(i, j)) = -i - j$; in figure 2.16, $Pri(\mathsf{v}(\ell, i)) = -i$; and in figure 2.18, $Pri(\mathsf{c}(N, i, k)) = i - k$. Hence, the agenda can simulate the method of tables. From a search perspective, this is much like breadth-first search, since every theorem that can be proved will be processed.

The table method, as noted above, does lead to exhaustive processing of all theorems. Processing any theorem that does not ultimately appear in the maximum-scoring proof is, in some sense, a waste of effort. Generally speaking, some such extra work is unavoidable. In the agenda setting, it is through the priority function that this kind of extra work may be avoided.

The real power of the agenda approach comes when we do not know a felicitous ordering, or one does not exist, or when there are simply more theorems than it is practical to process exhaustively. If the priority for a is set to $Ag[\mathsf{a}]$, we achieve the purest form of best-first search, generalized to the hypergraph case. Like any priority function that ensures every axiom and provable theorem is processed, this one is correct. However, it has the surprising property that it allows us to stop the algorithm early. As soon as goal is proved, its value will be correct. Although the agenda may not be empty, and the chart may not be otherwise correct, the algorithm can be stopped if only goal's value is of interest.

[28] Readers familiar with search will see that this is analogous to depth-first search.

Algorithm 1 A semiring-general algorithm for agenda-based deduction (Eisner et al., 2005). *Ag* and *Ch* are each maps from axioms and theorems to $\mathcal{K}$ values. "Antecedent-duplication" refers to the possibility that the same axiom or theorem can appear as an antecedent more than once within an instantiated inference rule. For modifications to handle side conditions (section 2.3.3), see Eisner et al. (2005).

Input: semiring-weighted logic program ($\mathcal{K}$-weighted axioms and inference rules), priority function *Pri* mapping axioms and theorems to $\mathbb{R}$

Output: *Ch*, a map from axioms and theorems to $\mathcal{K}$ values

```
for each axiom a do
  Ag[a] ← value of a
end for
while there is any a such that Ag[a] ≠ 0 do
  a ← argmax_a' Pri(a')
  u ← Ag[a] (the value of the update)
  agenda[a] ← 0
  if Ch[a] ≠ Ch[a] ⊕ u then
    old ← Ch[a]
    Ch[a] ← Ch[a] ⊕ u
    (compute new updates that result from the update to a, place on agenda)
    for each inference rule "c = ⊕_... a_1 ⊗ ··· ⊗ a_k" do
      for i = 1 to k do
        for each instantiation of the rule's variables s.t. a_i = a do
```

$$Ag[\mathsf{c}] \leftarrow Ag[\mathsf{c}] \oplus \bigotimes_{j=1}^{k} \begin{cases} \mathsf{old} & \text{if } j < i \text{ and } \mathsf{a}_j = \mathsf{a} \\ & \text{(ignore if no antecedent-duplication)} \\ \mathsf{u} & \text{if } j = i \\ Ch[\mathsf{a}_j] & \text{otherwise} \end{cases}$$

```
        end for
      end for
    end for
  end if
end while
```

2.3.5 APPROXIMATE SEARCH

$$
\begin{aligned}
\forall \ell \in \Lambda, \qquad \mathsf{v}(\langle \ell \rangle, 1) &= \left\{\mathbf{w}^\top \mathbf{g}_1(\boldsymbol{x}, \langle ⇨, \ell \rangle)\right\}_{\mathcal{K}} \\
\forall \ell \in \Lambda, i \in \{2, \ldots, n\}, \langle \ell_1, \ldots, \ell_{i-1} \rangle \in \Lambda^{i-1}, & \\
\mathsf{v}(\langle \ell_1, \ldots, \ell_{i-1}, \ell \rangle, i) &= \mathsf{v}(\langle \ell_1, \ldots, \ell_{i-1} \rangle, i-1) \\
&\quad \otimes \left\{\mathbf{w}^\top \mathbf{g}_i(\boldsymbol{x}, \langle ⇨, \ell_1, \ldots, \ell_{i-1}, \ell \rangle)\right\}_{\mathcal{K}} \\
\mathsf{goal} &= \bigoplus_{\langle \ell_1, \ldots, \ell_n \rangle \in \Lambda^n} \mathsf{v}(\langle \ell_1, \ldots, \ell_n \rangle, n) \\
&\quad \otimes \left\{\mathbf{w}^\top \mathbf{g}_{n+1}(\boldsymbol{x}, \langle ⇨, \ell_1, \ldots, \ell_n, ● \rangle)\right\}_{\mathcal{K}}
\end{aligned}
\tag{2.54}
$$

Figure 2.23: Sequence labeling DP equations suitable when $\mathbf{g}(\boldsymbol{x}, \boldsymbol{y})$ does not factor as in figures 2.16 and 2.17. Instead, we let $\mathbf{g}(\boldsymbol{x}, \boldsymbol{y}) = \sum_{i=1}^{n+1} \mathbf{g}_i(\boldsymbol{x}, \langle y_1, \ldots, y_i \rangle)$, which simply groups features by the minimum prefix needed to calculate their values. Note that the number of possible theorems is exponential in n. Although we use semiring notation, search algorithms generally assume the TROPICAL semiring.

Approximate methods are widely used to find a high-scoring $\boldsymbol{y}$, without the guarantee that it maximizes equation 2.3. This need may arise because the scoring function fails to factor (see, for example, figure 2.23). It may also happen that the observed runtime of a polynomial DP is simply too great to be practical. We consider some important approximate methods related to the DP view of decoding.

Heuristics and A*. Charniak et al. (1998) and Caraballo and Charniak (1998) showed that, in context-free parsing, alternative priority functions that estimate the value of the best parse resulting from a given theorem can be very effective. Their approach was to define

$$
Pri(\mathsf{a}) = Ag(\mathsf{a}) + \mathsf{h}(\mathsf{a}) \tag{2.55}
$$

where $\mathsf{h}(\mathsf{a})$ is a *heuristic*. In general, this approach may not discover the best proof of goal first. Klein and Manning (2003) analyzed such approaches in terms of a generalization of A* search (Hart et al., 1968) for hypergraphs, providing several admissible heuristics for CKY. Admissible heuristics have the attractive property that the first proof discovered for goal (the first time it comes off of the agenda) is the best one. Depending on the heuristic, then, A* search can be an approximate or exact decoding method. Prioritizing by $Ag(\mathsf{a})$, as noted previously, is admissible (it equates to setting $\mathsf{h}(\mathsf{a}) = 0$ for all a). There is a tradeoff between gains that come from faster runtime due to the use of an heuristic and the additional computation required for the heuristic itself, which may be substantial. Further, an inadmissible heuristic may lead to approximate results quickly, and the risk of search errors may be tolerable.

Beam search. **Beam search** is a popular approximate method that builds on the agenda (Lowerre, 1976). It is attractive because it is easy to implement. The key idea is to group search states together into a relatively small number of predefined successive stages, and to limit the number of states maintained at each stage. The search is essentially breadth-first, proceeding to each stage, in turn, but because each stage has only a limited number of states, the memory required for each stage and the time spent extending theorems from that stage are bounded. For the example in figure 2.23, we can group together v theorems by their second argument (the length of the prefix of labels in the term). The "beam" is defined by a thresholding function that determines which theorems will be used to generate the next stage's candidate theorems. A simple technique is to choose a fixed beam width k and extend only the k highest-scoring theorems from each stage. Another possibility is to use the highest-scoring theorem from a stage to define a threshold. For example, let $\mathcal{S}_j$ be the set of states at stage j and let $Ch[s]$ denote the value of state s. In the TROPICAL semiring, the threshold

$$\left(\max_{s \in \mathcal{S}_j} Ch[s]\right) - \alpha \tag{2.56}$$

maintains all competing theorems whose score is within α (a value greater than zero) of the best competing state at that stage. Note that because beam search is approximate, the "best" state among those known at a given stage is not necessarily the best among all states that *would* be assigned to that stage by an exact search algorithm. As the beam is widened—e.g., as k or α is increased to allow more theorems to pass the threshold—beam search tends toward breadth-first search. In the limit, the search is exhaustive. Beam search can be implemented in our agenda framework by giving priority $-\infty$ to any update with a value below the threshold.[29] Eliminating updates means we may eliminate some vertices (theorems) and hence any later vertices that depend on reaching them. Such vertices (and the hyperpaths that involve them) are said to have been *pruned*.

Note that if the entire best proof of each theorem (search state) is stored, then it is possible to include **non-local features** in the scoring function when conducting beam search.

Cube pruning. For problems that are nearly representable as parsing, best hyperpath, or weighted logic programs but for a few features that break the optimal substructure property, **cube pruning** has become a popular solution (Chiang, 2007). Cube pruning can be understood as solving the DP equations for a problem in a semiring that keeps track of the proofs of each theorem and their scores (Gimpel and Smith, 2009) and also as an heuristic search technique (Hopkins and Langmead, 2009). We define the semiring by proposing an exact method, then introducing approximations.

Let $\mathcal{L}$ denote the set of all proofs of all theorems, $\bigcup_{\mathrm{t}} \mathit{Proofs}(\mathrm{t})$. The semiring's values fall in $2^{(\mathbb{R} \cup \{-\infty\}) \times \mathcal{L}}$; that is, sets of reals paired with proofs. We will let $\langle u, \text{þ} \rangle$ denote such a pair and $\{\langle u_i, \text{þ}_i \rangle\}_{i=1}^{N}$ denote a set of N such pairs (a value in the semiring). The semiring is defined as

[29]Beam search is a general technique that can be applied to many search problems, not only those easily written with DP equations. We have chosen to highlight the connection to DP equations and linear models for notational convenience.

follows:

$$\mathbf{0} = \emptyset \tag{2.57}$$
$$\mathbf{1} = \{\langle 0, \epsilon \rangle\} \tag{2.58}$$
$$\{\langle u_i, \text{þ}_i \rangle\}_{i=1}^{N} \oplus \{\langle \bar{u}_j, \bar{\text{þ}}_j \rangle\}_{i=1}^{M} = \{\langle u_i, \text{þ}_i \rangle\}_{i=1}^{N} \cup \{\langle \bar{u}_j, \bar{\text{þ}}_j \rangle\}_{i=1}^{M} \tag{2.59}$$
$$\{\langle u_i, \text{þ}_i \rangle\}_{i=1}^{N} \otimes \{\langle \bar{u}_j, \bar{\text{þ}}_j \rangle\}_{j=1}^{M} = \left\{\langle u_i + \bar{u}_j, \text{þ}_i \smile \bar{\text{þ}}_j \rangle \mid 1 \leq i \leq N, 1 \leq j \leq M\right\} \tag{2.60}$$

where $\smile$ denotes proof combination or concatenation. The $\oplus$ operator simply merges the sets of proofs, and the $\otimes$ operator concatenates them. This semiring can be understood as a blend between the TROPICAL and ALL-PROOFS semirings (see figure 2.14).

If the entire proof of a theorem is available at the time we calculate the theorem's value, then it is easy to consider **non-local features** that depend on more than a single inference step in the proof. Such non-local features can be $\otimes$-factored into the first theorem whose proof contains sufficient information to know the feature value. In the sequence labeling example (figure 2.23), imagine a feature that fires for the second occurrence of label $\ell \in \Lambda$, wherever it may be or however far it is from the first occurrence. If the whole proof is available for any given v theorem, then it is easy to incorporate this feature into the score of a partial proof as soon as the second ℓ appears. The problem with this semiring, of course, is that storing the values requires exponential space, and performing $\otimes$ requires exponential runtime if the number of proofs is exponential.

Cube pruning makes two key approximations. The first is to limit the size of the set, instead letting values in the semiring be *lists* of only the k highest-scoring proofs for each theorem, $((\mathbb{R} \cup \{-\infty\}) \times \mathcal{L})^{\leq k}$. (The other proofs are said to have been "pruned.") We define an operator max-k that takes a set or list of $\langle u, \text{þ} \rangle$ objects and returns a list of at most k of the highest-scoring (by u), sorted in decreasing order. Then we redefine the operators as:

$$\{\langle u_i, \text{þ}_i \rangle\}_{i=1}^{N} \oplus \{\langle \bar{u}_j, \bar{\text{þ}}_j \rangle\}_{i=1}^{M} = \text{max-}k\left(\{\langle u_i, \text{þ}_i \rangle\}_{i=1}^{N} \cup \{\langle \bar{u}_j, \bar{\text{þ}}_j \rangle\}_{i=1}^{M}\right) \tag{2.61}$$
$$\{\langle u_i, \text{þ}_i \rangle\}_{i=1}^{N} \otimes \{\langle \bar{u}_j, \bar{\text{þ}}_j \rangle\}_{j=1}^{M} = \text{max-}k\left(\left\{\langle u_i + \bar{u}_j, \text{þ}_i \smile \bar{\text{þ}}_j \rangle \mid 1 \leq i \leq N, 1 \leq j \leq M\right\}\right) \tag{2.62}$$

The result is still a semiring, and it is quite similar to the "k-best proof" semiring of Goodman (1999). Gimpel and Smith (2009) refer to decoding with this approach **cube decoding**. It is an approximate technique in general: consider that it could always be the case that the $(k+1)$th proof would obtain a much higher score overall due to the introduction of a non-local feature, but that proof is lost.

The second approximation made in cube pruning is to more efficiently consider only $O(k)$ of the combined proofs for a theorem when incorporating the non-local factors for its score. Rather than calculating all of the k^2 proofs when performing the $\otimes$ operation, then $\otimes$-factoring in non-local features for each proof, Chiang (2007) produces the k-best first, then incorporates the non-local features. This results in additional approximation. This idea builds on important earlier developments for efficiently solving the "k-best" decoding problem (Huang and Chiang, 2005).

Again, we note that under special circumstances (the absence of non-local features), this technique is exact, generating the correct k-best list of scored proofs.

2.3.6 RERANKING AND COARSE-TO-FINE DECODING

For complex structured problems, an important development was **reranking** (Charniak and Johnson, 2005, Collins, 2000), which can be summed up mathematically as follows:

$$\bar{\mathcal{Y}}_{\boldsymbol{x}} = \text{max-}k\left(\left\{\langle \bar{\mathbf{w}}^\top \bar{\mathbf{g}}(\boldsymbol{x}, \boldsymbol{y}), \boldsymbol{y}\rangle \mid \boldsymbol{y} \in \mathcal{Y}_{\boldsymbol{x}}\right\}\right) \tag{2.63}$$

$$h(\boldsymbol{x}) = \operatorname*{argmax}_{\boldsymbol{y} \in \bar{\mathcal{Y}}_{\boldsymbol{x}}} \mathbf{w}^\top \mathbf{g}(\boldsymbol{x}, \boldsymbol{y}) \tag{2.64}$$

First, a k-best list of outputs is constructed using a model with features $\bar{\mathbf{g}}$ and weights $\bar{\mathbf{w}}$. Typically, this model uses highly factored feature functions so that k-best decoding is fast, using dynamic programming. Next, a more powerful model defined by features $\mathbf{g}$ and weights $\mathbf{w}$ is used to score each $\boldsymbol{y} \in \bar{\mathcal{Y}}_{\boldsymbol{x}}$. Usually $\mathbf{g}$ includes a richer set of features that would make search over $\mathcal{Y}_{\boldsymbol{x}}$ too expensive. The reranking phase is accomplished in $O(dk)$ time, where d is the number of features in $\mathbf{g}$.

A generalization of reranking is **hypergraph rescoring**, where the k-best list is replaced by a hypergraph constructed using the model with more local features (Huang and Chiang, 2007). This hypergraph represents the complete $\mathcal{Y}_{\boldsymbol{x}}$ (or a very large portion of it), and then calculations on the hypergraph using the more powerful model are used to select an approximate-best $\boldsymbol{y}$.

Another generalization of reranking is **coarse-to-fine** decoding. The coarse-to-fine approach replaces the k-best list $\bar{\mathcal{Y}}_{\boldsymbol{x}}$ with a restricted search space that is represented compactly. As in reranking, the first "coarse" stage can be implemented using dynamic programming with a simpler model (Goodman, 1997) and pruning. The main difference is that the DP data structure—the table or chart—can be used to store an exponentially large set of hypotheses to be scored by the second stage. Further, the simpler model can simplify the representation. For example, Charniak et al. (2006) and Petrov et al. (2006) used phrase-structure parses with a coarser, "projected" set of nonterminals, for the coarse stage, so that many $\boldsymbol{y} \in \mathcal{Y}_{\boldsymbol{x}}$ corresponded to each hypothesis encoded by the first stage. Often, the pruning of the hypothesis space is accomplished using a probabilistic interpretation of the scores, with hypotheses whose *posterior* probability is small being pruned away; we will return to posteriors in chapter 5. Recent work has sought to *learn* coarse models for the purpose of better prediction at later stages (Weiss and Taskar, 2010).

2.4 SPECIALIZED GRAPH ALGORITHMS

We saw in section 2.2.4 how some decoding problems can be understood as finding an optimal path in a graph. Similarly, some decoding problems can be understood naturally as other kinds of optimizations in a graph. Specialized algorithms have been developed for solving some such problems.

We consider three examples: bipartite matchings, spanning trees, and maximum flow/minimum cut problems. It is important to note that, while all three of these problems can be viewed as special cases of integer linear programming (see section 2.2.2), they each have a special structure that has allowed efficient algorithms to be developed. When considering a new decoding problem, it is helpful to consider whether there is an equivalent graph problem with known, specialized solutions.

2.4.1 BIPARTITE MATCHINGS

Consider an undirected graph with two sets of vertices, $\mathcal{U}$ and $\mathcal{V}$, and a set of edges $\mathcal{E}$, such that all edges are between one vertex in $\mathcal{U}$ and one vertex in $\mathcal{V}$. Let each edge $(u, v) \in \mathcal{E}$ have a weight associated with it, denoted $w_{(u,v)}$. A **matching** is a subset of edges $\mathcal{E}' \subseteq \mathcal{E}$ such that no two edges in $\mathcal{E}'$ share any vertices; let $\mathcal{M}(\mathcal{E})$ denote the set of all possible matchings for $\mathcal{E}$. The score of a matching is the weight of the edges it includes, and the maximum weighted bipartite matching is defined by:

$$\max_{\mathcal{E}' \in \mathcal{M}(\mathcal{E})} \sum_{(u,v) \in \mathcal{E}'} w_{(u,v)} \tag{2.65}$$

It was noted by Melamed (2000) that the problem of word alignment can be reduced to the maximum weighted bipartite matching problem if alignment scores can be factored into weights for pairs of words. More concretely, $\mathcal{U}$ corresponds to a bag of word tokens in one language (typically a sentence, but word order is irrelevant), and $\mathcal{V}$ corresponds to a bag of word tokens in the other language. Each edge between a word $u \in \mathcal{U}$ and a word $v \in \mathcal{V}$ is assigned an additive weight associated with the lexical types of those words, essentially encoding the strength of their translational equivalence.

The best known algorithm for this problem is the so-called "Hungarian" algorithm, due to Kuhn (1955); it runs in cubic time in the number of vertices. A greedy algorithm called "competitive linking," presented by Melamed (2000), is approximate but very fast and may be suitable for large-scale problems. A harder problem, alignment of *phrases*, has been shown to be NP-hard (DeNero and Klein, 2008).

2.4.2 SPANNING TREES

Consider a directed graph with vertices $\mathcal{V}$ and edges $\mathcal{E}$. Let $w_{(u,v)}$ denote the weight of the edge from $u \in \mathcal{V}$ to $v \in \mathcal{V}$. A directed **spanning tree** is a subset of edges $\mathcal{E}' \subseteq \mathcal{E}$ such that all vertices have exactly one incoming arc in $\mathcal{E}'$, except the root vertex (which has none), and such that $\mathcal{E}'$ contains no cycles.[30] Let $\mathcal{T}(\mathcal{E})$ denote the set of all possible directed spanning trees for $\mathcal{E}$. The total score of a spanning tree $\mathcal{E}'$ is the sum of the weights of the edges in $\mathcal{E}'$; the maximum[31] cost spanning tree

[30] Equivalently, we can say that all vertices have exactly one incoming arc in $\mathcal{E}'$, except the root vertex (which has none), and $\mathcal{E}'$ is connected.

[31] More commonly it is called a *minimum* cost spanning tree or minimum cost *arborescence*. We use the maximization form to emphasize the connection to other decoding problems, but it is trivial to convert between the two by negating the weights.

is defined by

$$\max_{\mathcal{E}' \in \mathcal{T}(\mathcal{E})} \sum_{(u,v) \in \mathcal{E}'} w_{(u,v)} \tag{2.66}$$

It was noted by McDonald et al. (2005b) that a specific dependency parsing decoding problem can be reduced to the minimum cost directed spanning tree problem. Consider finding a dependency parse for a sentence $\boldsymbol{x} = \langle x_1, \ldots, x_n \rangle$. We assume an invisible symbol at the left of the sentence, denoted $x_0 = ◈$. Any unlabeled dependency parse of $\boldsymbol{x}$ corresponds to a spanning tree with $\mathcal{V} = \{x_i\}_{i=0}^n$, with x_0 fixed to be the root of the tree. The space of possible trees is a subset of $\{0, 1, \ldots, n\}^n$. Hence, if $\boldsymbol{y} = \langle y_1, y_2, \ldots, y_n \rangle$ denotes a directed spanning tree for $\boldsymbol{x}$, then y_i is the index of x_i's parent.

Note that context-free approaches to dependency parsing are more restrictive, permitting only trees that are *projective*. The term **nonprojective parsing** refers to parsing methods that are not so-constrained. With a further stipulation on the form of the scoring function, nonprojective dependency parsing reduces trivially to the minimum cost directed spanning tree algorithm. This stipulation is that the scoring function factors into the edges $\mathcal{E}$, formally:

$$\mathbf{g}(\boldsymbol{x}, \boldsymbol{y}) = \sum_{i=1}^{n} \mathbf{f}(\boldsymbol{x}, i, y_i) \tag{2.67}$$

where $\boldsymbol{y}$ denotes any directed spanning tree for $\boldsymbol{x}$, represented in the form above.

It is straightforward to extend this approach to labeled dependency parsing, where each y_i corresponds to a pair: the index of x_i's parent and the type of the dependency (e.g., a symbol from alphabet Λ). In this case, we have $|\Lambda|$ edges for each pair of symbols in $\boldsymbol{x}$, one associated with each label. The same algorithm applies.

The most widely used algorithm for the spanning tree problem is the Chu-Liu-Edmonds algorithm (Chu and Liu, 1965, Edmonds, 1967), which runs in quadratic time with improvements by Tarjan (1977) and Camerini et al. (1980). For details, see Kübler et al. (2009, chapter 4). McDonald and Satta (2007) showed that exact decoding of nonprojective dependency trees with features that depend on two adjacent edges (i.e., features that do not factor as in equation 2.67) is NP-hard.

2.4.3 MAXIMUM FLOW AND MINIMUM CUT

Consider a directed graph with vertices $\mathcal{V}$ and edges $\mathcal{E}$. Let $w_{(u,v)}$ denote the *capacity* of the edge from $u \in \mathcal{V}$ to $v \in \mathcal{V}$. Let $s \in \mathcal{V}$ be a designated source node, and let $t \in \mathcal{V}$ be a designated sink node. A *flow* $\boldsymbol{y}$ through the graph is an assignment of nonnegative real values to edges $\mathcal{E}$ such that

$$\begin{aligned} \forall (u, v) \in \mathcal{E}, \quad & y_{(u,v)} \leq w_{(u,v)} \\ \forall (u, v) \in \mathcal{E}, \quad & y_{(u,v)} \geq 0 \\ \forall u \in \mathcal{V} \setminus \{s, t\}, \quad & \sum_{v \in \mathcal{V}:(u,v) \in \mathcal{E}} y_{(u,v)} = \sum_{v \in \mathcal{V}:(v,u) \in \mathcal{E}} y_{(v,u)} \end{aligned} \tag{2.68}$$

That is, each edge's flow is bounded by the edge's capacity, and the flow into of each node must match the flow out of that node, with the exceptions of s and t. The **maximum flow** problem involves finding the maximum of $\sum_{u \in \mathcal{V}} y_{(s,u)}$, subject to the constraints in equation 2.68. That is, we seek to maximize the amount of flow originating in s and traveling to t, respecting the capacity constraint on each edge.

A closely related problem is the **minumum cut** problem. A "cut" of the graph is defined as follows. Let $\mathcal{V}_1$ and $\mathcal{V}_2$ be a partition of $\mathcal{V}$ (i.e., $\mathcal{V}_1 \cup \mathcal{V}_2 = \mathcal{V}$ and $\mathcal{V}_1 \cap \mathcal{V}_2 = \emptyset$), such that $s \in \mathcal{V}_1$ and $t \in \mathcal{V}_2$. Let $\mathcal{E}' = \{(u, v) \in \mathcal{E} \mid u \in \mathcal{V}_1, v \in \mathcal{V}_2\}$. If the edges in $\mathcal{E}'$ are removed from the graph, then no flow is possible from s to t. If we let the capacity of the cut be denoted by the capacity of the edges in $\mathcal{E}'$, i.e.,

$$\sum_{(u,v) \in \mathcal{E} : u \in \mathcal{V}_1, v \in \mathcal{V}_2} w_{(u,v)} \tag{2.69}$$

then the minimum cut is the choice of $\mathcal{V}_1$ and $\mathcal{V}_2$ that minimizes the capacity.

A classic result is that there is a correspondence between flows and cuts: any flow $\boldsymbol{y}$ corresponds to a cut with capacity equal to $\sum_{u \in \mathcal{V}} y_{(s,u)}$ (Elias et al., 1956, Ford and Fulkerson, 1956). Specialized algorithms for maximizing flow or minimizing cut capacity have been studied extensively (see, e.g., Edmonds and Karp, 1972). Flows and cuts have been used in various NLP settings, from segmenting documents (Pang and Lee, 2004) to classification (Bansal et al., 2008) to alignment (Lacoste-Julien et al., 2006). The flow formulation can also be used to represent the bipartite matching and spanning tree problems discussed above.

2.5 CONCLUSION

There are many ways to think about decoding algorithms, and not much has been done to unify the literature. New developments in specialized domains arise frequently. We have sought here to present some of the most widely applied and formally coherent techniques and draw some connections among them. An exhaustive survey would probably require new research effort since so many current techniques exploit properties of a specific task.

Our emphasis has been on views of decoding in which the feasible space of outputs $\mathcal{Y}_x$ for input $\boldsymbol{x}$ can be encoded efficiently. As NLP moves to tackle more complex problems, we anticipate considerable research will be devoted to the challenge of much more complex spaces $\mathcal{Y}_{\boldsymbol{x}}$. For example, Rush et al. (2010) consider decoding problems that can be understood as two (or more) simpler decoding problems, each independently solvable by efficient means, and use a linear programming framework to enforce agreement between the subproblems' solutions.

It is hoped that future research will focus on abstractions that permit sharing of ideas across many linguistic (and non-linguistic) structure prediction scenarios as well as formal analysis.

In the next two chapters, we turn to learning. In the linear decoding framework, where our decoding problem is equation 2.3, learning involves the use of data to design the feature vector function $\mathbf{g}$ and to choose the weights $\mathbf{w}$. While some learning algorithms (notably, the perceptron, section 3.6.2) make direct use of decoding algorithms, the details of decoding are mostly orthogonal to learning. However, just as properties of the features in **g** can have a big effect on the availability of efficient decoding algorithms, the same will be true in learning, and indeed many of the algorithms required in learning have a close relationship to decoding algorithms.

Chapter 5 will present additional algorithms, including decoding techniques, based on a probabilistic interpretation of the scoring function. Their discussion is deferred because they relate more closely to foundations and techniques required for learning.

CHAPTER 3

Learning Structure from Annotated Data

Having given a framework for specifying what kinds of linguistic structures we might wish to predict and what kinds of algorithms might enable such predictions, we now turn to the question of learning.

The current paradigm for building linguistic structure predictors leans heavily on learning from **annotated datasets**. We denote such a dataset by $\langle\langle \tilde{\boldsymbol{x}}_1, \tilde{\boldsymbol{y}}_1\rangle, \langle \tilde{\boldsymbol{x}}_2, \tilde{\boldsymbol{y}}_2\rangle, \ldots, \langle \tilde{\boldsymbol{x}}_{\tilde{N}}, \tilde{\boldsymbol{y}}_{\tilde{N}}\rangle\rangle$, where each $\tilde{\boldsymbol{x}}_i$ is an example input and $\tilde{\boldsymbol{y}}$ its annotation, a gold-standard, manually assigned output. This chapter is about learning from annotated datasets.

3.1 ANNOTATED DATA

The following assumption is widely made in modern approaches to tackling the implementation question:

Assumption 3.1 *For a given linguistic structure prediction task, native speakers either have the ability to accurately complete the task for arbitrary inputs of sufficient linguistic well-formedness, or they can be so trained.*

The weakest form of this view holds that linguistic experts can confidently complete the task under reasonable input conditions, and will have high rates of agreement with each other. Assumption 3.1 is subject to debate for any particular linguistic structure prediction task, of course. It is usually left to the developers of the dataset to demonstrate that humans can competently and consistently perform the annotation.

Annotation projects ideally proceed through iterative refinement of an annotation scheme, codified in a set of guidelines for annotators. Inter-annotator agreement is checked frequently and sources of disagreement and confusion are addressed and conventions for resolving them are decided. From an engineering point of view, the usefulness of an annotated dataset depends on whether the annotations are internally consistent, and whether the phenomena that are annotated are relevant to a task or application.

If assumption 3.1 holds, it does not follow directly that automatic linguistic structure predictors can be built. It may be that human annotators rely on a vast amount of knowledge about the language the text is in, the world in which it was generated, and the textual context of each example, in order to complete a task. Given annotated data, the intermediate engineering goal is to construct linguistic structure predictors that accurately predict what a human annotator would do on as-yet-unannotated examples. The long-range goal is to build predictors that support useful text applications.

It is uncontroversial that annotated datasets are useful in NLP. Some debate revolves around the question of how much *additional* information must be made available to an automatic linguistic structure predictor. What level of knowledge must be made available, and in what form and what level of correctness, to complete any particular linguistic structure prediction task, is always open for debate.

In this chapter, we operate under an additional assumption:

Assumption 3.2 *The inputs and outputs provided by a dataset represent a learnable relation. In other words, the linguistic structure prediction task can be learned without recourse to additional information beyond the problem specification (definition of $\mathcal{X}$ and $\mathcal{Y}$) and the data.*

This assumption immediately invites connections to two related research topics: formal language learnability and human language acquisition.

Theoretical work in computer science. For some kinds of structure learning problems, most notably relating to formal grammars, there are theoretical results on learnability (e.g., Gold, 1967). We remark here only that such results typically rest on simplifying assumptions about the source of the data that are unlikely to hold for annotated datasets. Much remains to be done to connect learning theory with natural language-related learning.

Language acquisition in humans. Many researchers in theoretical linguistics have argued against the learnability of language by humans (Chomsky, 1965). Instead, they argue, children are endowed with extensive innate knowledge that makes the learning task easy. This view is controversial (Clark and Lappin, 2011), as it is built on assumptions that (i) language and learning are purely symbolic, (ii) children receive only positive evidence, and (iii) all native speakers of a language "know" the same grammar. More empirical research by psychologists and cognitive scientists focuses on the features children use to acquire linguistic proficiency, and at what stages these features come into play. Computational techniques from NLP are more closely related to this latter line of research.

Assumption 3.2 does not narrow the usefulness of the approaches we adopt. Most of the learning techniques proposed here welcome additional input information (i.e., enriched definitions of the input space $\mathcal{X}$), and can make use of it without much cost. Indeed, enriching the representations of the inputs and outputs is the focus of much current NLP research.

3.2 GENERIC FORMULATION OF LEARNING

Let $\mathcal{H}$ denote the set of all possible predictors that map $\mathcal{X} \rightarrow \mathcal{Y}$. Let *loss* be a **loss function** that maps $\mathcal{X} \times \mathcal{Y} \times (\mathcal{X} \rightarrow \mathcal{Y}) \rightarrow \mathbb{R}_{\geq 0}$, such that:

$$loss(\boldsymbol{x}, \boldsymbol{y}; h) = \text{given input } \boldsymbol{x}\text{, badness of the predictor } h \text{ when } \boldsymbol{y} \text{ is the correct output} \quad (3.1)$$

We describe loss abstractly because different learners quantify "badness" differently, with different results.

Given $\mathcal{H}$ and *loss*, the learning problem can then generically be framed as follows:

$$\min_{h \in \mathcal{H}} \mathbb{E}[\mathit{loss}(\boldsymbol{X}, \boldsymbol{Y}; h)] + \mathit{model\text{-}complexity}(h) \tag{3.2}$$

where the expectation is taken under the "true" distribution for $\boldsymbol{X}$ and $\boldsymbol{Y}$. We seek a linguistic structure predictor h that, in expectation, returns predictions with small cost (the first term), and that is no more complicated than necessary. The model complexity term serves to encourage good generalization (we will return to this idea later). The first term is usually approximated using the sample distribution in the training data:

$$\mathbb{E}[\mathit{loss}(\boldsymbol{X}, \boldsymbol{Y}; h)] \approx \frac{1}{\tilde{N}} \sum_{i=1}^{\tilde{N}} \mathit{loss}(\tilde{\boldsymbol{x}}_i, \tilde{\boldsymbol{y}}_i; h) \tag{3.3}$$

This quantity is called **empirical risk**; many machine learning algorithms can be understood as methods for minimizing the empirical risk, often subject to model complexity penalties as in equation 3.2.

Different approaches to learning vary in how they define the loss function, and more deeply in the formal foundations motivating the choice of *loss*.

3.3 GENERATIVE MODELS

Applied to a linguistic structure prediction task with input space $\mathcal{X}$ and output space $\mathcal{Y}$, a generative model p assigns probabilities to outcomes in $\mathcal{X} \times \mathcal{Y}$. We consider two interdependent random variables, $\boldsymbol{X}$ over $\mathcal{X}$ and $\boldsymbol{Y}$ over $\mathcal{Y}$. $p(\boldsymbol{X} = \boldsymbol{x}, \boldsymbol{Y} = \boldsymbol{y})$, or $p(\boldsymbol{x}, \boldsymbol{y})$ when the random variables are clear from context, denotes the joint probability of an input-output pair. Generative models typically (but do not always) assume that examples are drawn independently from the same distribution, so that the probability of the training data, for instance, can be factored:

$$p(\langle\langle \tilde{\boldsymbol{x}}_1, \tilde{\boldsymbol{y}}_1 \rangle, \ldots, \langle \tilde{\boldsymbol{x}}_{\tilde{N}}, \tilde{\boldsymbol{y}}_{\tilde{N}} \rangle\rangle) = \prod_{i=1}^{\tilde{N}} p(\boldsymbol{X} = \tilde{\boldsymbol{x}}_i, \boldsymbol{Y} = \tilde{\boldsymbol{y}}_i) \tag{3.4}$$

A proper generative model is a function $p : \mathcal{X} \times \mathcal{Y} \to \mathbb{R}_{\geq 0}$ such that

$$\sum_{\boldsymbol{x} \in \mathcal{X}} \sum_{\boldsymbol{y} \in \mathcal{Y}} p(\boldsymbol{X} = \boldsymbol{x}, \boldsymbol{Y} = \boldsymbol{y}) = 1 \tag{3.5}$$

We denote the set of all such proper models $\mathbb{P}_{\mathcal{X} \times \mathcal{Y}}$.

The simplest framework for generative learning requires specification of a family of probability models, $\mathcal{P} \subset \mathbb{P}_{\mathcal{X} \times \mathcal{Y}}$. This family encodes the allowed structures in $\mathcal{X}$ and $\mathcal{Y}$ and many, if not all, of the constraints on which $\boldsymbol{y} \in \mathcal{Y}$ are valid for a given $\boldsymbol{x} \in \mathcal{X}$. The choice of a model family implies **independence assumptions** about different parts of the structure.

In terms of equation 3.2, a generative model p defines

$$loss(\boldsymbol{x}, \boldsymbol{y}; h) = -\log p(\boldsymbol{X} = \boldsymbol{x}, \boldsymbol{Y} = \boldsymbol{y}) \tag{3.6}$$

This is sometimes called the **log loss.**

This formulation may seem rather odd; the loss function does not depend on the prediction made by h. The intuition behind this approach is best understood by imagining the following scenario. A predictor h corresponds to a probability distribution p over $\mathcal{X} \times \mathcal{Y}$. Minimizing the log-loss in equation 3.6 is a way of training the model to prefer $\langle \boldsymbol{x}, \boldsymbol{y} \rangle$ pairs it has seen before, by giving them higher probability. Taking this to the extreme, if $\mathcal{P}$ is sufficiently large, then the best distribution p from the perspective of equation 3.2 will be the empirical distribution that assigns probability to any pair $\langle \boldsymbol{x}, \boldsymbol{y} \rangle$ proportional to its occurrence in the training data:

$$\tilde{p}(\boldsymbol{x}, \boldsymbol{y}) = \frac{1}{\tilde{N}} \sum_{i=1}^{\tilde{N}} \mathbf{1}\left\{\boldsymbol{x} = \tilde{\boldsymbol{x}}_i \wedge \boldsymbol{y} = \tilde{\boldsymbol{y}}_i\right\} \tag{3.7}$$

This approach will assign zero probability to any $\langle \boldsymbol{x}, \boldsymbol{y} \rangle$ not seen in training data, and hence has nothing to say about *new* examples $\boldsymbol{x}$ not seen in training. By constraining $\mathcal{H}$ to correspond to those $p \in \mathcal{P}$, we hope that the learned model will prefer $\langle \boldsymbol{x}, \boldsymbol{y} \rangle$ pairs with favorable properties seen in training, even if $\langle \boldsymbol{x}, \boldsymbol{y} \rangle$ was not a pair seen in training. Further, the *model-complexity* term can also impose penalties on models that do not generalize well beyond the training data.

The theoretical motivation for this approach comes from statistics; learning with the log loss function of equation 3.6 equates to **maximum likelihood estimation** (MLE). Formally, given a model family $\mathcal{P}$ and a sample $\langle \langle \tilde{\boldsymbol{x}}_1, \tilde{\boldsymbol{y}}_1 \rangle, \ldots, \langle \tilde{\boldsymbol{x}}_{\tilde{N}}, \tilde{\boldsymbol{y}}_{\tilde{N}} \rangle \rangle$, maximum likelihood estimation chooses the model

$$\operatorname*{argmin}_{h \in \mathcal{H}} \frac{1}{\tilde{N}} \sum_{i=1}^{\tilde{N}} loss(\tilde{\boldsymbol{x}}_i, \tilde{\boldsymbol{y}}_i; h) \overset{\text{eq. 3.6}}{=} \operatorname*{argmax}_{p \in \mathcal{P}} \sum_{i=1}^{\tilde{N}} \log p(\tilde{\boldsymbol{x}}_i, \tilde{\boldsymbol{y}}_i) \tag{3.8}$$

$$= \operatorname*{argmax}_{p \in \mathcal{P}} \prod_{i=1}^{\tilde{N}} p(\tilde{\boldsymbol{x}}_i, \tilde{\boldsymbol{y}}_i) \tag{3.9}$$

$$\overset{\text{eq. 3.4}}{=} \operatorname*{argmax}_{p \in \mathcal{P}} p(\langle \tilde{\boldsymbol{x}}_i, \tilde{\boldsymbol{y}}_i \rangle_{i=1}^{\tilde{N}}) \tag{3.10}$$

Notice that the *model-complexity* term from equation 3.2 is not present. Maximum likelihood estimation can be understood to assign an equal model complexity score to every model in $\mathcal{P}$. We can alternatively write equation 3.9 as

$$\operatorname*{argmax}_{p \in \mathbb{P}_{\mathcal{X} \times \mathcal{Y}}} \sum_{i=1}^{\tilde{N}} \log p(\tilde{\boldsymbol{x}}_i, \tilde{\boldsymbol{y}}_i) - \begin{cases} 0 & \text{if } p \in \mathcal{P} \\ \infty & \text{otherwise} \end{cases} \tag{3.11}$$

In section 3.3.7 we will revisit this approach to model complexity.

A slight shift in notation is helpful. Let each $p \in \mathcal{P}$ correspond to a numerical parameter setting $\mathbf{w} \in \mathbb{R}^d$. Given $\mathbf{w}$, we denote its corresponding probability distribution $p_{\mathbf{w}}$, so that the model selection problem becomes one of **parameter estimation**:

$$\mathbf{w}^* = \underset{\mathbf{w} \in \mathbb{R}^d : p_{\mathbf{w}} \in \mathcal{P}}{\operatorname{argmax}} \; p_{\mathbf{w}}(\langle \tilde{\boldsymbol{x}}_i, \tilde{\boldsymbol{y}}_i \rangle_{i=1}^{\tilde{N}}) \overset{\text{eq. 3.4}}{=} \underset{\mathbf{w} \in \mathbb{R}^d : p_{\mathbf{w}} \in \mathcal{P}}{\operatorname{argmax}} \prod_{i=1}^{\tilde{N}} p_{\mathbf{w}}(\tilde{\boldsymbol{x}}_i, \tilde{\boldsymbol{y}}_i) \tag{3.12}$$

We will consider two different parameterizations of generative models. The first is based on multinomial distributions (section 3.3.2) and is the most widely used. The second is based on log-linear distributions (section 3.3.8) and is included to draw a connection between generative models and *conditional* models (discussed in section 3.4).

3.3.1 DECODING RULE

Generative models suggest that decoding—choosing $\boldsymbol{y}^*$ given $\boldsymbol{x}$—should be accomplished by taking the $\boldsymbol{y} \in \mathcal{Y}_{\boldsymbol{x}}$ that is most likely to have occurred with $\boldsymbol{x}$, under the model. This is given by the conditional probability $p_{\mathbf{w}}(\boldsymbol{Y} = \boldsymbol{y} \mid \boldsymbol{X} = \boldsymbol{x})$. Decoding can actually be simplified to use the joint probability defined by the model:

$$\boldsymbol{y}^* = \underset{\boldsymbol{y} \in \mathcal{Y}_{\boldsymbol{x}}}{\operatorname{argmax}} \; p_{\mathbf{w}}(\boldsymbol{Y} = \boldsymbol{y} \mid \boldsymbol{X} = \boldsymbol{x}) \tag{3.13}$$

$$= \underset{\boldsymbol{y} \in \mathcal{Y}_{\boldsymbol{x}}}{\operatorname{argmax}} \; \frac{p_{\mathbf{w}}(\boldsymbol{X} = \boldsymbol{x}, \boldsymbol{Y} = \boldsymbol{y})}{p_{\mathbf{w}}(\boldsymbol{X} = \boldsymbol{x})} \tag{3.14}$$

$$= \underset{\boldsymbol{y} \in \mathcal{Y}_{\boldsymbol{x}}}{\operatorname{argmax}} \; p_{\mathbf{w}}(\boldsymbol{X} = \boldsymbol{x}, \boldsymbol{Y} = \boldsymbol{y}) \tag{3.15}$$

This follows from the definition of conditional probability (applied in equation 3.14), and then ignoring the marginal $p_{\mathbf{w}}(\boldsymbol{x})$ in the denominator, which is constant with respect to $\boldsymbol{y}$ (equation 3.15).

3.3.2 MULTINOMIAL-BASED MODELS

A **multinomial distribution** assigns probability to a discrete, finite set of events $\mathcal{E}$; for each $e \in \mathcal{E}$,

$$p_{\boldsymbol{\theta}}(e) = \theta_e \tag{3.16}$$

where $\boldsymbol{\theta} \in \mathbb{R}^{|\mathcal{E}|}$. For $\boldsymbol{\theta}$ to be a proper parameterization, it must be the case that

$$\begin{aligned} \sum_{e \in \mathcal{E}} \theta_e &= 1 \\ \forall e \in \mathcal{E}, \quad \theta_e &\geq 0 \end{aligned} \tag{3.17}$$

It is helpful to think of a multinomial distribution as a many-sided die that is not (necessarily) weighted fairly. Each side of the die corresponds to a different $e \in \mathcal{E}$, and the probability of the die "coming up e" is θ_e. In NLP, we build more complex generative models by combining many multinomial distributions. This combination can involve repeated rolls of the die or using the outcome of one die to decide which die (or dice) to roll next.

The language models presented in section 1.1 exemplify multinomial-based generative models. We turn immediately to a more complex example that is frequently used in prediction of an output $\boldsymbol{y}$ given an input $\boldsymbol{x}$: hidden Markov models for sequence labeling.

3.3.3 HIDDEN MARKOV MODELS

Hidden Markov models (HMMs) are a key building block for statistical models that involve two or more sequences. They were first studied by Baum and colleagues (Baum and Petrie, 1966) and have been widely studied in information theory and machine learning and applied most famously in speech recognition (Baker, 1975, Jelinek, 1969) but also other areas such as computational biology (Durbin et al., 1998).

A (discrete) first-order HMM is defined by a finite set of states $\Lambda = \{\ell_1, \ldots, \ell_L\}$, a vocabulary of observable symbols $\Sigma = \{\sigma_1, \ldots, \sigma_V\}$, and real-valued parameters $\mathbf{w}$ explained as we proceed. The HMM defines a distribution over two random variables, $\boldsymbol{X}$ (ranging over Σ^*, sequences of symbols) and $\boldsymbol{Y}$ (ranging over Λ^*, sequences of states). We assume two additional variables: Y_0 is always equal to $\text{➲} \notin \Lambda$ and Y_{n+1} is always equal to $\bullet \notin \Lambda$ when the length of the sequence $\boldsymbol{X}$ is n. The first-order HMM defines the probability that $\boldsymbol{X} = \boldsymbol{x} \in \Sigma^n$ and $\boldsymbol{Y} = \boldsymbol{y} \in \{\text{➲}\} \times \Lambda \times \{\bullet\}$ as:

$$
\begin{aligned}
p(\boldsymbol{X} = \boldsymbol{x}, \boldsymbol{Y} = \boldsymbol{y}) &= p(\boldsymbol{Y} = \boldsymbol{y}) \times p(\boldsymbol{X} = \boldsymbol{x} \mid \boldsymbol{Y} = \boldsymbol{y}) \\
&= \left(\prod_{i=1}^{n+1} p(Y_i = y_i \mid Y_{i-1} = y_{i-1})\right) \times \left(\prod_{i=1}^{n} p(X_i = x_i \mid Y_i = y_i)\right)
\end{aligned}
\tag{3.18}
$$

Note that the first factor is a bigram model (see section 1.1) for sequences of states. The probabilities $p(Y_i = y_i \mid Y_{i-1} = y_{i-1})$ are often called **transition probabilities**. It is helpful to imagine the process by which values for $\boldsymbol{X}$ and $\boldsymbol{Y}$ are chosen as consisting of a random walk among states, with the probability of the "next" state given the "current" state defined by the transition probabilities. These probabilities are most often estimated as multinomial distributions, with the assumption that the state at position i in the sequence depends only on the state at position $i - 1$ and nothing else, not even the position i. We use the following notation to denote the transition probabilities for $\ell \in \{\text{➲}\} \cup \Lambda$ and $\ell' \in \Lambda \cup \{\bullet\}$.:

$$\gamma_{\ell,\ell'} = p(Y_{i+1} = \ell' \mid Y_i = \ell) \tag{3.19}$$

In many expositions of HMMs, these are understood as a matrix:

$$
\begin{array}{cc}
 & \text{transition } \textit{to}\text{:} \\
\text{transition } \textit{from}\text{:} & \begin{array}{ccccc} \ell_1 & \ell_2 & \cdots & \ell_L & \bullet \end{array}
\end{array}
$$

$$
\gamma = \begin{array}{c} \Rightarrow \\ \ell_1 \\ \vdots \\ \ell_L \end{array}
\begin{bmatrix}
\gamma_{\Rightarrow,\ell_1} & \gamma_{\Rightarrow,\ell_2} & \cdots & \gamma_{\Rightarrow,\ell_L} & \gamma_{\Rightarrow,\bullet} \\
\gamma_{\ell_1,\ell_1} & \gamma_{\ell_1,\ell_2} & \cdots & \gamma_{\ell_1,\ell_L} & \gamma_{\ell_1,\bullet} \\
\vdots & \ddots & \cdots & \vdots & \vdots \\
\gamma_{\ell_L,\ell_1} & \gamma_{\ell_L,\ell_2} & \cdots & \gamma_{\ell_L,\ell_L} & \gamma_{\ell_L,\bullet}
\end{bmatrix}
\tag{3.20}
$$

Note that each row sums to one. The top row is sometimes described as the **starting distribution** and the rightmost column the **stopping probabilities**. Note that $\gamma_{\Rightarrow,\bullet}$ is the probability of a zero-length sequence and would generally be set to 0.

The second factor in equation 3.18 consists of **emission probabilities**. Continuing with the random walk metaphor, whenever the random walk passes through state ℓ at time i, a symbol from Σ is emitted.[1] The symbol is chosen randomly based on that state's emission distribution—another multinomial—which we denote, for $\ell \in \Lambda$ and $\sigma \in \Sigma$:

$$
\eta_{\ell,\sigma} = p(X_i = \sigma \mid Y_i = \ell) \tag{3.21}
$$

A simpler form for equation 3.18 is therefore:

$$
p(\boldsymbol{X} = \boldsymbol{x}, \boldsymbol{Y} = \boldsymbol{y}) = \left(\prod_{i=1}^{n} \gamma_{y_{i-1},y_i} \eta_{y_i,x_i} \right) \times \gamma_{y_n,\bullet} \tag{3.22}
$$

Notice that the "random walk" metaphor for HMMs corresponds to a temporal sequence of events, the result of which is the appearance of the pair of sequences $\boldsymbol{x}$ and $\boldsymbol{y}$. This randomized event sequence is often specified as a generative process, which we show in algorithm 2.

(In a more general form, the choice of Y_i can depend on the previous m states, $\langle y_{i-m}, \ldots, y_{i-1} \rangle$. This equates to replacing the transition model $p(\boldsymbol{Y})$ with an $(m-1)$-gram model over states Λ. The distribution can then be written:

$$
p(\boldsymbol{X} = \boldsymbol{x}, \boldsymbol{Y} = \boldsymbol{y}) = \left(\prod_{i=1}^{n} \gamma_{y_{i-m},\ldots,y_{i-1},y_i} \eta_{y_i,x_i} \right) \times \gamma_{y_n,\bullet} \tag{3.23}
$$

Just as with an $(m-1)$-gram model over symbols, the number of parameters increases by a factor of Λ as m increases. "Trigram" ($m = 2$) HMMs are frequently found in the sequence labeling literature.)

We return to the $m = 1$ (first-order) HMM. An alternative to equations 3.18 and 3.22 is to write the probability based on frequences of events (i.e., transition and emission events), analogous

[1] Some formulations of HMMs permit the option of emitting nothing with some probability, called an ϵ-emission. States that always emit ϵ are called "silent." This variant is not widely used in NLP, so we skip it.

Algorithm 2 Stochastically generating a pair $\langle \boldsymbol{x}, \boldsymbol{y} \rangle$ from an HMM.

Input: transition probabilities $\boldsymbol{\gamma}$ and emission probabilities $\boldsymbol{\eta}$
Output: $\boldsymbol{x} \in \Sigma^*$ (and optionally $\boldsymbol{y} \in \Lambda^*$)

$y_0 \leftarrow$ ➾
$i \leftarrow 0$
while $y_i \neq$ ⬢ **do**
  $i \leftarrow i + 1$
  Transition: sample y_i from the distribution $p(Y_i \mid Y_{i-1} = y_{i-1})$, which we denote $\langle \gamma_{y_{i-1},\ell_1}, \ldots, \gamma_{y_{i-1},\ell_L}, \gamma_{y_{i-1},⬢} \rangle$
  Emission: sample x_i from the distribution $p(X_i \mid Y_i = y_i)$, which we denote $\langle \eta_{y_i,\sigma_1}, \ldots, \eta_{y_i,\sigma_V} \rangle$
end while
$n \leftarrow i - 1$
return $\boldsymbol{x} = \langle x_1, \ldots, x_n \rangle$ and optionally $\boldsymbol{y} = \langle y_0, \ldots, y_{n+1} \rangle$

to equation 1.4 for language modeling.

$$\mathit{freq}(\ell, \ell'; \boldsymbol{y}) = \left| \left\{ i \in \{1, 2, \ldots, n+1\} \mid y_{i-1} = \ell \wedge y_i = \ell' \right\} \right| \tag{3.24}$$

$$\mathit{freq}(\ell, \sigma; \boldsymbol{x}, \boldsymbol{y}) = \left| \left\{ i \in \{1, 2, \ldots, n\} \mid y_i = \ell \wedge x_i = \sigma \right\} \right| \tag{3.25}$$

$$p(\boldsymbol{X} = \boldsymbol{x}, \boldsymbol{Y} = \boldsymbol{y}) = \left(\prod_{\ell \in \Lambda \cup \{➾\}} \prod_{\ell' \in \Lambda \cup \{⬢\}} \gamma_{\ell,\ell'}^{\mathit{freq}(\ell,\ell';\boldsymbol{y})} \right) \times \left(\prod_{\ell \in \Lambda} \prod_{\sigma \in \Sigma} \eta_{\ell,\sigma}^{\mathit{freq}(\ell,\sigma;\boldsymbol{x},\boldsymbol{y})} \right) \tag{3.26}$$

As it happens, this event frequency-based view of the probability is particularly useful in mapping the HMM back to linear models for prediction. Taking the logarithm of $p(\boldsymbol{X} = \boldsymbol{x}, \boldsymbol{Y} = \boldsymbol{y})$ to be the score of $\boldsymbol{x}$ and $\boldsymbol{y}$, we have

$$\mathit{score}(\boldsymbol{x}, \boldsymbol{y}) = \sum_{\ell \in \Lambda \cup \{➾\}} \sum_{\ell' \in \Lambda \cup \{⬢\}} \mathit{freq}(\ell, \ell'; \boldsymbol{y}) \log \gamma_{\ell,\ell'} + \sum_{\ell \in \Lambda} \sum_{\sigma \in \Sigma} \mathit{freq}(\ell, \sigma; \boldsymbol{x}, \boldsymbol{y}) \log \eta_{\ell,\sigma} \tag{3.27}$$

It should be easy to see that this is a *linear* score in the frequencies of transition and emission events, with the role of the weights being filled by log-probabilities. In the notation of decoding with linear models in chapter 2,

$$\mathbf{g}(\boldsymbol{x}, \boldsymbol{y}) = \begin{bmatrix} \mathit{freq}(➡, \ell_1; \boldsymbol{y}) \\ \mathit{freq}(➡, \ell_2; \boldsymbol{y}) \\ \vdots \\ \mathit{freq}(\ell_L, ●; \boldsymbol{y}) \\ \mathit{freq}(\ell_1, \sigma_1; \boldsymbol{x}, \boldsymbol{y}) \\ \mathit{freq}(\ell_1, \sigma_2; \boldsymbol{x}, \boldsymbol{y}) \\ \vdots \\ \mathit{freq}(\ell_L, \sigma_V; \boldsymbol{x}, \boldsymbol{y}) \end{bmatrix} \quad (3.28)$$

$$\mathbf{w} = \begin{bmatrix} \log \gamma_{➡, \ell_1} \\ \log \gamma_{➡, \ell_2} \\ \vdots \\ \log \gamma_{\ell_L, ●} \\ \log \eta_{\ell_1, \sigma_1} \\ \log \eta_{\ell_1, \sigma_2} \\ \vdots \\ \log \eta_{\ell_L, \sigma_V} \end{bmatrix} \quad (3.29)$$

The inner product of $\mathbf{g}(\boldsymbol{x}, \boldsymbol{y})$ and $\mathbf{w}$ gives the score of equation 3.27, which in turn is the logarithm of $p(\boldsymbol{X} = \boldsymbol{x}, \boldsymbol{Y} = \boldsymbol{y})$.

We have already encountered the Viterbi algorithm for sequence labeling (section 2.3.3), though it was presented without mention of HMMs in order to show its full generality. We give the specific case of Viterbi for HMMs in our formulation in figure 3.1. Figure 2.16 (page 53) is the more general form.

$$\begin{aligned} \forall \ell \in \Lambda, \quad \mathsf{v}(\ell, 1) &= \log \gamma_{➡, \ell} \\ \forall \ell \in \Lambda, i \in \{2, \ldots, n\}, \quad \mathsf{v}(\ell, i) &= \max_{\ell' \in \Lambda} \mathsf{v}(\ell', i-1) + \log \gamma_{\ell', \ell} + \eta_{\ell, x_i} \\ \mathsf{goal} &= \max_{\ell \in \lambda} \mathsf{v}(\ell, n) + \log \gamma_{\ell, ●} \end{aligned}$$

Figure 3.1: Dynamic programming equations for the Viterbi algorithm for decoding HMMs. A more general form is given in figure 2.16; it abstracts away from the semiring and the features.

An HMM can therefore be seen as

- a probability distribution over $(\Lambda \times \Sigma)^*$, parameterized by the collections of multinomials $\boldsymbol{\gamma}$ and $\boldsymbol{\eta}$, and serving as a generative model; or

- a linear scoring function over Λ^* given Σ^*, allowing for the use of DP to predict $\boldsymbol{y} \in \Lambda^*$ given $\boldsymbol{x} \in \Sigma^*$.

3.3.4 PROBABILISTIC CONTEXT-FREE GRAMMARS

Probabilistic context-free grammars (PCFGs) are another generative model used widely in NLP, particularly as the basis for parsing models. As with HMMs, PCFGs generate data by repeatedly sampling from multinomial distributions based on what has been generated so far. Rather than a random walk through a graph, they can be understood as a *branching* process, with each state (called a "nonterminal") generating a sequence of new states to be visited recursively. Each visited state corresponds to a node in a phrase-structure tree ($\boldsymbol{y}$), as described in section 1.4.

We define context-free grammars as in section 2.2.3. Let Σ be a finite vocabulary of observable symbols, often called terminal symbols. Let $\mathcal{N}$ be a finite set of states, often called nonterminals, with $N_{\text{⇨}} \in \mathcal{N}$ the special start state. Let $\mathcal{R}$ be a set of production rules of the form "$N \rightarrow \alpha$" with $N \in \mathcal{N}$ and $\alpha \in (\mathcal{N} \cup \Sigma)^*$. Let $\mathcal{R}_N$ be the set of rules with N as the left-hand side. For each $N \in \mathcal{N}$, we associate a multinomial distribution over production rules with $\mathcal{R}_N$, so that

$$\forall (N \rightarrow \alpha) \in \mathcal{R}_N, \quad \theta_{N \rightarrow \alpha} \geq 0 \tag{3.30}$$

$$\sum_{(N \rightarrow \alpha) \in \mathcal{R}_N} \theta_{N \rightarrow \alpha} = 1 \tag{3.31}$$

We let $\boldsymbol{\theta}_N$ denote $\{\boldsymbol{\theta}_{N \rightarrow \alpha}\}_{(N \rightarrow \alpha) \in \mathcal{R}_N}$. The generative process begins with a node labeled with the start symbol $N_{\text{⇨}}$ and recursively samples rules given their left-hand sides. Each rule generates the children of a nonterminal node in the tree. The process continues until every nonterminal has been expanded. The leaves of the tree are labeled with terminal symbols, and, when read off in sequence, they correspond to a string in Σ^*.

Decoding algorithms for PCFGs were discussed at length in chapter 2; most notably they include the TROPICAL semiring variants of the CKY algorithm (figure 2.18) and the Earley algorithm (figure 2.19).

A formal description of the generative process (as in algorithm 2) is left as an exercise. Note that HMMs are a special case of PCFGs, with $\mathcal{N} = \Lambda \cup \{\text{⇨}, \text{●}\}$, $N_{\text{⇨}} = \text{⇨}$ and rules of the form

$$\begin{array}{lcll} \ell & \rightarrow & \sigma \ell' \quad \text{for } \ell \in \Lambda, \sigma \in \Sigma, \ell' \in \Lambda \cup \{\text{●}\} & \text{with probability } \eta_{\ell,\sigma} \gamma_{\ell,\ell'} \\ \text{⇨} & \rightarrow & \ell \quad \text{for } \ell \in \Lambda \cup \{\text{●}\} & \text{with probability } \gamma_{\text{⇨},\ell} \\ \text{●} & \rightarrow & \epsilon \quad \text{with probability } 1 & \end{array}$$

where ϵ denotes the empty string.

3.3.5 OTHER GENERATIVE MULTINOMIAL-BASED MODELS

Many other generative models are used in NLP. For example, **naïve Bayes** is an appropriate model when $\mathcal{X}$ is a fixed-length tuple of K attribute-value pairs and $\mathcal{Y}$ is a finite discrete set of C classes.

Letting $\boldsymbol{x} = \langle x_1, \ldots, x_k \rangle$ denote a value in $\mathcal{X}$,

$$\begin{aligned} p(\boldsymbol{X} = \boldsymbol{x}, \boldsymbol{Y} = \boldsymbol{y}) &= p(\boldsymbol{Y} = \boldsymbol{y}) \times p(\boldsymbol{X} = \boldsymbol{x} \mid \boldsymbol{Y} = \boldsymbol{y}) \\ &= p(\boldsymbol{Y} = \boldsymbol{y}) \prod_{i=1}^{k} p(X_i = x_i \mid \boldsymbol{Y} = \boldsymbol{y}) \end{aligned}$$

The parameterization of $p(\boldsymbol{Y})$ (known as the class prior) and $p(X_k \mid \boldsymbol{Y} = \boldsymbol{y})$ for each of the K features are problem-specific, though they are often multinomial distributions when the data are discrete. Decoding can be performed in $O(CK)$ runtime, for C classes, by calculating the score for each class. An excellent source of examples of generative models over structures that are built from multinomial distributions is the collection of so-called "IBM models" for translation (Brown et al., 1990).

3.3.6 MAXIMUM LIKELIHOOD ESTIMATION BY COUNTING

Multinomials make maximum likelihood estimation (equation 3.9) very simple in the case of fully observed data. Consider a discrete random variable $\boldsymbol{E}$ over the discrete finite space $\mathcal{E} = \{\mathrm{e}_1, \ldots, \mathrm{e}_d\}$. We are interested in estimating $\boldsymbol{\theta} = \langle \theta_{\mathrm{e}_1}, \theta_{\mathrm{e}_2}, \ldots, \theta_{\mathrm{e}_d} \rangle$, corresponding to the probabilities of the d outcomes for $\boldsymbol{E}$. $\boldsymbol{\theta}$ must satisfy the sum-to-one and nonnegativity constraints in equation 3.17.

The maximum likelihood estimate of $\boldsymbol{\theta}$, given training data $\langle \tilde{e}_1, \tilde{e}_2, \ldots, \tilde{e}_{\tilde{N}} \rangle$, is equal to the vector of **relative frequencies** of each event occuring in the data:

$$\operatorname*{argmax}_{\boldsymbol{\theta}} p_{\boldsymbol{\theta}}(\langle \tilde{e}_1, \ldots, \tilde{e}_{\tilde{N}} \rangle) = \left\langle \frac{\sum_{i=1}^{\tilde{N}} \mathbf{1}\{\tilde{e}_i = \mathrm{e}_1\}}{\tilde{N}}, \frac{\sum_{i=1}^{\tilde{N}} \mathbf{1}\{\tilde{e}_i = \mathrm{e}_2\}}{\tilde{N}}, \ldots, \frac{\sum_{i=1}^{\tilde{N}} \mathbf{1}\{\tilde{e}_i = \mathrm{e}_d\}}{\tilde{N}} \right\rangle \tag{3.32}$$

Using the notation of frequencies directly, we can also write:

$$\operatorname*{argmax}_{\boldsymbol{\theta}} p_{\boldsymbol{\theta}}(\langle \tilde{e}_1, \ldots, \tilde{e}_{\tilde{N}} \rangle) = \left\langle \frac{\mathit{freq}(\mathrm{e}_1; \langle \tilde{e}_i \rangle_{i=1}^{\tilde{N}})}{\tilde{N}}, \frac{\mathit{freq}(\mathrm{e}_2; \langle \tilde{e}_i \rangle_{i=1}^{\tilde{N}})}{\tilde{N}}, \ldots, \frac{\mathit{freq}(\mathrm{e}_d; \langle \tilde{e}_i \rangle_{i=1}^{\tilde{N}})}{\tilde{N}} \right\rangle \tag{3.33}$$

Given the counts of the events of a multinomial distribution, then, all we need to do to calculate the parameters $\boldsymbol{\theta}$ is normalize the counts by dividing each by $\tilde{N}$ (the size of the training sample). Note that if an event e_j is not seen in the training data, its probability will be estimated as 0.

We include the derivation of the above in our notation. Assuming the observed events $\langle \tilde{\mathbf{e}}_1, \ldots, \tilde{\mathbf{e}}_{\tilde{N}} \rangle$ are independent, maximizing likelihood equates to finding the value of $\boldsymbol{\theta}$ that solves

$$\begin{pmatrix} \operatorname*{argmax}_{\boldsymbol{\theta} \in \mathbb{R}^d_{\geq 0}} & \prod_{i=1}^{\tilde{N}} p_{\boldsymbol{\theta}}(\tilde{\mathbf{e}}_i) \\ \text{such that} & \sum_{j=1}^{d} \theta_{\mathbf{e}_j} = 1 \end{pmatrix} = \begin{pmatrix} \operatorname*{argmax}_{\boldsymbol{\theta} \in \mathbb{R}^d_{\geq 0}} & \sum_{i=1}^{\tilde{N}} \log p_{\boldsymbol{\theta}}(\tilde{\mathbf{e}}_i) \\ \text{such that} & \sum_{j=1}^{d} \theta_{\mathbf{e}_j} = 1 \end{pmatrix} \tag{3.34}$$

$$= \begin{pmatrix} \operatorname*{argmax}_{\boldsymbol{\theta} \in \mathbb{R}^d_{\geq 0}} & \sum_{j=1}^{d} \mathit{freq}(\mathbf{e}_j; \langle \tilde{\mathbf{e}}_i \rangle_{i=1}^{\tilde{N}}) \log \theta_{\mathbf{e}_j} \\ \text{such that} & \sum_{j=1}^{d} \theta_{\mathbf{e}_j} = 1 \end{pmatrix} \tag{3.35}$$

$$= \operatorname*{argmax}_{\boldsymbol{\theta} \in \mathbb{R}^d_{\geq 0}} \sum_{j=1}^{d} \mathit{freq}(\mathbf{e}_j; \langle \tilde{\mathbf{e}}_i \rangle_{i=1}^{\tilde{N}}) \log \theta_{\mathbf{e}_j} + \min_{\nu} \nu \left(1 - \sum_{j=1}^{d} \theta_{\mathbf{e}_j}\right)$$

The last step replaces the constraint that $\boldsymbol{\theta}$ sum to one with a term in the objective function. This term can be understood as a penalty. When the sum of $\boldsymbol{\theta}$ is equal to one, the penalty is zero. If $\sum_{j=1}^{d} \theta_{\mathbf{e}_j} > 1$, then the value of ν that minimizes the penalty will be ∞, so that the entire objective goes to $-\infty$. If $\sum_{j=1}^{d} \theta_{\mathbf{e}_j} < 1$, then ν will go to ∞ and the entire objective again goes to $-\infty$. ν is "adversarial" in the sense that it works against optimizing likelihood whenever the sum-to-one constraint is not met. ν is called a **Lagrangian multiplier**. The theory of Lagrangian duality allows us to rearrange the objective as follows:

$$\min_{\nu} \max_{\boldsymbol{\theta} \in \mathbb{R}^d_{\geq 0}} \sum_{j=1}^{d} \mathit{freq}(\mathbf{e}_j; \langle \tilde{\mathbf{e}}_i \rangle_{i=1}^{\tilde{N}}) \log \theta_{\mathbf{e}_j} + \nu \left(1 - \sum_{j=1}^{d} \theta_{\mathbf{e}_j}\right) \tag{3.36}$$

We now solve the inner problem analytically. This is accomplished by differentiating with respect to each $\theta_{\mathbf{e}}$ in turn. For an arbitrary $\mathbf{e} \in \mathcal{E}$,

$$\frac{\partial}{\partial \theta_{\mathbf{e}}} = \frac{\mathit{freq}(\mathbf{e}; \langle \tilde{\mathbf{e}}_i \rangle_{i=1}^{\tilde{N}})}{\theta_{\mathbf{e}}} - \nu \tag{3.37}$$

At the optimal $\boldsymbol{\theta}$, the partial derivatives will be equal to zero. This leads to setting

$$\theta_{\mathbf{e}} = \frac{\mathit{freq}(\mathbf{e}; \langle \tilde{\mathbf{e}}_i \rangle_{i=1}^{\tilde{N}})}{\nu} \tag{3.38}$$

Finally, note that the constraint that $\sum_{j=1}^{d} \theta_{\mathbf{e}_j} = 1$ can be satisfied if $\nu = \tilde{N}$, and the nonnegativity of $\boldsymbol{\theta}$ follows because the frequencies and $\tilde{N}$ are nonnegative.

3.3.7 MAXIMUM *A POSTERIORI* ESTIMATION

A major disadvantage of maximum likelihood estimation is its tendency to **overfit** the training data. Overfitting is the situation in which a model learns to perform well on the training data but fails to generalize to new data. In data with very large event spaces (notably, word vocabularies in natural languages), the fact that many relative frequencies are zero, even for events that are in principle possible, is a major cause of overfitting. Overfitting becomes less of a problem as the training sample grows.

A widely-used solution to overfitting is to introduce a model complexity term that penalizes models that are undesirable. One way to frame this notion of "undesirable" models is to say that we have a prior belief about what a good model will look like, and models that deviate from that prior will receive a larger penalty.[2] This prior belief can be encoded as a probability distribution over models in $\mathcal{P}$.

If we are using a parametric family such that each model $p \in \mathcal{P}$ is parameterized by a fixed-length real vector $\mathbf{w}$, then we seek a distribution over different $\mathbf{w}$. For example, $\mathbf{w}$ might be the concatenation of all the multinomial parameters for a collection of multinomial distributions defining the model. We now consider $\mathbf{W}$ to be a random variable taking values in $\mathbb{R}^d$. The prior is a distribution $p(\mathbf{W} = \mathbf{w})$, for each value of $\mathbf{w}$. We further reinterpret any model $p \in \mathcal{P}$ over $\boldsymbol{X}$ and $\boldsymbol{Y}$ as a conditional distribution $p(\boldsymbol{X}, \boldsymbol{Y} \mid \mathbf{W})$.

Maximum *a posteriori* (MAP) estimation can now be understood in two ways. The probabilistic view, comparable to equation 3.12, tells us to choose

$$\begin{aligned}
\mathbf{w}^* &= \underset{\mathbf{w} \in \mathbb{R}^d}{\operatorname{argmax}}\, p(\mathbf{W} = \mathbf{w} \mid \boldsymbol{X}_1 = \tilde{\boldsymbol{x}}_1, \boldsymbol{Y}_1 = \tilde{\boldsymbol{y}}_1, \ldots, \boldsymbol{X}_{\tilde{N}} = \boldsymbol{x}_{\tilde{N}}, \boldsymbol{Y}_{\tilde{N}} = \boldsymbol{y}_{\tilde{N}}) \\
&= \underset{\text{models}}{\operatorname{argmax}}\, p(\text{model} \mid \text{data}) \\
&= \underset{\text{models}}{\operatorname{argmax}}\, \frac{p(\text{model, data})}{p(\text{data})} \\
&= \underset{\text{models}}{\operatorname{argmax}}\, p(\text{model, data}) \\
&= \underset{\text{models}}{\operatorname{argmax}}\, p(\text{data} \mid \text{model}) \times p(\text{model}) \\
&= \underset{\mathbf{w} \in \mathbb{R}^d}{\operatorname{argmax}} \left(\prod_{i=1}^{\tilde{N}} p(\boldsymbol{X} = \tilde{\boldsymbol{x}}_i, \boldsymbol{Y} = \tilde{\boldsymbol{y}}_i \mid \mathbf{W} = \mathbf{w}) \right) \times p(\mathbf{W} = \mathbf{w}) \qquad (3.39)
\end{aligned}$$

This is equivalent to equation 3.12 (maximum likelihood estimation), except that the prior term is factored in.[3]

The second view, which is equivalent, instantiates equation 3.2. The expected loss is exactly as in maximum likelihood estimation, but we now include the model complexity term, *model-complexity*,

[2] A related idea is **minimum description length**: models that require many bits to encode are to be penalized (Rissanen, 1978).
[3] The reader may recall seeing the term "MAP" used to refer to the decoding problem in section 2.2.1. The principle is exactly the same. There, we wanted the most likely $\boldsymbol{y}$ given $\boldsymbol{x}$. Here, we want the most likely $\mathbf{w}$ given the training data.

by defining

$$model\text{-}complexity(p_{\mathbf{w}}) = -\frac{1}{\tilde{N}} \log p(\mathbf{W} = \mathbf{w}) \tag{3.40}$$

The result is equivalent to applying the logarithm function to equation 3.39 and scaling by $\frac{1}{\tilde{N}}$:

$$\mathbf{w}^* = \underset{\mathbf{w} \in \mathbb{R}^d}{\operatorname{argmax}} \frac{1}{\tilde{N}} \sum_{i=1}^{\tilde{N}} \log p_{\mathbf{w}}(\boldsymbol{X} = \tilde{\boldsymbol{x}}_i, \boldsymbol{Y} = \tilde{\boldsymbol{y}}_i) + \underbrace{\frac{1}{\tilde{N}} \log p(\mathbf{W} = \mathbf{w})}_{-model\text{-}complexity(p_{\mathbf{w}})} \tag{3.41}$$

What form should $p(\mathbf{W} = \mathbf{w})$ take? Many NLP models (including the examples above) are based on multinomial distributions. A very natural and convenient parametric prior for a multinomial distribution is the **Dirichlet distribution**. Let $\mathcal{P}$ denote the set of multinomial distributions over events in $\mathcal{E} = \{e_1, \ldots, e_d\}$. A Dirichlet is parameterized by a mean $\boldsymbol{\rho} \in \mathcal{P}$ and a concentration parameter $\alpha > 0$ that encodes the tendency for the outcome of the Dirichlet to be close to the mean (when α is large) or farther away (as α tends to 0).[4]

Letting $\boldsymbol{\Theta}$ be the random variable ranging over multinomials over $\mathcal{E}$, the Dirichlet assigns:[5]

$$p_{\alpha,\boldsymbol{\rho}}(\boldsymbol{\Theta} = \boldsymbol{\theta}) = \frac{\Gamma(\alpha)}{\prod_{e \in \mathcal{E}} \Gamma(\alpha \rho_e)} \prod_{e \in \mathcal{E}} (\theta_e)^{(\alpha \rho_e - 1)} \tag{3.43}$$

Written out in full, the Dirichlet is rather daunting. It is helpful to consider it as a model complexity penalty on the multinomial probability vector $\boldsymbol{\theta}$, obtained by taking the logarithm as in equation 3.41, where $\log p(\mathbf{W} = \mathbf{w}) = -\tilde{N}\, model\text{-}complexity(\mathbf{w})$:

$$\begin{aligned}
\log p_{\alpha,\boldsymbol{\rho}}(\boldsymbol{\Theta} = \boldsymbol{\theta}) &= \log \Gamma(\alpha) + \sum_{e \in \mathcal{E}} (-\log \Gamma(\alpha \rho_e) + (\alpha \rho_e - 1) \log \theta_e) \\
&= \text{constant}(\boldsymbol{\theta}) + \sum_{e \in \mathcal{E}} (\alpha \rho_e - 1) \log \theta_e
\end{aligned} \tag{3.44}$$

A simple way to understand the Dirichlet distribution is as a series of draws from $|\mathcal{E}|$ Gamma distributions.[6] There is one draw per e, with parameters $shape = \alpha \rho_e$ and $scale = 1$. After these independent draws, the values are renormalized to sum to one.

[4]Rather than the standard notation, we separate the mean of the Dirichlet, $\boldsymbol{\rho}$, from the concentration parameter, α. The standard notation uses a vector $\boldsymbol{\alpha} \in \mathbb{R}^d_{\geq 0}$, such that for $j \in \{1, \ldots, d\}$, α_j in standard notation equates to $\alpha \rho_j$ in our notation.

[5]Γ denotes the Gamma function, defined by

$$\Gamma(x) = \int_0^\infty u^{x-1} e^{-u}\, du \tag{3.42}$$

The Gamma function is an extension of the factorial function to the nonnegative reals; note that $\Gamma(n) = (n-1)!$ for $n \in \mathbb{N}$.

[6]A Gamma distribution is a continuous distribution over $[0, \infty)$. It has two parameters, $shape > 0$ and $scale > 0$. Its probability density function is:

$$p_{shape,scale}(v) = v^{shape-1} \frac{\exp(-v/scale)}{scale^{shape}\, \Gamma(shape)} \tag{3.45}$$

If we think of the above as a penalty function on values of $\mathbf{\Theta}$, what kinds of distributions receive a penalty? Three special cases are illuminating.

Uninformative prior. When $\boldsymbol{\rho} = \langle \frac{1}{d}, \frac{1}{d}, \ldots, \frac{1}{d} \rangle$ and $\alpha = d$, the penalty is 0 for all values $\boldsymbol{\theta}$. This is sometimes called an uninformative or flat prior, and using it makes MAP equivalent to maximum likelihood estimation.

Smoothing. When $\alpha\boldsymbol{\rho} > \mathbf{1}$, the penalty term approaches $-\infty$ as any θ_e approaches 0. (As $x \rightarrow^{+} 0$, $\log x \rightarrow -\infty$.) Hence, distributions are pushed toward giving some nonzero probability to each of the d multinomial outcomes. In MAP estimation, the most frequent use of the Dirichlet is for smoothing, or choosing model parameters in a way that allocates probability mass more evenly across the event space than MLE. Whenever $\alpha\boldsymbol{\rho} \geq \mathbf{1}$, MAP estimation has a closed form that is as easy to calculate as maximum likelihood estimation (equation 3.32):

$$\underset{\boldsymbol{\theta}}{\operatorname{argmax}}\ p_{\boldsymbol{\theta}}(\langle \tilde{e}_1, \ldots, \tilde{e}_{\tilde{N}} \rangle) \times p_{\alpha,\boldsymbol{\rho}}(\boldsymbol{\Theta} = \boldsymbol{\theta}) = \left\langle \frac{\alpha\rho_1 - 1 + \mathit{freq}(e_1; \langle \tilde{e}_i \rangle_{i=1}^{\tilde{N}})}{\alpha - 1 + \tilde{N}}, \ldots, \frac{\alpha\rho_d - 1 + \mathit{freq}(e_d; \langle \tilde{e}_i \rangle_{i=1}^{\tilde{N}})}{\alpha - 1 + \tilde{N}} \right\rangle \tag{3.46}$$

The special case where $\boldsymbol{\rho} = \langle \frac{1}{d}, \frac{1}{d}, \ldots, \frac{1}{d} \rangle$ and $\alpha = 2d$ is the simplest kind of smoothing, **Laplace smoothing**. Laplace smoothing simply adds 1 to each frequency before normalizing. More generally, when $\boldsymbol{\rho}$ is uniform and $\alpha > d$, MAP estimation equates to adding $\alpha/d - 1$ to each frequency before normalizing; this is known as **add-λ smoothing**, where $\lambda = \alpha/d - 1$. In general, the vector of values $\langle \alpha\rho_1 - 1, \alpha\rho_2 - 1, \ldots, \alpha\rho_d - 1 \rangle$ is known as a vector of **pseudocounts** added to the frequencies of events in training data before normalization. Note that many other smoothing methods are available for multinomial distributions; see Chen and Goodman (1998) for a survey in the context of language modeling.

Sparse prior. When $\alpha\rho_j < 1$ for some or all $\boldsymbol{e}_j \in \mathcal{E}$, the sign of the penalty term reverses, so that θ_j becomes more favorable when approaching 0. Hence, distributions are pushed to assign 0 to as many events as possible, while still maintaining the ability to account for the training data. Note that the closed form solution of equation 3.46 does not apply in this case (see, for instance, Johnson et al., 2007b).

3.3.8 ALTERNATIVE PARAMETERIZATION: LOG-LINEAR MODELS

So far, we have assumed that a generative model for discrete events in $\mathcal{X} \times \mathcal{Y}$ is built out of multinomial distributions. We connected multinomials to linear decoding by pointing out that if $\mathbf{w}$ takes the value of $\log \boldsymbol{\theta}$ (possibly concatenating together the parameters of more than one multinomial distribution, with each multinomial summing to one), and if $\mathbf{g}$ counts the frequency of each multinomial event in the generative model, one per dimension, then the result will be that

$$\log p(\boldsymbol{X} = \boldsymbol{x}, \boldsymbol{Y} = \boldsymbol{y}) = \mathbf{w}^\top \mathbf{g}(\boldsymbol{x}, \boldsymbol{y}) \tag{3.47}$$

$$p(\boldsymbol{X} = \boldsymbol{x}, \boldsymbol{Y} = \boldsymbol{y}) = \exp \mathbf{w}^\top \mathbf{g}(\boldsymbol{x}, \boldsymbol{y}) \tag{3.48}$$

It is easy, however, to imagine alternative features that might be informative for linguistic structure prediction, features that do not easily fit the generative story. Suppose, for example, in the HMM case, that we wish to increase the score of labeling a word with $\ell \in \Lambda$ if it is capitalized (see, e.g., the example in section 2.1). The decision to capitalize the word is already modeled, assuming that its uncapitalized and capitalized versions are two separate elements of Σ. But there is no elegant way to tie together the events of all capitalized word forms; each has its own separate value in the HMM's emission distribution $\boldsymbol{\eta}_\ell$. One possibility would be to follow the kinds of assumptions made by a naïve Bayes model for the emission distribution, letting

$$p(X_i = \sigma \mid Y_i = \ell) = p(\sigma \mid \ell) \times p(\mathit{capitalized}(\sigma) \mid \ell) \tag{3.49}$$

Additional features of the word might similarly be generated by multiplying in additional factors. This model is naïve in that it ignores all correlations among surface features, and it allows some probability mass to go to combinations of features that are impossible (e.g., it is possible to generate the string *Blei* and simultaneously decide that it should be uncapitalized and contain a numeric digit, despite the fact that it is inherently capitalized and contains no digits). Such a model wastes probability mass on events that are logical impossibilities (e.g., the string *Blei* and "not capitalized").[7]

Log-linear models offer a more expressive approach to generative modeling.[8] The basic idea is to start with equation 3.47 but remove any restrictions on the weights and the features. That is, the weights no longer need to be understood as log-probabilities, and the features can be any functions $\mathcal{X} \times \mathcal{Y} \rightarrow \mathbb{R}$ (not just frequencies of events in a generative modeling story about derivations). This means, of course, that the exponential of the score $\mathbf{w}^\top \mathbf{g}(\boldsymbol{x}, \boldsymbol{y})$ cannot be treated as a well-formed probability. Although $\exp \mathbf{w}^\top \mathbf{g}(\boldsymbol{x}, \boldsymbol{y})$ will always be nonnegative, the values cannot in general be guaranteed to sum to one. So we introduce a normalizer, which depends on the weights $\mathbf{w}$:

$$z_{\mathbf{w}} = \sum_{\boldsymbol{x} \in \mathcal{X}} \sum_{\boldsymbol{y} \in \mathcal{Y}_{\boldsymbol{x}}} \exp \mathbf{w}^\top \mathbf{g}(\boldsymbol{x}, \boldsymbol{y}) \tag{3.50}$$

[7] One answer to this problem is to alter the generative story, saying that first the model generates the word, then it generates the capitalization feature. If they are inconsistent, it starts over, repeating until a consistent outcome is achieved. This story is perfectly acceptable, but it implies that the event space is restricted in a way that is not reflected in the relative frequency estimation. More precisely, relative frequency estimation assumes each multinomial can be estimated independently, but the consistency check and "starting over" clearly break that independence. In order to accomplish true maximum likelihood estimation under this story, we must perform operations much more complex than relative frequency estimation. When we simply apply relative frequency estimation anyway, ignoring the statistical dependencies introduced by the consistency check, we have something known historically as a **deficient** model. It would be more accurate to describe the *estimation* as deficient, not the model. Thanks to David Blei for this explanation.

[8] We note that it is not traditional to present them as generative models first; they are usually used as *conditional* models (section 3.4), and most of our discussion about them (section 3.5) will use that interpretation. The general idea, however, can be understood in a generative framework.

This is sometimes called a partition function (it is a function of $\mathbf{w}$). If we use it to scale the exponentiated scores, we arrive at a well-formed probability distribution:

$$p_{\mathbf{w}}(\boldsymbol{X} = \boldsymbol{x}, \boldsymbol{Y} = \boldsymbol{y}) = \frac{1}{z_{\mathbf{w}}} \exp \mathbf{w}^\top \mathbf{g}(\boldsymbol{x}, \boldsymbol{y}) \tag{3.51}$$

The central idea is to transform the linear score used in decoding into a probability by exponentiation and renormalization.

The same techniques for training multinomial-based generative models are available, at least in principle, for log-linear models. One important challenge is the choice of the feature functions $\mathbf{g}$. As for parameter estimation, an important difference is that the maximum likelihood estimate for a log-linear model does not have a closed-form solution (cf. relative frequencies as in section 3.3.6), and numerical optimization techniques must be used to find the optimum. Maximum *a posteriori* estimation is available as well, and it is widely used, though the form of the prior distribution is different (we will return to this matter in section 3.5.5).

Log-linear models can be applied in (at least) two ways in the generative setting. The first is to define a single "global" model over the entire event space $\mathcal{X} \times \mathcal{Y}$. This is rarely done, because the resulting partition function ($z_{\mathbf{w}}$) must sum over a very large, perhaps infinite, space, and approximations are almost always required. A classic example is the "whole sentence language model" of Rosenfeld et al. (2001). Smith et al. (2007) applied an alternative estimation criterion based on M-estimation (Jeon and Lin, 2006) that avoids calculating the partition function and is very fast to train.

The second way to use log-linear models in the generative setting is to use log-linear distributions over derivation steps in the generative process. For example, the distribution over symbols to be emitted by an HMM state could be parameterized log-linearly. The partition function in this case will be much more manageable since the number of outcomes ($|\Sigma|$ for each HMM state's emission distribution) is finite.

Log-linear models are often called "maximum entropy" models. For further discussion, see appendix C.

Because log-linear models are so much more frequently used in *conditional modeling*, we will discuss them in that setting in much more detail (section 3.5). Indeed, conditional models—which perform well and, when log-linear parameterizations are used, offer more straightforward decoding and learning algorithms—have mostly eclipsed research on generative log-linear approaches.

3.3.9 COMMENTS

One advantage of generative models is that they can answer many questions. Our starting point was the goal of building a decoder $h : \mathcal{X} \to \mathcal{Y}$ to use for prediction. Generative models indeed offer a solution to that problem, as discussed in section 3.3.1. But a generative model can, at least in principle, solve many other problems, such as finding the most likely value of $\boldsymbol{X}$ given that $\boldsymbol{Y} = \boldsymbol{y}$. Given a generative model, the problem of finding the values of some random variables given the values of others is called **probabilistic inference**. In some settings we do have many questions, and the ability to use a single model to answer all of them is attractive.[9,10]

If we know in advance that our model will *only* be used to model the prediction of $\boldsymbol{Y}$ from $\boldsymbol{X}$, then the generative model may be doing too much work, with the result of decreased predictive accuracy on the $\boldsymbol{X}$-to-$\boldsymbol{Y}$ task. Consider that, for any joint model p, the following holds:

$$p(\boldsymbol{X} = \boldsymbol{x}, \boldsymbol{Y} = \boldsymbol{y}) = p(\boldsymbol{X} = \boldsymbol{x}) \times p(\boldsymbol{Y} = \boldsymbol{y} \mid \boldsymbol{X} = \boldsymbol{x}) \tag{3.53}$$

A generative model aims to accurately fit both factors of the joint distribution: the marginal over $\boldsymbol{X}$ and the conditional over $\boldsymbol{Y}$ given $\boldsymbol{X}$. (Note that it may not be *parameterized* into these factors.) Yet if the model only needs to be used for prediction of $\boldsymbol{Y}$'s value from $\boldsymbol{X}$'s value, the former factor is unnecessary. Put another way, there is no reason to model the input $\boldsymbol{X}$ if it is *always* observed. For the prediction task, we only really need $p(\boldsymbol{Y} \mid \boldsymbol{X})$.

Consider, for example, a situation in which we discover a new source of information for the input to our system. In other words, we have an augmented representation of $\boldsymbol{X}$. Our hope is that such information will be useful and improve the accuracy of our model's predictions. Unfortunately, we now have an expanded (or more detailed) input event space $\mathcal{X}$, and the model must be extended to explain the new information. Further, if the new information is not useful to the prediction, we still must do the extra work of explaining it in the generative story.

Conditional models, to which we turn next, keep the probabilistic view of prediction but do not attempt to build a model to explain the input random variable $\boldsymbol{X}$.

3.4 CONDITIONAL MODELS

A conditional model for predicting output $\boldsymbol{Y}$ from a given input $\boldsymbol{X} = \boldsymbol{x}$ is one that defines, usually using a parametric model, the distribution

$$p(\boldsymbol{Y} = \boldsymbol{y} \mid \boldsymbol{X} = \boldsymbol{x}) \tag{3.54}$$

instead of the joint distribution $p(\boldsymbol{X} = \boldsymbol{x}, \boldsymbol{Y} = \boldsymbol{y})$. A well-formed conditional model is a function $p : \mathcal{X} \times \mathcal{Y} \rightarrow \mathbb{R}_{\geq 0}$ such that

$$\forall \boldsymbol{x} \in \mathcal{X}, \qquad \sum_{\boldsymbol{y} \in \mathcal{Y}_{\boldsymbol{x}}} p(\boldsymbol{Y} = \boldsymbol{y} \mid \boldsymbol{X} = \boldsymbol{x}) = 1 \tag{3.55}$$

[9]In section 3.3.7, when we started treating the parameters $\mathbf{w}$ as the value taken by random variable $\mathbf{W}$, the problem of MAP estimation is another inference problem, where we choose the most likely value of $\mathbf{W}$ given the empirical distribution over $\boldsymbol{X}$ and $\boldsymbol{Y}$.

[10]Another example of an "alternative question" is the alternative decoding rule known as **minimum Bayes risk** decoding:

$$\begin{aligned} h(\boldsymbol{x}) &= \operatorname*{argmin}_{\boldsymbol{y} \in \mathcal{Y}_{\boldsymbol{x}}} \mathbb{E}_{p_{\mathbf{w}}(\boldsymbol{Y} \mid \boldsymbol{X} = \boldsymbol{x})}[\mathit{cost}(\boldsymbol{x}, \boldsymbol{Y}; h)] \\ &= \operatorname*{argmin}_{\boldsymbol{y} \in \mathcal{Y}_{\boldsymbol{x}}} \sum_{\boldsymbol{y}' \in \mathcal{Y}_{\boldsymbol{x}}} p_{\mathbf{w}}(\boldsymbol{Y} = \boldsymbol{y}' \mid \boldsymbol{X} = \boldsymbol{x}) \mathit{cost}(\boldsymbol{x}, \boldsymbol{y}, \boldsymbol{y}') \end{aligned} \tag{3.52}$$

The idea is to imagine that the true value of $\boldsymbol{Y}$ is distributed randomly according to the model's distribution $p(\boldsymbol{Y} \mid \boldsymbol{X} = \boldsymbol{x})$, and choose the $\boldsymbol{y}$ that minimizes the risk, or expected value (under that distribution) of a cost or error function. In section 5.3, we will consider minimum Bayes risk decoding.

Compare this to equation 3.5 for joint models. Designing models this way is similar to generative approaches, but leads to some surprising advantages. We denote the set of proper conditional models $\mathbb{P}_{\mathcal{Y}|\mathcal{X}}$.

To see this approach as an instantiation of equation 3.2, let

$$loss(\boldsymbol{x}, \boldsymbol{y}; h) = -\log p(\boldsymbol{Y} = \boldsymbol{y} \mid \boldsymbol{X} = \boldsymbol{x}) \tag{3.56}$$

This is another form of the log loss (equation 3.6). Interestingly, equation 3.6 can be understood as including two terms: equation 3.56 and $-\log p(\boldsymbol{X} = \boldsymbol{x})$. The conditional version in equation 3.56 has no penalty for an unlikely value of $\boldsymbol{X}$, and the conditional model has nothing to say about different values of $\boldsymbol{X}$.

The conditional modeling technique suggests the decoding rule:

$$\boldsymbol{y}^* = \operatorname*{argmax}_{\boldsymbol{y} \in \mathcal{Y}_{\boldsymbol{x}}} p(\boldsymbol{Y} = \boldsymbol{y} \mid \boldsymbol{X} = \boldsymbol{x}) \tag{3.57}$$

This is just like equation 3.13, except that we do not need to use the definition of conditional probability to arrive at the joint probability $p(\boldsymbol{X} = \boldsymbol{x}, \boldsymbol{Y} = \boldsymbol{y})$, which the conditional model does not even define.

Given a parametric family $\mathcal{P} \subset \mathbb{P}_{\mathcal{Y}|\mathcal{X}}$, maximum likelihood estimation for this model maximizes the conditional likelihood of the observed outputs given their respective inputs:

$$\max_{p \in \mathcal{P}} \prod_{i=1}^{\tilde{N}} p(\boldsymbol{Y} = \tilde{\boldsymbol{y}}_i \mid \boldsymbol{X} = \tilde{\boldsymbol{x}}_i) = \max_{p \in \mathcal{P}} \sum_{i=1}^{\tilde{N}} \log p(\boldsymbol{Y} = \tilde{\boldsymbol{y}}_i \mid \boldsymbol{X} = \tilde{\boldsymbol{x}}_i) \tag{3.58}$$

This is equivalent to a model in which the marginal probability over $\boldsymbol{X}$ is fixed rather than learned. (It does not matter the values $p(\boldsymbol{X})$ is "fixed" to, as long as each training example $\tilde{\boldsymbol{x}}_i$ has nonzero probability.)

Maximizing likelihood for a conditional model corresponds to minimizing the expectation of equation 3.56 over the training sample:

$$\operatorname*{argmax}_{p \in \mathcal{P}} \sum_{i=1}^{\tilde{N}} \log p(\boldsymbol{Y} = \tilde{\boldsymbol{y}}_i \mid \boldsymbol{X} = \tilde{\boldsymbol{x}}_i) = \operatorname*{argmin}_{p \in \mathcal{P}} \frac{1}{\tilde{N}} \sum_{i=1}^{\tilde{N}} loss(\tilde{\boldsymbol{x}}_i, \tilde{\boldsymbol{y}}_i; h) \tag{3.59}$$

As in the generative case, this training criterion does not directly depend on h.

Conditional models are attractive in that they do not do "extra work" aiming to explain the distribution of inputs $\boldsymbol{X}$. They still model uncertainty using probability, and (like generative models) permit probabilistic inference (not just decoding).

Conditional models may be parameterized using multinomials or log-linear models. They may be factored into derivation steps (as in section 3.3), or not. The most powerful and widely used conditional models are built from log-linear models and do not factor into derivation steps. We turn to this approach next. A contrasting approach, where the conditional probability distribution *does* factor into derivation steps, is presented in appendix D.

3.5 GLOBALLY NORMALIZED CONDITIONAL LOG-LINEAR MODELS

One dominant approach to conditional models is based on **log-linear models** that are **globally normalized**. Log-linear models were introduced in section 3.3.8 in the generative setting. Here we consider them in a conditional setting.

The basic idea of conditional log-linear modeling is to turn the linear score in equation 2.3 into a conditional probability distribution over output values of $\boldsymbol{Y}$ given input values of $\boldsymbol{X}$. The distribution is defined as follows:

$$p_{\mathbf{w}}(\boldsymbol{Y} = \boldsymbol{y} \mid \boldsymbol{X} = \boldsymbol{x}) = \frac{\exp \mathbf{w}^\top \mathbf{g}(\boldsymbol{x}, \boldsymbol{y})}{\sum_{\boldsymbol{y}' \in \mathcal{Y}_{\boldsymbol{x}}} \exp \mathbf{w}^\top \mathbf{g}(\boldsymbol{x}, \boldsymbol{y}')} \tag{3.60}$$

The normalizer, the denominator in equation 3.60, is often referred to as the **partition function**; we will use the notation

$$z_{\mathbf{w}}(\boldsymbol{x}) = \sum_{\boldsymbol{y}' \in \mathcal{Y}_{\boldsymbol{x}}} \exp \mathbf{w}^\top \mathbf{g}(\boldsymbol{x}, \boldsymbol{y}') \tag{3.61}$$

Comparing to section 3.3.8, note that the partition function here is specific to each $\boldsymbol{x} \in \mathcal{X}$. Earlier, we introduced log-linear distributions as an alternative to conditional multinomial distributions. Here, we propose to use a single log-linear model for the whole distribution over the structured random variable $\boldsymbol{Y}$ given the structured random variable $\boldsymbol{X}$. The score may factor into local parts (this is important for efficient exact decoding), but the probability does not factor into derivation steps or a generative process.

Given the above model, we can derive the decoding rule of equation 2.3 by taking the most probable $\boldsymbol{y}$ given $\boldsymbol{x}$:

$$\begin{aligned}
\operatorname*{argmax}_{\boldsymbol{y} \in \mathcal{Y}_{\boldsymbol{x}}} p_{\mathbf{w}}(\boldsymbol{Y} = \boldsymbol{y} \mid \boldsymbol{X} = \boldsymbol{x}) &= \operatorname*{argmax}_{\boldsymbol{y} \in \mathcal{Y}_{\boldsymbol{x}}} \frac{\exp \mathbf{w}^\top \mathbf{g}(\boldsymbol{x}, \boldsymbol{y})}{z_{\mathbf{w}}(\boldsymbol{x})} \\
&= \operatorname*{argmax}_{\boldsymbol{y} \in \mathcal{Y}_{\boldsymbol{x}}} \log \frac{\exp \mathbf{w}^\top \mathbf{g}(\boldsymbol{x}, \boldsymbol{y})}{z_{\mathbf{w}}(\boldsymbol{x})} \\
&= \operatorname*{argmax}_{\boldsymbol{y} \in \mathcal{Y}_{\boldsymbol{x}}} \mathbf{w}^\top \mathbf{g}(\boldsymbol{x}, \boldsymbol{y}) - \log z_{\mathbf{w}}(\boldsymbol{x}) \\
&= \operatorname*{argmax}_{\boldsymbol{y} \in \mathcal{Y}_{\boldsymbol{x}}} \mathbf{w}^\top \mathbf{g}(\boldsymbol{x}, \boldsymbol{y})
\end{aligned} \tag{3.62}$$

The $\log z_{\mathbf{w}}(\boldsymbol{x})$ term can be ignored because it is constant in $\boldsymbol{y}$.

3.5.1 LOGISTIC REGRESSION

Log-linear models are a generalization of a binary classification technique called **logistic regression**.[11] Let $\boldsymbol{X}$ be the input random variable ranging over $\mathbb{R}^d$, and let $\boldsymbol{Y}$ be the output random

[11] Confusingly, logistic regression is a classification technique, not a regression technique as the name suggests.

variable, ranging over $\{-1, +1\}$ (typically corresponding to a negative class label and a positive class label).

$$
\begin{aligned}
p(\boldsymbol{Y} = +1 \mid \boldsymbol{X} = \boldsymbol{x}) &= \frac{\exp \mathbf{w}^\top \boldsymbol{x}}{\exp \mathbf{w}^\top \boldsymbol{x} + 1} = \frac{1}{1 + \exp(-\mathbf{w}^\top \boldsymbol{x})} \\
p(\boldsymbol{Y} = -1 \mid \boldsymbol{X} = \boldsymbol{x}) &= \frac{1}{\exp \mathbf{w}^\top \boldsymbol{x} + 1}
\end{aligned}
\tag{3.63}
$$

Equation 3.63 is equivalent to a log-linear model with d features, such that, for each j:

$$
g_j(\boldsymbol{x}, \boldsymbol{y}) = \begin{cases} x_j & \text{if } \boldsymbol{y} = +1 \\ 0 & \text{otherwise} \end{cases} \tag{3.64}
$$

Multinomial logistic regression is a generalization that allows $\boldsymbol{Y}$ to range over a discrete finite set $\mathcal{Y} = \{\boldsymbol{y}_1, \ldots, \boldsymbol{y}_K\}$. Each $\boldsymbol{y} \in \mathcal{Y}$ has its own weight vector, so that

$$
\mathrm{p}(\boldsymbol{Y} = \boldsymbol{y} \mid \boldsymbol{X} = \boldsymbol{x}) = \frac{\exp \mathbf{w}_{\boldsymbol{y}}^\top \boldsymbol{x}}{\sum_{k=1}^{K} \exp \mathbf{w}_{\boldsymbol{y}_k}^\top \boldsymbol{x}} \tag{3.65}
$$

This is equivalent to a log-linear model with $|\mathcal{Y}| \times d$ features,

$$
g_{k,j}(\boldsymbol{x}, \boldsymbol{y}) = \begin{cases} x_j & \text{if } \boldsymbol{y} = \boldsymbol{y}_k \\ 0 & \text{otherwise} \end{cases} \tag{3.66}
$$

and the weights concatenated together:

$$
\mathbf{w} = \langle \mathbf{w}_{\boldsymbol{y}_1}, \mathbf{w}_{\boldsymbol{y}_2}, \ldots, \mathbf{w}_{\boldsymbol{y}_K} \rangle \tag{3.67}
$$

3.5.2 CONDITIONAL RANDOM FIELDS

Conditional random fields (CRFs), strictly speaking, are a variation on undirected graphical models (also called Markov random fields or Markov networks) in which some random variables are observed and others are modeled probabilistically. CRFs were introduced by Lafferty et al. (2001) for sequence labeling; they have been generalized in many ways for other structured problems. We give the original version first, then a more general notation.

The original CRFs defined the distribution over label sequences in Λ^*, given an observed sequence $\boldsymbol{x} \in \Sigma^n$ (for arbitrary n), by:

$$
p_{\mathbf{w}}(\boldsymbol{Y} = \boldsymbol{y} \mid \boldsymbol{X} = \boldsymbol{x}) = \frac{\exp \sum_{i=1}^{n+1} \mathbf{w}^\top \mathbf{f}(\boldsymbol{x}, y_{i-1}, y_i, i)}{\sum_{\boldsymbol{y}' \in \Lambda^n} \exp \sum_{i=1}^{n+1} \mathbf{w}^\top \mathbf{f}(\boldsymbol{x}, y'_{i-1}, y'_i, i)} \tag{3.68}
$$

(As before we assume $y_0 =$ ⬗ and $y_{n+1} =$ ◉.) The attraction of the CRF is that it permits the inclusion of any (local) features. Compared to the HMM, this is a significant advantage; HMMs only include transition and emission features, since the generative process (to be proper) must account for each piece of structure (each x_i and each y_i) exactly once, no more and no less. The CRF has no such interpretation, so features that "overlap" and are redundant can be included without any naïve assumptions about feature independence. To take an example, Lafferty et al. (2001) modeled part of speech tagging with standard HMM features (pairs of adjacent tags are transitions, word-tag pairs are emissions) but extended the feature set to include spelling features, such as whether the word starts with a capital letter or contains a digit. In the generative story, these features would have been redundant (once the word is emitted, its spelling is fully determined), but the CRF permits them and learns to balance their effect on prediction against the other features.

The above is a special case of the general log-linear formulation in equation 3.60. The key assumption is that the feature vector function $\mathbf{g}$ *factors* into local parts of the output structure. For the original CRF, this permitted the use of dynamic programming to perform exact inference for decoding and for learning. In the notation of chapter 2, traditional CRFs have $n + 1$ projections of $\langle \boldsymbol{x}, \boldsymbol{y} \rangle$ when n is the length of $\boldsymbol{x}$, and

$$\Pi_i(\boldsymbol{x}, \boldsymbol{y}) = \langle \boldsymbol{x}, y_i, y_{i-1}, i \rangle \tag{3.69}$$

In the language of graphical models, we consider each of the projection functions Π_i to correspond to an assignment of values to a clique in the chain-structured undirected graphical model (see section 2.2.1).

The general form for CRFs with projection functions $\Pi_1, \ldots, \Pi_{\#parts(\boldsymbol{x})}$ is:

$$p_{\mathbf{w}}(\boldsymbol{Y} = \boldsymbol{y} \mid \boldsymbol{X} = \boldsymbol{x}) = \frac{\exp \sum_{j=1}^{\#parts(\boldsymbol{x})} \mathbf{w}^\top \mathbf{f}(\Pi_j(\boldsymbol{x}, \boldsymbol{y}))}{\sum_{\boldsymbol{y}' \in \mathcal{Y}_{\boldsymbol{x}}} \exp \sum_{j=1}^{\#parts(\boldsymbol{x})} \mathbf{w}^\top \mathbf{f}(\Pi_j(\boldsymbol{x}, \boldsymbol{y}'))} \tag{3.70}$$

If

$$\mathbf{g}(\boldsymbol{x}, \boldsymbol{y}) = \sum_{j=1}^{\#parts(\boldsymbol{x})} \mathbf{f}(\Pi_j(\boldsymbol{x}, \boldsymbol{y})) = \sum_{i=1}^{n+1} \mathbf{f}(\boldsymbol{x}, y_{i-1}, y_i, i) \tag{3.71}$$

then the general Viterbi algorithm (figure 2.16) can be applied without modification for decoding with a CRF.

We turn next to learning log-linear models from data. Constructing a log-linear model requires a specification of

- the input space ($\mathcal{X}$) and output space ($\mathcal{Y}$), possibly with some constraints on the $\mathcal{Y}_{\boldsymbol{x}} \subseteq \mathcal{Y}$ that is valid for a each $\boldsymbol{x} \in \mathcal{X}$;

- the feature vector function $\mathbf{g} : \mathcal{X} \times \mathcal{Y} \rightarrow \mathbb{R}^d$; and
- the weight vector $\mathbf{w} \in \mathbb{R}^d$.

The first two are normally defined by the model builder, though we will discuss the choice of features briefly in section 3.5.3. The weight vector is generally acquired automatically through parameter estimation, discussed in sections 3.5.4– 3.5.5.

3.5.3 FEATURE CHOICE

The choice of features is central to the performance of a model, and many research questions involve primarily the exploration of new features for a particular task. Indeed, without knowing the features a model includes, we can say very little about the linguistic viability of a model, the computational expense of its decoding and learning algorithms, or the learnability of the model from available data. Changing the features in a model can have a huge effect on its performance.

In natural language processing, feature choice is, at this writing, largely a matter of manual development guided by linguistic expertise and task performance. Computational expense plays a big role in feature design for models of structure since efficient decoding and learning hinge on the factoring property of equation 3.70. "Non-local" features, ones that require projections Π that depend on large, disparate parts of $\boldsymbol{y}$, make efficient inference (such as dynamic programming) asymptotically more expensive, if not intractable, and therefore may require novel inference algorithms, often with approximations. If a new feature requires reimplementing the decoder and loss of efficiency, it may not be worth adding to a model.

Nonetheless, as seen in chapter 2, there has been a trend toward decoding algorithms that are capable of handling features that are less and less local. As the projections Π_j become larger, more features become available.

To take a simple example, consider dependency parsing. At first, the score of a dependency parse $\boldsymbol{y}$ coupled with input sentence $\boldsymbol{x}$ was taken to factor into the arcs of the parse (see section 2.4.2). This implies that each feature can consider one arc at a time and any part of $\boldsymbol{x}$. With even this strong feature locality constraint, there is a combinatorial explosion of features. For each possible arc, the following elements are readily available:

- for each word involved, the surface form, its lemma, its part of speech, and any shape, spelling, or morphological features;
- words involved include the parent, the child, context words on either side of the parent and child, words in between the parent and child;
- the length of the arc (number of words between the parent and child), its direction, and (if the parse is to be labeled) the grammatical relation type.

More recently, exact and approximate decoding algorithms have been developed to allow features that involve two adjacent edges (i.e., a parent and multiple children, or a grandparent, parent, and child) or more global properties of the graph such as the number of nonprojective arcs (Carreras et al., 2008, Koo and Collins, 2010, Martins et al., 2009, McDonald and Pereira, 2006). Even beyond the matter of decoding algorithms, even with arc-factored features alone, tens of millions of features can easily be instantiated on a sizeable dataset; with more kinds of features, the length of $\mathbf{g}$ and $\mathbf{w}$ may become unwieldly.

The term "feature engineering" has come about as a fair description of the amount of linguistic expertise that has gone into designing features for various linguistic structure prediction tasks. As the accuracy of some types of linguistic predictors has achieved acceptably high levels, we often see the output of one predictor incorporated as the input of another. English part of speech tagging, for instance, is now generally believed to be sufficiently accurate, at least on data in the same domain as the training data, that automatically predicted tags are often included as part of the input $\boldsymbol{x}$ for syntactic parsing, whose output is often included as input to semantic processing, translation, and other downstream predictors. As this trend continues, the possibilities for features that may go into any given model increase.

The centrality of features in linguistic structure modeling is belied by the dearth of research on systematic approaches to feature engineering and *automatic* feature selection using data. While some literature in machine learning addresses feature selection at length (Guyon and Elisseeff, 2003), and some work in NLP has sought to infer new, complex features by combining simpler ones during learning (Della Pietra et al., 1997, McCallum, 2003), such approaches receive little attention in current NLP research. Indeed, NLP researchers tend to adopt the strategy of incorporating as many features as they can think of into learning and allowing the parameter estimation method to determine which features are helpful and which should be ignored. Perhaps because of the heavy-tailed nature of linguistic phenomena and the continued growth in computational power available to researchers, the current consensus seems to be that more features are always welcome in an NLP model, especially in frameworks like log-linear models that can incorporate them. This consensus must be met with some caution: adding more features can only help a model fit the training data better, but at the risk of *overfitting*, with negative effects on performance on new data (see section 3.5.5).

We conjecture that automatic feature selection must attract greater attention in the future, particularly if we wish our learned models to be intelligible to their human designers. A key recent trend is the use of unlabeled data to infer features (Koo et al., 2008, Liang et al., 2008, *inter alia*). We will see below that, for log-linear models, feature selection is closely related to parameter estimation.

3.5.4 MAXIMUM LIKELIHOOD ESTIMATION

Because log-linear models are probabilistic and the weight vector $\mathbf{w} = \langle w_1, \ldots, w_d \rangle$ constitutes the parameters of the model, parameter estimation by **maximum likelihood estimation** (MLE) is a natural place to start. Let the training data consist of $\langle \langle \tilde{\boldsymbol{x}}_1, \tilde{\boldsymbol{y}}_1 \rangle, \ldots, \langle \tilde{\boldsymbol{x}}_{\tilde{N}}, \tilde{\boldsymbol{y}}_{\tilde{N}} \rangle \rangle$, as before. The model only predicts $\boldsymbol{Y}$ given $\boldsymbol{X}$, so MLE corresponds to

$$\mathbf{w}^* = \operatorname*{argmax}_{\mathbf{w}} \prod_{i=1}^{\tilde{N}} p_{\mathbf{w}}(\tilde{\boldsymbol{y}}_i \mid \tilde{\boldsymbol{x}}_i) = \operatorname*{argmax}_{\mathbf{w}} \frac{1}{\tilde{N}} \sum_{i=1}^{\tilde{N}} \log p_{\mathbf{w}}(\tilde{\boldsymbol{y}}_i \mid \tilde{\boldsymbol{x}}_i) \tag{3.72}$$

(since log is a monotonic transformation).[12] Given the log-linear form of the model, this equates to:

$$\mathbf{w}^* = \operatorname*{argmax}_{\mathbf{w}} \frac{1}{\tilde{N}} \sum_{i=1}^{\tilde{N}} \mathbf{w}^\top \mathbf{g}(\tilde{\boldsymbol{x}}_i, \tilde{\boldsymbol{y}}_i) - \log z_{\mathbf{w}}(\tilde{\boldsymbol{x}}_i) \tag{3.74}$$

Unlike joint models based on multinomial distributions, maximum likelihood estimation for conditional log-linear models does not have a closed-form solution. This is the price to be paid for allowing arbitrary features that may be redundant or interdependent of each other. Equation 3.74 does, however, have several useful properties. First, it is an unconstrained optimization problem; $\mathbf{w}$ can take any value in $\mathbb{R}^d$. Second, the function is smooth and differentiable. Third, it is globally concave. This means that a wide range of numerical optimization algorithms are available to solve equation 3.74.[13] In most cases, those algorithms will require the calculation of the objective function (log-likelihood) and its first derivatives with respect to each w_j:

$$\begin{aligned}
\Phi_{\text{LL}}(\mathbf{w}) &= \frac{1}{\tilde{N}} \sum_{i=1}^{\tilde{N}} \mathbf{w}^\top \mathbf{g}(\tilde{\boldsymbol{x}}_i, \tilde{\boldsymbol{y}}_i) - \log z_{\mathbf{w}}(\tilde{\boldsymbol{x}}_i) & (3.75)\\
\frac{\partial \Phi_{\text{LL}}}{\partial w_j}(\mathbf{w}) &= \frac{1}{\tilde{N}} \sum_{i=1}^{\tilde{N}} g_j(\tilde{\boldsymbol{x}}_i, \tilde{\boldsymbol{y}}_i) - \sum_{\boldsymbol{y} \in \mathcal{Y}_{\boldsymbol{x}}} p_{\mathbf{w}}(\boldsymbol{Y} = \boldsymbol{y} \mid \boldsymbol{X} = \tilde{\boldsymbol{x}}_i) g_j(\tilde{\boldsymbol{x}}_i, \boldsymbol{y}) & (3.76)\\
&= \frac{1}{\tilde{N}} \sum_{i=1}^{\tilde{N}} g_j(\tilde{\boldsymbol{x}}_i, \tilde{\boldsymbol{y}}_i) - \mathbb{E}_{p_{\mathbf{w}}(\boldsymbol{Y} \mid \boldsymbol{X} = \tilde{\boldsymbol{x}}_i)}[g_j(\tilde{\boldsymbol{x}}_i, \boldsymbol{Y})] & (3.77)\\
&= \mathbb{E}_{\tilde{p}(\boldsymbol{X}, \boldsymbol{Y})}[g_j(\boldsymbol{X}, \boldsymbol{Y})] - \mathbb{E}_{\tilde{p}(\boldsymbol{X}) \cdot p_{\mathbf{w}}(\boldsymbol{Y} \mid \boldsymbol{X})}[g_j(\boldsymbol{X}, \boldsymbol{Y})] & (3.78)
\end{aligned}$$

The first derivative with respect to the jth weight is the difference in expectations of the jth feature between the empirical distribution and the model distribution.

Recall from calculus that a smooth, concave function like Φ_{LL} is maximized at the $\mathbf{w}$ where the first derivatives are all zero. Setting expression 3.78 equal to zero implies that the maximum

[12]Note that this is equivalent to a generative (joint) model over both $\boldsymbol{X}$ and $\boldsymbol{Y}$, while fixing the marginal distribution over $\boldsymbol{X}$ to be the empirical distribution:

$$\operatorname*{argmax}_{\mathbf{w}} \sum_{i=1}^{\tilde{N}} \log \tilde{p}(\tilde{\boldsymbol{x}}_i) + \log p_{\mathbf{w}}(\tilde{\boldsymbol{y}}_i \mid \tilde{\boldsymbol{x}}_i) \tag{3.73}$$

The $\log \tilde{p}(\tilde{\boldsymbol{x}}_i)$ terms are constant in $\mathbf{w}$ and so may be ignored. If we think of this as an approach to generative modeling, then note that it will horribly overfit the training data, assigning probability 0 to any new input $\boldsymbol{x}$ not seen in training. Under this interpretation, we might say that the decoding rule simply ignores the $p(\boldsymbol{X})$ factor, even if it is zero.

[13]Optimization is discussed in greater depth in appendix A.

likelihood $\mathbf{w}$ is the weight vector that makes the model's expectations of feature values equal to the empirical expectations. This is simply an alternative way to understand the idea of "fitting the data."

Efficiently training a log-linear model hinges on the efficiency of calculating the partition function and expected feature values, which typically must be done many times as the inner loop of an optimization algorithm. For globally normalized models like CRFs, this often can be accomplished by dynamic programming (see chapter 5). For non-structured models like logistic regression, these computations are polynomial in the number of features and the cardinality of $\mathcal{Y}$.

3.5.5 MAXIMUM *A POSTERIORI* ESTIMATION

We discussed overfitting by maximum likelihood estimation for generative models and the maximum *a posteriori* solution in section 3.3.7. Recall that the basic idea is to define a probability distribution over model parameter values ($\mathbf{w}$) and augment the log-likelihood objective with a penalty:

$$\textit{model-complexity}(p_{\mathbf{w}}) = -\frac{1}{\tilde{N}} \log p(\mathbf{W} = \mathbf{w}) \tag{3.79}$$

This change to the objective function encourages models that don't just fit the data well (maximum likelihood), but also are *a priori* deemed to be good (likely) models.

Log-linear models estimated by MLE suffer from overfitting in a particular way: in some situations, Φ_{LL} can be increased by increasing some weights arbitrarily toward $+\infty$ or by decreasing some weights arbitrarily toward $-\infty$. Consider, for example, a feature g_6 with value 1 on a single training example, say $\langle \tilde{\boldsymbol{x}}_9, \tilde{\boldsymbol{y}}_9 \rangle$ in the training data but that is always zero on $\langle \tilde{\boldsymbol{x}}_9, \boldsymbol{y} \rangle$, for all $\boldsymbol{y} \neq \tilde{\boldsymbol{y}}_9$ and for all $\langle \tilde{\boldsymbol{x}}_i, \boldsymbol{y} \rangle$ where $i \neq 9$ and for all $\boldsymbol{y} \in \mathcal{Y}$. The first derivative for this feature will be

$$\begin{aligned}\sum_{i=1}^{\tilde{N}} g_6(\tilde{\boldsymbol{x}}_i, \tilde{\boldsymbol{y}}_i) - \mathbb{E}_{p_{\mathbf{w}}(\boldsymbol{Y} \mid \boldsymbol{X} = \tilde{\boldsymbol{x}}_i)}[g_6(\tilde{\boldsymbol{x}}_i, \boldsymbol{Y})] &= g_6(\tilde{\boldsymbol{x}}_9, \tilde{\boldsymbol{y}}_9) - \mathbb{E}_{p_{\mathbf{w}}(\boldsymbol{Y} \mid \boldsymbol{X} = \tilde{\boldsymbol{x}}_9)}[g_6(\tilde{\boldsymbol{x}}_9, \boldsymbol{Y})] \\ &= 1 - p(\boldsymbol{Y} = \tilde{\boldsymbol{y}}_9 \mid \boldsymbol{X} = \tilde{\boldsymbol{x}}_9)\end{aligned}$$

This value can approach 0, but the only way to achieve 0 is to give $\tilde{\boldsymbol{y}}_9$ *all* of the probability for $\tilde{\boldsymbol{x}}_9$. That can only happen as w_9 approaches $+\infty$. The opposite problem will happen for weights of features that are zero for all training examples and nonzero for some competing $\boldsymbol{y} \in \mathcal{Y}$: such weights will be pushed toward $-\infty$.

Infinite-valued weights can be understood as hard constraints since they drive the probability of some structures to zero. They are analogous to multinomial parameters set to zero, which forbid particular stochastic events. (Remember that log-probabilities of multinomials are similar to weights in a linear model.) While such hard constraints may be desirable, in most settings we prefer constraints to be specified by the engineer, not discovered from the training data. Extreme weights are normally taken to be a sign of overfitting.

This suggests the use of a technique called **regularization** (also called "penalization"), in which we penalize weights that grow too large in magnitude. This can be accomplished using a penalized objective function. The two most commonly used are:

$$\max_{\mathbf{w}} \Phi_{\text{LL}}(\mathbf{w}) - \frac{C}{2}\sum_{j=1}^{d} w_j^2 = \max_{\mathbf{w}} \Phi_{\text{LL}}(\mathbf{w}) - \frac{C}{2}\|\mathbf{w}\|_2^2 \quad (3.80)$$

$$\max_{\mathbf{w}} \Phi_{\text{LL}}(\mathbf{w}) - C\sum_{j=1}^{d} |w_j| = \max_{\mathbf{w}} \Phi_{\text{LL}}(\mathbf{w}) - C\|\mathbf{w}\|_1 \quad (3.81)$$

These are typically referred to as L_2 and L_1 regularization, respectively, because they penalize proportional to the L_2 and L_1 norms of the weight vector.[14]

Both kinds of regularization above can be shown to instantiate **maximum *a posteriori*** (MAP) estimation for log-linear models. Recall from section 3.3.7 that MAP seeks to maximize the probability of the model given the data (cf. equation 3.39). The only difference with conditional models is that $\boldsymbol{X}$ remains on the right-hand side of the conditional; it is conditioned *against*, not modeled.

$$\begin{aligned}
\mathbf{w}^* &= \operatorname*{argmax}_{\mathbf{w}\in\mathbb{R}^d} p(\mathbf{W} = \mathbf{w} \mid \boldsymbol{X}_1 = \tilde{\boldsymbol{x}}_1, \boldsymbol{Y}_1 = \tilde{\boldsymbol{y}}_1, \ldots, \boldsymbol{X}_{\tilde{N}} = \boldsymbol{x}_{\tilde{N}}, \boldsymbol{Y}_{\tilde{N}} = \boldsymbol{y}_{\tilde{N}}) \\
&= \operatorname*{argmax}_{\text{models}} p(\text{model} \mid \text{data}) \\
&= = \operatorname*{argmax}_{\text{models}} \frac{p(\text{model, outputs} \mid \text{inputs})}{p(\text{outputs} \mid \text{inputs})} \\
&= \operatorname*{argmax}_{\text{models}} p(\text{model, outputs} \mid \text{inputs}) \\
&= \operatorname*{argmax}_{\text{models}} p(\text{outputs} \mid \text{model, inputs}) \times p(\text{model}) \\
&= \operatorname*{argmax}_{\mathbf{w}\in\mathbb{R}^d} \left(\prod_{i=1}^{\tilde{N}} p(\boldsymbol{Y} = \tilde{\boldsymbol{y}}_i \mid \mathbf{W} = \mathbf{w}, \boldsymbol{X} = \tilde{\boldsymbol{x}}_i)\right) \times p(\mathbf{W} = \mathbf{w}) \\
&= \operatorname*{argmax}_{\mathbf{w}\in\mathbb{R}^d} \sum_{i=1}^{\tilde{N}} \log p_{\mathbf{w}}(\boldsymbol{Y} = \tilde{\boldsymbol{y}}_i \mid \boldsymbol{X} = \tilde{\boldsymbol{x}}_i) + \log p(\mathbf{W} = \mathbf{w}) \quad (3.82)
\end{aligned}$$

What remains is how we choose the form of the prior distribution $p(\mathbf{W} = \mathbf{w})$—a probability distribution over the real-valued weight vector $\mathbf{w}$—and that choice is how we can arrive at equations 3.80–3.81. In section 3.3.7 we used one or more Dirichlet distributions because we needed the real-vector to correspond to one or more proper multinomial distributions. Here we have no such constraint.

Equation 3.80 is equivalent to the choice of a d-dimensional **Gaussian distribution** with mean vector $\mathbf{0}$ and diagonal covariance matrix $\frac{1}{C}\mathbf{I}_d$, where $\mathbf{I}_d$ is the $d \times d$ identity matrix. This was noted by Chen and Rosenfeld (2000). The Gaussian distribution could, of course, be generalized to use a different mean vector or covariance matrix; see Chelba and Acero (2006) for an example in which the Gaussian prior is defined by a model trained on the same task in a different text domain.

[14] These can also be additively combined; see Friedman et al. (2008).

In general, with mean vector $\boldsymbol{\mu}$ and covariance matrix $\boldsymbol{\Sigma}$, the Gaussian prior has the form:

$$
\begin{aligned}
p_{\boldsymbol{\mu},\boldsymbol{\Sigma}}(\mathbf{W} = \mathbf{w}) &= \frac{1}{\sqrt{(2\pi)^d |\boldsymbol{\Sigma}|}} \exp\left(-\frac{1}{2}(\mathbf{w} - \boldsymbol{\mu})^\top \boldsymbol{\Sigma}^{-1} (\mathbf{w} - \boldsymbol{\mu})\right) && (3.83) \\
\log p_{\boldsymbol{\mu},\boldsymbol{\Sigma}}(\mathbf{W} = \mathbf{w}) &= -\frac{1}{2}\log((2\pi)^d |\boldsymbol{\Sigma}|) - \frac{1}{2}(\mathbf{w} - \boldsymbol{\mu})^\top \boldsymbol{\Sigma}^{-1} (\mathbf{w} - \boldsymbol{\mu}) \\
&= \text{constant}(\mathbf{w}) - \frac{1}{2}(\mathbf{w} - \boldsymbol{\mu})^\top \boldsymbol{\Sigma}^{-1} (\mathbf{w} - \boldsymbol{\mu}) && (3.84)
\end{aligned}
$$

The above is continuous, concave, and differentiable; the first derivative of the above with respect to w_j is straightforward to compute (it is left as an exercise). Similar techniques for optimizing Φ_{LL} can therefore be applied to solve equation 3.80, which sets $\boldsymbol{\mu} = \mathbf{0}$ and $\boldsymbol{\Sigma} = \frac{1}{C}\mathbf{I}_d$.

Equation 3.81 corresponds to the choice of d **Laplacian distributions** with mean 0 and scale parameter $\frac{1}{C}$. There is one such distribution for each weight (equivalently, we can say that each weight is drawn independently from the same Laplacian distribution). More generally, one might choose a different set of means $\boldsymbol{\mu}$ and scale parameters $\boldsymbol{b}$, and they need not be identical for all weights. The form of such a prior is:

$$
\begin{aligned}
p_{\boldsymbol{\mu},\boldsymbol{b}}(\mathbf{W} = \mathbf{w}) &= \prod_{j=1}^{d} \frac{1}{2b_j} \exp \frac{-|w_j - \mu_j|}{b_j} && (3.85) \\
\log p_{\boldsymbol{\mu},\boldsymbol{b}}(\mathbf{W} = \mathbf{w}) &= \sum_{j=1}^{d} \left(-\log 2b_j - \frac{|w_j - \mu_j|}{b_j}\right) \\
&= \text{constant}(\mathbf{w}) - \sum_{j=1}^{d} \frac{|w_j - \mu_j|}{b_j} && (3.86)
\end{aligned}
$$

The L_1 regularizer in equation 3.81 equates to setting $\boldsymbol{\mu} = \mathbf{0}$ and all $b_j = \frac{1}{C}$.

The absolute value in the equation 3.86 renders the function non-differentiable at some points (though it is continuous and concave), so that some gradient-based optimization methods are not applicable.

An interesting effect of using this approach is that many weights will be forced to have values exactly 0, effectively removing those features from the model. This is often taken as a form of automatic feature selection. The use of L_1 regularization in NLP was explored by Kazama and Tsujii (2003) and Goodman (2004), both of whom present specialized optimization methods for dealing with the non-differentiability problem. Andrew and Gao (2007) present an approach based on quasi-Newton methods. At this writing, an active area of research is regularization that promotes sparsity in the weight vector of a linear model, building on L_1.

For problems with many features, these two different priors perform differently. As noted, the Laplacian prior can drive many feature weights to zero, leading to a more sparse model with fewer effective features. This can be understood as a kind of feature selection, accomplished as by-product of parameter estimation. The Gaussian tends to drive many weights close to zero, but not all the way. The Laplacian has a "fatter tail," meaning that large feature weights are acceptable for features that the data strongly support. Both priors prevent weights from going to $\pm\infty$.

In both L_2 and L_1 regularization, the choice of C can be important; while any positive value of C will prevent weights from going to $\pm\infty$, a larger value of C corresponds to a prior with smaller variance. This means that it takes more data to overcome the prior belief that all weights should be close to zero. If C is too large, not much will be learned, as the prior will dominate the optimization and keep the weights close to their means ($\boldsymbol{\mu}$ in both cases). If C is too small, the prior may not prevent overfitting. It is usually wise to tune the value of C on some held out data but never the test data.[15]

3.5.6 PSEUDOLIKELIHOOD

Training log-linear models is computationally expensive, largely because of the calculation of the partition functions $z_{\mathbf{w}}(\tilde{\boldsymbol{x}}_i)$ and the expected values of the features under the model, $\mathbb{E}_{p_{\mathbf{w}}(\boldsymbol{Y}|\boldsymbol{X}=\tilde{\boldsymbol{x}}_i)}[\mathbf{g}(\tilde{\boldsymbol{x}}_i, \boldsymbol{Y})]$. **Pseudolikelihood** is an alternative approach to training. It is a general technique that is available for joint models as well as conditional models; we consider it here for the case of conditional models.

Let the random variable $\boldsymbol{Y}$ be defined by a collection of m random variables $\langle Y_1, Y_2, \ldots, Y_m\rangle$. (In sequence labeling, each Y_i might be the label for one element of the sequence.) Consider the following approximate model:

$$p(\boldsymbol{Y} = \boldsymbol{y} \mid \boldsymbol{X} = \boldsymbol{x}) \approx \prod_{k=1}^{m} p\left(Y_k = y_k \mid \boldsymbol{X} = \boldsymbol{x}, \{Y_j = y_j\}_{j\in\{1,\ldots,m\}\setminus\{k\}}\right) \quad (3.87)$$

$$= \prod_{k=1}^{m} \frac{\exp \sum_{j:Y_k\in\Pi_j(\boldsymbol{x},\boldsymbol{Y})} \mathbf{w}^\top \mathbf{f}(\Pi_j(\boldsymbol{x}, \boldsymbol{y}))}{z_{\mathbf{w}}(\boldsymbol{x}, y_1, \ldots, y_{k-1}, y_{k+1}, \ldots, y_m)} \quad (3.88)$$

where "$Y_k \in \Pi_j(\boldsymbol{x}, \boldsymbol{Y})$" means that the jth part of the structure includes the kth Y random variable.

While this model resembles locally normalized models, it is quite different; each Y_k is generated based on all the others, so that there are many cyclic dependencies. The form of the local model here is log-linear, and all of the local models share the same weight vector. The central idea of pseudolikelihood is to carry out maximum likelihood estimation on the approximate model's weights, then use the estimated weights in the globally normalized model for decoding. The approximate model in equation 3.88 is locally normalized, and feature expectations will only be required per-label, not per-sequence. This means that, for sequence labeling, calculating the gradient for training will require only $O(n|\Lambda|)$ runtime, compared to $O(n|\Lambda|^2)$ for CRFs with first-order dependencies.

Because pseudolikelihood training of CRFs does not depend on strong independence assumptions (dynamic programming is not used at all), the inclusion of "non-local" features does not affect training time. Hence, $\mathbf{f}$ can depend on the entire prefix of labels preceding the one to be predicted. This gives such models the ability to model very rich non-local phenomena without necessarily

[15] See Appendix B for further discussion.

affecting the cost of training. The effect on decoding, of course, will be a sacrifice in efficiency or exactness.

Pseudolikelihood also has the desirable property of **statistical consistency**. A consistent estimator is one that converges to the true distribution as the training sample size goes to $+\infty$, under the assumption that the true distribution is in the model family the estimator considers. Pseudolikelihood was proposed by Besag (1975) and has been applied in NLP by Toutanova et al. (2003) and others. See Sutton and McCallum (2007) for a variety of approximate training methods building on the idea of using local models to approximate a global one.

3.5.7 TOWARD DISCRIMINATIVE LEARNING

The log-linear modeling approach is very attractive because it permits, in principle, the inclusion of any features at all. This is is in contrast to multinomial-based models, which require the specification of a sequence of steps explaining the derivation of the structure y (and, in the generative setting, the structure $\boldsymbol{x}$ as well). While rich, nonindependent features can be shoehorned into multinomial-based models, this often requires inaccurate independence assumptions to be made. A recurring theme has been that the locality of features in a model influences very strongly the efficiency of training and decoding algorithms.

Another attraction of log-linear models is that they are built on a probabilistic framework, allowing not just the standard decoding problem to be solved but also probabilistic inference. Conditional log-linear models do not allow *any* question to be answered (unlike generative models; see section 3.3.9) since the input random variable $\boldsymbol{X}$ is not modeled, but any questions about the distribution of the output $\boldsymbol{Y}$, given $\boldsymbol{X}$, can in principle be answered.

As for performance, conditional models have been found to work very well for linguistic structure prediction tasks. By avoiding the problem of estimating the input distribution $p(\boldsymbol{X})$, conditional models take a step in the direction of **discriminative** machine learning. Discriminative learning uses knowledge of the final task—here, prediction of $\boldsymbol{Y}$ given $\boldsymbol{X}$—during training. This is accomplished through creative use of the loss function.

So far we have seen two loss functions in learning, both based on negated log-probabilities (see equations 3.6 and 3.56). Both of these loss functions will be diminished when the probability model makes training outputs $\tilde{\boldsymbol{y}}_i$ more probable given $\tilde{\boldsymbol{x}}_i$. In the generative case, making $\tilde{\boldsymbol{x}}_i$ more probable also diminishes the training objective. There are two failings of both of these log loss functions. The first is that, even if the model correctly makes $\tilde{\boldsymbol{y}}_i$ more probable than any other $\boldsymbol{y} \in \mathcal{Y}$, given $\tilde{\boldsymbol{x}}_i$, there is still pressure to diminish the loss function as long as the alternatives receive nonzero probability. That is, the log loss goes to zero only when $p(\boldsymbol{Y} = \tilde{\boldsymbol{y}}_i \mid \boldsymbol{X} = \tilde{\boldsymbol{x}}_i) = 1$.

The second failing is that the loss function ignores the prediction function h and our criteria for judging its quality. Consider a situation where the correct output $\tilde{\boldsymbol{y}}_i$ can never be the most probable output, because of limitations of the model family. Not all alternatives are equally bad; let $\boldsymbol{y}$ and $\boldsymbol{y}' \in \mathcal{Y}$ be two imperfect outputs such that $\boldsymbol{y}$ is less errorful or "closer" to the correct answer $\tilde{\boldsymbol{y}}_i$ than $\boldsymbol{y}'$. The log loss is insensitive to this fact (it has no notion of "badness" of alternatives); it only knows about the right answer and pays no attention to the allocation of probability mass among the competitors in $\mathcal{Y} \setminus \{\tilde{\boldsymbol{y}}_i\}$.

We turn next to discrimative feature-based models that forgo the probabilistic interpretation altogether, instead focusing on the predictive task of choosing the right $\boldsymbol{y}$, including explicit incorporation of engineer-defined *error* or *cost* in the loss function, and on generalization ability of those predictive models. For theoretical analyses of generative and discriminative approaches, we refer the reader to Ng and Jordan (2002) and Liang and Jordan (2008).

3.6 LARGE MARGIN METHODS

The simplest case of a large margin model is the **support vector machine** (SVM; Cortes and Vapnik, 1995), which is often closely associated with kernel representations. Here we will only consider linear models, which are dominant in NLP; many other discussions of large margin methods focus on abstract kernel functions.[16]

Our starting point is the linear decoding problem (equation 2.3). Instead of a probabilistic view that transforms $\mathbf{w}^\top \mathbf{g}(\boldsymbol{x}, \boldsymbol{y})$ into a probability, we take a *geometric* view in which $\mathbf{g}(\boldsymbol{x}, \boldsymbol{y})$ is an embedding of $\langle \boldsymbol{x}, \boldsymbol{y} \rangle$ into $\mathbb{R}^d$. During training, we consider the point $\mathbf{g}(\tilde{\boldsymbol{x}}_i, \tilde{\boldsymbol{y}}_i)$ and all competing points $\mathbf{g}(\tilde{\boldsymbol{x}}_i, \boldsymbol{y})$ for $\boldsymbol{y} \in \mathcal{Y} \setminus \{\tilde{\boldsymbol{y}}_i\}$. The goal is to choose a direction (encoded in the weight vector $\mathbf{w}$) along which the point $\mathbf{g}(\tilde{\boldsymbol{x}}_i, \tilde{\boldsymbol{y}}_i)$ is at one extreme, i.e., $\mathbf{w}^\top \mathbf{g}(\tilde{\boldsymbol{x}}_i, \tilde{\boldsymbol{y}}_i)$ has a high value. Furthermore, the alternative points $\mathbf{g}(\tilde{\boldsymbol{x}}_i, \boldsymbol{y})$ should all receive scores $\mathbf{w}^\top \mathbf{g}(\tilde{\boldsymbol{x}}_i, \boldsymbol{y})$ that are inversely proportional to the amount of error incurred in labeling $\tilde{\boldsymbol{x}}_i$ with $\boldsymbol{y}$ when the true answer is $\tilde{\boldsymbol{y}}_i$. This is naturally encoded in a cost function $cost(\tilde{\boldsymbol{x}}_i, \boldsymbol{y}, \tilde{\boldsymbol{y}}_i; h)$, which now becomes an abstract component of the learner.

3.6.1 BINARY CLASSIFICATION

For binary classification, the large margin approach can be easily understood and visualized. Let $\mathcal{Y} = \{-1, +1\}$, corresponding to negative and positive class labels. We let $\mathcal{X} = \mathbb{R}^d$ and define the model score to be

$$score(\boldsymbol{x}, \boldsymbol{y}) = \begin{cases} \mathbf{w}^\top \boldsymbol{x} & \text{if } \boldsymbol{y} = +1 \\ \mathbf{0} & \text{otherwise} \end{cases} \tag{3.90}$$

This is very similar to logistic regression, section 3.5.1, but without the probabilistic interpretation.

[16] For completeness: for a set of objects $\mathcal{U}$, a kernel function $K : \mathcal{U} \times \mathcal{U} \rightarrow \mathbb{R}_{\geq 0}$ is a special kind of similarity function such that, for all $\boldsymbol{u}, \boldsymbol{v} \in \mathcal{U}$,

$$K(\boldsymbol{u}, \boldsymbol{v}) = \mathbf{g}(\boldsymbol{u})^\top \mathbf{g}(\boldsymbol{v}) \tag{3.89}$$

for some feature function $\mathbf{g} : \mathcal{U} \rightarrow \mathbb{R}^d$. In the linear case considered in this book, $\mathbf{g}$ is represented explicitly. For many other kernels, $\mathbf{g}$ is implied by the kernel function, which is selected to satisfy certain mathematical properties (including equation 3.89) and to be very efficient to calculate, usually much less than linear in the (implied) value of d. If all necessary calculations can be understood in terms of cheaply evaluating K rather than representing $\mathbf{g}$, as in the case of learning SVMs, then we obtain richer representations at low computational cost; see Schölkopf and Smola (2001). The linear models discussed here correspond to a linear kernel. For structured output spaces, non-linear kernels can severely complicate decoding algorithms. In NLP, kernels have mostly been used either in ranking (Collins and Duffy, 2002) or in rather different ways from the typical application within SVMs.

The classifier will be a weight vector $\mathbf{w} \in \mathbb{R}^d$ used as follows:

$$h(\boldsymbol{x}) = \begin{cases} +1 & \text{if } \mathbf{w}^\top \boldsymbol{x} > \mathbf{w}^\top \mathbf{0} = 0 \\ -1 & \text{otherwise} \end{cases} = \text{sign}(\mathbf{w}^\top \boldsymbol{x}) \tag{3.91}$$

We can therefore think of $\mathbf{w}$ as defining a hyperplane $\{\mathbf{u} \in \mathbb{R}^d \mid \mathbf{w}^\top \mathbf{u} = 0\}$. Points on one side of the hyperplane, $\{\mathbf{u} \in \mathbb{R}^d \mid \mathbf{w}^\top \mathbf{u} > 0\}$, will be classified as positive, and points on the other side, $\{\mathbf{u} \in \mathbb{R}^d \mid \mathbf{w}^\top \mathbf{u} < 0\}$, will be classified as negative. The goal of learning is to place the positive examples (where $\tilde{\boldsymbol{y}}_i = +1$) on the former side of the hyperplane and the negative examples (where $\tilde{\boldsymbol{y}}_i = -1$) on the latter side. Choosing $\mathbf{w}$ defines the hyperplane.

Note that we can interpret this as a feature-based model:

$$g_j(\boldsymbol{x}, \boldsymbol{y}) = \begin{cases} x_j & \text{if } \boldsymbol{y} = +1 \\ 0 & \text{otherwise} \end{cases} \tag{3.92}$$

$$\mathit{score}(\boldsymbol{x}, \boldsymbol{y}) = \mathbf{w}^\top \mathbf{g}(\boldsymbol{x}, \boldsymbol{y}) \tag{3.93}$$

This is exactly like logistic regression (section 3.5.1), but we have emphasized the hyperplane that separates the positive examples from the negative ones rather than the probability distribution over $\boldsymbol{Y}$ given $\boldsymbol{X}$.

The hyperplane view is less intuitive when we move to structured data and more complex loss functions. In the above, there is an implied loss function that follows from the definition of the decoding rule. Specifically, the above can be understood as choosing

$$\mathit{loss}(\tilde{\boldsymbol{x}}_i, \tilde{\boldsymbol{y}}_i; h) = \max \left\{0, 1 - \mathbf{w}^\top \mathbf{g}(\tilde{\boldsymbol{x}}_i, \tilde{\boldsymbol{y}}_i)\right\} \tag{3.94}$$

This is known as the **hinge loss**. It can equivalently be written as

$$\mathit{loss}(\tilde{\boldsymbol{x}}_i, \tilde{\boldsymbol{y}}_i; h) = \max_{\boldsymbol{y} \in \mathcal{Y}_{\tilde{\boldsymbol{x}}_i}} \mathit{score}(\tilde{\boldsymbol{x}}_i, \boldsymbol{y}) + \underbrace{\mathbf{1}\left\{\boldsymbol{y} \neq \tilde{\boldsymbol{y}}_i\right\}}_{\mathit{cost}(\tilde{\boldsymbol{x}}_i, \boldsymbol{y}, \tilde{\boldsymbol{y}}_i)} - \mathbf{w}^\top \mathbf{g}(\tilde{\boldsymbol{x}}_i, \tilde{\boldsymbol{y}}_i) \tag{3.95}$$

where $\mathit{cost} : \mathcal{X} \times \mathcal{Y} \times \mathcal{Y}$ returns 1 for a misclassification error and 0 when the model's hypothesis matches the true answer. The ability of large margin models to take into account different cost functions as part of *loss* is one of their main advantages. In the binary case, choosing a hyperplane that separates the positive examples from the negative ones is, in more general terms, a way of defining a positive spectrum that makes each correct answer (such that $\mathit{cost} = 0$) receive a higher score than each incorrect answer (such that $\mathit{cost} = 1$).

More generally, we might have a larger output space $\mathcal{Y}$ and a more fine-grained cost function that we seek to capture in learning $\mathbf{w}$. *cost* is a way of showing the learner that some bad answers (e.g., mislabeling every word in a sentence) are worse than others (e.g., mislabeling only one word). Compare the case of the log loss (equations 3.6 and 3.56), which does not encode any knowledge about the relative "wrongness" of different wrong answers.

While there is much to be said about binary classification, we will assume structured output spaces $\mathcal{Y}$.

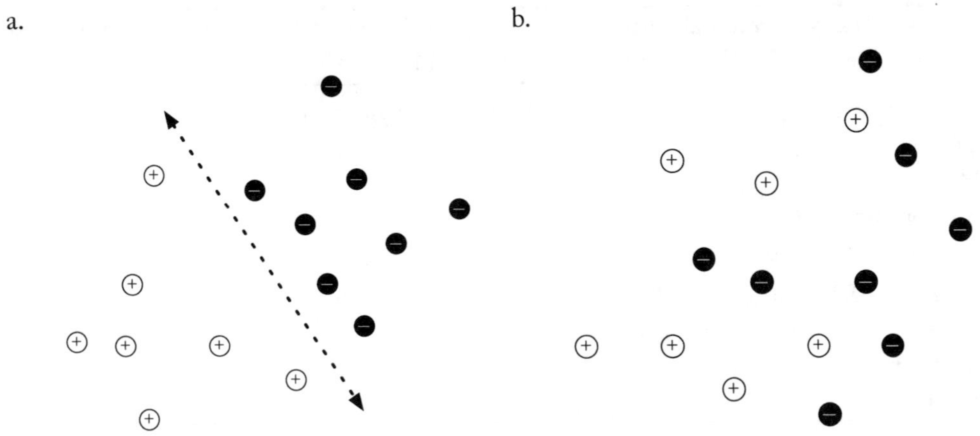

Figure 3.2: A visualization of some points $\boldsymbol{x} \in \mathbb{R}^2$ with outputs in $\{-1, +1\}$ marked as $-$ and $+$. (a) The points are separable, and a separating hyperplane (in two dimensions, a line) is shown. (b) The points are not separable.

3.6.2 PERCEPTRON

In binary classification, we may ask whether such a hyperplane even exists; that is, are the data linearly separable? Consider, for the binary case and only two features, figure 3.2. More generally, for structure prediction, does there exist some $\mathbf{w}$ such that, for all $i \in \{1, \ldots, \tilde{N}\}$,

$$h(\tilde{\boldsymbol{x}}_i) = \operatorname*{argmax}_{\boldsymbol{y} \in \mathcal{Y}_{\tilde{\boldsymbol{x}}_i}} \mathbf{w}^\top \mathbf{g}(\tilde{\boldsymbol{x}}_i, \boldsymbol{y}) = \operatorname*{argmin}_{\boldsymbol{y} \in \mathcal{Y}_{\tilde{\boldsymbol{x}}_i}} \mathit{cost}(\tilde{\boldsymbol{x}}_i, \boldsymbol{y}, \tilde{\boldsymbol{y}}_i) = \tilde{\boldsymbol{y}}_i \tag{3.96}$$

Collins (2002) showed how the classic **perceptron algorithm** for finding a separating hyperplane (if it exists) can be generalized to problems with structured output spaces. The perceptron algorithm (algorithm 3) iteratively updates weights by considering each training example in turn. On each round, it uses the current model to make a prediction. If the prediction is correct, there is no change to the weights. If the prediction is incorrect, the weights are updated proportional to the difference between the correct feature vector $\mathbf{g}(\tilde{\boldsymbol{x}}_i, \tilde{\boldsymbol{y}}_i)$ and the predicted feature vector.

An attractive property of the perceptron algorithm is that it has some theoretical guarantees. We discuss these because they introduce the notion of **margin**, which will be useful in later sections.

Let $\bar{\mathcal{Y}}_i$ denote the set of incorrect outputs for input $\tilde{\boldsymbol{x}}_i$, that is, $\bar{\mathcal{Y}}_i = \mathcal{Y}_{\tilde{\boldsymbol{x}}_i} \setminus \{\tilde{\boldsymbol{y}}_i\}$. For some value $\delta > 0$, we say that a training dataset is **separable with margin** δ if there exists a weight vector $\mathbf{w}$ such that:

$$\|\mathbf{w}\|_2 = 1 \tag{3.97}$$

$$\forall i \in \{1, \ldots, \tilde{N}\}, \forall \boldsymbol{y} \in \bar{\mathcal{Y}}_i, \qquad \mathbf{w}^\top \mathbf{g}(\tilde{\boldsymbol{x}}_i, \tilde{\boldsymbol{y}}_i) - \mathbf{w}^\top (\tilde{\boldsymbol{x}}_i, \boldsymbol{y}) > \delta \tag{3.98}$$

Algorithm 3 The perceptron algorithm for learning a structure predictor based on a linear score. Following Collins (2002). Note that the update to $\mathbf{w}$ will be $\mathbf{0}$ when $\boldsymbol{y}' = \tilde{\boldsymbol{y}}_i$.

Input: Training data $\langle\langle \tilde{\boldsymbol{x}}_i, \tilde{\boldsymbol{y}}_i \rangle\rangle_{i=1}^{\tilde{N}}$, number of iterations T, learning rate $\alpha > 0$
Output: $\mathbf{w}$
  $\mathbf{w}^{(0)} \leftarrow \mathbf{0}$
  for t from 1 to T **do**
    for i from 1 to $\tilde{N}$ **do**
      $\boldsymbol{y}' \leftarrow \text{argmax}_{\boldsymbol{y} \in \mathcal{Y}_{\tilde{\boldsymbol{x}}_i}} \mathbf{w}^\top \mathbf{g}(\tilde{\boldsymbol{x}}_i, \boldsymbol{y})$
      $\mathbf{w} \leftarrow \mathbf{w} + \alpha(\mathbf{g}(\tilde{\boldsymbol{x}}_i, \tilde{\boldsymbol{y}}_i) - \mathbf{g}(\tilde{\boldsymbol{x}}_i, \boldsymbol{y}'))$
    end for
  end for

Further, let R be a constant such that

$$\forall i \in \{1, \ldots, \tilde{N}\}, \forall \boldsymbol{y} \in \bar{\mathcal{Y}}_i, \qquad \left\| \mathbf{w}^\top \mathbf{g}(\tilde{\boldsymbol{x}}_i, \tilde{\boldsymbol{y}}_i) - \mathbf{w}^\top (\tilde{\boldsymbol{x}}_i, \boldsymbol{y}) \right\|_2 \leq R \tag{3.99}$$

For a training dataset separable with margin δ, the number of mistakes of the perceptron algorithm is bounded by R^2/δ^2. This implies that the algorithm will converge to a weight vector that makes no mistakes on the training data.

When the training data are not separable, there is also a bound on the number of mistakes. See Collins (2002) for more details. In practice, when the data are not separable, the perceptron algorithm can oscillate among different solutions, depending on which examples it has considered most recently. Two solutions that are often used to overcome this problem are:

- **averaging,** in which the weight vectors over time are accumulated and averaged together at the end to produce the final weights; and

- **voting,** a more expensive variant in which different weight vectors over time are stored, and finally (after training) used to make T different predictions, with the majority prediction being chosen.

The perceptron algorithm is very easy to implement given a decoder (chapter 2), and it is easy to understand. In the learning scenario of section 3.2, the perceptron aims to minimize the expected zero-one loss

$$\mathit{loss}(\boldsymbol{x}, \boldsymbol{y}; h) = \begin{cases} 0 & \text{if } h(\boldsymbol{x}) = \boldsymbol{y} \\ 1 & \text{otherwise} \end{cases} \tag{3.100}$$

The actual loss function of the perceptron (in the empirical risk minimization view of section 3.2) is the following approximation to the zero-one loss:

$$\mathit{loss}(\boldsymbol{x}, \boldsymbol{y}; h) = -\mathbf{w}^\top \mathbf{g}(\boldsymbol{x}, \boldsymbol{y}) + \mathbf{w}^\top \mathbf{g}(\boldsymbol{x}, h(\boldsymbol{x})) \tag{3.101}$$

This is just like the hinge loss (equation 3.95), but without the *cost* term.

In the perceptron, here is no explicit penalty for model complexity.[17] In summary, the perceptron will find weights that separate each $\tilde{\boldsymbol{y}}_i$ from the corresponding $\bar{\mathcal{Y}}_i$, if such weights exist, but it has no preference among such possibilities and has no internal mechanism to deal with non-separable data.

The idea of *maximizing* the margin is a way of stating a preference among the models that separate the training data. Rather than simply seeking such a model $\mathbf{w}$, we return to optimization as a way to declare the constraints on the model and an objective function it should optimize.

3.6.3 MULTI-CLASS SUPPORT VECTOR MACHINES

We begin with a model used in classification, the multi-class support vector machine (Crammer and Singer, 2001). The optimization problem is as follows:

$$\begin{aligned} \min_{\mathbf{w}} \quad & \frac{C}{2}\|\mathbf{w}\|_2^2 \\ \text{such that} \quad & \forall i \in \{1, \ldots, \tilde{N}\}, \forall \boldsymbol{y} \in \mathcal{Y}_{\tilde{\boldsymbol{x}}_i}, \\ & \mathbf{w}^\top \mathbf{g}(\tilde{\boldsymbol{x}}_i, \tilde{\boldsymbol{y}}_i) - \mathbf{w}^\top \mathbf{g}(\tilde{\boldsymbol{x}}_i, \boldsymbol{y}) \geq \mathit{cost}(\tilde{\boldsymbol{x}}_i, \boldsymbol{y}, \tilde{\boldsymbol{y}}_i) \end{aligned} \tag{3.102}$$

Note that the cost function is known by the learner. Intuitively, the goal is to find a weight vector that is not extreme—the objective criterion is essentially an L_2 penalty that prefers weights closer to zero—while making sure that each incorrect $\boldsymbol{y}$ is punished (pushed away from the correct answer) proportional to its level of error (loss). This can be visualized as choosing a direction in $\mathbb{R}^d$ such that $\mathbf{g}(\tilde{\boldsymbol{x}}_i, \tilde{\boldsymbol{y}}_i)$ is at one extreme of the direction, while all alternative $\{\mathbf{g}(\tilde{\boldsymbol{x}}_i, \boldsymbol{y}) \mid \boldsymbol{y} \in \bar{\mathcal{Y}}_i\}$ are positioned so that the ones with the most error are more distant from the extreme.

We can recover the satisfiability problem the perceptron aims to solve by instantiating $\mathit{cost}(\tilde{\boldsymbol{x}}_i, \boldsymbol{y}, \tilde{\boldsymbol{y}}_i)$ as equation 3.101 and eliminating the objective criterion. The perceptron seeks to ensure that the score difference is positive for all alternative $\boldsymbol{y} \in \bar{\mathcal{Y}}_i$. It does not optimize an objective; it simply seeks a satisfying vector $\mathbf{w}$.

It is possible that the constraints in equation 3.102 cannot be satisfied. We therefore relax them slightly, allowing the margin not to be exactly proportional to the loss on every example, but penalizing the amount by which it fails. One formulation, due to Crammer and Singer (2001) and used in the structured case by Taskar et al. (2004b), permits a linear decrease in the loss function for purposes of the constraints:

$$\begin{aligned} \min_{\mathbf{w}, \boldsymbol{\xi} \geq \mathbf{0}} \quad & \frac{C}{2}\|\mathbf{w}\|_2^2 + \frac{1}{\tilde{N}}\sum_{i=1}^{\tilde{N}} \xi_i \\ \text{such that} \quad & \forall i \in \{1, \ldots, \tilde{N}\}, \forall \boldsymbol{y} \in \mathcal{Y}_{\tilde{\boldsymbol{x}}_i}, \\ & \mathbf{w}^\top \mathbf{g}(\tilde{\boldsymbol{x}}_i, \tilde{\boldsymbol{y}}_i) - \mathbf{w}^\top \mathbf{g}(\tilde{\boldsymbol{x}}_i, \boldsymbol{y}) \geq \mathit{cost}(\tilde{\boldsymbol{x}}_i, \boldsymbol{y}, \tilde{\boldsymbol{y}}_i) - \xi_i \end{aligned} \tag{3.103}$$

[17] Averaging and voting can be understood as accomplishing a kind of penalty on complex models in a less declarative fashion.

The variables $\boldsymbol{\xi} = \langle \xi_1, \ldots, \xi_{\tilde{N}} \rangle$ are known as **slack variables**. An alternative form for the constraints is due to Tsochantaridis et al. (2004):

$$\begin{array}{ll} \min\limits_{\mathbf{w}, \boldsymbol{\xi} \geq \mathbf{0}} & \frac{C}{2}\|\mathbf{w}\|_2^2 + \frac{1}{\tilde{N}} \sum_{i=1}^{\tilde{N}} \xi_i \\ \text{such that} & \forall i \in \{1, \ldots, \tilde{N}\}, \forall \boldsymbol{y} \in \mathcal{Y}_{\tilde{\boldsymbol{x}}_i}, \\ & \mathbf{w}^\top \mathbf{g}(\tilde{\boldsymbol{x}}_i, \tilde{\boldsymbol{y}}_i) - \mathbf{w}^\top \mathbf{g}(\tilde{\boldsymbol{x}}_i, \boldsymbol{y}) \geq 1 - \frac{\xi_i}{\mathit{cost}(\tilde{\boldsymbol{x}}_i, \boldsymbol{y}, \tilde{\boldsymbol{y}}_i)} \end{array} \tag{3.104}$$

Here we focus on the "margin rescaling" variant (equation 3.103); the "slack rescaling" variant (equation 3.104) is more computationally challenging for structure prediction problems.

3.6.4 STRUCTURAL SVM

We now move to the structured case. Because the space $\mathcal{Y}_{\boldsymbol{x}}$ can be exponentially large, problems 3.103–3.104 have exponentially many constraints in the size of the training data and are not directly solvable. There is considerable literature on specialized optimization algorithms for solving large margin learning problems. We will focus here on the ones that have been most useful for linguistic structure prediction and that bear the strongest similarity to training algorithms for other models.

The first step is to solve for each ξ_i in terms of known quantities. Taking together all of the constraints relating to ξ_i, the following bound is straightforward. For all $\boldsymbol{y} \in \mathcal{Y}_{\tilde{\boldsymbol{x}}_i}$,

$$\begin{aligned} & -\mathbf{w}^\top \mathbf{g}(\tilde{\boldsymbol{x}}_i, \tilde{\boldsymbol{y}}_i) + \max_{\boldsymbol{y}' \in \mathcal{Y}_{\tilde{\boldsymbol{x}}_i}} \left(\mathbf{w}^\top \mathbf{g}(\tilde{\boldsymbol{x}}_i, \boldsymbol{y}') + \mathit{cost}(\tilde{\boldsymbol{x}}_i, \boldsymbol{y}', \tilde{\boldsymbol{y}}_i) \right) \\ \geq \; & -\mathbf{w}^\top \mathbf{g}(\tilde{\boldsymbol{x}}_i, \tilde{\boldsymbol{y}}_i) + \mathbf{w}^\top \mathbf{g}(\tilde{\boldsymbol{x}}_i, \boldsymbol{y}) + \mathit{cost}(\tilde{\boldsymbol{x}}_i, \boldsymbol{y}, \tilde{\boldsymbol{y}}_i) \end{aligned} \tag{3.105}$$

Therefore, setting ξ_i to be the value on the left-hand side will achieve the constraints. We no longer view the slack variables $\boldsymbol{\xi}$ as free variables, but rather as functions of $\mathbf{w}$ that are used to penalize models that do not meet the constraints. (Can we hope to solve the maximization problem in equation 3.105 efficiently? Yes; we will return to this matter in section 3.6.5.)

Substituting the values of $\boldsymbol{\xi}$ into equation 3.103, we now have the following *unconstrained* objective function:

$$\begin{aligned} & \operatorname*{argmin}_{\mathbf{w}} \frac{C}{2}\|\mathbf{w}\|_2^2 + \frac{1}{\tilde{N}} \sum_{i=1}^{\tilde{N}} \overbrace{-\mathbf{w}^\top \mathbf{g}(\tilde{\boldsymbol{x}}_i, \tilde{\boldsymbol{y}}_i) + \max_{\boldsymbol{y} \in \mathcal{Y}_{\tilde{\boldsymbol{x}}_i}} \mathbf{w}^\top \mathbf{g}(\tilde{\boldsymbol{x}}_i, \boldsymbol{y}) + \mathit{cost}(\tilde{\boldsymbol{x}}_i, \boldsymbol{y}, \tilde{\boldsymbol{y}}_i)}^{\mathit{loss}(\tilde{\boldsymbol{x}}_i, \tilde{\boldsymbol{y}}_i; h)} \\ = \; & \operatorname*{argmax}_{\mathbf{w}} \underbrace{\frac{1}{\tilde{N}} \sum_{i=1}^{\tilde{N}} \left(\mathbf{w}^\top \mathbf{g}(\tilde{\boldsymbol{x}}_i, \tilde{\boldsymbol{y}}_i) - \left(\max_{\boldsymbol{y} \in \mathcal{Y}_{\tilde{\boldsymbol{x}}_i}} \mathbf{w}^\top \mathbf{g}(\tilde{\boldsymbol{x}}_i, \boldsymbol{y}) + \mathit{cost}(\tilde{\boldsymbol{x}}_i, \boldsymbol{y}, \tilde{\boldsymbol{y}}_i) \right) \right)}_{\Phi_{\mathrm{MM}}} - \frac{C}{2}\|\mathbf{w}\|_2^2 \end{aligned} \tag{3.106}$$

A model trained this way is often called a **structural SVM** (emphasizing the hyperplane view; Tsochantaridis et al., 2004) or a **max-margin Markov network** (emphasizing the connection to probabilistic graphical models, without a probabilistic objective function; Taskar et al., 2004b). Intuitively, the goal is to find weights $\mathbf{w}$ that make each $\langle \tilde{\boldsymbol{x}}_i, \tilde{\boldsymbol{y}}_i \rangle$ score well (first term inside the sum of equation 3.106) and alternatives score badly (maximizing term inside the sum of equation 3.106) without $\mathbf{w}$ becoming too large in magnitude (last term of equation 3.106). The second term inside the sum is slightly counterintuitive. It considers the $\boldsymbol{y}$ with the highest score plus cost and tries to diminish its score. In other words, it seeks for each training example an alternative $\boldsymbol{y}$ from $\bar{\mathcal{Y}}_i$ that scores well and also has high cost; this is a "dangerous" alternative, because it is both "close" to the correct answer $\tilde{\boldsymbol{y}}_i$ and will incur high cost if it is chosen. It serves as a proxy in the objective for the full set of exponentially many other incorrect answers.

Equation 3.106 can be understood in the empirical risk minimization framework of section 3.2. Within a factor of $\frac{1}{\tilde{N}}$, the expression within the sum corresponds to a loss function known as the structured hinge loss, and the model complexity penalty is the familiar quadratic function on the weights (section 3.5.5).

3.6.5 OPTIMIZATION

As an optimization problem, equation 3.106 has some attractive properties. It is convex and continuous. It is not, however, differentiable at all points. The reason is the max operator. At certain points in parameter space, the maximizer from $\mathcal{Y}$ will change from one candidate to another, giving the function a "cusp." Note that, apart from the quadratic term at the end, the function is piecewise linear.

Gradient ascent and other methods that rely on differentiability, therefore, will not help us solve this problem. A generalization called **subgradient ascent**, discussed in appendix section A.3.1, can be applied and has been found to work well in practice, particularly when used in an "online" mode that makes an update to $\mathbf{w}$ after considering each example in turn (Ratliff et al., 2006). Another online method developed specifically for the purpose of maximizing the margin is the **margin-infused relaxation algorithm** (MIRA; Crammer and Singer, 2003), which instantiates a larger class of so-called "aggressive" algorithms (Crammer et al., 2006). Some discussion can be found in section A.5.

Calculating the structural SVM objective in equation 3.106 requires us to solve the following problem for a given training example $\langle \tilde{\boldsymbol{x}}_i, \tilde{\boldsymbol{y}}_i \rangle$:

$$\operatorname*{argmax}_{\boldsymbol{y} \in \mathcal{Y}_{\tilde{\boldsymbol{x}}_i}} \mathbf{w}^\top \mathbf{g}(\tilde{\boldsymbol{x}}_i, \boldsymbol{y}) + \mathit{cost}(\tilde{\boldsymbol{x}}_i, \boldsymbol{y}, \tilde{\boldsymbol{y}}_i) \tag{3.107}$$

This is known as **cost-augmented decoding**. If *cost* factors the same way that the feature vector function $\mathbf{g}$ factors, then the complexity of cost-augmented decoding (with respect to $\tilde{\boldsymbol{x}}_i$) will be the same as standard decoding. Further discussion can be found in section 5.4.

3.6.6 DISCUSSION

It is worth pointing out that equation 3.106 is very similar to the maximum *a posteriori* objective for L_2-regularized CRFs (equations 3.75 and 3.80, repeated here):

$$\max_{\mathbf{w}} \frac{1}{\tilde{N}} \sum_{i=1}^{\tilde{N}} \left(\mathbf{w}^\top \mathbf{g}(\tilde{\boldsymbol{x}}_i, \tilde{\boldsymbol{y}}_i) - \left(\log \sum_{\boldsymbol{y} \in \mathcal{Y}_{\tilde{\boldsymbol{x}}_i}} \exp \mathbf{w}^\top \mathbf{g}(\tilde{\boldsymbol{x}}_i, \boldsymbol{y}) \right) \right) - \frac{C}{2} \|\mathbf{w}\|_2^2 \tag{3.108}$$

For a generalizing framework that places the two approaches in a larger family of discriminative objectives, see Gimpel and Smith (2010).

The perceptron and large margin approaches to learning weights $\mathbf{w}$ for a linear model are very attractive because of their ease of implementation. If there is a decoder implemented, the perceptron can be used. If the decoder can be modified to allow for cost-augmented decoding, the margin can be maximized. Unlike other learning methods discussed in this chapter, large margin learning can incorporate into training a cost function. The structural SVM is a purely discriminative method that aims to perform well (and generalize well) on exactly the task defined by that cost function. In other words, if we know how a model is to be evaluated at decoding time, a cost function can be defined for use at training time, providing an opportunity to better inform the learner about its real goals.

There are a few limitations of large margin techniques. Because they do not have a probabilistic interpretation, they can only be used to answer one question—the decoding question, "Which $\boldsymbol{y}$ is best for a given $\boldsymbol{x}$?" They do not provide joint or conditional likelihoods. The techniques we have described here depend heavily on the factorization of the features and the cost function into the same local parts. Recent research, e.g., by Daumé et al. (2009), has sought to break this dependence, drawing a tighter connection between the search performed in decoding and discriminative learning algorithms.

3.7 CONCLUSION

This chapter has covered key approaches to supervised learning for linguistic structure prediction (see figure 3.3). Our approach has been to assume from the start that the input and output spaces are structured, which leads immediately to keeping questions about the computational efficiency of learning at the fore. We note that there are many more topics in machine learning involving structure that have not been considered here, since our focus is on techniques for natural language processing. Bakır et al. (2007) offer a broad collection of advances in general structured learning.

Supervised learning for structures is still an active area of research. Important topics include the effects of approximate inference on learning, scalability to very large training datasets, learning models that are "sparse" (i.e., exclude features that are not helpful), and models that are non-linear (e.g., through the use of kernels).

approach	$loss(\boldsymbol{x}, \boldsymbol{y}; h)$	**training expense**	**notes**
generative models (3.3)	$-\log p_{\mathbf{w}}(\boldsymbol{x}, \boldsymbol{y})$	if multinomial-based, easy to train	can answer "many questions," but the model must explain all evidence
globally normalized conditional models (3.5)	$-\log p_{\mathbf{w}}(\boldsymbol{y} \mid \boldsymbol{x}) = -\mathbf{w}^\top \mathbf{g}(\boldsymbol{x}, \boldsymbol{y}) + z_{\mathbf{w}}(\boldsymbol{x})$	require inference for feature expectations and $z_{\mathbf{w}}$	allow arbitrary local features; hybridize generative and discriminative approaches
perceptron (3.6.2)	$-\mathbf{w}^\top \mathbf{g}(\boldsymbol{x}, \boldsymbol{y}) + \max_{\boldsymbol{y}' \in \mathcal{Y}_{\boldsymbol{x}}} \mathbf{w}^\top \mathbf{g}(\boldsymbol{x}, \boldsymbol{y}')$	only requires a decoder	no probabilistic interpretation or explicit regularization
large margin models (3.6)	$-\mathbf{w}^\top \mathbf{g}(\boldsymbol{x}, \boldsymbol{y}) + \max_{\boldsymbol{y}' \in \mathcal{Y}_{\boldsymbol{x}}} \mathbf{w}^\top \mathbf{g}(\boldsymbol{x}, \boldsymbol{y}') + cost(\boldsymbol{x}, \boldsymbol{y}', \boldsymbol{y})$	only require a cost-augmented decoder	incorporate cost function; no probabilistic interpretation

Figure 3.3: A comparison of the main learning methods discussed in this chapter. The form of the predictor $h(\boldsymbol{x})$ is assumed to be a linear decoder, $\text{argmax}_{\boldsymbol{y} \in \mathcal{Y}_{\boldsymbol{x}}} \mathbf{w}^\top \mathbf{g}(\boldsymbol{x}, \boldsymbol{y})$.

CHAPTER 4

Learning Structure from Incomplete Data

In chapter 3, we considered a wide range of techniques for learning to predict linguistic structure from annotated datasets. Such datasets can be costly to produce, and very often the developer of an annotated linguistic dataset will be faced with many decisions about the annotation scheme. These can range from deep theoretical questions about linguistic structure to mundane matters of convention, either of which may affect the usefulness of the resulting annotated data.

Learning linguistic structure from incomplete data—whether a blend of annotated and unannotated text, or unannotated text alone—offers the possibility of building natural language processing more cheaply. We emphasize that, in most cases, this is a long-term bet, and supervised learning is the advised starting point. The main alternatives are as follows.

Semisupervised learning usually refers to a setting where some annotated examples $\{\langle \tilde{\boldsymbol{x}}_i, \tilde{\boldsymbol{y}}_i \rangle\}_{i \in \mathcal{L}}$ are available, along with a pool of inputs $\{\tilde{\boldsymbol{x}}_i\}_{i \in \mathcal{U}}$ that lack outputs (unannotated data). At this writing, it is difficult to give a unified treatment semisupervised learning approaches used in linguistic models. We do not cover semisupervised learning here, instead referring to Abney (2007) and Zhu and Goldberg (2009) as two recent surveys. We note that many semisupervised learning techniques make use of supervised and/or unsupervised learning as subroutines, and therefore understanding supervised (chapter 3) and unsupervised (this chapter) techniques is essential to understanding semisupervised learning.

Unsupervised learning refers to a setting where outputs are not observed for *any* training examples. In some cases, we presume that true outputs could, in principle and perhaps at great expense, be obtained; evaluation of the learned predictor on annotated data is therefore possible. An example of this is unsupervised grammar induction, where we seek to infer grammatical structure for sentences without the use of a treebank. In other cases, like clustering and dimensionality reduction, "correct" solutions are not presumably knowable by humans, and evaluation must be conducted extrinsically, within some larger task.

Hidden variable learning involves learning from data for which outputs are observed, but some parts of the desired input representation are not. Learning to translate from pairs of translated sentences (parallel text) is a frequently cited example: correspondences between words or phrases in the two sentences are often desired for reasoning about translating a sentence, but these correspondences are not directly observed in most datasets.

Figure 4.1 contrasts these settings.

In this chapter, we will first discuss unsupervised learning with generative models. We then discuss the main ideas behind Bayesian unsupervised learning, which has recently attracted interest in NLP. Finally, we consider supervised learning with hidden variables.

what is missing from the training data?	terminology	example
nothing	supervised learning (chapter 3)	training a parser from a treebank
$\tilde{\boldsymbol{y}}_i$ for some i	semisupervised learning (not covered in this book)	... plus a collection of unparsed sentences
$\tilde{\boldsymbol{y}}_i$ for all i	unsupervised learning (sections 4.1–4.2)	training a parser from unparsed text
part of $\tilde{\boldsymbol{x}}_i$ for some or all i	hidden variable learning (section 4.3)	inducing word alignments in parallel sentences

Figure 4.1: Different types of learning, as defined in this book. Another variation on semisupervised, unsupervised, and hidden variable scenarios is when some (or all) $\tilde{\boldsymbol{y}}_i$ are *incomplete*. For example, we might wish to train a parser from data that includes partially parsed sentences.

4.1 UNSUPERVISED GENERATIVE MODELS

In this discussion of unsupervised learning, we assume our training data consist only of $\langle \tilde{\boldsymbol{x}}_1, \ldots, \tilde{\boldsymbol{x}}_{\tilde{N}} \rangle$, with no examples of the desired output random variable $\boldsymbol{Y}$. Usually, the aim is to learn a predictor of $\boldsymbol{Y}$, and evaluation is conducted on an annotated test set $\langle \langle \dot{\boldsymbol{x}}_1, \dot{\boldsymbol{y}}_1 \rangle, \ldots, \langle \dot{\boldsymbol{x}}_{\dot{N}}, \dot{\boldsymbol{y}}_{\dot{N}} \rangle$.

When a novice first encounters the idea of unsupervised learning, the reaction is often one of disbelief: how could it be possible to learn to predict an outcome without ever having seen one? It is important to remember that unsupervised learning is not "free." It requires some understanding of the domain, and the development of an algorithm that incorporates prior knowledge, or inductive bias, to guide the learner toward a solution that has the desired properties. Although many techniques have been developed for unsupervised learning, here we focus on those for which the inductive bias can be stated through objective functions and which are extensible as our linguistic structure prediction tasks evolve.

A typical starting place for unsupervised learning is to design a generative model that assigns joint probabilities to input-output pairs in $\mathcal{X} \times \mathcal{Y}$, just as in section 3.3. Sometimes these generative models are very similar to the ones we would estimate if we had annotated training data, but the difficulty of unsupervised learning has generally led to the use of simpler models for the unsupervised case than are used in supervised learning. As before, we let $\mathcal{P}$ denote the model family, and we select a model from $\mathcal{P}$ to maximize the log-likelihood of the data we observe:

$$\operatorname*{argmax}_{p \in \mathcal{P}} \sum_{i=1}^{\tilde{N}} \log p(\tilde{\boldsymbol{x}}_i) \tag{4.1}$$

Note that there is no mention of the $\boldsymbol{Y}$ random variable. In the above, we treat $\boldsymbol{Y}$ as a **hidden variable**;[1] it is marginalized out in the definition of $p(\boldsymbol{X})$. We can expand equation 4.1 to make the dependence on $\boldsymbol{Y}$ explicit:

$$\operatorname*{argmax}_{p \in \mathcal{P}} \sum_{i=1}^{\tilde{N}} \log \sum_{\boldsymbol{y} \in \mathcal{Y}_{\tilde{\boldsymbol{x}}_i}} p(\tilde{\boldsymbol{x}}_i, \boldsymbol{y}) \tag{4.2}$$

The central idea of this approach to learning is to build a probabilistic model over both the observable part of the data $\boldsymbol{X}$ and the hidden part $\boldsymbol{Y}$. This will allow us to (i) calculate posterior probability distributions over the value of $\boldsymbol{Y}$ given $\boldsymbol{X}$ and (ii) learn the parameters of the model using the same maximum likelihood principle we used in chapter 3. We assume a parametric model over $\boldsymbol{X}$ and $\boldsymbol{Y}$, with parameters $\mathbf{w}$, so that equation 4.2 becomes:

$$\operatorname*{argmax}_{\mathbf{w}} \sum_{i=1}^{\tilde{N}} \log \sum_{\boldsymbol{y} \in \mathcal{Y}_{\tilde{\boldsymbol{x}}_i}} p_{\mathbf{w}}(\tilde{\boldsymbol{x}}_i, \boldsymbol{y}) \tag{4.3}$$

From a practical perspective, the major difference between maximum likelihood estimation in the unsupervised case, compared to the supervised case (equation 3.9), is the non-convexity of the objective function in equation 4.3 with respect to $\mathbf{w}$. In general, the unsupervised likelihood objective is not concave in the parameters of the probability distribution $p_{\mathbf{w}}$. This means that estimation of parameters in unsupervised learning is necessarily approximate; there is no known, general algorithm to efficiently find the global maximum of equation 4.3, and in some cases, it has been shown to be NP-hard (for HMMs, see Day, 1983; for PCFGs, see Cohen and Smith, 2010).

4.1.1 EXPECTATION MAXIMIZATION

There is, however, a widely used approximate technique for *locally* optimizing the unsupervised likelihood function: the **Expectation Maximization** (EM) algorithm (Dempster et al., 1977). EM can be understood in several different ways; here we describe it as a specialized coordinate ascent algorithm for the unsupervised likelihood function. Throughout the text, we have relegated most optimization algorithms to appendix A, but because EM is so tightly coupled with incomplete data MLE, we include it here. It is important to remember that other optimization algorithms can be

[1]The meaning of "hidden variable" here is the same as it will be in section 4.3 when we focus on supervised learning with hidden variables. From the perspective of probabilstic inference and maximum likelihood estimation, it makes no difference whether the hidden variable is the output variable (as here) or not (as in section 4.3).

applied to this problem as well (e.g., we might apply some form of gradient ascent). EM is the usual starting place, perhaps because it is intuitive and relatively easy to derive. Further, its convergence does not hinge on well-chosen parameters, and its inputs are merely the data and some initial parameter estimate.

EM iterates between calculating the posterior distributions over the hidden variables Y_i (for each example $\tilde{\boldsymbol{x}}_i$) and updating the model parameters $\mathbf{w}$. The posterior distribution for example i is simply $p_{\mathbf{w}}(\boldsymbol{Y}_i \mid \tilde{\boldsymbol{x}}_i)$. The calculation of the posterior is called the "E step," and the reestimation of model parameters is called the "M step." The high level steps are shown in algorithm 4. The attraction of the EM algorithm is that the E step and the M step are each intuitive and easy to implement:

- If we know the model parameters ($\mathbf{w}$), then calculating the posterior distribution over $\boldsymbol{Y}$, given $\tilde{\boldsymbol{x}}_i$ and $\mathbf{w}$, is a matter of inference (E step).
- If we know the complete data distribution over $\boldsymbol{X}$ and $\boldsymbol{Y}$, then solving for the best parameters $\mathbf{w}$ is a matter of MLE (M step).

Algorithm 4 Expectation Maximization at a high level. For models of structure, the E step is often accomplished indirectly, and for some model families, the M step may not have a closed-form solution.

Input: initial model parameters $\mathbf{w}^{(0)}$, training data $\langle \tilde{\boldsymbol{x}}_1, \ldots, \tilde{\boldsymbol{x}}_{\tilde{N}} \rangle$
Output: learned parameters $\mathbf{w}$

$t \leftarrow 0$
repeat
E step:
for $i = 1$ to $\tilde{N}$ **do**

$$\forall \boldsymbol{y} \in \mathcal{Y}_{\tilde{\boldsymbol{x}}_i}, q_i^{(t)}(\boldsymbol{y}) \leftarrow p_{\mathbf{w}^{(t)}}(\boldsymbol{y} \mid \tilde{\boldsymbol{x}}_i) = \frac{p_{\mathbf{w}^{(t)}}(\tilde{\boldsymbol{x}}_i, \boldsymbol{y})}{\sum_{\boldsymbol{y}' \in \mathcal{Y}_{\tilde{\boldsymbol{x}}_i}} p_{\mathbf{w}^{(t)}}(\tilde{\boldsymbol{x}}_i, \boldsymbol{y}')}$$

end for

$$\textit{M step: } \mathbf{w}^{(t+1)} \leftarrow \operatorname*{argmax}_{\mathbf{w}} \sum_{i=1}^{\tilde{N}} \sum_{\boldsymbol{y} \in \mathcal{Y}_{\tilde{\boldsymbol{x}}_i}} q_i^{(t)}(\boldsymbol{y}) \log p_{\mathbf{w}}(\tilde{\boldsymbol{x}}_i, \boldsymbol{y})$$

$t \leftarrow t + 1$
until $\mathbf{w}^{(t)} \approx \mathbf{w}^{(t-1)}$
$\mathbf{w} \leftarrow \mathbf{w}^{(t)}$

4.1.2 WORD CLUSTERING

We consider an example of a word clustering model based on the "aggregate Markov model" of Saul and Pereira (1997). Let $\boldsymbol{X}$ correspond to a random variable over sequences of words, $\mathcal{X} = \Sigma^*$.

We let $\boldsymbol{Y}$ correspond to a sequence of clusters for the words, so that $\boldsymbol{Y} = \langle Y_1, \ldots, Y_n \rangle$. $\boldsymbol{X}$ and $\boldsymbol{Y}$ will be the same length; Y_i corresponds to the cluster for the ith word in $\boldsymbol{X}$ and takes values in $\{1, \ldots, K\}$. The sequence $\boldsymbol{Y}$ is never observed in training data.

The model can be understood as a bigram model (section 1.1),

$$p(\boldsymbol{X} = \boldsymbol{x}) = \prod_{i=1}^{n+1} p(X_i = x_i \mid X_{i-1} = x_{i-1}) \tag{4.4}$$

for an n-length sequence $\boldsymbol{x}$, with $x_0 = ⊲$ and $x_{n+1} = ⊙$. The bigram probabilities are further broken down by introducing the cluster variable:

$$p(X_i = x_i \mid X_{i-1} = x_{i-1}) = \sum_{c=1}^{K} \underbrace{p(X_i = x_i \mid Y_i = c)}_{\eta_{c,x_i}} \underbrace{p(Y_i = c \mid X_{i-1} = x_{i-1})}_{\psi_{x_i,c}} \tag{4.5}$$

Hence, word clusters are associated with the positions *between* words. The model is equivalent to a bigram model that alternates between generating words and clusters. For this reason, the model has $O(|\Sigma|K)$ parameters rather than the $O(|\Sigma|^2)$ of a standard bigram model. In the training data, the clusters are unknown.

The following is a generative model for this clustering scheme:

1. Let $x_0 = ⊲$.
2. For $i \in \{1, 2, \ldots\}$, until $x_{i-1} = ⊙$:
   (a) Draw a cluster $y_i \in \{1, \ldots K\}$ according to the multinomial distribution $p(Y_i \mid X_{i-1} = x_{i-1}) = \boldsymbol{\psi}_{x_{i-1},\cdot}$.
   (b) Draw a word $x_i \in \Sigma$ according to the multinomial distribution $p(X_i \mid Y_i = y_i) = \boldsymbol{\eta}_{y_i,\cdot}$.

The parameters of the model are $\mathbf{w} = \langle \boldsymbol{\eta}, \boldsymbol{\psi} \rangle$; unsupervised learning in this setting requires that we choose the parameters to maximize the likelihood of the observed data:

$$\begin{aligned}
\operatorname*{argmax}_{\mathbf{w}} \sum_{i=1}^{\tilde{N}} \log p_{\mathbf{w}}(\tilde{\boldsymbol{x}}_i) &= \operatorname*{argmax}_{\boldsymbol{\eta},\boldsymbol{\psi}} \sum_{i=1}^{\tilde{N}} \log \sum_{\boldsymbol{y} \in \{1,\ldots,K\}^{|\tilde{\boldsymbol{x}}_i|}} \prod_{k=1}^{|\tilde{\boldsymbol{x}}_i|+1} \psi_{\tilde{x}_{i,k-1},y_k} \eta_{y_k,\tilde{x}_{i,k}} && (4.6)\\
&= \operatorname*{argmax}_{\boldsymbol{\eta},\boldsymbol{\psi}} \sum_{i=1}^{\tilde{N}} \sum_{k=1}^{|\tilde{\boldsymbol{x}}_i|+1} \log \sum_{c \in \{1,\ldots,K\}} \psi_{\tilde{x}_{i,k-1},c} \eta_{c,\tilde{x}_{i,k}} && (4.7)
\end{aligned}$$

The latter equality holds because the cluster for each word is conditionally independent of all other word clusters, given the words. This allows us to move the summation over word positions outside the logarithm, and greatly simplifies the EM algorithm compared to models in which the $Y_{i,k}$ are interdependent (upcoming in section 4.1.4).

On round t, the E step for this model requires us to calculate $\langle q_{i,k}^{(t)}(1), \ldots, q_{i,k}^{(t)}(K) \rangle$, the posterior probability of the ith sentence's kth word belonging to each cluster. The formula is simple:

$$q_{i,k}^{(t)}(c) \leftarrow \frac{\psi_{\tilde{x}_{i,k-1},c}\eta_{c,\tilde{x}_{i,k}}}{\sum_{c'=1}^{K} \psi_{\tilde{x}_{i,k-1},c'}\eta_{c',\tilde{x}_{i,k}}} = p_{\mathbf{w}}(Y_{k,i} = c \mid X_{i,k-1} = \tilde{x}_{i,k-1}, X_{i,k} = \tilde{x}_{i,k}) \tag{4.8}$$

The full posterior, for all i and all c, can therefore be calculated in $O(NK)$ time, where $N = \sum_{i=1}^{\tilde{N}} |\tilde{\boldsymbol{x}}_i|$. The q values can then be aggregated into "soft counts" of model events. We use "$\widehat{freq}_{q^{(t)}}$" to denote these soft counts because they are expectations of frequencies under the distribution q.

$$\widehat{freq}_{q^{(t)}}\left(c; \langle \tilde{\boldsymbol{x}} \rangle_{i=1}^{\tilde{N}}\right) = \sum_{i=1}^{\tilde{N}} \sum_{k=1}^{|\tilde{\boldsymbol{x}}_i|+1} q_{i,k}^{(t)}(c) = \sum_{i=1}^{\tilde{N}} \sum_{k=1}^{|\tilde{\boldsymbol{x}}_i|+1} \mathbb{E}_{p_{\mathbf{w}^{(t)}}(Y_{i,k} \mid \boldsymbol{X} = \tilde{\boldsymbol{x}}_i)}[\mathbf{1}\{Y = c\}] \tag{4.9}$$

is the expectation, under the model, of the number of words in the training data belonging to cluster c. For a given $\sigma \in \Sigma$, $y \in \{1, \ldots, K\}$,[2]

$$\widehat{freq}_{q^{(t)}}\left(c, \sigma; \langle \tilde{\boldsymbol{x}}_1, \ldots, \tilde{\boldsymbol{x}}_i \rangle_{i=1}^{\tilde{N}}\right) = \sum_{(i,k):\tilde{x}_{i,k}=\sigma} q_{i,k}^{(t)}(c) \tag{4.10}$$

$$\widehat{freq}_{q^{(t)}}\left(\sigma, c; \langle \tilde{\boldsymbol{x}}_1, \ldots, \tilde{\boldsymbol{x}}_i \rangle_{i=1}^{\tilde{N}}\right) = \sum_{(i,k):\tilde{x}_{i,k}=\sigma} q_{i,k+1}^{(t)}(c) \tag{4.11}$$

These are expected values of the number of times cluster c precedes σ or follows it, respectively.

Because this clustering model is based entirely on multinomials, the M step is accomplished by normalizing the soft counts of events. This is exactly like MLE by counting described in section 3.3.6, except our counts are "soft."

$$\forall c \in \{1, \ldots, K\}, \sigma \in \Sigma \cup \{\text{●}\}, \quad \eta_{c,\sigma}^{(t+1)} \leftarrow \frac{\widehat{freq}_{q^{(t)}}\left(c, \sigma; \langle \tilde{\boldsymbol{x}}_i \rangle_{i=1}^{\tilde{N}}\right)}{\widehat{freq}_{q^{(t)}}(c; \langle \tilde{\boldsymbol{x}}_i \rangle_{i=1}^{\tilde{N}})} \tag{4.12}$$

$$\forall c \in \{1, \ldots, K\}, \sigma \in \Sigma \cup \{\text{➾}\}, \quad \psi_{\sigma,c}^{(t+1)} \leftarrow \frac{\widehat{freq}_{q^{(t)}}\left(\sigma, c; \langle \tilde{\boldsymbol{x}}_i \rangle_{i=1}^{\tilde{N}}\right)}{freq(\sigma; \langle \tilde{\boldsymbol{x}}_i \rangle_{i=1}^{\tilde{N}})} \tag{4.13}$$

In equation 4.13, an actual ("hard") frequency is used because we condition against an event that is always observed (a word).

Notice that both steps are accomplished by applying straightforward, intuitive calculations. The E step performs a particular kind of inference, calculating the posteriors over the hidden variable. The M step is maximum likelihood estimation, where we assume the model posteriors "fill in" the

[2]Equation 4.10 is also applicable to $\sigma = $ ● and equation 4.11 to $\sigma = $ ➾.

missing distributional information about the hidden variable. The simplicity of the two steps masks the approximate nature of the EM algorithm, which taken as a whole can be understood as a hill-climber of the non-convex likelihood objective in equation 4.3.

It is important to remember that the objective function may have many local optima, and depending on the initialization of the model parameters, EM will converge to very different parameter estimates.[3] Therefore, initialization is very important. In the case of clustering, in particular, initialization must not be naïve. If, for instance, the parameters relating to each cluster are initialized identically, then the model will not be able to distinguish among the different clusters. Initialization must break symmetry, so that each cluster is perturbed away from the others, or all of the clusters will remain identical throughout EM iterations. The problem of underlying symmetries is part of the challenge of unsupervised learning; two models that are equivalent but swap two clusters' parameters (here $\boldsymbol{\eta}_{y,\cdot}$ and $\boldsymbol{\psi}_{\cdot,y}$) will achieve exactly the same likelihood.

Broadly speaking, EM is successful only under two scenarios. In the first, the initialization takes into account prior knowledge about the problem or the data, so that the local optimum achieved is an improvement on an already reasonable starting point. One classic example is the gradual introduction of more complex models, initialized by EM-trained simpler ones, in the statistical machine translation models of Brown et al. (1990). In the second scenario, the structure of the model—its independence assumptions or features—impose strong bias or constraints, so that the model does not have inherent symmetries. The unsupervised syntactic bracketing model of Klein and Manning (2002b) exemplifies this kind of successful model design.

4.1.3 HARD AND SOFT K-MEANS

Because the K-means clustering algorithm is so widely known, it is helpful to relate it to the EM algorithm. The K-means algorithm assumes training examples that are numerical vectors, i.e., $\mathcal{X} = \mathbb{R}^d$. It is assumed that there are K clusters, so that $\mathcal{Y} = \{1, \ldots, K\}$. The parameters of the model are the *centroids* associated with each cluster; we will let $\mathbf{w}_y \in \mathbb{R}^d$ denote the centroid for cluster $y \in \mathcal{Y}$. K-means assumes one additional piece of information is provided: a distance function $\Delta : \mathbb{R}^d \times \mathbb{R}^d \rightarrow \mathbb{R}_{\geq 0}$. See algorithm 5.

The K-means algorithm has a structure similar to EM, and it is annotated as such in algorithm 5. The main differences are (i) there is no explicit probabilistic story, and hence (ii) the E step does not involve posteriors. The M step estimates the parameters using something like maximum likelihood estimation. If we were to assume that each cluster y's weight vector $\mathbf{w}_y$ is the mean of a Gaussian distribution, and that all $\tilde{\boldsymbol{x}}_i$ such that $\hat{y}_i = y$ were drawn from that Gaussian, then the M step would correspond exactly to MLE for the mean of the Gaussian. Indeed, this is where the name "K-means" comes from; it follows from choosing Δ to be Euclidean distance:

$$\Delta(\mathbf{w}_y, \boldsymbol{x}) = \sqrt{\sum_{j=1}^{d} (w_{y,j} - x_j)^2} = \left\| \mathbf{w}_y - \boldsymbol{x} \right\|_2 \tag{4.14}$$

[3]This is true in general, but there are interesting special cases where the objective function is actually convex.

Algorithm 5 The K-means algorithm.

Input: number of clusters K, initial centroids $\langle \mathbf{w}_y^{(0)} \rangle_{y=1}^{K}$, training data $\langle \tilde{\boldsymbol{x}}_1, \ldots, \tilde{\boldsymbol{x}}_{\tilde{N}} \rangle$, distance function $\Delta : \mathbb{R}^d \times \mathbb{R}^d \rightarrow \mathbb{R}_{\geq 0}$

Output: learned centroids $\langle \mathbf{w}_y \rangle_{y=1}^{K}$

$t \leftarrow 0$

repeat

"E step":

for $i = 1$ to $\tilde{N}$ **do**

$\hat{y}_i^{(t)} \leftarrow \underset{y \in \{1,\ldots,K\}}{\text{argmin}} \; \Delta(\mathbf{w}_y^{(t)}, \tilde{\boldsymbol{x}}_i)$

end for

"M step":

for $y = 1$ to K **do**

$$\mathbf{w}_y^{(t+1)} \leftarrow \left(\sum_{i : \hat{y}_i^{(t)} = y} \tilde{\boldsymbol{x}}_i \right) \Bigg/ |\{i \mid \hat{y}_i^{(t)} = y\}|$$

end for

$t \leftarrow t + 1$

until $\mathbf{w}^{(t)} \approx \mathbf{w}^{(t-1)}$

$\mathbf{w} \leftarrow \mathbf{w}^{(t)}$

Under the Gaussian interpretation, we can understand the K-means E step as an alternative to calculating the posterior over Y_i under the current model: it finds the *mode* of Y_i under the current model. That is, it calculates

$$\underset{y \in \{1,\ldots,K\}}{\text{argmax}} \; p_{\mathbf{w}}(Y_i = y \mid \boldsymbol{X} = \tilde{\boldsymbol{x}}_i) \tag{4.15}$$

This will hold if we define the model probabilities using (i) a uniform distribution over Y and (ii) a multivariate Gaussian over $\boldsymbol{X}$ for each Y, with the covariance matrix fixed at $\mathbf{I}$:

$$p_{\mathbf{w}}(Y = y \mid \boldsymbol{X} = \boldsymbol{x}) \propto p_{\text{uniform}}(Y = y) \times p_{\mathbf{w}}(\boldsymbol{X} = \boldsymbol{x} \mid Y = y) \tag{4.16}$$

$$= \frac{1}{K} \times \frac{1}{\sqrt{(2\pi)^d |\boldsymbol{\Sigma}|}} \exp\left(-\frac{1}{2} (\boldsymbol{x} - \mathbf{w}_y)^\top \boldsymbol{\Sigma}^{-1} (\boldsymbol{x} - \mathbf{w}_y) \right) \tag{4.17}$$

$$\propto \exp\left(-\frac{1}{2} \left\| \boldsymbol{x} - \mathbf{w}_y \right\|_2^2 \right) \tag{4.18}$$

It should be clear that the most likely y for a given $\boldsymbol{x}$ will be the one whose centroid $\mathbf{w}_y$ is closest in Euclidean distance to $\boldsymbol{x}$.

To transform K-means into an EM algorithm, we can replace the "hard" E step with a traditional E step, calculating a posterior probability that each example belongs to each cluster:

$$q_i^{(t)}(y) \leftarrow \exp\left(-\frac{1}{2}\left\|\tilde{\boldsymbol{x}}_i - \mathbf{w}_y^{(t)}\right\|_2^2\right) \Big/ \sum_{y'=1}^{K} \exp\left(-\frac{1}{2}\left\|\tilde{\boldsymbol{x}}_i - \mathbf{w}_{y'}^{(t)}\right\|_2^2\right) \tag{4.19}$$

The M step would then use these posteriors to count each example fractionally toward each cluster:

$$\mathbf{w}_y^{(t+1)} \leftarrow \sum_{i=1}^{\tilde{N}} q_i^{(t)}(y)\tilde{\boldsymbol{x}}_i \Big/ \sum_{i=1}^{\tilde{N}} q_i^{(t)}(\boldsymbol{y}) \tag{4.20}$$

The use of the mode to choose a single value of $\hat{y}_i$, instead of calculating a posterior $q_i : \mathcal{Y} \rightarrow \mathbb{R}_{\geq 0}$, suggests a variation on the EM algorithm that is sometimes called **hard** or **winner-take-all** EM. This approach can be understood as a greedy approximation to the following optimization problem:

$$\underset{p \in \mathcal{P}, \boldsymbol{y}_1 \in \mathcal{Y}_{\tilde{\boldsymbol{x}}_1}, \ldots, \boldsymbol{y}_{\tilde{N}} \in \mathcal{Y}_{\tilde{\boldsymbol{x}}_{\tilde{N}}}}{\operatorname{argmax}} \sum_{i=1}^{\tilde{N}} \log p(\tilde{\boldsymbol{x}}_i, \boldsymbol{y}_i) \tag{4.21}$$

In the hard E step, the maximizing $\boldsymbol{y}_1, \ldots, \boldsymbol{y}_{\tilde{N}}$ are selected for fixed p. In the hard M step, the $\boldsymbol{y}_i$ are held fixed, and p is chosen using maximum likelihood estimation exactly as in the supervised case.

4.1.4 THE STRUCTURED CASE

Interestingly, the beginnings of the EM algorithm can be found in the hidden Markov model literature (Baum et al., 1970), and it has been applied to probabilistic grammars almost since its inception (Baker, 1979). Algorithm 4 obscures some important details when we move to *structured* output spaces. We consider the E step and the M step each in more detail.

E step. In the E step, the current model is used to calculate, for each training example $\tilde{\boldsymbol{x}}_i$, the posterior probability of each $\boldsymbol{y} \in \mathcal{Y}_{\tilde{\boldsymbol{x}}_i}$. This is an instance of *inference*, discussed more generally in chapter 5. A naïve approach to calculating $q_i^{(t)}$ would be to consider each $\boldsymbol{y} \in \mathcal{Y}_{\tilde{\boldsymbol{x}}_i}$ in turn and calculate $p_{\mathbf{w}^{(t)}}(\tilde{\boldsymbol{x}}_i, \boldsymbol{y})$; imagine a very long vector containing these values:

$$\begin{bmatrix} \vdots \\ p_{\mathbf{w}^{(t)}}(\tilde{\boldsymbol{x}}_i, \boldsymbol{y}) \\ \vdots \\ p_{\mathbf{w}^{(t)}}(\tilde{\boldsymbol{x}}_i, \boldsymbol{y}') \\ \vdots \end{bmatrix} \tag{4.22}$$

We would then renormalize by the marginal $p_{\mathbf{w}^{(t)}}(\tilde{\boldsymbol{x}}_i)$ (the sum of the elements of the vector). While this is a reasonable approach for clustering models with relatively few clusters, this is grossly inefficient when $\mathcal{Y}_{\tilde{\boldsymbol{x}}_i}$ is an exponentially large structured space.

Instead, we do not calculate the distribution $q_i^{(t)}$ directly, but rather calculate only what is needed to accomplish the M step. For multinomial-based models (section 3.3.2), this corresponds to the expected frequency of each model event, summed over all examples. We can therefore redefine $q^{(t)}$ to store aggregate expected frequencies of model events. Let $j \in \{1, \ldots, d\}$ range over model events:

$$\widehat{freq}_{p_{\mathbf{w}^{(t)}}}\left(\text{event } j;\, \langle \tilde{\boldsymbol{x}}_i \rangle_{i=1}^{\tilde{N}}\right) = \sum_{i=1}^{\tilde{N}} \frac{\displaystyle\sum_{\boldsymbol{y} \in \mathcal{Y}_{\tilde{\boldsymbol{x}}_i}} p_{\mathbf{w}^{(t)}}(\tilde{\boldsymbol{x}}_i, \boldsymbol{y}) \times freq(\text{event } j;\, \tilde{\boldsymbol{x}}_i, \boldsymbol{y})}{\displaystyle\sum_{\boldsymbol{y} \in \mathcal{Y}_{\tilde{\boldsymbol{x}}_i}} p_{\mathbf{w}^{(t)}}(\tilde{\boldsymbol{x}}_i, \boldsymbol{y})} \tag{4.23}$$

Note that we have dropped all mention of q here, instead calculating sufficient statistics using the model distribution $p_{\mathbf{w}^{(t)}}$ to fill in the distribution over $\boldsymbol{Y}$. The fact that q is implied is a source of confusion for many newcomers to EM; without recognizing that the E step is performing inference under the (now implied) distribution q, the calculations may seem magical. Another source of confusion is that the inference algorithms we use to calculate the above soft frequencies are non-trivial (e.g., involving dynamic programming) and incur most of the overall computational expense of EM. These complexities make it easy to lose sight of what EM is really doing: locally optimizing equation 4.3.

Of course, multinomial-based models are not the only option; generative log-linear models are an alternative. If the model family is log-linear, then the required quantities take the more general form of feature expectations. For the jth feature function:

$$\begin{aligned}
\mathbb{E}_{\tilde{p}(\boldsymbol{X}) p_{\mathbf{w}^{(t)}}(\boldsymbol{Y} \mid \boldsymbol{X})}[g_j(\boldsymbol{X}, \boldsymbol{Y})] &= \sum_{i=1}^{\tilde{N}} \frac{1}{\tilde{N}} \frac{\displaystyle\sum_{\boldsymbol{y} \in \mathcal{Y}_{\tilde{\boldsymbol{x}}_i}} p_{\mathbf{w}^{(t)}}(\tilde{\boldsymbol{x}}_i, \boldsymbol{y}) g_j(\tilde{\boldsymbol{x}}_i, \boldsymbol{y})}{\displaystyle\sum_{\boldsymbol{y} \in \mathcal{Y}_{\tilde{\boldsymbol{x}}_i}} p_{\mathbf{w}^{(t)}}(\tilde{\boldsymbol{x}}_i, \boldsymbol{y})} \\
&= \sum_{i=1}^{\tilde{N}} \frac{1}{\tilde{N}} \frac{\displaystyle\sum_{\boldsymbol{y} \in \mathcal{Y}_{\tilde{\boldsymbol{x}}_i}} \left(\exp \mathbf{w}^\top \mathbf{g}(\tilde{\boldsymbol{x}}_i, \boldsymbol{y})\right) g_j(\tilde{\boldsymbol{x}}_i, \boldsymbol{y})}{\displaystyle\sum_{\boldsymbol{y} \in \mathcal{Y}_{\tilde{\boldsymbol{x}}_i}} \exp \mathbf{w}^\top \mathbf{g}(\tilde{\boldsymbol{x}}_i, \boldsymbol{y})}
\end{aligned} \tag{4.24}$$

(The "required quantities" for a given model family's M step are known as **sufficient statistics**. For a given parameter, a sufficient statistic is one that summarizes the sample perfectly well; i.e., no additional information about the parameter can be inferred from the sample beyond the statistic.)

In both the multinomial and log-linear variations, efficiently solving the E step hinges on the ability to calculate feature expectations (section 5.2). Hence, the very same factoring assumptions that have enabled efficient decoding and supervised learning may now exploited in unsupervised learning.

M step. The key innovation of the EM algorithm is to make unsupervised learning look like a series of supervised learning problems. Supervised learning requires that we have a sample of paired values for $\boldsymbol{X}$ and $\boldsymbol{Y}$, or, more generally, an empirical distribution $\tilde{p}(\boldsymbol{X}, \boldsymbol{Y})$. In unsupervised learning, we have an incomplete sample where only $\tilde{p}(\boldsymbol{X})$ is given. The E step provides an estimate of the conditional probability of $\boldsymbol{Y}$ given X, allowing us to define a complete distribution "$\tilde{p}(\boldsymbol{X}, \boldsymbol{Y})$" $= \tilde{p}(\boldsymbol{X}) \cdot q(\boldsymbol{Y} \mid \boldsymbol{X})$. Given the complete distribution, the M step simply performs supervised learning, finding the maximum likelihood estimate from the model family $\mathcal{P}$, given the now "complete" sample. Most commonly in linguistic structure prediction, the model family is multinomial-based, and the M step is accomplished by normalizing the expected frequencies. As noted, it is also possible to use other model families, such as a log-linear family, in which case the M step may require an auxiliary optimization routine to find the maximum likelihood estimate (see section 3.5.4).

EM feels circular, and it is. The current model $\mathbf{w}^{(t)}$ is used to find a distribution $q^{(t)}$ over the missing information, which is then used to find the next model $\mathbf{w}^{(t+1)}$. This circularity is really no different from the iterative procedures we used to optimize various criteria in supervised learning (chapter 3). Note again that alternatives for MLE with incomplete data are available; equation 4.3 is an optimization problem that could be solved in many ways. The EM algorithm is attractive because it is understandable and easy to implement. For more discussion about EM as a coordinate ascent method, see section A.2.

4.1.5 HIDDEN MARKOV MODELS

We consider next EM applied to HMMs. In this case, the model family is specified by the number of states, $L = |\Lambda|$,[4] and the vocabulary of observable symbols, $\Sigma = \langle \sigma_1, \ldots, \sigma_V \rangle$. Here we assume a first-order HMM, so that the set of parameters to be estimated are:

$$\begin{aligned}
\boldsymbol{\gamma} &= \langle \gamma_{\ell,\ell'} \rangle_{\ell \in \{\text{➾}\} \cup \Lambda, \ell' \in \{\text{●}\} \cup \Lambda} \\
\boldsymbol{\eta} &= \langle \eta_{\ell,\sigma} \rangle_{\ell \in \Lambda, \sigma \in \Sigma}
\end{aligned}$$

We assume a training dataset $\langle \tilde{\boldsymbol{x}}_1, \ldots, \tilde{\boldsymbol{x}}_{\tilde{N}} \rangle$, each $\tilde{\boldsymbol{x}}_i \in \Sigma^*$.

As in the clustering case, initialization is important and should be done so as to break symmetry among the L different states. It is helpful to think of each state L as analogous to one of the K clusters in K-means; here, however, each cluster-state is statistically dependent on the cluster-states preceding and following it, as well as the symbol it emits.

[4] Note that without any labeled data, there is nothing to distinguish any state in Λ from any other. This is an example of a symmetry problem that makes many of the possible solutions that EM might find functionally equivalent.

The E step requires that we calculate sufficient statistics for the model. These are the expected frequencies of the transition and emission events, summed over all training examples:

$$\widehat{freq}(\ell, \ell'; \langle \tilde{\boldsymbol{x}}_i \rangle_{i=1}^{\tilde{N}}) \leftarrow \sum_{i=1}^{\tilde{N}} \mathbb{E}_{p_{\gamma,\eta}(\boldsymbol{Y} \mid \tilde{\boldsymbol{x}}_i)}[freq(\ell, \ell'; \boldsymbol{Y})] \tag{4.25}$$

$$\widehat{freq}(\ell, \sigma; \langle \tilde{\boldsymbol{x}}_i \rangle_{i=1}^{\tilde{N}}) \leftarrow \sum_{i=1}^{\tilde{N}} \mathbb{E}_{p_{\gamma,\eta}(\boldsymbol{Y} \mid \tilde{\boldsymbol{x}}_i)}[freq(\ell, \sigma; \tilde{\boldsymbol{x}}_i, \boldsymbol{Y})] \tag{4.26}$$

We defer discussion of *how* these expected frequencies are calculated to section 5.2 (essentially, the forward and backward algorithms are invoked for each example $\tilde{\boldsymbol{x}}_i$).

The renormalization required by the M step is straightforward:

$$\begin{array}{rrcl} \forall \ell \in \{\text{⇨}\} \cup \Lambda, \ell' \in \{\text{●}\} \cup \Lambda, & \gamma_{\ell,\ell'} & \leftarrow & \widehat{freq}(\ell, \ell'; \langle \tilde{\boldsymbol{x}}_i \rangle_{i=1}^{\tilde{N}}) \Big/ \widehat{freq}(\ell; \langle \tilde{\boldsymbol{x}}_i \rangle_{i=1}^{\tilde{N}}) \\ \forall \ell \in \Lambda, \sigma \in \Sigma, & \eta_{\ell,\sigma} & \leftarrow & \widehat{freq}(\ell, \sigma; \langle \tilde{\boldsymbol{x}}_i \rangle_{i=1}^{\tilde{N}}) \Big/ \widehat{freq}(\ell; \langle \tilde{\boldsymbol{x}}_i \rangle_{i=1}^{\tilde{N}}) \end{array}$$

Two classic papers exploring unsupervised (and semisupervised) learning of HMM parameters with EM are Merialdo (1994) and Elworthy (1994). EM for HMMs is sometimes called **Baum-Welch** training.

4.1.6 EM ITERATIONS IMPROVE LIKELIHOOD

Returning to the general problem of maximizing likelihood (equation 4.3), it is not obvious that the procedure in algorithm 4 finds a local optimum of this objective function, as we have claimed. Here we show that each iteration of EM improves the likelihood objective.

Let

$$\Phi_{\mathrm{ML}}(\mathbf{w}) = \sum_{i=1}^{\tilde{N}} \log \sum_{\boldsymbol{y} \in \mathcal{Y}_{\tilde{\boldsymbol{x}}_i}} p_{\mathbf{w}}(\tilde{\boldsymbol{x}}_i, \boldsymbol{y}) \tag{4.27}$$

where $\mathbf{w}$ are the parameters of the probabilistic model $p \in \mathcal{P}$ (a valid model in equation 4.2). "ML" here stands for "marginal likelihood."

Theorem 4.1 When performing the EM algorithm (algorithm 4), each iteration of an E step and an M step will find $\mathbf{w}^{(t+1)}$ such that

$$\Phi_{\mathrm{ML}}(\mathbf{w}^{(t+1)}) \geq \Phi_{\mathrm{ML}}(\mathbf{w}^{(t)})$$

Proof: Let $Q^{(t)} : \mathbb{R}^d \to \mathbb{R}$ be the function defined by:

$$Q^{(t)}(\mathbf{w}) = \sum_{i=1}^{\tilde{N}} \sum_{\boldsymbol{y} \in \mathcal{Y}_{\tilde{\boldsymbol{x}}_i}} q_i^{(t)}(\boldsymbol{y}) \log p_{\mathbf{w}}(\tilde{\boldsymbol{x}}_i, \boldsymbol{y}) \tag{4.28}$$

$Q^{(t)}$ is maximized with respect to weights $\mathbf{w}$ on the tth M step (see algorithm 4). Let us consider the *difference* between the likelihood objective $\Phi_{\mathrm{ML}}(\mathbf{w})$ and the tth M step's objective $Q^{(t)}(\mathbf{w})$:

$$
\begin{aligned}
\Phi_{\mathrm{ML}}(\mathbf{w}) - Q^{(t)}(\mathbf{w}) & \\
&= \sum_{i=1}^{\tilde{N}} \log \sum_{\boldsymbol{y}' \in \mathcal{Y}_{\tilde{\boldsymbol{x}}_i}} p_{\mathbf{w}}(\tilde{\boldsymbol{x}}_i, \boldsymbol{y}') - \sum_{i=1}^{\tilde{N}} \sum_{\boldsymbol{y} \in \mathcal{Y}_{\tilde{\boldsymbol{x}}_i}} q_i^{(t)}(\boldsymbol{y}) \log p_{\mathbf{w}}(\tilde{\boldsymbol{x}}_i, \boldsymbol{y}) \\
&= \sum_{i=1}^{\tilde{N}} \sum_{\boldsymbol{y} \in \mathcal{Y}_{\tilde{\boldsymbol{x}}_i}} q_i^{(t)}(\boldsymbol{y}) \log \sum_{\boldsymbol{y}' \in \mathcal{Y}_{\tilde{\boldsymbol{x}}_i}} p_{\mathbf{w}}(\tilde{\boldsymbol{x}}_i, \boldsymbol{y}') - \sum_{i=1}^{\tilde{N}} \sum_{\boldsymbol{y} \in \mathcal{Y}_{\tilde{\boldsymbol{x}}_i}} q_i^{(t)}(\boldsymbol{y}) \log p_{\mathbf{w}}(\tilde{\boldsymbol{x}}_i, \boldsymbol{y}) \\
&= \sum_{i=1}^{\tilde{N}} \sum_{\boldsymbol{y} \in \mathcal{Y}_{\tilde{\boldsymbol{x}}_i}} q_i^{(t)}(\boldsymbol{y}) \log \frac{\sum_{\boldsymbol{y}' \in \mathcal{Y}_{\tilde{\boldsymbol{x}}_i}} p_{\mathbf{w}}(\tilde{\boldsymbol{x}}_i, \boldsymbol{y}')}{p_{\mathbf{w}}(\tilde{\boldsymbol{x}}_i, \boldsymbol{y})} \\
&= -\sum_{i=1}^{\tilde{N}} \sum_{\boldsymbol{y} \in \mathcal{Y}_{\tilde{\boldsymbol{x}}_i}} q_i^{(t)}(\boldsymbol{y}) \log p_{\mathbf{w}}(\boldsymbol{y} \mid \tilde{\boldsymbol{x}}_i) \\
\Phi_{\mathrm{ML}}(\mathbf{w}) &= \underbrace{Q^{(t)}(\mathbf{w})}_{\text{term 1}} \underbrace{- \sum_{i=1}^{\tilde{N}} \sum_{\boldsymbol{y} \in \mathcal{Y}_{\tilde{\boldsymbol{x}}_i}} q_i^{(t)}(\boldsymbol{y}) \log p_{\mathbf{w}}(\boldsymbol{y} \mid \tilde{\boldsymbol{x}}_i)}_{\text{term 2}}
\end{aligned}
$$

The second equality introduces a summation over $q_i^{(t)}$, equivalent to multiplying by one. The third collapses the logarithms. The fourth uses the definition of conditional probability. The above will hold for any iteration t. We can think of each E step as redefining Φ_{ML} through the choice of a new set of $q_i^{(t)}$ distributions. The M step updates the weights $\mathbf{w}$, keeping $q_i^{(t)}$ and the definitions of terms 1 and 2 (as functions of $\mathbf{w}$) fixed. We already know that the M step sets $\mathbf{w}^{(t+1)} = \operatorname{argmax}_{\mathbf{w}} Q^{(t)}(\mathbf{w})$, so we know that

$$
Q^{(t)}(\mathbf{w}^{(t+1)}) = \max_{\mathbf{w}} Q^{(t)}(\mathbf{w}) \geq Q^{(t)}(\mathbf{w}^{(t)}) \tag{4.29}
$$

We next need to show that term 2 also improves (the quantity at left depends on $\mathbf{w}^{(t+1)}$, and the one at right depends on $\mathbf{w}^{(t)}$):

$$
-\sum_{i=1}^{\tilde{N}} \sum_{\boldsymbol{y} \in \mathcal{Y}_{\tilde{\boldsymbol{x}}_i}} q_i^{(t)}(\boldsymbol{y}) \log p_{\mathbf{w}^{(t+1)}}(\boldsymbol{y} \mid \tilde{\boldsymbol{x}}_i) \geq -\sum_{i=1}^{\tilde{N}} \sum_{\boldsymbol{y} \in \mathcal{Y}_{\tilde{\boldsymbol{x}}_i}} q_i^{(t)}(\boldsymbol{y}) \log p_{\mathbf{w}^{(t)}}(\boldsymbol{y} \mid \tilde{\boldsymbol{x}}_i) \tag{4.30}
$$

Consider the difference:

$$
\begin{aligned}
& \left(-\sum_{i=1}^{\tilde{N}} \sum_{\boldsymbol{y} \in \mathcal{Y}_{\tilde{\boldsymbol{x}}_i}} q_i^{(t)}(\boldsymbol{y}) \log p_{\mathbf{w}^{(t+1)}}(\boldsymbol{y} \mid \tilde{\boldsymbol{x}}_i)\right) - \left(-\sum_{i=1}^{\tilde{N}} \sum_{\boldsymbol{y} \in \mathcal{Y}_{\tilde{\boldsymbol{x}}_i}} q_i^{(t)}(\boldsymbol{y}) \log p_{\mathbf{w}^{(t)}}(\boldsymbol{y} \mid \tilde{\boldsymbol{x}}_i)\right) \\
= & \sum_{i=1}^{\tilde{N}} \sum_{\boldsymbol{y} \in \mathcal{Y}_{\tilde{\boldsymbol{x}}_i}} q_i^{(t)}(\boldsymbol{y}) \log p_{\mathbf{w}^{(t)}}(\boldsymbol{y} \mid \tilde{\boldsymbol{x}}_i) - \sum_{i=1}^{\tilde{N}} \sum_{\boldsymbol{y} \in \mathcal{Y}_{\tilde{\boldsymbol{x}}_i}} q_i^{(t)}(\boldsymbol{y}) \log p_{\mathbf{w}^{(t+1)}}(\boldsymbol{y} \mid \tilde{\boldsymbol{x}}_i) \\
= & \sum_{i=1}^{\tilde{N}} \sum_{\boldsymbol{y} \in \mathcal{Y}_{\tilde{\boldsymbol{x}}_i}} q_i^{(t)}(\boldsymbol{y}) \log \frac{p_{\mathbf{w}^{(t)}}(\boldsymbol{y} \mid \tilde{\boldsymbol{x}}_i)}{p_{\mathbf{w}^{(t+1)}}(\boldsymbol{y} \mid \tilde{\boldsymbol{x}}_i)} \\
= & \sum_{i=1}^{\tilde{N}} \sum_{\boldsymbol{y} \in \mathcal{Y}_{\tilde{\boldsymbol{x}}_i}} q_i^{(t)}(\boldsymbol{y}) \log \frac{q_i^{(t)}(\boldsymbol{y})}{p_{\mathbf{w}^{(t+1)}}(\boldsymbol{y} \mid \tilde{\boldsymbol{x}}_i)} \\
= & \sum_{i=1}^{\tilde{N}} D_{KL}\left(q_i^{(t)}(\boldsymbol{Y}) \| p_{\mathbf{w}^{(t+1)}}(\boldsymbol{Y} \mid \tilde{\boldsymbol{x}}_i)\right) \\
\geq & \; 0
\end{aligned}
$$

Because the KL divergence is always nonnegative, the difference is a sum of nonnegative terms and therefore is nonnegative. Therefore, term 2 cannot decrease on an EM iteration. □

This proof is not quite as strong as one might hope for, and, in fact, EM may converge to a *saddle point* of the likelihood function rather than a true local maximum.[5] In practice, these concerns are usually ignored. For more discussion, see Wu (1983) and Collins (1997). Bishop (2006, section 9.4) provides an elegant visualization of the relevant quantities.

4.1.7 EXTENSIONS AND IMPROVEMENTS

We have already noted the challenge of local optima when maximizing Φ_{ML}. In practice, this concern is often ignored. Anecdotal evidence suggests that, for structured problems, EM is extremely sensitive to the initial parameter setting $\mathbf{w}^{(0)}$ (Carroll and Charniak, 1992). A few techniques have been used to mitigate this problem, though none have theoretical guarantees.

The simplest is to run EM multiple times with different initializers. After obtaining M different parameter estimates from M different runs, $\langle \mathbf{w}_1, \mathbf{w}_2, \ldots, \mathbf{w}_M \rangle$, we can select among them using the likelihood criterion: $\mathbf{w} \leftarrow \mathbf{w}_{\text{argmax}_i \, \Phi_{\text{ML}}(\mathbf{w}_i)}$. Alternately, if some annotated data are available, we can use them to select among models, leading to a semisupervised blend of unannotated data for training and annotated data for model selection. If the initializers are chosen as a random sample from the family of models $\mathcal{P}$, more runs should imply improvements in likelihood. Prior knowledge might be sacrificed in random initialization, or the random sampling of initial weights could be biased by prior knowledge.

[5] A saddle point is a point that is a local maximum in some dimensions but a local minimum in others.

Deterministic annealing is a general technique for non-convex optimization (Rose et al., 1990, Ueda and Nakano, 1998). The basic idea is to define a sequence of objective functions $\langle \Phi_1, \Phi_2, \ldots, \Phi_T \rangle$ such that Φ_T is equal to the objective of interest, here Φ_{ML}. The first function is convex, and each Φ_j is only slightly different from Φ_{j-1}. The hope is to follow a path from the (single) global optimum of Φ_1 to a competitive local optimum of Φ_{ML}. Smith and Eisner (2004) describe a straightforward deterministic annealing technique involving only slight modifications to the EM algorithm.

Another approach to avoiding local optima is to introduce random perturbations to the empirical distribution $\tilde{p}(\boldsymbol{X})$ between each iteration. Related to this idea, some research has recently turned to "online" variants of EM, where the model is improved after running E step inference on one example per iteration. For further discussion about variations on EM, see Neal and Hinton (1998) and Liang and Klein (2009).

Researchers have also sought to impose bias on generative models during EM learning, to improve the accuracy of the learned predictor. One example is work by Smith and Eisner (2006) on unsupervised dependency parsing. They imposed a dependency length bias by altering the posterior distributions $q^{(t)}$ to favor dependency trees with shorter attachments. A more general idea was proposed by Graça et al. (2008), who imposed constraints on certain of the model's posterior probabilities, giving an alternative objective function. They interpret the new objective as a regularized version of likelihood.

4.1.8 LOG-LINEAR EM

Unsupervised generative models tend to make use of multinomial parameterizations rather than log-linear ones. This is surprising since feature-based models (see section 3.3.8) are intuitive, particularly in unsupervised learning where redundant patterns ought to help a learner discover structural regularities. Berg-Kirkpatrick et al. (2010) describe the use of generative models built out of locally normalized log-linear distributions in unsupervised learning for a variety of problems.

One reason that globally normalized, generative log-linear models are not widely used in unsupervised learning is the computational expense. Consider the log-likelihood objective:

$$\max_{\mathbf{w}} \sum_{i=1}^{\tilde{N}} \left(\log \sum_{\boldsymbol{y} \in \mathcal{Y}_{\tilde{\boldsymbol{x}}_i}} \exp \mathbf{w}^\top \mathbf{g}(\tilde{\boldsymbol{x}}_i, \boldsymbol{y}) - \log z_{\mathbf{w}} \right) \tag{4.31}$$

As in the supervised case, the partition function $z_{\mathbf{w}}$ poses a challenge, requiring a costly joint summation:

$$z_{\mathbf{w}} = \sum_{\boldsymbol{x} \in \mathcal{X}} \sum_{\boldsymbol{y} \in \mathcal{Y}_{\boldsymbol{x}}} \exp \mathbf{w}^\top \mathbf{g}(\boldsymbol{x}, \boldsymbol{y}) \tag{4.32}$$

Although not widely used in NLP at this writing, there are techniques for maximizing the log-likelihood without directly calculating $z_{\mathbf{w}}$. Consider that the first derivative of the log-likelihood objective with respect to an arbitrary w_j is a difference of feature expectations:

$$\mathbb{E}_{\tilde{p}(\boldsymbol{X})p_{\mathbf{w}}(\boldsymbol{Y}|\boldsymbol{X})}[g_j(\boldsymbol{X}, \boldsymbol{Y})] - \mathbb{E}_{p_{\mathbf{w}}(\boldsymbol{X},\boldsymbol{Y})}[g_j(\boldsymbol{X}, \boldsymbol{Y})] \tag{4.33}$$

Exact calculation of the second term is especially hard (it hinges on $z_{\mathbf{w}}$), but it can often be approximated. Later in this chapter we will discuss approximate inference algorithms (e.g., Gibbs sampling) that may be applicable for sampling from distributions like $p_{\mathbf{w}}(\boldsymbol{Y} \mid \boldsymbol{X} = \tilde{\boldsymbol{x}}_i)$ and $p_{\mathbf{w}}(\boldsymbol{X}, \boldsymbol{Y})$. Another possibility is pseudolikelihood (section 3.5.6), which approximates the full model by a collection of simpler models. While these techniques are well understood in machine learning (see, e.g., the contrastive divergence method of Hinton, 2002), their application to structured problems is still under exploration.

4.1.9 CONTRASTIVE ESTIMATION

Recall that globally-normalized *conditional* log-linear models (section 3.5) avoid $z_{\mathbf{w}}$, requiring only a summation over analyses in $\mathcal{Y}_{\tilde{\boldsymbol{x}}_i}$ for each training example $\tilde{\boldsymbol{x}}_i$. We noted that they also move toward *discriminative* modeling and are therefore very popular for supervised NLP.

Contrastive estimation is a technique that transforms a generative model over $\boldsymbol{X}$ and $\boldsymbol{Y}$ into a conditional model (Smith and Eisner, 2005) but in the context of unsupervised learning. From an objective function point of view, it replaces $z_{\mathbf{w}}$ with a more tractable summation over structures similar to $\tilde{\boldsymbol{x}}_i$, called its "neighborhood." Let $\mathcal{N}_{\boldsymbol{x}} \subset \mathcal{X}$ be the neighborhood for input $\boldsymbol{x}$. The learning problem is

$$\max_{\mathbf{w}} \sum_{i=1}^{\tilde{N}} \left(\log \sum_{\boldsymbol{y} \in \mathcal{Y}_{\tilde{\boldsymbol{x}}_i}} \exp \mathbf{w}^\top \mathbf{g}(\tilde{\boldsymbol{x}}_i, \boldsymbol{y}) - \log \sum_{\boldsymbol{x} \in \mathcal{N}_{\tilde{\boldsymbol{x}}_i}} \sum_{\boldsymbol{y} \in \mathcal{Y}_{\boldsymbol{x}}} \exp \mathbf{w}^\top \mathbf{g}(\boldsymbol{x}, \boldsymbol{y}) \right) \tag{4.34}$$

The above is equivalent to maximizing the likelihood of a *conditional* model (section 3.4) where the conditioned-upon variable is an indicator of whether $\boldsymbol{X}$ falls in the neighborhood of $\tilde{\boldsymbol{x}}_i$:

$$\max_{\mathbf{w}} \sum_{i=1}^{\tilde{N}} \log p_{\mathbf{w}}(\boldsymbol{X} = \tilde{\boldsymbol{x}}_i \mid \boldsymbol{X} \in \mathcal{N}_{\tilde{\boldsymbol{x}}_i}) \tag{4.35}$$

Intuitively, training this model moves probability mass away from $\mathcal{N}_{\tilde{\boldsymbol{x}}_i} \setminus \{\tilde{\boldsymbol{x}}_i\}$ onto $\tilde{\boldsymbol{x}}_i$. The random variable $\boldsymbol{Y}$ is a hidden variable in this model, and the distribution over $\mathcal{Y}_{\tilde{\boldsymbol{x}}_i}$ is manipulated in service of optimizing the conditional likelihood above.

Although it offers computational benefits, contrastive estimation was introduced as a way of introducing "implicit negative evidence" as a form of bias into unsupervised learning. The contrastive neighborhood $\mathcal{N}_{\tilde{\boldsymbol{x}}_i} \setminus \{\tilde{\boldsymbol{x}}_i\}$ is understood as a set of negative examples (or at least, "negative on average"), and the goal of learning is to make $\tilde{\boldsymbol{x}}_i$ more probable at their expense.

For syntax learning, Smith and Eisner (2005) and Smith (2006) used neighborhoods of sentences that were efficiently representable using finite-state lattices. This permits efficient inference of the feature expectations that arise in the gradient of the log-likelihood objective, using dynamic programming.

4.2 BAYESIAN UNSUPERVISED LEARNING

The term "Bayesian" is potentially confusing, in part because its meaning has drifted over time. For a long time, it was associated with the idea of learning with a **prior** over models, either model structure (independence assumptions, features, etc.) or model parameters. There was and is nothing inherently unsupervised about this idea; we considered the use of a prior in supervised learning by maximum *a posteriori* estimation for generative models (section 3.3.7) and conditional models (section 3.5.5). The use of a prior is also possible in unsupervised learning with generative models. If we think of the parameters $\mathbf{w}$ as the value taken by random variable $\mathbf{W}$, we can define a parameterized model over $\mathbf{W}$, $p_{\mathbf{v}}(\mathbf{W})$. This prior probability of $\mathbf{W}$ becomes a factor in the objective function, so that the learning problem becomes:

$$\max_{\mathbf{w}} p_{\mathbf{v}}(\mathbf{W} = \mathbf{w}) \times \prod_{i=1}^{\tilde{N}} \sum_{\boldsymbol{y} \in \mathcal{Y}_{\tilde{\boldsymbol{x}}_i}} p_{\mathbf{w}}(\boldsymbol{X} = \tilde{\boldsymbol{x}}_i, \boldsymbol{Y} = \boldsymbol{y}) \tag{4.36}$$

The above can be solved (approximately) using the EM algorithm if maximum *a posterior* estimation can be accomplished with the given prior $p_{\mathbf{v}}$. The change is simple: rather than MLE on the M step, we perform MAP estimation. For multinomial-based models, priors built out of Dirichlet distributions with $\alpha\boldsymbol{\rho} > \mathbf{1}$ give a closed form for the MAP estimate, and "MAP EM" is no more difficult than classical EM.

In current literature, the term "Bayesian" usually implies something more than the use of a prior; it implies that the parameters $\mathbf{W}$ are treated as a hidden variable in the same way that $\boldsymbol{Y}$ is treated as a hidden variable. This means that all values of $\mathbf{W}$ are to be considered, and we take an average weighted by the probability of each. The generative process is typically as follows:

1. Draw numerical vector $\mathbf{w}$ from the distribution $p_{\mathbf{v}}(\mathbf{W})$. (The parameters $\mathbf{v}$ define the prior over $\mathbf{W}$ and are typically specified in advance.)

2. For $i \in \{1, \ldots, \tilde{N}\}$, draw $\langle \tilde{\boldsymbol{x}}_i, \boldsymbol{y}_i \rangle$ from $p_{\mathbf{w}}(\boldsymbol{X}, \boldsymbol{Y})$. Hide $\boldsymbol{y}_i$, so that only $\tilde{\boldsymbol{x}}_i$ is observed.

The likelihood here is similar to the one in equation 4.36, only now we integrate over all values of $\mathbf{W}$ instead of maximizing:

$$\int_{\mathbf{w}} p_{\mathbf{v}}(\mathbf{W} = \mathbf{w}) \prod_{i=1}^{\tilde{N}} \sum_{\boldsymbol{y} \in \mathcal{Y}_{\tilde{\boldsymbol{x}}_i}} p_{\mathbf{w}}(\boldsymbol{X} = \tilde{\boldsymbol{x}}_i, \boldsymbol{Y} = \boldsymbol{y}) \tag{4.37}$$

The full Bayesian approach does not seek to optimize anything; instead, it offers inference over the missing values: the collection of $\boldsymbol{Y}_i$ and $\mathbf{W}$. For all possible values of the missing outputs,

$\langle \boldsymbol{y}_1, \ldots \boldsymbol{y}_{\tilde{N}} \rangle \in \mathcal{Y}_{\tilde{\boldsymbol{x}}_1} \times \cdots \times \mathcal{Y}_{\tilde{\boldsymbol{x}}_{\tilde{N}}}$,

$$p(\boldsymbol{Y}_1 = \boldsymbol{y}_1, \ldots, \boldsymbol{Y}_{\tilde{N}} = \boldsymbol{y}_{\tilde{N}} \mid \boldsymbol{X}_1 = \tilde{\boldsymbol{x}}_1, \ldots, \boldsymbol{X}_{\tilde{N}} = \tilde{\boldsymbol{x}}_{\tilde{N}}, \mathbf{v}) = \frac{\int_{\mathbf{w}} p_{\mathbf{v}}(\mathbf{W} = \mathbf{w}) \prod_{i=1}^{\tilde{N}} p_{\mathbf{w}}(\boldsymbol{X} = \tilde{\boldsymbol{x}}_i, \boldsymbol{Y} = \boldsymbol{y}_i)}{\int_{\mathbf{w}} p_{\mathbf{v}}(\mathbf{W} = \mathbf{w}) \prod_{i=1}^{\tilde{N}} \sum_{\boldsymbol{y}' \in \mathcal{Y}_{\tilde{\boldsymbol{x}}_i}} p_{\mathbf{w}}(\boldsymbol{X} = \tilde{\boldsymbol{x}}_i, \boldsymbol{Y} = \boldsymbol{y}')} \tag{4.38}$$

All examples are conditionally independent of each other only through the random variable $\mathbf{W}$, which is hidden. We do not fix a particular value for $\mathbf{W}$, and therefore we cannot perform inference separately for each example. We can also infer the posterior probability of different values of $\mathbf{W}$:

$$p(\mathbf{W} = \mathbf{w} \mid \boldsymbol{X}_1 = \tilde{\boldsymbol{x}}_1, \ldots, \boldsymbol{X}_{\tilde{N}} = \tilde{\boldsymbol{x}}_{\tilde{N}}, \mathbf{v}) = \frac{p_{\mathbf{v}}(\mathbf{W} = \mathbf{w}) \prod_{i=1}^{\tilde{N}} \sum_{\boldsymbol{y} \in \mathcal{Y}_{\tilde{\boldsymbol{x}}_i}} p_{\mathbf{w}}(\boldsymbol{X} = \tilde{\boldsymbol{x}}_i, \boldsymbol{Y} = \boldsymbol{y})}{\int_{\mathbf{w}} p_{\mathbf{v}}(\mathbf{W} = \mathbf{w}) \prod_{i=1}^{\tilde{N}} \sum_{\boldsymbol{y}' \in \mathcal{Y}_{\tilde{\boldsymbol{x}}_i}} p_{\mathbf{w}}(\boldsymbol{X} = \tilde{\boldsymbol{x}}_i, \boldsymbol{Y} = \boldsymbol{y}')} \tag{4.39}$$

And, more generally, we can infer the posterior probability of both the collection of $\boldsymbol{Y}_i$ and $\mathbf{W}$, jointly:

$$p(\boldsymbol{Y}_1 = \boldsymbol{y}_1, \ldots, \boldsymbol{Y}_{\tilde{N}} = \boldsymbol{y}_{\tilde{N}}, \mathbf{W} = \mathbf{w} \mid \boldsymbol{X}_1 = \tilde{\boldsymbol{x}}_1, \ldots, \boldsymbol{X}_{\tilde{N}} = \tilde{\boldsymbol{x}}_{\tilde{N}}, \mathbf{v}) = \frac{p_{\mathbf{v}}(\mathbf{W} = \mathbf{w}) \prod_{i=1}^{\tilde{N}} p_{\mathbf{w}}(\boldsymbol{X} = \tilde{\boldsymbol{x}}_i, \boldsymbol{Y} = \boldsymbol{y}_i)}{\int_{\mathbf{w}} p_{\mathbf{v}}(\mathbf{W} = \mathbf{w}) \prod_{i=1}^{\tilde{N}} \sum_{\boldsymbol{y}' \in \mathcal{Y}_{\tilde{\boldsymbol{x}}_i}} p_{\mathbf{w}}(\boldsymbol{X} = \tilde{\boldsymbol{x}}_i, \boldsymbol{Y} = \boldsymbol{y}')} \tag{4.40}$$

(Finding the best assignment of all $\boldsymbol{Y}_i$ and $\mathbf{W}$ is an example of "most probable explanation" inference, discussed below.)

The value of $\mathbf{W}$ is never actually *decided* in a fully Bayesian treatment; we only calculate a posterior distribution over $\mathbf{W}$ (equation 4.39), or over $\boldsymbol{Y}$ (equation 4.38), or over both (equation 4.40). Hence, this approach falls short of learning a predictor h that maps $\mathcal{X}$ to $\mathcal{Y}$. Bayesian inference is not learning *per se*, though one obvious way to choose $\mathbf{w}$ after performing Bayesian inference is to take the most probable value of $\mathbf{w}$ (apply $\text{argmax}_{\mathbf{w}}$ to equation 4.39).

An advantage of Bayesian modeling is that uncertainty about everything—the missing parts of the data, the missing parameter values—can all be handled using the same basic principles. Further, it allows the encoding of prior knowledge in the form of the prior distribution $p_{\mathbf{v}}$ (either the family or the choice of $\mathbf{v}$). For complex problems like linguistic structure prediction, the Bayesian approach is an attractive way of thinking because (as in all generative models) simple components can be combined to jointly model complex data. Particularly in exploratory settings, considering the full posterior over $\boldsymbol{Y}$ or $\mathbf{W}$ may provide insight into the problem or the model.

4.2.1 EMPIRICAL BAYES

In practice, **empirical Bayesian** methods are more frequently used than the full Bayesian approach. In empirical Bayesian learning, we perform maximum likelihood (or, alternatively, maximum *a posteriori*) inference for some variables; in the above abstract example, we might choose $\mathbf{v}$ to make the observed data $\langle \tilde{\boldsymbol{x}}_1, \ldots, \tilde{\boldsymbol{x}}_{\tilde{N}} \rangle$ as likely as possible:

$$\operatorname*{argmax}_{\mathbf{v}} \int_{\mathbf{w}} p_{\mathbf{v}}(\mathbf{W} = \mathbf{w}) \prod_{i=1}^{\tilde{N}} \sum_{\boldsymbol{y} \in \mathcal{Y}_{\tilde{\boldsymbol{x}}_i}} p_{\mathbf{w}}(\boldsymbol{X} = \tilde{\boldsymbol{x}}_i, \boldsymbol{Y} = \boldsymbol{y}) \tag{4.41}$$

When we take the view that $\mathbf{v}$ is a model parameter, empirical Bayesian estimation is no different in principle than maximum likelihood estimation (equation 4.3). In both cases, the value of $\boldsymbol{X}$ is observed. In MLE, $\boldsymbol{Y}$ is hidden and all possible values are considered in a weighted average by their probability, and we aim to find the likelihood-maximizing $\mathbf{w}$. In empirical Bayesian learning, $\boldsymbol{Y}$ and $\mathbf{W}$ are both hidden, with all possible values considered in a weighted average, and we aim to find the likelihood-maximizing $\mathbf{v}$. Empirical Bayes is sometimes called "type II maximum likelihood." After performing empirical Bayesian learning to choose $\mathbf{v}$, it is common to use MAP inference to extract values for, or distributions over, $\boldsymbol{y}$ and/or $\mathbf{w}$ (equations 4.38–4.39). If we seek the most probable values for all unknowns, the inference problem is called **most probable explanation** (MPE); the more general problem of finding some variables (and possibly marginalizing out others) is maximum *a posteriori* inference, of which maximum *a posteriori* estimation (discussed in section 3.3.7) is a special case.

4.2.2 LATENT DIRICHLET ALLOCATION

Latent Dirichlet allocation (LDA; Blei et al., 2003) is one of the simplest Bayesian models for text. Here we describe it as a Bayesian version of a unigram language model that is trained on a collection of documents that are assumed to each have an individual blend of "topics" that influence their different word histograms. Let $\Sigma = \{\sigma_1, \ldots, \sigma_V\}$ denote the vocabulary. Let K be a fixed number of topics. Let the training data consist of $\langle \tilde{\boldsymbol{x}}_1, \ldots, \tilde{\boldsymbol{x}}_{\tilde{N}} \rangle$, where each $\tilde{\boldsymbol{x}}_i$ is a *document*. Let $\tilde{\boldsymbol{x}}_i = \langle \tilde{x}_{i,1}, \ldots, \tilde{x}_{i,|\tilde{\boldsymbol{x}}_i|} \rangle$, each $\tilde{x}_{i,j} \in \Sigma$. The generative process is as follows:[6]

1. For $k \in \{1, \ldots, K\}$, draw a multinomial distribution $\boldsymbol{\beta}_k = \langle \beta_{k,1}, \ldots, \beta_{k,V} \rangle$ from the V-dimensional Dirichlet distribution parameterized by α_{u} and $\boldsymbol{\rho}_{\mathrm{u}}$. $\boldsymbol{\beta}_k$ is the unigram distribution

[6]We use the version with "smoothing" described in section 5.4 of Blei et al. (2003). Our notation is somewhat different, however, in order to elucidate the connection between LDA and other NLP models.

over words in Σ specific to the kth topic. (In our notation, α_u and $\boldsymbol{\rho}_\text{u}$ are part of "**v**," and each $\boldsymbol{\beta}_k$ is part of "**w**.")

2. For $i \in \{1, \ldots, \tilde{N}\}$:

   (a) Draw a multinomial distribution over topics $\boldsymbol{\theta}_i = \langle \theta_{i,1}, \ldots, \theta_{i,K} \rangle$ from the K-dimensional Dirichlet distribution parameterized by α_t and $\boldsymbol{\rho}_\text{t}$. This represents the relative proportions of each of the K topics to appear in the ith document. (In our notation, α_t and $\boldsymbol{\rho}_\text{t}$ are part of "**v**," and each $\boldsymbol{\theta}_i$ is part of "**w**" or, possibly, "$\boldsymbol{y}$.")

   (b) Choose a document length n_i from some distribution. (The lengths are not explicitly modeled; because document lengths are always observed, there is no need to make this distribution explicit or estimate it, as the probability over n_i will always cancel out.)

   (c) For $j \in \{1, \ldots, n_i\}$:

      i. Draw a topic $y_{i,j}$ according to $\boldsymbol{\theta}_i$.

      ii. Draw a word $\tilde{x}_{i,j}$ according to $\boldsymbol{\beta}_{y_{i,j}}$.

      iii. Hide $y_{i,j}$ (it is unobserved).

   (d) Hide $\boldsymbol{\theta}_i$ (it is unobserved).

The probability model, then, is given by:

$$p(\tilde{\boldsymbol{x}}_1, \ldots, \tilde{\boldsymbol{x}}_{\tilde{N}} \mid \alpha_\text{u}, \boldsymbol{\rho}_\text{u}, \alpha_\text{t}, \boldsymbol{\rho}_\text{t}) = \tag{4.42}$$
$$\int_{\boldsymbol{\beta}} \underbrace{\left(\prod_{k=1}^{K} p_{\alpha_\text{u}, \boldsymbol{\rho}_\text{u}}(\boldsymbol{\beta}_k) \right)}_{\text{step 1}} \left(\prod_{i=1}^{\tilde{N}} \int_{\boldsymbol{\theta}_i} \underbrace{p_{\alpha_\text{t}, \boldsymbol{\rho}_\text{t}}(\boldsymbol{\theta}_i)}_{\text{step 2a}} \prod_{j=1}^{n_i} \sum_{y_{i,j} \in \{1, \ldots, K\}} \underbrace{p_{\boldsymbol{\theta}_i}(y_{i,j})}_{\text{step 2(c)i}} \underbrace{p_{\boldsymbol{\beta}_{y_{i,j}}}(\tilde{x}_{i,j})}_{\text{step 2(c)ii}} \right)$$

The result of LDA is a probabilistic model that breaks word distributions down into topic-specific unigram models. The topics are discovered unsupervisedly and, in many settings, have been shown to be remarkably intuitive. Topics can alternately be understood as word *clusters*, where the cluster a word belongs in is essentially determined by the documents it tends to occur in. The $\boldsymbol{\theta}_i$ variables can be understood either as document-specific weights or as part of the structure to be inferred; mathematically the result is the same.

LDA can be understood as a generative, Bayesian approach to **dimensionality reduction**. Other such techniques include principle component analysis (Pearson, 1901), latent semantic analysis (Deerwester et al., 1990), and probabilistic variants (Hofmann, 1999).

Note that LDA can be applied in a "full" Bayesian way, where α_t, $\boldsymbol{\rho}_\text{t}$, α_u, and $\boldsymbol{\rho}_\text{u}$ are fixed in advance, or in an empirical Bayesian way (section 4.2.1), where they chosen to maximize the likelihood of the data. LDA has been extended in many ways; the ability to augment a model with new evidence and experiment with variations on its independence assumptions are key advantages of probabilistic models in general. Most relevant to the examples considered in this book, we direct the reader to Goldwater and Griffiths (2007), who give a Dirichlet-based treatment of hidden Markov models. Cohen et al. (2009) give a Bayesian treatment of probabilistic context-free grammars, using Dirichlet and other priors.

4.2.3 EM IN THE EMPIRICAL BAYESIAN SETTING

In the empirical Bayesian setting, EM does not fundamentally change. The E step still calculates posteriors over hidden variables, and the M step still uses those posteriors to fill in the missing information and update the maximum likelihood estimate of the parameters to be optimized. Consider LDA (in the notation of section 4.2.2):

- In the E step, we require a posterior distribution over all the missing information: $q(\langle \boldsymbol{\beta}_k \rangle_{k=1}^{K}, \langle \boldsymbol{\theta}_i, \langle y_{i,j} \rangle_{j=1}^{n_i} \rangle_{i=1}^{\tilde{N}})$.

- In the M step, we use the empirical distribution over the observables and q to find the maximum likelihood estimate of the free parameters α_{t}, $\boldsymbol{\rho}_{\mathrm{t}}$, α_{u}, and $\boldsymbol{\rho}_{\mathrm{u}}$.

Compared to more traditional forms of EM, e.g., for parameter estimation as in section 4.1.5, the posterior distribution q is considerably more complex to represent and to calculate. Further, the M step may require an auxiliary optimization routine, as there is no closed form for the update to the Dirichlet parameters. A full discussion of each of these is out of scope; we refer to Blei et al. (2003) for a discussion of EM for LDA, in particular, and briefly discuss techniques the kind of inference required by the E step in empirical Bayesian estimation.

4.2.4 INFERENCE

At a high level of abstraction, Bayesian and empirical Bayesian methods require us to do inference, calculating distributions over some variables given some other variables, with the rest marginalized out (see equations 4.38–4.40). This is not, in principle, different from the inference methods we need for feature expectations when training log-linear models (to be discussed in chapter 5). For example, if we think of G_j as a random variable corresponding to the jth feature function value $g_j(\boldsymbol{X}, \boldsymbol{Y})$, then feature expectation calculations (section 5.2) are a statistic derived from the following distribution over feature values: $\forall a \in \mathrm{Range}(g_j)$,

$$p(g_j(\boldsymbol{X}, \boldsymbol{Y}) = a \mid \boldsymbol{X} = \tilde{\boldsymbol{x}}) = \sum_{\boldsymbol{y} \in \mathcal{Y}_{\tilde{\boldsymbol{x}}}} p(g_j(\boldsymbol{X}, \boldsymbol{Y}) = a \mid \boldsymbol{X} = \tilde{\boldsymbol{x}}, \boldsymbol{Y} = \boldsymbol{y}) \tag{4.43}$$

$$= \frac{\displaystyle\sum_{\boldsymbol{y} \in \mathcal{Y}_{\tilde{\boldsymbol{x}}} : g_j(\tilde{\boldsymbol{x}}, \boldsymbol{y}) = a} p(\boldsymbol{X} = \tilde{\boldsymbol{x}}, \boldsymbol{Y} = \boldsymbol{y})}{\displaystyle\sum_{\boldsymbol{y} \in \mathcal{Y}_{\tilde{\boldsymbol{x}}}} p(\boldsymbol{X} = \tilde{\boldsymbol{x}}, \boldsymbol{Y} = \boldsymbol{y})} \tag{4.44}$$

In general, the expectation statistic, $\int_a p(g_j(\boldsymbol{X}, \boldsymbol{Y}) = a) \times a$, would not be calculated as an explicit integral of terms like those above, but rather through a more efficient summation over structures, $\sum_{\boldsymbol{x}} \sum_{\boldsymbol{y}} p(\boldsymbol{x}, \boldsymbol{y}) \times g_j(\boldsymbol{x}, \boldsymbol{y})$.

The difference between the inference problem faced when summing over values of $\mathbf{W}$, compared with summing over values of $\boldsymbol{Y}$, is that $\mathbf{W}$ ranges over $\mathbb{R}^d$, a continuous space, while $\boldsymbol{Y}$ ranges over a discrete structured space. Combinatorial summing algorithms are often helpful in the latter case, but integrals are a different kind of calculation.

In current research, there are two broad classes of approaches to inference with continuous variables: **Markov chain Monte Carlo** (MCMC) methods, and **variational inference**. We cover each only briefly, presenting the key underlying ideas and directing the reader to more thorough treatments for details.

Markov Chain Monte Carlo

MCMC methods approximate the posterior distribution over a complex set of interdependent variables by generating random samples from the posterior. Consider the scenario of equation 4.40 where Bayesian inference requires calculating distributions over the interdependent random variables $\boldsymbol{Y}_1, \ldots, \boldsymbol{Y}_{\tilde{N}}, \mathbf{W}$. If we have M samples from the posterior, then we can let

$$\begin{aligned} & p(\boldsymbol{Y}_1 = \boldsymbol{y}_1, \ldots, \boldsymbol{Y}_{\tilde{N}} = \boldsymbol{y}_{\tilde{N}}, \mathbf{W} = \mathbf{w} \mid \boldsymbol{X}_1 = \tilde{\boldsymbol{x}}_1, \ldots, \boldsymbol{X}_{\tilde{N}} = \tilde{\boldsymbol{x}}_{\tilde{N}}, \mathbf{v}) \\ & \quad \approx \frac{1}{M} \sum_{m=1}^{M} \mathbf{1}\left\{\boldsymbol{y}_1 = \hat{\boldsymbol{y}}_1^{(m)} \wedge \cdots \wedge \boldsymbol{y}_{\tilde{N}} = \hat{\boldsymbol{y}}_{\tilde{N}}^{(m)} \wedge \mathbf{w} = \hat{\mathbf{w}}^{(m)}\right\} \end{aligned} \tag{4.45}$$

where $\hat{\boldsymbol{y}}_i^{(m)}$ is the mth sample for random variable $\boldsymbol{Y}_i$. This approach lets us approximate marginals as well:

$$p(\boldsymbol{Y}_i = \boldsymbol{y}_i \mid \boldsymbol{X}_1 = \tilde{\boldsymbol{x}}_1, \ldots, \boldsymbol{X}_{\tilde{N}} = \tilde{\boldsymbol{x}}_{\tilde{N}}, \mathbf{v}) \approx \frac{1}{M} \sum_{m=1}^{M} \mathbf{1}\left\{\boldsymbol{y}_i = \hat{\boldsymbol{y}}_i^{(m)}\right\} \tag{4.46}$$

$$p(\mathbf{W} = \mathbf{w} \mid \boldsymbol{X}_1 = \tilde{\boldsymbol{x}}_1, \ldots, \boldsymbol{X}_{\tilde{N}} = \tilde{\boldsymbol{x}}_{\tilde{N}}, \mathbf{v}) \approx \frac{1}{M} \sum_{m=1}^{M} \mathbf{1}\left\{\mathbf{w} = \hat{\mathbf{w}}^{(m)}\right\} \tag{4.47}$$

Expectations can also be approximated:

$$\mathbb{E}\left[g_j(\tilde{\boldsymbol{x}}_i, \boldsymbol{Y})\right] \approx \frac{1}{M} \sum_{m=1}^{M} g_j(\tilde{\boldsymbol{x}}_i, \hat{\boldsymbol{y}}_i^{(m)}) \tag{4.48}$$

Given a sufficiently large sample size M, we can approximate the posterior with high accuracy. The idea underlying MCMC methods is to consider a very large (and possibly infinite) state space $\mathcal{S}$. Let each state $s \in \mathcal{S}$ correspond to an assignment of values to *all* missing variables (in our running example, all $\boldsymbol{Y}_i$ and $\mathbf{W}$); so an arbitrary s is defined by $\langle \hat{\boldsymbol{y}}_1^{(s)}, \ldots, \hat{\boldsymbol{y}}_{\tilde{N}}^{(s)}, \hat{\mathbf{w}}^{(s)} \rangle$. Next, we imagine a random walk among the states $\mathcal{S}$. The random walk never ends, and each step only depends on the previous state. If we design the transition probabilities correctly, then the result is an ergodic Markov chain, so that a sufficiently long random walk will lead to any state $s \in \mathcal{S}$ with probability $p(s)$, the stationary probability of s.

In designing the Markov chain, we want for the stationary probability to be equal to the posterior from which we aim to sample.

$$p(s) = p(\boldsymbol{Y}_1 = \hat{\boldsymbol{y}}_1^{(s)}, \ldots, \boldsymbol{Y}_{\tilde{N}}^{(s)} = \hat{\boldsymbol{y}}_{\tilde{N}}^{(s)}, \mathbf{W} = \hat{\mathbf{w}}^{(s)} \mid \boldsymbol{X}_1 = \tilde{\boldsymbol{x}}_1, \ldots, \boldsymbol{X}_{\tilde{N}} = \boldsymbol{x}_{\tilde{N}}, \mathbf{v}) \tag{4.49}$$

It turns out that it is relatively easy to implement a sampler that will accomplish equation 4.49. **Gibbs sampling** is a technique that defines the sampler in terms of local changes to the assignment. Given the current state, a Gibbs sampler chooses one random variable (either randomly or according to a fixed schedule) and resamples its value conditioned on the current values of all the others. For example, consider a time step in the random walk where we are at state s, and random variable $\boldsymbol{Y}_2$ has been chosen for resampling. We randomly draw $\boldsymbol{Y}_2$'s new value according to:

$$p(\boldsymbol{Y}_2 \mid \boldsymbol{Y}_1 = \hat{\boldsymbol{y}}_1^{(s)}, \boldsymbol{Y}_3 = \hat{\boldsymbol{y}}_3^{(s)}, \ldots, \boldsymbol{Y}_{\tilde{N}} = \hat{\boldsymbol{y}}_{\tilde{N}}^{(s)}, \mathbf{W} = \hat{\mathbf{w}}^{(s)}, \boldsymbol{X}_1 = \tilde{\boldsymbol{x}}_1, \ldots, \boldsymbol{X}_{\tilde{N}} = \tilde{\boldsymbol{x}}_{\tilde{N}}, \mathbf{v}) \tag{4.50}$$

This distribution is over a relatively small space ($\mathcal{Y}_{\tilde{\boldsymbol{x}}_2}$), and it is often manageable to sample from it. Given the new value $\hat{\boldsymbol{y}}_2$, the state in $\mathcal{S}$ to which the random walk proceeds is defined by

$$\left\langle \hat{\boldsymbol{y}}_1^{(s)}, \hat{\boldsymbol{y}}_2, \hat{\boldsymbol{y}}_3^{(s)}, \ldots, \hat{\boldsymbol{y}}_{\tilde{N}}^{(s)}, \hat{\mathbf{w}}^{(s)} \right\rangle$$

Hence, Gibbs sampling can be understood as two reductions: (i) approximating inference by sampling from the posterior and (ii) sampling from the posterior by sampling each random variable, many times.

A big advantage of MCMC sampling methods is that they are often easy to implement; sampling from a single random variable at a time given all the others is usually straightforward. It is also guaranteed to give a sample from the desired distribution, provided that the random walk is long enough. Unfortunately, that can take a long time in practice, and it is generally not easy to tell when the sampler has run "long enough" that the samples are coming from the true posterior distribution. This issue is usually ignored in practice, and it is unknown whether this should affect conclusions drawn from experiments that use MCMC methods.

There are many ways to build MCMC samplers, and much research has focused on speeding their convergence. Important tricks include sampling many random variables at once ("blocked" sampling) and integrating out some random variables during sampling ("collapsed" sampling). There are also generalizations of Gibbs sampling for situations where sampling over a particular random variable exactly is not tractable.

For example, one more general technique often used in NLP is **Metropolis-Hastings sampling** (Hastings, 1970). Consider a scenario where the transition distribution over next states in $\mathcal{S}$ from state s (e.g., equation 4.50) is too expensive to compute. Let $p(S)$ denote the distribution from which we wish to sample, as before, with S ranging over $\mathcal{S}$. Assume that, for any $s \in \mathcal{S}$, $p(s)$ can be computed. Now suppose that we have a proposal distribution $q(S_t \mid S_{t-1})$ that is not equivalent to the desired transition distribution for the Markov chain. A single step in Metropolis-Hastings sampling consists of:

1. Let s denote the current state. Draw a proposal state $s' \in \mathcal{S}$ according to $q(\cdot \mid S_{t-1} = s)$.

2. With the following probability, move to s':

$$\min \left\{ 1, \frac{p(s')q(s \mid s')}{p(s)q(s' \mid s)} \right\} \tag{4.51}$$

(Otherwise, stay in s.)

Metropolis-Hastings is useful when the desired transition distribution is difficult to sample from, but there is a simpler distribution that is a fair approximation of it. If the approximation is poor, the result will be a slower sampler, perhaps much slower. Note that $p(s)$ and $p(s')$ only need to be calculated up to a constant factor, which will cancel out. Note also that Gibbs sampling is a special case of Metropolis-Hastings sampling where the probability of moving from s to s' is 1 (by definition of the proposal distribution).

For more extensive introductions to MCMC methods, we recommend Robert and Casella (2004), Heinrich (2008), and Resnik and Hardisty (2010).

Variational Inference

The second main approximate inference technique used in Bayesian modeling is **variational inference,** which transforms inference calculations like equation 4.40 into an optimization problem. The idea is to first define an alternative distribution q over the variables of interest (the $\boldsymbol{Y}_i$ and $\mathbf{W}$), then optimize the parameters of q to be as close as possible to the "real" model p under which we seek to perform inference. This is accomplished using the variational bound (assume one training example $\tilde{\boldsymbol{x}}$ for simplicity):

$$\begin{aligned}
&\log p(\boldsymbol{X} = \tilde{\boldsymbol{x}} \mid \mathbf{v}) \\
&= \log \int_{\mathbf{w}} \sum_{\boldsymbol{y}} p(\mathbf{W} = \mathbf{w}, \boldsymbol{X} = \tilde{\boldsymbol{x}}, \boldsymbol{Y} = \boldsymbol{y} \mid \mathbf{v}) && (4.52) \\
&= \log \int_{\mathbf{w}} \sum_{\boldsymbol{y}} \frac{p(\mathbf{W} = \mathbf{w}, \boldsymbol{X} = \tilde{\boldsymbol{x}}, \boldsymbol{Y} = \boldsymbol{y} \mid \mathbf{v}) q(\mathbf{W} = \mathbf{w}, \boldsymbol{Y} = \boldsymbol{y})}{q(\mathbf{W} = \mathbf{w}, \boldsymbol{Y} = \boldsymbol{y})} && (4.53) \\
&\geq \int_{\mathbf{w}} \sum_{\boldsymbol{y}} q(\mathbf{W} = \mathbf{w}, \boldsymbol{Y} = \boldsymbol{y}) \log \frac{p(\mathbf{W} = \mathbf{w}, \boldsymbol{X} = \tilde{\boldsymbol{x}}, \boldsymbol{Y} = \boldsymbol{y} \mid \mathbf{v})}{q(\mathbf{W} = \mathbf{w}, \boldsymbol{Y} = \boldsymbol{y})} && (4.54) \\
&= \int_{\mathbf{w}} \sum_{\boldsymbol{y}} q(\mathbf{W} = \mathbf{w}, \boldsymbol{Y} = \boldsymbol{y}) \log \frac{p(\boldsymbol{X} = \tilde{\boldsymbol{x}} \mid \mathbf{v}) \times p(\mathbf{W} = \mathbf{w}, \boldsymbol{Y} = \boldsymbol{y} \mid \boldsymbol{X} = \tilde{\boldsymbol{x}}, \mathbf{v})}{q(\mathbf{W} = \mathbf{w}, \boldsymbol{Y} = \boldsymbol{y})} \\
&= \log p(\boldsymbol{X} = \tilde{\boldsymbol{x}} \mid \mathbf{v}) - D_{KL}\left(q(\mathbf{W}, \boldsymbol{Y}) \| p(\mathbf{W}, \boldsymbol{Y} \mid \boldsymbol{X} = \tilde{\boldsymbol{x}}, \mathbf{v})\right) && (4.55)
\end{aligned}$$

The inequality in equation 4.54 follows from Jensen's inequality. The key insight is that maximizing the variational bound in equation 4.55 equates to minimizing the KL divergence between the alternative distribution q and the model we care about. This breaks down further into two terms:

$$\mathbb{E}_{q(\mathbf{W},\boldsymbol{Y})}[\log p(\mathbf{W},\boldsymbol{Y} \mid \boldsymbol{X} = \tilde{\boldsymbol{x}}, \mathbf{v})] + \boldsymbol{H}(q(\mathbf{W},\boldsymbol{Y})) \tag{4.56}$$

Letting $\mathcal{Q}$ denote the family to which the distribution q belongs, variational inference seeks to solve:

$$\operatorname*{argmax}_{q \in \mathcal{Q}} \mathbb{E}_{q(\mathbf{W},\boldsymbol{Y})}[\log p(\mathbf{W},\boldsymbol{Y} \mid \boldsymbol{X} = \tilde{\boldsymbol{x}}, \mathbf{v})] + \boldsymbol{H}(q(\mathbf{W},\boldsymbol{Y})) \tag{4.57}$$

After solving for q, the approximate posterior is given by q:

$$p(\boldsymbol{Y}_1 = \boldsymbol{y}_1, \ldots, \boldsymbol{Y}_{\tilde{N}} = \boldsymbol{y}_{\tilde{N}}, \mathbf{W} = \mathbf{w} \mid \boldsymbol{X}_1 = \tilde{\boldsymbol{x}}_1, \ldots, \boldsymbol{X}_{\tilde{N}} = \tilde{\boldsymbol{x}}_{\tilde{N}}, \mathbf{v}) \quad \approx \quad q(\mathbf{w}, \boldsymbol{y}_1, \ldots, \boldsymbol{y}_{\tilde{N}})$$

Other posteriors can be derived from q by marginalizing:

$$\begin{aligned} p(\boldsymbol{Y}_i = \boldsymbol{y}_i \mid \boldsymbol{X}_1 = \tilde{\boldsymbol{x}}_1, \ldots, \boldsymbol{X}_{\tilde{N}} = \tilde{\boldsymbol{x}}_{\tilde{N}}, \mathbf{v}) \quad &\approx \quad \sum_{\boldsymbol{y}_1} \cdots \sum_{\boldsymbol{y}_{i-1}} \sum_{\boldsymbol{y}_{i+1}} \cdots \sum_{\boldsymbol{y}_{\tilde{N}}} \int_{\mathbf{w}} q(\mathbf{w}, \boldsymbol{y}_1, \ldots, \boldsymbol{y}_{\tilde{N}}) \\ p(\mathbf{W} = \mathbf{w} \mid \boldsymbol{X}_1 = \tilde{\boldsymbol{x}}_1, \ldots, \boldsymbol{X}_{\tilde{N}} = \tilde{\boldsymbol{x}}_{\tilde{N}}, \mathbf{v}) \quad &\approx \quad \sum_{\boldsymbol{y}_1} \cdots \sum_{\boldsymbol{y}_{\tilde{N}}} q(\mathbf{w}, \boldsymbol{y}_1, \ldots, \boldsymbol{y}_{\tilde{N}}) \end{aligned}$$

Mean field variational inference is the most widely used instance of variational inference; it uses a fully factored form for q; in the scenario of equation 4.40,

$$q(\mathbf{W}, \boldsymbol{Y}_1, \ldots, \boldsymbol{Y}_{\tilde{N}}) = q(\mathbf{W}) \prod_{i=1}^{\tilde{N}} q(\boldsymbol{Y}_i) \tag{4.58}$$

This is part of a choice about the family $\mathcal{Q}$. These strong independence assumptions are computationally convenient. Often the marginals $q(\boldsymbol{Y}_i)$ and $q(\mathbf{W})$ are all that are required for the algorithm calling the variational inference routine (e.g., EM). The form of each q factor must also be decided, and this is usually chosen for computational convenience, as well. It is important to remember that we are not making these assumptions in the model of interest, only in the variational distribution q. Often, mean field variational inference can be used to derive iterative updates for each of the factored q distributions. These are often made in turn, one after another, in a fashion reminiscent of both E step updates in EM and random updates in Gibbs sampling. Indeed, these updates can look strikingly similar to the updates made during the E step of the EM algorithm. Somewhat confusingly, variational inference is often used as an approximate E step for the empirical Bayesian EM algorithm (see section 4.2.3). This embedding of variational inference (which happens to itself resemble some EM algorithms) within EM is sometimes called **variational EM**.

Variational inference can be faster than Gibbs sampling, although it, too, is an iterative algorithm and can require considerable time to converge—though it is an *optimization* algorithm, and it is therefore possible to track changes in the free variables to detect when some convergence threshold has been reached (unlike Gibbs sampling). One flaw is that it is biased; unlike MCMC methods, it is not guaranteed to eventually converge to the desired posterior. Another challenge is that the mechanical steps to derive variational EM can require considerable arithmetic with some sophisticated tricks. This can make variational EM rather difficult to implement correctly. For a more extensive introduction to variational inference, see Wainwright and Jordan (2008).

We close this section by noting that approximate inference is an area of active research. The techniques described above are not limited to Bayesian methods or to unsupervised learning; in fact, Gibbs sampling has been exploited for training and decoding in supervised NLP models with non-local features (Finkel et al., 2005), and many approximate inference algorithms used in supervised learning can be understood as variational approximations (Martins et al., 2010).

4.2.5 NONPARAMETRIC BAYESIAN METHODS

A loose end in unsupervised structure learning is often the dimensionality of the hidden variable. How many topics K should be used in LDA? How many states should be used in an HMM? The Bayesian approach provides a solution in the form of **nonparametric** models. The term "nonparametric" is potentially confusing. It does *not* mean that the model has no parameters. It rather suggests that we make weaker assumptions about the family $\mathcal{P}$ of models we might learn, allowing the family to become more complex when warranted by the data. For hidden variable models, this often means that the dimensionality of the hidden space can be arbitrarily large, and "grows" with the data. The word "infinite" is often used when naming nonparametric models, to evoke this "growing with the data" metaphor (Beal et al., 2002). Nonparametric models should not be confused with nonparametric statistical hypothesis tests (discussed in appendix section B.2.5).

In nonparametric modeling, the dimensionality of the hidden variable is inferred rather than fixed. Bayesian models need not be nonparametric (those discussed above were generally parametric), and nonparametric models need not be Bayesian (the K nearest neighbors technique, used rarely in NLP, is not Bayesian). One possibility in the generative modeling approach we consider here is to define a random variable K over $\mathbb{N}$ corresponding to the number of clusters or HMM states. By performing maximum *a posteriori* estimation, we can optimize the value of K:

$$\max_{k,\mathbf{w}} \log p_{\mathbf{v}}(k, \mathbf{w}) + \sum_{i=1}^{\tilde{N}} \log \sum_{\boldsymbol{y}} p_{\mathbf{w}}(\tilde{\boldsymbol{x}}_i, \boldsymbol{y}) \tag{4.59}$$

This idea is closely related to the information-theoretic principle of minimum description length (Rissanen, 1978); it is instantiated in statistics as the Akaike (1974) information criterion and the Bayesian information criterion (Schwarz, 1978). The choice of k is also sometimes called "model selection," though it a special case of a wider class of model selection problems. Note that in this setting, increasing k can never decrease the second term; more possible hidden variables allow more expressive models and therefore the possibility of improving fit to the data. (A $(k+1)$-state model can always simulate a k-state model by ignoring one state, and thus can achieve at least as high a likelihood score.) The prior over models is typically designed to prefer smaller k, so depending on the strength of the prior, the learner will try to strike a balance between fitting the data and choosing a more concise model.

The Bayesian approach to nonparametric modeling does not "choose" K's value, but instead: (i) defines a prior over models with all possible values of K, and (ii) sums over $k \in \mathbb{N}$, weighting each by its probability. The most common tool for this in NLP to date has been the **Dirichlet process** (not to be confused with the Dirichlet distribution, though the two are connected, as we will see). Here, we briefly describe models based on the **Pitman-Yor process**, of which the Dirichlet process is a special case. We do not discuss inference with these models, instead directing the interested reader to papers where they are applied.

GEM Stick-Breaking Process

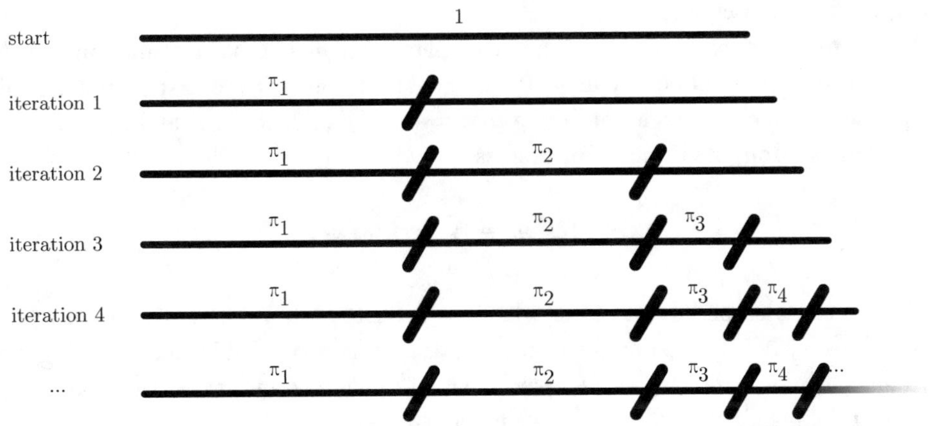

Figure 4.2: An illustration of the first four rounds of the stick-breaking process. Each of the infinitely many iterations breaks off a portion of the remainder of the stick, giving an infinitely long vector of stick lengths $\langle \pi_1, \pi_2, \ldots \rangle$ that sums to one.

Consider a stick of length one unit that can be broken anywhere. A **GEM distribution** defines a probability distribution over the many ways to break the stick into a sequence of countably infinite pieces. It is known as a "stick-breaking" process. It has two parameters, $b \in [0, 1]$ (the "discount" parameter) and $\alpha \in (-b, +\infty)$ (the "concentration" parameter), and the generative process is as follows:

1. For $i \in \{1, 2, \ldots\}$:

(a) Draw v_i from the Beta distribution $\text{Beta}(1 - b, \alpha + ib)$.[7] Note that the distribution's parameters depend on the iteration number i.

(b) Define the ith stick length π_i to be $v_i \prod_{j=1}^{i-1}(1 - v_j)$.

For an illustration, see figure 4.2. The result is an infinitely long vector of values $\boldsymbol{\pi} = \langle \pi_1, \pi_2, \ldots \rangle$. On average, the stick lengths will decay as i increases. If the reader is tempted to puzzle over how we might represent this infinitely long vector, note that we will not directly represent $\boldsymbol{\pi}$; it will be (approximately) marginalized out by the inference algorithm.

Infinite Mixture

Continuing the definition of a Pitman-Yor process, we next let $\mathcal{U}$ denote an event space. A draw from the Pitman-Yor will return a distribution over $\mathcal{U}$. $\mathcal{U}$ may be continuous or discrete, but it is guaranteed that a distribution over $\mathcal{U}$ drawn from the Pitman-Yor process will be nonzero for (only) a countably infinite subset of $\mathcal{U}$.

To accomplish this, the Pitman-Yor uses a parameter $\boldsymbol{\rho}$, a "base" distribution over $\mathcal{U}$. The parametric form of $\boldsymbol{\rho}$ could be anything. In the generative process, we first sample an infinitely long sequence of elements of $\mathcal{U}$, according to $\boldsymbol{\rho}$: $\boldsymbol{u} = \langle u_1, u_2, \ldots \rangle$. Given $\boldsymbol{\pi}$ and $\boldsymbol{u}$, let $\boldsymbol{\theta}$ denote the distribution drawn from the Pitman-Yor process:

$$\forall u \in \mathcal{U}, \; \theta_u = \sum_{i=1}^{\infty} \pi_i \mathbf{1}\{u_i = u\} \tag{4.61}$$

We next consider special cases. First, when $b = 0$, the Pitman-Yor process becomes a **Dirichlet process** (Ferguson, 1973). The Dirichlet process was originally defined by the following property: for any finite partition of $\mathcal{U}$, $\langle \mathcal{U}_1, \ldots \mathcal{U}_n \rangle$ (such that $\bigcup_{i=1}^{n} \mathcal{U}_i = \mathcal{U}$ and if $i \neq j$ then $\mathcal{U}_i \cap \mathcal{U}_j = \emptyset$), then consider the marginals of $\boldsymbol{\theta}$ over the n partitioned events:

$$\theta_{\mathcal{U}_1} = \sum_{u \in \mathcal{U}_1} \theta_u, \theta_{\mathcal{U}_2} = \sum_{u \in \mathcal{U}_2} \theta_u, \ldots, \theta_{\mathcal{U}_n} = \sum_{u \in \mathcal{U}_n} \theta_u,$$

The above n-dimensional multinomial distribution is distributed according to a Dirichlet distribution with parameters $\langle \alpha \sum_{u \in \mathcal{U}_1} \rho_u, \ldots, \alpha \sum_{u \in \mathcal{U}_n} \rho_u \rangle$. This is how the Dirichlet process was originally defined, and it highlights the connection between the Dirichlet *distribution* and the Dirichlet *process*; namely, if $\mathcal{U}$ is finite, then the Dirichlet process is simply a Dirichlet distribution with concentration parameter α and mean $\boldsymbol{\rho}$ (see section 3.3.7).

[7] The Beta distribution is a continuous distribution over values in $(0, 1)$. It defines:

$$p_{\alpha_0,\alpha_1}(x) = \frac{x^{\alpha_0 - 1}(1 - x)^{\alpha_1 - 1}}{\text{B}(\alpha_0, \alpha_1)} = \frac{x^{\alpha_0 - 1}(1 - x)^{\alpha_1 - 1}}{\int_{t=0}^{1} t^{\alpha_0 - 1}(1 - t)^{\alpha_1 - 1}} \tag{4.60}$$

where the denominator is known as the Beta function. It is the special case of a Dirichlet distribution over binomial distributions as outcomes (two events).

Pitman-Yor Language Model

We consider the use of a Pitman-Yor process as a prior distribution over unigram language models. Consider an observation of a corpus $\boldsymbol{x} = \langle x_1, x_2, \ldots, x_n \rangle$, each word $x_i \in \Sigma$. We let Σ, which is $\mathcal{U}$ in the notation above, be defined by all sequences of characters in Υ: $\Sigma = \Upsilon^*$.

Let $\boldsymbol{\rho}$, the base distribution over words, be defined by:

1. Let $t = 1$.
2. Draw the tth character in the word uniformly from $\Upsilon \cup \{\text{◉}\}$.
3. If ◉ was not drawn, increment t and go to step 2. Otherwise, stop.

The full generative process for the corpus is:[8,9]

- Draw an infinitely long sequence of values $\boldsymbol{\pi} = \langle \pi_1, \pi_2, \ldots \rangle$, according to a GEM distribution with parameters b and α.
- Draw an infinitely long sequence of words from $\boldsymbol{\rho}$, denoted by $\langle \sigma_1, \sigma_2, \ldots \rangle$. Note that the same word may be drawn more than once.
- Define the unigram distribution $\boldsymbol{\theta}$ over words by:

$$\forall \sigma \in \Sigma, \qquad \theta_\sigma = \sum_{i=1}^{\infty} \pi_i \mathbf{1}\{\sigma_i = \sigma\} \tag{4.62}$$

- For $i = 1$ to n: draw x_i from the distribution $\boldsymbol{\theta}$.

Alternative Story: Chinese Restaurant Process

The above generative story is not practical because of the infinitely long sequences $\boldsymbol{\pi}$ and $\boldsymbol{\sigma}$, both of which are hidden variables. It is therefore helpful to describe a variant of the above story that marginalizes out $\boldsymbol{\theta}$, rather than representing it directly. The **Chinese restaurant process** is a generative story that defines the same distribution without explicitly representing $\boldsymbol{\theta}$ (or $\boldsymbol{\pi}$ or $\boldsymbol{\sigma}$), by instead considering only the distribution over a word token x_i given the words previously generated:

1. Draw σ_1 from $\boldsymbol{\rho}$, and let $x_1 = \sigma_1$. Let t denote the number of draws from the base distribution $\boldsymbol{\rho}$ that have occurred so far, so $t = 1$. Let $\mathit{freq}(1; \langle x_1 \rangle) = 1$. In the "Chinese restaurant" analogy, the first customer has entered a restaurant and seated himself at the first table.
2. For $i = 2$ to n:

[8]We assume n is fixed, but it could be effectively generated by including a stop symbol ◉ in Σ or sampling it directly from a distribution over whole numbers.

[9]This model closely follows a simple example from Teh (2006).

(a) We consider a random variable Y_i that takes a value in $\{1, 2, \ldots, t, t+1\}$. In the Chinese restaurant analogy, this is the number of the table that the ith customer will sit, and we will set the value of the ith word x_i to be σ_{y_i}. For each $j \in \{1, \ldots, t+1\}$, assign probability $Y_i = j$ according to:

$$p(Y_i = j \mid y_1, \ldots, y_{i-1}) = \begin{cases} \dfrac{freq(j; \langle y_1, \ldots, y_{i-1} \rangle) - b}{\alpha + i - 1} & \text{if } j \in \{1, \ldots, t\} \\ \dfrac{\alpha + bt}{\alpha + i - 1} & \text{if } j = t + 1 \end{cases} \tag{4.63}$$

This corresponds to the ith customer joining the jth table, the probability of which is dependent on how many previous customers have already joined that table. There is some probability reserved for the customer choosing to be the first to sit at a new table that is as-yet unoccupied ($Y_i = t + 1$).

(b) If $y_i = t + 1$, then sample σ_{t+1} from the base distribution $\boldsymbol{\rho}$ and increment t. Whatever the value of y_i is, let $x_i = \sigma_{y_i}$.

The Chinese restaurant process is an alternative view of the same probability distribution as the infinite mixture. It replaces the infinite hidden variables $\boldsymbol{\pi}$ and $\boldsymbol{\sigma}$ with the n-length sequence of hidden variables $\boldsymbol{Y}$. It highlights the fact that the words in the corpus are not distributed independently of each other; each word's distribution depends on all the previous words. This view is used to design Monte Carlo inference algorithms for models that are based on Pitman-Yor processes. Such algorithms take advantage of the exchangeability property of Pitman-Yor processes: the order of the observed x_is makes no difference to the probability $p_{b,\alpha}(\boldsymbol{x})$.

Infinite-State Models in NLP

Nonparametric Bayesian models based on Pitman-Yor or Dirichlet processes have been explored widely in natural language processing. They are attractive for two reasons: (i) they provide a well-founded method for inferring the dimensionality of a hidden variable (or, more generally, the complexity of the model), and (ii) they provide a framework for modeling a common phenomenon in linguistic data of discrete power-law distributions. This effect, sometimes called **Zipf's law** after the linguist who observed it, is a tendency for the empirical probability of an event to be inversely proportional to its *rank*. That is, the nth most frequent event will have probability proportional, roughly, to $\frac{1}{n}$. Zipf (1935) noted this tendency in the distribution of words in text. The same kind of power-law distribution is observable in the posterior distribution over events resulting from the Pitman-Yor process-based infinite mixtures discussed above. This property is sometimes called a "rich get richer" dynamic: as more data is generated, events that are frequent become even more so, though the tail of infrequent events becomes ever longer.

Examples of infinite-state models applied to linguistic structure are often based on *hierarchical* Pitman-Yor and Dirichlet processes (Teh et al., 2005), where the base distribution of one Pitman-Yor process is defined using another, to permit sharing. Example applications include language modeling (Goldwater et al., 2006a, Teh, 2006), segmentation (Goldwater et al., 2006b), part of speech tagging (Goldwater and Griffiths, 2007), coreference and entity resolution (Daumé and Marcu, 2005, Haghighi and Klein, 2007), unsupervised refinements of syntactic parse structure (Cohn et al., 2009, Finkel et al., 2007, Liang et al., 2007), and synchronous grammar induction (Blunsom et al., 2009).

Adaptor Grammars

Adaptor grammars are a model due to Johnson et al. (2007a) that bring together probabilistic context-free grammars (section 3.3.4) and Pitman-Yor processes. Rather than having an arbitrary number of values of a hidden state variable (cf. Finkel et al., 2007, Liang et al., 2007), adaptor grammars have an arbitrarily large number of structural elements used in deriving grammatical structures.

We give a simple version first, and then the more general form. Consider a PCFG with nonterminals $\mathcal{N}$, terminals Σ, and start symbol $S \in \mathcal{N}$. Let $\mathcal{R}$ denote the production rules, and for any rule $\boldsymbol{r} \in \mathcal{R}$, let $\rho_{\boldsymbol{r}}$ be the rule's probability (conditioned on its lefthand side).

In our simple adaptor grammar, we let the PCFG be the base distribution $\boldsymbol{\rho}$. After the GEM process allocates probability to countably infinitely many mixture components, each mixture component is assigned a parse tree drawn from the PCFG. The result is a distribution over trees that tend to repeat, verbatim, with a long tail of utterances that occur very few times.

In the general setting, some subset of the nonterminals, $\mathcal{M} \subseteq \mathcal{N}$, is chosen to be "adaptable." This means that there is a separate Pitman-Yor process for each adaptable nonterminal, and when the time comes to expand an instance of some nonterminal $M \in \mathcal{M}$, we draw from its own infinite mixture. As a result, constituents rooted in adapted nonterminals will be distributed in a Zipfian way, with a few very common phrases repeated often.

In the Chinese restaurant view, each adaptable nonterminal $M \in \mathcal{M}$ has its own restaurant, and each M generated corresponds to a customer entering the M-restaurant. When a customer sits at a new table, this triggers the generation of a new tree rooted in M, which may involve customers entering other nonterminals' restaurants.

Adaptor grammars have been applied to the problem of inferring hidden grammatical derivations for unparsed strings. Johnson et al. (2007a) first applied them to a word segmentation task; they have also been applied to named entity structure learning by Elsner et al. (2009) and dependency grammar induction by Cohen et al. (2010).

4.2.6 DISCUSSION

Nonparametric Bayesian methods are attractive in unsupervised linguistic structure prediction because they allow some of the difficult decisions—how many states should be in the model?—to be made empirically. The Pitman-Yor process (and Dirichlet process) that underlies most of the research in this area to date has the attractive property of heavy-tailed, Zipfian posteriors that intuitively match what we observe in real natural language data. It is important to keep in mind that many priors are possible for Bayesian inference, that nonparametric modeling and Bayesian modeling are two orthogonal choices about models, and that there is more than one way to apply Bayesian thinking (e.g., MAP estimation, empirical Bayesian learning, full Bayesian inference).

4.3 HIDDEN VARIABLE LEARNING

A recent and highly promising direction in supervised learning has been the combination of discriminative learning criteria with hidden variables. In section 4.1, when considering unsupervised learning, we treated $\boldsymbol{Y}$, the desired output, as a hidden variable, and in section 4.2 we made the parameters of our linear prediction model into a random variable $\mathbf{W}$ that was also hidden. Here we consider the case where the model is augmented with additional hidden variables that are interpreted not as the desired output ($\boldsymbol{Y}$), but rather as information missing from the incomplete *input* $\boldsymbol{X}$. A classic example is in translation, where the alignments between words and phrases in an input sentence $\boldsymbol{x}$ and an output sentence $\boldsymbol{y}$ (in a different language) are posited by the model, but are not required to be reported in the final output. Structured hidden variables are, at this writing, now used in many NLP problems, including those where the output random variable $\boldsymbol{Y}$ is a binary decision (Chang et al., 2010, Das and Smith, 2009).

Recall that in chapter 3, the learning problem for input random variable $\boldsymbol{X}$ and output random variable $\boldsymbol{Y}$ was framed as

$$\begin{aligned} &\min_{h \in \mathcal{H}} \mathbb{E}[\mathit{loss}(\boldsymbol{X}, \boldsymbol{Y}; h)] + \mathit{model\text{-}complexity}(h) \\ &\approx \min_{h \in \mathcal{H}} \frac{1}{\tilde{N}} \sum_{i=1}^{\tilde{N}} \mathit{loss}(\tilde{\boldsymbol{x}}_i, \tilde{\boldsymbol{y}}_i; h) + \mathit{model\text{-}complexity}(h) \end{aligned} \tag{4.64}$$

where the training sample distribution approximates the expectation over values of $\boldsymbol{X}$ and $\boldsymbol{Y}$, and many options exist for the loss and the model complexity.

In hidden variable learning, we add a third random variable, denoted here by $\boldsymbol{Z}$, whose value is "hidden" or "latent," meaning that its value is not known even at training time. A classic example of this idea is a mixture model, in which the distribution over $\boldsymbol{X}$ and $\boldsymbol{Y}$ depends on the choice of one of several mixture components:

$$p(\boldsymbol{X} = \boldsymbol{x}, \boldsymbol{Y} = \boldsymbol{y}) = \sum_{\boldsymbol{z} \in \mathcal{Z}} p(\boldsymbol{Z} = \boldsymbol{z}) p(\boldsymbol{X} = \boldsymbol{x}, \boldsymbol{Y} = \boldsymbol{y} \mid \boldsymbol{Z} = \boldsymbol{z}) \tag{4.65}$$

$\mathcal{Z}$ might be binary or range over a large structured space (similar to $\mathcal{X}$ and $\mathcal{Y}$), or even be continuous. The model might also take a different generative structure, e.g., choosing $\boldsymbol{X}$ first, $\boldsymbol{Z}$ conditioned on $\boldsymbol{X}$, and $\boldsymbol{Y}$ conditioned on $\boldsymbol{Z}$:

$$p(\boldsymbol{X} = \boldsymbol{x}, \boldsymbol{Y} = \boldsymbol{y}) = p(\boldsymbol{X} = \boldsymbol{x}) \sum_{\boldsymbol{z} \in \mathcal{Z}} p(\boldsymbol{Z} = \boldsymbol{z} \mid \boldsymbol{X} = \boldsymbol{x}) p(\boldsymbol{Y} = \boldsymbol{y} \mid \boldsymbol{Z} = \boldsymbol{z}) \tag{4.66}$$

Or it might be an undirected model defined using features on $\boldsymbol{X}, \boldsymbol{Y}$, and $\boldsymbol{Z}$:

$$p(\boldsymbol{X} = \boldsymbol{x}, \boldsymbol{Y} = \boldsymbol{y}) = \frac{1}{z_{\mathbf{w}}} \sum_{\boldsymbol{z} \in \mathcal{Z}} \exp \mathbf{w}^\top \mathbf{g}(\boldsymbol{x}, \boldsymbol{y}, \boldsymbol{z}) \tag{4.67}$$

We can think of $\boldsymbol{Z}$ as a part of the input which is unknown, or part of the output which is uninteresting except for its help in predicting $\boldsymbol{Y}$ from $\boldsymbol{X}$.

Normally, the choice to use a hidden variable is driven by hopes of making the model over $\boldsymbol{Y}$ given $\boldsymbol{X}$ more expressive. The most commonly cited example in NLP is **word alignment**. For NLP tasks involving two sentences, like translation (where $\boldsymbol{X}$ is one sentence and $\boldsymbol{Y}$ is its translation in another language), it is often helpful to posit a correspondence between words in the two sentences. In section 1.9, we discussed correspondences as structures that might be predicted. In the hidden variable view, we do not actually wish to predict the correspondence as an end in itself, we simply view it as a useful part of the description of how our two sentences relate to each other, to be used for the purpose of predicting $\boldsymbol{y}$ from $\boldsymbol{x}$.

For a true hidden variable, whose value is of no consequence to the final task, the loss function remains unchanged and still takes the form $loss(\boldsymbol{x}, \boldsymbol{y}; h)$. We briefly consider extensions of generative, conditional, and large margin discriminative models to the hidden variable case.

4.3.1 GENERATIVE MODELS WITH HIDDEN VARIABLES

In the generative setting, the model does not distinguish between inputs and outputs; they are all generated randomly according to the joint distribution the model defines. Including a hidden variable, then, is no different than solving an unsupervised learning problem. Techniques like EM (section 4.1.1) can be applied for parameter estimation, solving the marginalized maximum likelihood estimation problem:

$$\max_{p_{\mathbf{w}} \in \mathcal{P}} \sum_{i=1}^{\tilde{N}} \log \sum_{z \in \mathcal{Z}} p_{\mathbf{w}}(\boldsymbol{X} = \tilde{\boldsymbol{x}}_i, \boldsymbol{Y} = \tilde{\boldsymbol{y}}_i, \boldsymbol{Z} = \boldsymbol{z}) \tag{4.68}$$

This objective is well-motivated in the same way that maximum likelihood learning of a mixture model is motivated: we have some uncertainty about each training example, so we use our model of the various possible analyses ($\boldsymbol{z} \in \mathcal{Z}$) to consider each in turn and take a probablistically weighted average. Unlike a classic mixture model where $\mathcal{Z} = \{1, \ldots, K\}$ for K mixture components, $\mathcal{Z}$ is often a combinatorial space of possible hidden values.

In the loss function view, we can view this approach as a generalized log loss function (just as in equation 3.6):

$$loss(\boldsymbol{x}, \boldsymbol{y}; h = p_{\mathbf{w}}) = -\log \sum_{\boldsymbol{z} \in \mathcal{Z}} p_{\mathbf{w}}(\boldsymbol{x}, \boldsymbol{y}, \boldsymbol{z}) \tag{4.69}$$

Unlike the loss functions in chapter 3, this loss function is not convex in general, and therefore equation 4.68 is not globally concave. As in unsupervised learning, a local maximum is the best we can hope for.

To date, the most successful application of this approach has been in parsing. Since Johnson (1998), it has been well understood that context-free grammars extracted directly from expert-annotated treebanks can be greatly improved by transforming the nonterminal set into more fine-grained categories. For instance, Johnson achieved significant parsing performance improvements by augmenting each nonterminal token with the label of its parent. (For example, under the rule S $\rightarrow$ NP VP, the NP becomes NP^{S}, while under VP $\rightarrow$ VBD NP, the NP becomes NP^{VP}. Therefore, the categories of subject NPs and object NPs are distinguished.) Klein and Manning (2003) accomplished many more gains by exploring similar grammar transformations. These techniques effectively pass information around the tree, weakening the effective independence assumptions about different parts of the structure without giving up the CFG formalism. Of course, increasing the size of the nonterminal set *does* increase the expressive power of the model, but the basic inference and learning algorithms are the same.

More recently, attempts to automatically improve the nonterminal labels have met with success. Chiang and Bikel (2002) sought to infer lexical heads of constituents as latent variables associated with nonterminals. Matsuzaki et al. (2005), Prescher (2005), Dreyer and Eisner (2006), and Petrov et al. (2006) augmented the nonterminal states each with a discrete hidden variable, often called a "latent annotation." These latent variables are interdependent through the weights of the rich production rules, and by applying the EM algorithm, these models essentially perform soft clustering on the nonterminal tokens to maximize the likelihood of the observable part of the trees. Note that, for a sentence $\tilde{\boldsymbol{x}}$ and its tree $\tilde{\boldsymbol{y}}$, the E step sums only over labelings of $\tilde{\boldsymbol{y}}$ (denoted, perhaps, $\boldsymbol{z} \in \mathcal{Z}_{\tilde{\boldsymbol{y}}}$), which does not require inference over all the parse trees for $\tilde{\boldsymbol{x}}$. Instead, a dynamic programming algorithm that traverses the fixed tree $\tilde{\boldsymbol{y}}$ in an upward pass and then a downward pass reverse algorithm can calculate the required posteriors (to be discussed in section 5.2.1).

4.3.2 CONDITIONAL LOG-LINEAR MODELS WITH HIDDEN VARIABLES

The log-linear modeling approach described in section 3.5 is straightforward to extend with hidden variables. In the classic setting, we define a distribution over outputs given inputs as in equation 3.60, repeated here:

$$p(\boldsymbol{Y} = \boldsymbol{y} \mid \boldsymbol{X} = \boldsymbol{x}) = \frac{\exp \mathbf{w}^\top \mathbf{g}(\boldsymbol{x}, \boldsymbol{y})}{z_{\mathbf{w}}(\boldsymbol{x})} \tag{4.70}$$

The additional variable $\boldsymbol{Z}$ can be included, though we are still interested only in the conditional distribution of $\boldsymbol{Y}$ given $\boldsymbol{X}$. The new form is:

$$p(\boldsymbol{Y} = \boldsymbol{y} \mid \boldsymbol{X} = \boldsymbol{x}) = \frac{\sum_{\boldsymbol{z} \in \mathcal{Z}} \exp \mathbf{w}^\top \mathbf{g}(\boldsymbol{x}, \boldsymbol{y}, \boldsymbol{z})}{z_{\mathbf{w}}(\boldsymbol{x})} \tag{4.71}$$

$$z_{\mathbf{w}}(\boldsymbol{x}) = \sum_{\boldsymbol{y} \in \mathcal{Y}} \sum_{\boldsymbol{z} \in \mathcal{Z}} \exp \mathbf{w}^\top \mathbf{g}(\boldsymbol{x}, \boldsymbol{y}, \boldsymbol{z}) \tag{4.72}$$

Note that we use an undirected, feature-based linear model to score complete configurations $\langle \boldsymbol{x}, \boldsymbol{y}, \boldsymbol{z} \rangle$ just as we did in the fully-observable case.

The objective function for learning is:

$$\max_{\mathbf{w}} \sum_{i=1}^{\tilde{N}} \log \sum_{z \in \mathcal{Z}} p(\tilde{\boldsymbol{y}}_i, \boldsymbol{z} \mid \tilde{\boldsymbol{x}}_i) \tag{4.73}$$

$$= \max_{\mathbf{w}} \sum_{i=1}^{\tilde{N}} \left(\log \left(\sum_{z \in \mathcal{Z}} \exp \mathbf{w}^\top \mathbf{g}(\tilde{\boldsymbol{x}}_i, \tilde{\boldsymbol{y}}_i, \boldsymbol{z}) \right) - \log \left(\sum_{\boldsymbol{y} \in \mathcal{Y}} \sum_{z \in \mathcal{Z}} \exp \mathbf{w}^\top \mathbf{g}(\tilde{\boldsymbol{x}}_i, \boldsymbol{y}, \boldsymbol{z}) \right) \right)$$

Just like generative models with hidden variables, the above objective is non-convex in the model parameters $\mathbf{w}$. To see this, consider that functions of the form

$$-\log \sum_i \exp \left(\mathbf{w}^\top \mathbf{g}_i \right) \tag{4.74}$$

are globally concave (Boyd and Vandenberghe, 2004, section 3.1.5). The partition function $z_{\mathbf{w}}(\boldsymbol{x})$ takes this form. Naturally, negating such a function results in a globally *convex* function. Equation 4.73 replaces equation 3.60's linear first term with a globally convex function, making the objective neither globally concave nor globally convex. (See figure 4.3 for an illustrative example.) We therefore resort to algorithms that find a local optimum given some starting point, just as in the unsupervised case.

The hidden-variable conditional modeling approach has been applied in many scenarios (Blunsom et al., 2008, Clark and Curran, 2004, Koo and Collins, 2005, Quattoni et al., 2007, Sutton et al., 2007, Wang et al., 2007, *inter alia*).

4.3.3 LARGE MARGIN METHODS WITH HIDDEN VARIABLES

While the name "hidden variable learning" suggests a probabilistic treatment of $\boldsymbol{Z}$ as a random variable, it is also possible to think of $\boldsymbol{Z}$ as missing information when learning within the non-probabilistic large margin framework. Here the idea is to score $\langle \boldsymbol{y}, \boldsymbol{z} \rangle$ pairs much as we scored outputs $\boldsymbol{Y}$ previously, using the linear model formulation of the score, $\mathbf{w}^\top \mathbf{g}(\boldsymbol{x}, \boldsymbol{y}, \boldsymbol{z})$.

In the training data, values of $\boldsymbol{Z}$ are not known, so we optimize over them. Yu and Joachims (2009) describe a framework for this, generalizing margin-rescaled structural SVMs (section 3.6.4). One way to view their approach is to alternate between optimizing the values of $\boldsymbol{z}$ (for each training example $\tilde{\boldsymbol{x}}_i$) and the values of the weights $\mathbf{w}$. Their objective takes the form:

$$\min_{\mathbf{w}} \frac{1}{2} \|\mathbf{w}\|^2 + C \sum_{i=1}^{\tilde{N}} \left(\max_{\langle \boldsymbol{y}, \boldsymbol{z} \rangle \in \mathcal{Y} \times \mathcal{Z}} \mathit{cost}(\tilde{\boldsymbol{x}}_i, \boldsymbol{y}, \boldsymbol{z}, \tilde{\boldsymbol{y}}_i) + \mathbf{w}^\top \mathbf{g}(\tilde{\boldsymbol{x}}_i, \boldsymbol{y}, \boldsymbol{z}) \right) - \left(\max_{z \in \mathcal{Z}} \mathbf{w}^\top \mathbf{g}(\tilde{\boldsymbol{x}}_i, \tilde{\boldsymbol{y}}_i, \boldsymbol{z}) \right) \tag{4.75}$$

Note that the cost function may depend on the predicted hidden variable value, but not the "true" one (which is assumed not to be known). The above formulation reduces to the structural SVM formulation of equation 3.103 if $\mathcal{Z}$ contains a single trivial value. Yu and Joachims (2009) propose an alternating optimization procedure not unlike EM. Their E-like step chooses the values of $\boldsymbol{z}_i$

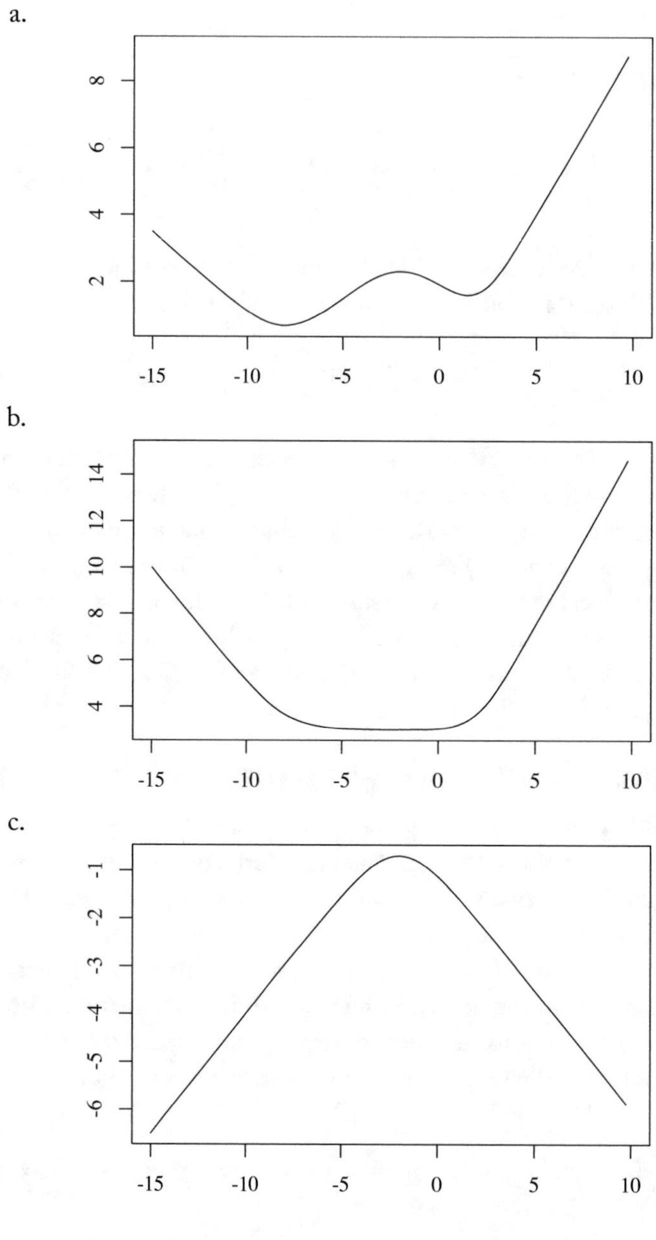

Figure 4.3: (a) A function $f = f_{convex} + f_{concave}$ that is neither globally concave nor convex; (b) $f_{convex}(x) = \log(e^{3x/2} + e^{-x-5} + e^3)$; (c) $f_{concave}(x) = -\log(e^{x/2+1} + e^{-x/2-1})$, which has the form of equation 4.74.

for each $\tilde{x}_i$, then their M-like step improves the weights in a manner similar to structural SVM learning.

4.4 CONCLUSION

This chapter has surveyed some techniques for learning models of linguistic structure from incomplete data. A summary is shown in figure 4.4. We focused on homogeneous training data, where all training examples are missing the same information from outputs or inputs. Unsupervised (and semisupervised) NLP is, at this writing, an intense area of research; the basic ideas put forward here underlie much of the current work and have been included to provide a foundation for understanding the challenges of learning linguistic structure models when some or all of the structure is unseen in the training sample.

technique	fixed in training	optimized or inferred	integrated out	formula
supervised MLE (section 4.3):				
joint model	$\boldsymbol{x}, \boldsymbol{y}$	w	z	$\max_{\mathrm{w}} \sum_{\boldsymbol{z}} p_{\mathrm{w}}(\boldsymbol{x}, \boldsymbol{y}, z)$
conditional model	$\boldsymbol{x}, \boldsymbol{y}$	w	z	$\max_{\mathrm{w}} \sum_{\boldsymbol{z}} p_{\mathrm{w}}(\boldsymbol{y}, z \mid \boldsymbol{x})$
unsupervised:				
MLE	$\boldsymbol{x}$	w	y	$\max_{\mathrm{w}} \sum_{y} p_{\mathrm{w}}(\boldsymbol{x}, y)$
"winner-take-all"	$\boldsymbol{x}$	w, y	–	$\max_{\mathrm{w}, y} p_{\mathrm{w}}(\boldsymbol{x}, y)$
MAP	$\boldsymbol{x}$, **v**	w	y	$\max_{\mathrm{w}} p_{\mathbf{v}}(\mathrm{w}) \sum_{y} p_{\mathrm{w}}(\boldsymbol{x}, y)$
contrastive	$\boldsymbol{x}, \mathcal{N}_{\boldsymbol{x}}$	w	y	$\max_{\mathrm{w}} \sum_{y} p_{\mathrm{w}}(\boldsymbol{x}, y \mid \boldsymbol{x} \in \mathcal{N}_{\boldsymbol{x}})$
empirical Bayesian	$\boldsymbol{x}$	v	w, y	$\max_{\mathrm{v}} \int_{\mathrm{w}} p_{\mathrm{v}}(\mathrm{w}) \sum_{y} p_{\mathrm{w}}(\boldsymbol{x}, y)$
fully Bayesian	$\boldsymbol{x}$, **v**	w	y	$\forall \mathrm{w}, \dfrac{p_{\mathbf{v}}(\mathrm{w}) \sum_{y} p_{\mathrm{w}}(\boldsymbol{x}, y)}{\int_{\mathrm{w}'} p_{\mathbf{v}}(\mathrm{w}') \sum_{y'} p_{\mathrm{w}'}(\boldsymbol{x}, y')}$

Figure 4.4: Probabilistic learning methods. The supervised methods generalize those in chapter 3 by adding hidden variable $\boldsymbol{Z}$; in chapter 3, $\boldsymbol{Z}$ is empty. "Inferred" means that the probability distribution over values is calculated. "Winner-take-all" is exemplified by (hard) K-means (section 4.1.3).

CHAPTER 5

Beyond Decoding: Inference

In chapter 2, we discussed at length algorithms for finding the solution to the decoding problem,

$$\operatorname*{argmax}_{y \in \mathcal{Y}} \mathbf{w}^\top \mathbf{g}(\boldsymbol{x}, \boldsymbol{y}) \tag{5.1}$$

for some input $\boldsymbol{x}$ in structured space $\mathcal{X}$. In chapters 3 and 4, we discussed a variety of learning algorithms, some of which required calculations quite different from equation 5.1. In particular, these inference problems included:

- Partition functions for globally-normalized conditional log-linear models (section 3.5):

$$z_{\mathbf{w}}(\boldsymbol{x}) = \sum_{\boldsymbol{y}' \in \mathcal{Y}} \exp \mathbf{w}^\top \mathbf{g}(\boldsymbol{x}, \boldsymbol{y}') \tag{5.2}$$

- Feature expectations for globally normalized conditional log-linear models (section 3.5.4):

$$\begin{aligned} \mathbb{E}_{\tilde{p}(\boldsymbol{X}) \cdot p_{\mathbf{w}}(\boldsymbol{Y} \mid \boldsymbol{X})}[g_j(\boldsymbol{X}, \boldsymbol{Y})] &= \frac{1}{\tilde{N}} \sum_{i=1}^{\tilde{N}} \sum_{\boldsymbol{y} \in \mathcal{Y}} p_{\mathbf{w}}(\boldsymbol{Y} = \boldsymbol{y} \mid \boldsymbol{X} = \tilde{\boldsymbol{x}}_i) g_j(\tilde{\boldsymbol{x}}_i, \boldsymbol{y}) \\ &= \frac{1}{\tilde{N}} \sum_{i=1}^{\tilde{N}} \sum_{\boldsymbol{y} \in \mathcal{Y}} \frac{\exp \mathbf{w}^\top \mathbf{g}(\tilde{\boldsymbol{x}}_i, \boldsymbol{y})}{z_{\mathbf{w}}(\tilde{\boldsymbol{x}}_i)} g_j(\tilde{\boldsymbol{x}}_i, \boldsymbol{y}) \end{aligned} \tag{5.3}$$

- Minimum Bayes risk decoding (mentioned briefly in section 3.3.9, footnote 10), an alternative to the usual decoding rule of equation 5.1:

$$\operatorname*{argmin}_{\boldsymbol{y} \in \mathcal{Y}} \sum_{\boldsymbol{y}' \in \mathcal{Y}} p_{\mathbf{w}}(\boldsymbol{Y} = \boldsymbol{y}' \mid \boldsymbol{X} = \boldsymbol{x}) \mathit{cost}(\boldsymbol{x}, \boldsymbol{y}, \boldsymbol{y}') \tag{5.4}$$

- Cost-augmented decoding, used in training large margin models (section 3.6):

$$\operatorname*{argmax}_{\boldsymbol{y} \in \mathcal{Y}} \mathbf{w}^\top \mathbf{g}(\boldsymbol{x}, \boldsymbol{y}) + \mathit{cost}(\boldsymbol{x}, \boldsymbol{y}, \boldsymbol{y}^*) \tag{5.5}$$

- Decoding with hidden variables (relevant to hidden variable models in section 4.3):

$$\operatorname*{argmax}_{\boldsymbol{y} \in \mathcal{Y}} \sum_{\boldsymbol{z} \in \mathcal{Z}} \exp \mathbf{w}^\top \mathbf{g}(\boldsymbol{x}, \boldsymbol{y}, \boldsymbol{z}) \tag{5.6}$$

Here we discuss each of these problems in turn.

5.1 PARTITION FUNCTIONS: SUMMING OVER $\mathcal{Y}$

Given an input $\boldsymbol{x} \in \mathcal{X}$, we are interested in the summation of the exponentiated scores $\exp \mathbf{w}^\top \mathbf{g}(\boldsymbol{x}, \boldsymbol{y})$, over all valid $\boldsymbol{y} \in \mathcal{Y}_{\boldsymbol{x}} \subseteq \mathcal{Y}$ that can be paired with $\boldsymbol{x}$. This is known as the partition function:

$$z_{\mathbf{w}}(\boldsymbol{x}) = \sum_{\boldsymbol{y} \in \mathcal{Y}_{\boldsymbol{x}}} \exp \mathbf{w}^\top \mathbf{g}(\boldsymbol{x}, \boldsymbol{y}) \tag{5.7}$$

The set of NLP problems for which the above sum can be calculated efficiently is relatively restricted.

5.1.1 SUMMING BY DYNAMIC PROGRAMMING

When $\mathcal{Y}_{\boldsymbol{x}}$ can be efficiently represented as a weighted graph or a weighted hypergraph, dynamic programming is available. Recall that, in this problem representation, each hyperpath corresponds to one $\boldsymbol{y} \in \mathcal{Y}_{\boldsymbol{x}}$. The sum over hyperpaths, then, corresponds to the sum over $\mathcal{Y}_{\boldsymbol{x}}$. The only alteration to the semiring DP equations (e.g., those used in section 2.3) is the change to either the REAL or LOG-REAL semiring.

If we use the REAL semiring, each hyperpath's score is the exponentiated linear score of the corresponding $\boldsymbol{y}$ with $\boldsymbol{x}$, $\exp \mathbf{w}^\top \mathbf{g}(\boldsymbol{x}, \boldsymbol{y})$. The $\oplus$ operator is $+$, so that aggregating over hyperpaths corresponds to summing over their scores. We interpret $\{v\}_{\mathcal{K}}$ as $\exp v$. The result will be that $\mathsf{goal} = z_{\mathbf{w}}(\boldsymbol{x})$.

If we use the LOG-REAL semiring, each hyperpath's score is the linear score of the corresponding $\boldsymbol{y}$ with $\boldsymbol{x}$, $\mathbf{w}^\top \mathbf{g}(\boldsymbol{x}, \boldsymbol{y})$. The $\oplus$ operator is the "log-add" operation, $\mathsf{u} \oplus \mathsf{v} = \log(e^{\mathsf{u}} + e^{\mathsf{v}})$, so that aggregating over hyperpaths corresponds to "log-summing" over their scores. We interpret $\{v\}_{\mathcal{K}}$ as v. The result will be that $\mathsf{goal} = \log z_{\mathbf{w}}(\boldsymbol{x})$. The LOG-REAL semiring is sometimes preferable for avoiding underflow due to floating point arithmetic, though the log-add operation is somewhat more expensive than simple addition.

Two classic algorithms are special cases:

- The **forward algorithm**, which sums over the HMM-assigned probabilities of all label sequences for $\boldsymbol{x}$, is simply the DP of figure 2.16 (or figure 2.17 for the second-order case) instantiated with the REAL or LOG-REAL semiring. See figure 5.1.

- The **inside algorithm**, which sums over the PCFG-assigned probabilities of all phrase-structure parses (derivations) for $\boldsymbol{x}$, is simply the DP of figure 2.18 instantiated with the REAL or LOG-REAL semiring.

It is important to remember that these are special cases; there are many combinatorial structured models for which dynamic programming is available; these two summing algorithms are merely the best known.

Interestingly, for weighted graph problems, the REAL-semiring DP can also be represented as a linear system of equations (inspection of figure 5.1 should make this clear for the forward algorithm). One of the variables in the system is goal, and the rest are the values of the other theorems. For weighted hypergraph problems, the equations become polynomial in the variables. We know of no attempts to solve for $z_{\mathbf{w}}(\boldsymbol{x})$ by directly solving these systems of equations using numerical methods, but we note the connection for completeness.

$$\begin{aligned}
\forall \ell \in \Lambda, \quad \mathsf{v}(\ell, 1) &= \left(\exp \mathbf{w}^\top \mathbf{f}(\boldsymbol{x}, ⬗, \ell, 1)\right) \\
\forall \ell \in \Lambda, i \in \{2, \ldots, n\}, \quad \mathsf{v}(\ell, i) &= \sum_{\ell' \in \Lambda} \mathsf{v}(\ell', i-1) \times \left(\exp \mathbf{w}^\top \mathbf{f}(\boldsymbol{x}, \ell', \ell, i)\right) \\
\mathsf{goal} &= \sum_{\ell \in \Lambda} \mathsf{v}(\ell, n) \times \left(\exp \mathbf{w}^\top \mathbf{f}(\boldsymbol{x}, \ell, ●, n+1)\right)
\end{aligned} \tag{5.8}$$

Figure 5.1: The forward algorithm: an instantiation of figure 2.16, with the REAL semiring. Note that this is a linear system of $|\Lambda|n + 1$ variables (the $\mathsf{v}(\ell, i)$ and goal) related through $|\Lambda|n + 1$ linear equations. Each of the exp factors is a constant in the linear system. In the special case of HMMs, $\exp \mathbf{w}^\top \mathbf{f}(\boldsymbol{x}, \ell', \ell, i) = \gamma_{\ell',\ell}\eta_{\ell,x_i}$, in the notation of section 3.3.3.

Any scoring function that factors sufficiently locally will support the use of dynamic programming for summing. While many approaches are used for solving TROPICAL-semiring problems, REAL/LOG-REAL-semiring problems are usually solved by first identifying a felicitous ordering and then using tabling methods (section 2.3.4). In the context of decoding we noted two challenges of tabling methods. The first is that felicitous orderings are not always apparent, and cycles in the hypergraph typically require iterative approximations (Goodman, 1999). This problem is even more of a challenge for summing than for decoding since decoding algorithms can often take advantage of "dampening" in cycles (longer cycles receive lower scores and hence do not maximize the DP equations). Exact summing algorithms must include all hyperpaths, though in practice most NLP models do not involve cycles in the hypergraph.

The second challenge is the requirement that—in the weighted logic programming jargon—every provable theorem's value be calculated in the process of solving for goal's value. When summing, we *must* solve the values of all provable and useful theorems if we are to exactly calculate $z_{\mathbf{w}}(\boldsymbol{x})$. All theorems that lead to a proof of goal must have their values calculated, or the sum will not be correct. While this requirement leads to unnecessary work in the decoding case, for summing it *is* necessary. Indeed, agenda-based "search" approaches to solving DPs (section 2.3.4) are less attractive for summing. Making agenda solvers efficient hinges on having a well-constructed priority function that avoids updating any theorem's value more than once. Repeated updates to the same theorem can trigger repeated updates to all theorems it helps prove, and therefore repeated repropagation of updates through the proof structure. This gross inefficiency is to be avoided, and the only way to do so is to order the computation felicitously. If we have a felicitous ordering and know that each provable theorem must be visited at least once, then we know the agenda must be exhausted before the value of goal converges. Therefore, for exact summing, the agenda approach, at best, simulates exactly the tabling approach. An alternative, discussed by Eisner et al. (2005), is to stop the agenda algorithm early and obtain an approximate value for the sum.

5.1.2 OTHER SUMMING ALGORITHMS

There are a small number of special cases where summing over structures can be accomplished efficiently, or where it is known to be computationally hard.

For instance, summing over edge-factored bipartite matching scores (see section 2.4.1 for discussion about decoding) is known to be #P-complete,[1] through its connection to (i) *counting* the number of matchings and (ii) calculating the permanent of a matrix (Valiant, 1979).

Summing over edge-factored directed spanning tree scores (section 2.4.2), can be accomplished efficiently. A result due to Tutte (1984) shows that the determinant of a matrix called the "Kirchhoff matrix" is equal to the logarithm of the partition function. This is known as the **matrix-tree theorem**. The Kirchhoff matrix is of size $n \times n$ for an n-length input sentence, and its determinant can be calculated in $O(n^3)$ time. This connection was pointed out by McDonald and Satta (2007), Smith and Smith (2007), and Koo et al. (2007), to which we refer the reader for details.

In summary, $z_{\mathbf{w}}(\boldsymbol{x})$ is in general an expensive quantity to calculate. Its efficiency depends on the local factoring of features $\mathbf{g}$. When summing is efficient, the algorithms are often closely related to decoding algorithms for the same model, but summing algorithms are usually more expensive than decoding algorithms in practice.

5.2 FEATURE EXPECTATIONS

A summation over all of $\mathcal{Y}_{\boldsymbol{x}}$ is useful if we wish to explicitly calculate probabilities of the form $p_{\mathbf{w}}(\boldsymbol{y} \mid \boldsymbol{x})$. As we have noted, this is not necessary for decoding. Choosing the best $\boldsymbol{y}$ can be done on the basis of the linear scores without exponentiating or normalizing them into probabilities. The time we are most likely to need the quantity $z_{\mathbf{w}}(\boldsymbol{x})$ is during parameter estimation, particularly if we seek to optimize the conditional likelihood (Φ_{LL}; see equation 3.74).

Many current techniques for optimizing Φ_{LL} are based on gradient ascent (discussed at greater length in appendix A). Recall from section 3.5.4 that the first derivative of Φ_{LL} with respect to an arbitrary weight w_j is proportional to:

$$\sum_{i=1}^{\tilde{N}} g_j(\tilde{\boldsymbol{x}}_i, \tilde{\boldsymbol{y}}_i) - \mathbb{E}_{p_{\mathbf{w}}(\boldsymbol{Y} \mid \boldsymbol{X} = \tilde{\boldsymbol{x}}_i)}[g_j(\tilde{\boldsymbol{x}}_i, \boldsymbol{Y})] \tag{5.9}$$

(See the derivation in equation 3.77.) We turn next to **feature expectations** of the form $\mathbb{E}_{p_{\mathbf{w}}(\boldsymbol{Y} \mid \boldsymbol{X} = \boldsymbol{x})}[g_j(\tilde{\boldsymbol{x}}, \boldsymbol{Y})]$. Written out more explicitly, these can be understood as the average value of the feature g_j across all $\boldsymbol{y} \in \mathcal{Y}_{\boldsymbol{x}}$, with each $\boldsymbol{y}$ weighted by its conditional probability given $\boldsymbol{x}$.

[1]A discussion of this complexity class is out of scope; it suffices to say that, if P $\neq$ NP, then an efficient solution does not exist.

Invoking the log-linear form of the model first, then the local factoring assumption,

$$\mathbb{E}_{p_{\mathbf{w}}(\boldsymbol{Y}|\boldsymbol{X}=\boldsymbol{x})}[g_j(\boldsymbol{x},\boldsymbol{Y})] = \left(\frac{1}{z_{\mathbf{w}}(\boldsymbol{x})}\right)\sum_{\boldsymbol{y}\in\mathcal{Y}_{\boldsymbol{x}}}\left(\exp\mathbf{w}^{\top}\mathbf{g}(\boldsymbol{x},\ y)\right)g_j(\boldsymbol{x},\boldsymbol{y}) \tag{5.10}$$

It is convenient to switch notation at this point. We assume that for any $\boldsymbol{x} \in \mathcal{X}$ and any $\boldsymbol{y} \in \mathcal{Y}_{\boldsymbol{x}}$, the feature vector function $\mathbf{g}$ breaks into $\#parts(\boldsymbol{x})$ local parts:

$$\mathbf{g}(\boldsymbol{x},\boldsymbol{y}) = \sum_{i=1}^{\#parts(\boldsymbol{x})}\mathbf{f}(\Pi_i(\boldsymbol{x},\boldsymbol{y})) \tag{5.11}$$

Then:

$$\mathbb{E}_{p_{\mathbf{w}}(\boldsymbol{Y}|\boldsymbol{X}=\boldsymbol{x})}[g_j(\boldsymbol{x},\boldsymbol{Y})] = \left(\frac{1}{z_{\mathbf{w}}(\boldsymbol{x})}\right)\sum_{\boldsymbol{y}\in\mathcal{Y}_{\boldsymbol{x}}}\sum_{i=1}^{\#parts(\boldsymbol{x})}\left(\exp\mathbf{w}^{\top}\mathbf{g}(\boldsymbol{x},\boldsymbol{y})\right)f_j(\Pi_i(\boldsymbol{x},\boldsymbol{y})) \tag{5.12}$$

Let $\mathcal{R}_i(\boldsymbol{x})$ denote the set of possible values for the ith projected part of $\boldsymbol{x}$ with any $\boldsymbol{y}$,

$$\mathcal{R}_i(\boldsymbol{x}) = \{\boldsymbol{\pi} \mid \exists \boldsymbol{y} \in \mathcal{Y}_{\boldsymbol{x}}, \Pi_i(\boldsymbol{x},\boldsymbol{y}) = \boldsymbol{\pi}\} \tag{5.13}$$

and let $\mathcal{R}(\boldsymbol{x})$ denote all possible values for any projected part of $\langle\boldsymbol{x},\boldsymbol{y}\rangle$:

$$\mathcal{R}(\boldsymbol{x}) = \bigcup_{i=1}^{\#parts(\boldsymbol{x})}\mathcal{R}_i(\boldsymbol{x}) \tag{5.14}$$

Generally, speaking, while $|\mathcal{Y}_{\boldsymbol{x}}|$ is usually exponential in the size of $\boldsymbol{x}$, $|\mathcal{R}(\boldsymbol{x})|$ is polynomial-sized. Crucially, each $\boldsymbol{y} \in \mathcal{Y}_{\boldsymbol{x}}$ corresponds exactly to an assignment of $\Pi_i(\boldsymbol{x},\boldsymbol{y})$ to some value $\boldsymbol{\pi}_i \in \mathcal{R}_i(\boldsymbol{x})$. We therefore think of Π_i as a random variable whose value is conditioned on $\boldsymbol{x}$, ranging over $\mathcal{R}_i(\boldsymbol{x})$. Of course, given the values of $\boldsymbol{X}$ and $\boldsymbol{Y}$, the value of Π_i is known (it is, after all, a function of $\boldsymbol{X}$ and $\boldsymbol{Y}$). The different Π_i are *not*, in general, conditionally independent of each other.

$$\begin{aligned}
\mathbb{E}_{p_{\mathbf{w}}(\boldsymbol{Y}|\boldsymbol{X}=\boldsymbol{x})}[g_j(\boldsymbol{x},\boldsymbol{Y})] &= \sum_{i=1}^{\#parts(\boldsymbol{x})}\mathbb{E}_{p_{\mathbf{w}}(\Pi_i|\boldsymbol{X}=\boldsymbol{x})}[f_j(\Pi_i)] \\
&= \frac{\displaystyle\sum_{i=1}^{\#parts(\boldsymbol{x})}\sum_{\boldsymbol{\pi}\in\mathcal{R}_i(\boldsymbol{x})}\left(\sum_{\boldsymbol{y}\in\mathcal{Y}_{\boldsymbol{x}}:\Pi_i(\boldsymbol{x},\boldsymbol{y})=\boldsymbol{\pi}}\exp\mathbf{w}^{\top}\mathbf{g}(\boldsymbol{x},\boldsymbol{y})\right)f_j(\boldsymbol{\pi})}{z_{\mathbf{w}}(\boldsymbol{x})}
\end{aligned} \tag{5.15}$$

It should now be clear that, under local factoring assumptions, if the number of possible "parts" is manageably small, then feature expectations can be calculated by summing over the expectations of features on local parts. Such expectations require us to sum over *subsets* of structures $\boldsymbol{y}$, specifically, one subset per possible part. There are cases where exact calculation of expectations is intractable; for example, DeNero and Klein (2008) showed that calculating expectations under phrase alignments is #P-hard.

In the probabilistic setting, feature expectations are closely related to marginal probabilities. Note that a portion of equation 5.15 is exactly the marginal probability that $\Pi_i(\boldsymbol{x}, \boldsymbol{Y})$ is equal to $\boldsymbol{\pi}$:

$$\frac{\sum_{\boldsymbol{y} \in \mathcal{Y}_{\boldsymbol{x}}:\Pi_i(\boldsymbol{x},\boldsymbol{y})=\boldsymbol{\pi}} \exp \mathbf{w}^\top \mathbf{g}(\boldsymbol{x}, \boldsymbol{y})}{z_{\mathbf{w}}(\boldsymbol{x})} = p_{\mathbf{w}}(\Pi_i(\boldsymbol{x}, \boldsymbol{Y}) = \boldsymbol{\pi} \mid \boldsymbol{X} = \boldsymbol{x}) \tag{5.16}$$

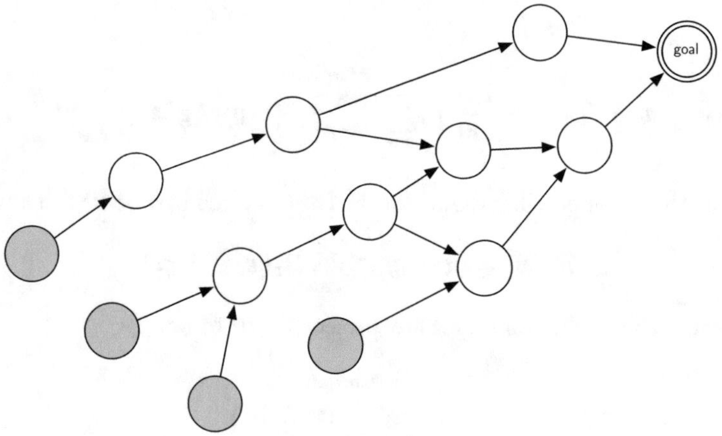

Figure 5.2: A hypothetical path problem. Each path from a gray node to goal corresponds to a proof of goal.

5.2.1 REVERSE DPS

For feature functions that factor locally, dynamic programming can be used to calculate local feature expectations, but we must first extend our repertoire of dynamic programming algorithms to include **reverse DPs**. The way we defined DPs in chapter 2 was as equations for calculating the semiring-sum over scores of proofs of a special goal theorem. DP equations related the value (proof-score $\oplus$-sum) for goal recursively to the values of theorems and axioms that were used in any proof. A reverse DP calculates similar quantities, but the values now correspond always to *subsets* of proofs of goal. Specifically, the reverse value for a theorem is the semiring-sum of scores of proofs of goal *starting from* that theorem.

We consider the case of graph (rather than hypergraph) DPs first. Figure 5.2 shows a directed graph; we can think of each white node as a theorem and each gray node as an axiom. The goal theorem is marked with a double-line. A DP on this graph will calculate the semiring-sum of scores

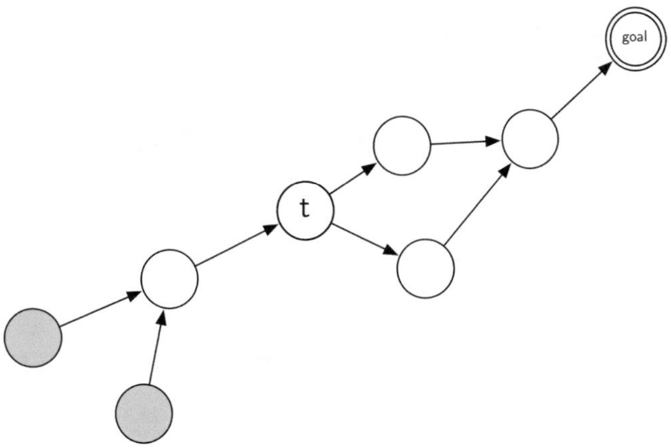

Figure 5.3: A hypothetical path problem. We are interested in calculating the semiring-sum of scores of paths from any gray node through t to goal.

of paths (proofs) into each vertex (theorem). Consider a specific theorem t (see figure 5.3). We are interested in the proof-score sum for goal, restricted to proof-paths that pass through t.

Any proof of goal that uses t corresponds to a path from some start node (axiom) to t to goal. We can therefore break every such proof into two parts: a proof of t and a proof of goal *given* t. These two parts of the proof are separate and independent. Getting to t does not depend on how we later move from t to goal. Once we have t, it does not make any difference which path got us there when we continue onward toward goal. Therefore:

$$\bigoplus_{\text{proofs } p \text{ of goal that depend on t}} \mathit{score}(p) = \left(\bigoplus_{\text{proofs } p' \text{ of t}} \mathit{score}(p') \right) \otimes \left(\bigoplus_{\text{proofs } p'' \text{ of goal given t}} \mathit{score}(p'') \right) \tag{5.17}$$

Note further that other proofs of goal that do not depend on t have no effect on the sum of proof-scores that pass through t. Figure 5.4 illustrates the separation of the two terms in equation 5.17.

It should be clear that the first term in equation 5.17 is the path sum for t, i.e., its value. (In figures 5.2–5.4, there are two such paths.) The second term is the **reverse value**. It can be understood as the semiring-sum of proofs of goal where t is treated as a **1**-valued axiom that must be used in the proof of goal. Equivalently, it is the semiring-sum over paths to goal starting from t.

In the case of figure 2.16, for example, the reverse value of $\mathsf{v}(\ell, i)$ will be the semiring-sum of scores of sequence labelings of $\langle x_{i+1}, \ldots, x_n \rangle$, assuming that $y_i = \ell$ and ignoring the score of

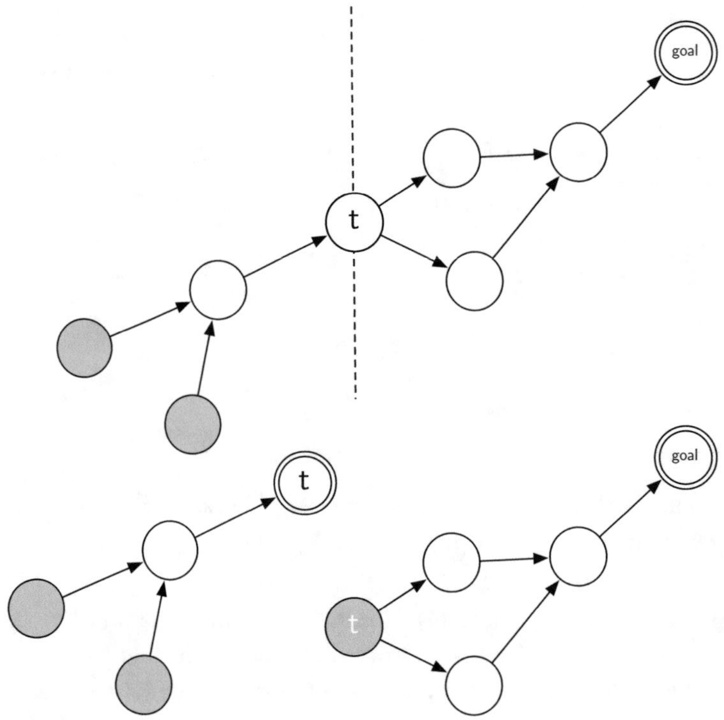

Figure 5.4: A hypothetical path problem. A path from a gray node to t to goal breaks into two parts: a path from a gray node to t and a path from t to goal. Semiring-summing over such paths can be accomplished by $\oplus$-summing over the two types of subpaths separately, then taking the $\otimes$-product of the resulting values.

$\langle x_1, \ldots, x_i \rangle$. It is only possible to calculate such a quantity because of the local factoring assumptions that permitted dynamic programming in the first place.

Interestingly, the reverse values for a DP's theorems can be calculated using another DP, often called the *reverse* DP. The reverse DP can be derived mechanically from the original DP, as we will see. The **backward algorithm**, shown in figure 5.5, is a DP that calculates the reverse values for all of the theorems in figure 2.16. In most scenarios, this program is instantiated with the REAL or LOG-REAL semiring.

The hypergraph case is similar to the graph case, only now the reverse value of a theorem t is understood as the semiring-sum of scores of *hyperpaths* ending in goal where t is now a start-node. Again, the local factoring property is required to hold if we are to separate a complete proof of goal into two parts: the proof of a particular theorem t and the proof of goal that builds on t as if it were an axiom. The classic example of a reverse DP for a hyperpath problem is the **outside algorithm**

$$
\begin{aligned}
\forall \ell \in \Lambda, \quad \mathsf{v}'(\ell, n) &= \left\{\mathbf{w}^\top \mathbf{f}(\boldsymbol{x}, \ell, \bullet, n+1)\right\}_{\mathcal{K}} && (5.18)\\
\forall \ell \in \Lambda, i \in \{n-1, \ldots, 1\}, \quad \mathsf{v}'(\ell, i) &= \bigoplus_{\ell' \in \Lambda} \mathsf{v}'(\ell', i+1) \otimes \left\{\mathbf{w}^\top \mathbf{f}(\boldsymbol{x}, \ell, \ell', i)\right\}_{\mathcal{K}} && (5.19)\\
\mathsf{goal} &= \bigoplus_{\ell \in \Lambda} \mathsf{v}'(\ell, 1) \otimes \left\{\mathbf{w}^\top \mathbf{f}(\boldsymbol{x}, \Rightarrow, \ell, 1)\right\}_{\mathcal{K}} && (5.20)
\end{aligned}
$$

Figure 5.5: The reverse DP for figure 2.16. Under the LOG-REAL semiring, figure 2.16 is the forward algorithm and this is the backward algorithm. The value of $\mathsf{v}'(\ell, i)$ is precisely the reverse value of the theorem $\mathsf{v}(\ell, i)$. $\{p\}_{\mathcal{K}}$ denotes the value of p as interpreted in the semiring; in the LOG-REAL semiring, $\{p\}_{\mathcal{K}} = p$.

shown in figure 5.6. In the hypergraph case, the reverse values depend directly on the original DP's values.

In both the graph and hypergraph cases, it is possible for a theorem to be used more than once to prove goal. The reverse value's definition must be refined slightly to handle this possibility. In a semiring DP, the reverse value of theorem t is the semiring-sum of all scores of all partial proofs of goal such that t is treated not as a theorem whose proof-score contributes to the total, but rather as an axiom with semiring value **1**. If t is used n times in a proof, then each of the n partial proofs will, in general, have a different score, and each must be counted separately.

The reverse value of goal is **1** since the hyperpath from goal to itself is empty and incurs no cost (its score is semiring-**1**).

Reverse values can be calculated in any semiring, but they are mostly used in the REAL and LOG-REAL semirings. One application of TROPICAL-semiring reverse values is in calculating heuristics that may help speed up decoding (see section 2.3.5).

5.2.2 ANOTHER INTERPRETATION OF REVERSE VALUES

Consider a theorem t; t also denotes the value of the theorem. We will let t′ denote the theorem's reverse value. Let us assume the REAL semiring. *Proofs*(t) will denote the set of valid proofs of t, and *Proofs*$_{\mathsf{u}}$(t) will denote the proofs of t that rely on some other theorem u. For a proof p, we let *Axioms*(p) denote the bag of axioms used in p (note that some axioms may be used more than once).

Then:

$$\mathsf{t} = \sum_{p \in Proofs(\mathsf{t})} \prod_{\mathsf{u} \in Axioms(p)} \mathsf{u} \tag{5.21}$$

$$\mathsf{goal} = \sum_{p \in Proofs_{\mathsf{t}}(\mathsf{goal})} \prod_{\mathsf{u} \in Axioms(p)} \mathsf{u} + \sum_{p \in Proofs(\mathsf{goal}) \setminus Proofs_{\mathsf{t}}(\mathsf{goal})} \prod_{\mathsf{u} \in Axioms(p)} \mathsf{u} \tag{5.22}$$

$$= \mathsf{t} \times \mathsf{t}' + \sum_{p \in Proofs(\mathsf{goal}) \setminus Proofs_{\mathsf{t}}(\mathsf{goal})} \prod_{\mathsf{u} \in Axioms(p)} \mathsf{u} \tag{5.23}$$

$$= \mathsf{t} \times \mathsf{t}' + \text{constant}(\mathsf{t}) \tag{5.24}$$

If we wish to take the derivative of goal's value with respect to t's value, we have:

$$\frac{\partial \mathsf{goal}}{\partial \mathsf{t}} = \mathsf{t}' \tag{5.25}$$

In the LOG-REAL semiring, a similar result will hold:

$$\begin{aligned}
\mathsf{t} &= \log \sum_{p \in Proofs(\mathsf{t})} \prod_{\mathsf{u} \in Axioms(p)} \exp \mathsf{u} \\
\mathsf{goal} &= \log \sum_{p \in Proofs(\mathsf{goal})} \prod_{\mathsf{u} \in Axioms(p)} \exp \mathsf{u} \\
&= \log \left(\sum_{p \in Proofs_{\mathsf{t}}(\mathsf{goal})} \prod_{\mathsf{u} \in Axioms(p)} \exp \mathsf{u} + \sum_{p \in Proofs(\mathsf{goal}) \setminus Proofs_{\mathsf{t}}(\mathsf{goal})} \prod_{\mathsf{u} \in Axioms(p)} \exp \mathsf{u} \right) \\
&= \log \left(\exp \mathsf{t} + \mathsf{t}' + \sum_{p \in Proofs(\mathsf{goal}) \setminus Proofs_{\mathsf{t}}(\mathsf{goal})} \prod_{\mathsf{u} \in Axioms(p)} \exp \mathsf{u} \right) \\
\frac{\partial \mathsf{goal}}{\partial \mathsf{t}} &= \frac{1}{\sum_{p \in Proofs(\mathsf{goal})} \prod_{\mathsf{u} \in Axioms(p)} \exp \mathsf{u}} \exp(\mathsf{t} + \mathsf{t}') \\
&= \frac{\exp(\mathsf{t} + \mathsf{t}')}{\exp \mathsf{goal}}
\end{aligned}$$

The above hold for any t at all. Consider these special cases:

- $\mathsf{t} = \mathsf{goal}$. Then $\mathsf{t}' = \mathsf{goal}' = \mathbf{1}$, as noted in section 5.2.1. Therefore, $\frac{\partial \mathsf{goal}}{\partial \mathsf{t}} = 1$ in the REAL semiring and $\exp(\mathsf{goal} + 0) / \exp(\mathsf{goal}) = 1$ in the LOG-REAL semiring.
- t is not used in any proof of goal, i.e., $Proofs_{\mathsf{t}}(\mathsf{goal}) = \emptyset$. Then $\mathsf{t}' = \mathbf{0}$ and $\frac{\partial \mathsf{goal}}{\partial \mathsf{t}} = 0$ in the REAL semiring and $\exp(\mathsf{t} - \infty) / \exp(\mathsf{goal}) = 0$ in the LOG-REAL semiring.

- t is an axiom of the form $\left\{\mathbf{w}^\top \mathbf{f}(\boldsymbol{\pi}_\mathsf{t})\right\}_\mathcal{K}$ for some possible output "part" $\boldsymbol{\pi}_\mathsf{t} \in \mathcal{R}_i(\boldsymbol{x})$ for some i. We let

$$\mathcal{Y}_{\boldsymbol{x},i,\mathsf{t}} = \{\boldsymbol{y} \in \mathcal{Y}_{\boldsymbol{x}} \mid \Pi_i(\boldsymbol{x}, \boldsymbol{y}) = \boldsymbol{\pi}_\mathsf{t}\} \tag{5.26}$$

Since $\mathsf{t} \otimes \mathsf{t}'$ is the semiring-sum of all values of proofs that rely on axiom t, the LOG-REAL-semiring version can be interpreted as

$$\begin{aligned}
\frac{\partial \mathsf{goal}}{\partial \mathsf{t}} &= \frac{\exp(\mathsf{t} + \mathsf{t}')}{\exp \mathsf{goal}} \\
&= \frac{\sum_{\boldsymbol{y} \in \mathcal{Y}_{\boldsymbol{x},i,\mathsf{t}}} \exp \mathbf{w}^\top \mathbf{g}(\boldsymbol{x}, \boldsymbol{y})}{\sum_{\boldsymbol{y} \in \mathcal{Y}_{\boldsymbol{x}}} \exp \mathbf{w}^\top \mathbf{g}(\boldsymbol{x}, \boldsymbol{y})} \\
&= \sum_{\boldsymbol{y} \in \mathcal{Y}_{\boldsymbol{x},i,\mathsf{t}}} p_\mathbf{w}(\boldsymbol{Y} = \boldsymbol{y} \mid \boldsymbol{X} = \boldsymbol{x}) \\
&= p_\mathbf{w}(\boldsymbol{Y} \in \mathcal{Y}_{\boldsymbol{x},i,\mathsf{t}} \mid \boldsymbol{X} = \boldsymbol{x}) \\
&= p_\mathbf{w}(\Pi_i = \boldsymbol{\pi}_\mathsf{t} \mid \boldsymbol{X} = \boldsymbol{x}) && (5.27) \\
&= \mathbb{E}_{p_\mathbf{w}(\Pi_i \mid \boldsymbol{X} = \boldsymbol{x})}[\mathbf{1}\{\Pi_i = \boldsymbol{\pi}_\mathsf{t}\}] && (5.28)
\end{aligned}$$

Hence, the reverse value for an axiom that corresponds to a local factor in a linear model is a posterior probability that projection i of $\langle \boldsymbol{x}, \boldsymbol{Y} \rangle$ takes a certain value, under the model.

5.2.3 FROM REVERSE VALUES TO EXPECTATIONS

We have seen that reverse values in the REAL and LOG-REAL semirings can be understood as first derivatives of goal with respect to theorem and axiom values. We are specifically interested in the following quantities:

$$\frac{\partial \log z_\mathbf{w}(\boldsymbol{x})}{\partial w_j} = \mathbb{E}_{p_\mathbf{w}(\boldsymbol{Y} \mid \boldsymbol{X} = \boldsymbol{x})}[g_j(\boldsymbol{x}, \boldsymbol{Y})] \tag{5.29}$$

In the above, we saw that the reverse value for a local factor axiom t of the form $\left\{\mathbf{w}^\top \mathbf{f}(\boldsymbol{\pi}_\mathsf{t})\right\}_\mathcal{K}$ is equal to the model probability of a "local match" of the ith part of the structure $\boldsymbol{Y}$ to $\boldsymbol{\pi}_\mathsf{t}$ (for some i). The result in equation 5.28 gets us most of the way to equation 5.10.

The next step is to note that local factor axioms are assigned scores based on the local feature functions and weight vectors. In the LOG-REAL semiring,

$$\mathsf{t} = \left\{\mathbf{w}^\top \mathbf{f}(\boldsymbol{\pi}_\mathsf{t})\right\}_\mathcal{K} \tag{5.30}$$

and therefore

$$\frac{\partial \mathsf{t}}{\partial w_j} = f_j(\boldsymbol{\pi}_\mathsf{t}) \tag{5.31}$$

We can put these two pieces together through the chain rule from differential calculus. The value of goal depends on $\mathbf{w}$ through the local factor axioms. For a particular weight w_j, goal may be affected through any or all of these axioms since

$$\mathsf{goal} = \log \sum_{\boldsymbol{y} \in \mathcal{Y}} \exp \mathbf{w}^\top \mathbf{g}(\boldsymbol{x}, \boldsymbol{y}) = \log \sum_{\boldsymbol{y} \in \mathcal{Y}} \exp \sum_{i=1}^{\#parts(\boldsymbol{x})} \mathbf{w}^\top \mathbf{f}(\Pi_i(\boldsymbol{x}, \boldsymbol{y})) \tag{5.32}$$

The chain rule for multiple variables tells us that

$$\frac{\partial \mathsf{goal}}{\partial w_j} = \sum_{i=1}^{\#parts(\boldsymbol{x})} \sum_{\mathsf{t}:\mathsf{t}=\{\mathbf{w}^\top \mathbf{f}(\boldsymbol{\pi}_\mathsf{t})\}_\mathcal{K}} \frac{\partial \mathsf{goal}}{\partial \mathsf{t}} \frac{\partial \mathsf{t}}{\partial w_j} \tag{5.33}$$

and therefore

$$\begin{aligned}
\frac{\partial \mathsf{goal}}{\partial w_j} &= \sum_{i=1}^{\#parts(\boldsymbol{x})} \sum_{\mathsf{t}:\mathsf{t}=\{\mathbf{w}^\top \mathbf{f}(\boldsymbol{\pi}_\mathsf{t})\}_\mathcal{K}} \mathsf{t}' f_j(\boldsymbol{\pi}_\mathsf{t}) & (5.34)\\
&= \sum_{i=1}^{\#parts(\boldsymbol{x})} \sum_{\mathsf{t}:\mathsf{t}=\{\mathbf{w}^\top \mathbf{f}(\boldsymbol{\pi}_\mathsf{t})\}_\mathcal{K}} p_\mathbf{w}(\Pi_i(\boldsymbol{x}, \boldsymbol{Y}) = \boldsymbol{\pi}_\mathsf{t} \mid \boldsymbol{X} = \boldsymbol{x}) f_j(\boldsymbol{\pi}_\mathsf{t}) & (5.35)\\
&= \sum_{i=1}^{\#parts(\boldsymbol{x})} \sum_{\boldsymbol{\pi}} p_\mathbf{w}(\Pi_i(\boldsymbol{x}, \boldsymbol{Y}) = \boldsymbol{\pi} \mid \boldsymbol{X} = \boldsymbol{x}) f_j(\boldsymbol{\pi}) & (5.36)\\
&= \sum_{i=1}^{\#parts(\boldsymbol{x})} \sum_{\boldsymbol{\pi}} \sum_{\boldsymbol{y} \in \mathcal{Y}_{\boldsymbol{x}} : \Pi_i(\boldsymbol{x}, \boldsymbol{y}) = \boldsymbol{\pi}} p_\mathbf{w}(\boldsymbol{Y} = \boldsymbol{y} \mid \boldsymbol{X} = \boldsymbol{x}) f_j(\boldsymbol{\pi}) & (5.37)\\
&= \sum_{i=1}^{\#parts(\boldsymbol{x})} \sum_{\boldsymbol{y} \in \mathcal{Y}_{\boldsymbol{x}}} p_\mathbf{w}(\boldsymbol{Y} = \boldsymbol{y} \mid \boldsymbol{X} = \boldsymbol{x}) f_j(\Pi_i(\boldsymbol{x}, \boldsymbol{y})) & (5.38)\\
&= \sum_{\boldsymbol{y} \in \mathcal{Y}_{\boldsymbol{x}}} p_\mathbf{w}(\boldsymbol{Y} = \boldsymbol{y} \mid \boldsymbol{X} = \boldsymbol{x}) \sum_{i=1}^{\#parts(\boldsymbol{x})} f_j(\Pi_i(\boldsymbol{x}, \boldsymbol{y})) & (5.39)\\
&= \sum_{\boldsymbol{y} \in \mathcal{Y}_{\boldsymbol{x}}} p_\mathbf{w}(\boldsymbol{Y} = \boldsymbol{y} \mid \boldsymbol{X} = \boldsymbol{x}) g_j(\boldsymbol{x}, \boldsymbol{y}) & (5.40)
\end{aligned}$$

where the last line holds by the definition of $\mathbf{g}$ as a sum of local features. Equation 5.34 provides for efficient calculation of $\frac{\partial \mathsf{goal}}{\partial w_j}$; each local factor axiom contributes to the first derivatives of weights that are involved in the local factor. If $\mathbf{f}$ tends to return sparse vectors at local factors, then the feature expectations will be efficient to calculate.

To conclude so far, solving the reverse DP allows straightforward calculation of feature expectations.

5.2.4 DERIVING THE REVERSE DP

The view of a reverse value t' as the first derivative of goal's value with respect to t's value leads to a startlingly simple derivation of a DP for solving *all* of the reverse values in a DP. This is an example of automatic differentiation (Corliss et al., 2002). We will work in the REAL semiring here, then return to the LOG-REAL semiring. The key is to apply the chain rule on the DP equations (leaving variables intact). Consider the following DP inference rule:

$$\mathsf{c}(\boldsymbol{i}) = \sum_{\boldsymbol{j}} \mathsf{a}_1(\boldsymbol{k}_1) \times \mathsf{a}_2(\boldsymbol{k}_2) \times \cdots \times \mathsf{a}_L(\boldsymbol{k}_L) \tag{5.41}$$

Here we use $\boldsymbol{i}$, $\boldsymbol{j}$, $\boldsymbol{k}_1$, and so on, to denote tuples of arguments, which may overlap. Letting $\boldsymbol{k} = \bigcup_{\ell=1}^{L} \boldsymbol{k}_\ell$, it holds that $\boldsymbol{k} = \boldsymbol{i} \cup \boldsymbol{j}$ and $\boldsymbol{i} \cap \boldsymbol{j} = \emptyset$.

Each fully instantiated inference rule in the DP describes an update to one theorem—here, $\mathsf{c}(\boldsymbol{i})$—with the right-hand side corresponding to the quantity by which $\mathsf{c}(\boldsymbol{i})$ is updated. The chain rule tells us that

$$\frac{\partial \mathsf{goal}}{\partial \mathsf{a}_\ell(\boldsymbol{k}_\ell)} = \sum_{\boldsymbol{k} \setminus \boldsymbol{k}_\ell} \frac{\partial \mathsf{goal}}{\partial \mathsf{c}(\boldsymbol{i})} \times \frac{\partial \mathsf{c}(\boldsymbol{i})}{\partial \mathsf{a}_\ell(\boldsymbol{k}_\ell)} \tag{5.42}$$

where the summation is over bindings of all variables that are consistent with $\boldsymbol{k}_\ell$. Making use of reverse values, this gives:

$$\begin{aligned} \mathsf{a}'_\ell(\boldsymbol{k}_\ell) &= \sum_{\boldsymbol{k} \setminus \boldsymbol{k}_\ell} \mathsf{c}'(\boldsymbol{i}) \times \frac{\partial \mathsf{c}(\boldsymbol{i})}{\partial \mathsf{a}_\ell(\boldsymbol{k}_\ell)} & (5.43)\\ &= \sum_{\boldsymbol{k} \setminus \boldsymbol{k}_\ell} \mathsf{c}'(\boldsymbol{i}) \times \prod_{\ell' \in \{1,\ldots,L\} \setminus \{\ell\}} \mathsf{a}_{\ell'}(\boldsymbol{k}_{\ell'}) & (5.44) \end{aligned}$$

Note that the above expression is in exactly the required form for a DP; it is a sum of products. To obtain the reverse DP, we begin with the rules for the original DP, and add in the transformed rules. The original rules must be kept since, in general, the reverse DP will depend on the values of theorems from the original DP.

If $\mathsf{a}_\ell(\boldsymbol{k}_\ell)$ appears as an antecedent in other inference rules, those must be transformed as well, contributing further to $\mathsf{a}'_\ell(\boldsymbol{k}_\ell)$. For example, if these two rules are in the original DP:

$$\begin{aligned} \mathsf{c}(i) &= \sum_{j} \mathsf{a}(i, j) \times \mathsf{b}(j) \\ \mathsf{d}(j) &= \sum_{i} \mathsf{e}(i) \times \mathsf{a}(i, j) \end{aligned}$$

then the reverse rules will include:

$$\begin{aligned}
\mathsf{a}'(i,j) &= \left(\mathsf{c}'(i) \times \mathsf{b}(j)\right) + \left(\mathsf{d}'(j) \times \mathsf{e}(i)\right) + \cdots \\
\mathsf{b}'(j) &= \left(\sum_i \mathsf{c}'(i) \times \mathsf{a}(i,j)\right) + \cdots \\
\mathsf{e}'(i) &= \left(\sum_j \mathsf{d}'(j) \times \mathsf{a}(i,j)\right) + \cdots
\end{aligned}$$

where further rules with a, b, and e as antecedents may contribute further to the values of a', b', and e', respectively. A case where this happens is in the reverse DP for the CKY algorithm (shown in figure 5.6), in which $\mathsf{c}(N, i, j)$ can correspond to either the left child or the right child of a larger constituent.

For completeness, we give the LOG-REAL derivation as well. The form of the original DP rule will be

$$\mathsf{c}(\boldsymbol{i}) = \log \sum_{\boldsymbol{j}} \exp\left(\mathsf{a}_1(\boldsymbol{k}_1) + \mathsf{a}_2(\boldsymbol{k}_2) + \cdots + \mathsf{a}_L(\boldsymbol{k}_L)\right) \tag{5.45}$$

Starting from equation 5.42, we have:

$$\begin{aligned}
\frac{\exp(\mathsf{a}_\ell(\boldsymbol{k}_\ell) + \mathsf{a}'_\ell(\boldsymbol{k}_\ell))}{\exp \mathsf{goal}} &= \sum_{\boldsymbol{k}\setminus\boldsymbol{k}_\ell} \frac{\exp(\mathsf{c}(\boldsymbol{i}) + \mathsf{c}'(\boldsymbol{i}))}{\exp \mathsf{goal}} \times \frac{\partial \mathsf{c}(\boldsymbol{i})}{\partial \mathsf{a}_\ell(\boldsymbol{k}_\ell)} \\
&= \sum_{\boldsymbol{k}\setminus\boldsymbol{k}_\ell} \frac{\exp(\mathsf{c}(\boldsymbol{i}) + \mathsf{c}'(\boldsymbol{i}))}{\exp \mathsf{goal}} \times \frac{\exp(\mathsf{a}_1(\boldsymbol{k}_1) + \mathsf{a}_2(\boldsymbol{k}_2) + \cdots + \mathsf{a}_L(\boldsymbol{k}_L))}{\exp \mathsf{c}(\boldsymbol{i})} \\
&= \sum_{\boldsymbol{k}\setminus\boldsymbol{k}_\ell} \frac{\exp(\mathsf{c}'(\boldsymbol{i}) + \mathsf{a}_1(\boldsymbol{k}_1) + \mathsf{a}_2(\boldsymbol{k}_2) + \cdots + \mathsf{a}_L(\boldsymbol{k}_L))}{\exp \mathsf{goal}} \\
\mathsf{a}'_\ell(\boldsymbol{k}_\ell) &= \log \sum_{\boldsymbol{k}\setminus\boldsymbol{k}_\ell} \exp\left(\mathsf{c}'(\boldsymbol{i}) + \sum_{\ell' \in \{1,\ldots,L\}\setminus\{\ell\}} \mathsf{a}_{\ell'}(\boldsymbol{k}_{\ell'})\right)
\end{aligned}$$

An alternative approach to calculating reverse values is to keep track of updates during runtime of the original DP, then calculate the corresponding reverse value updates, in reverse, after the original DP finishes. This technique was proposed by Eisner et al. (2005).

5.2.5 NON-DP EXPECTATIONS

Dynamic programming is not available for all models. **Cube summing** is general technique based on dynamic programming that allows the incorporation of non-local features on a dynamic programming "skeleton" (Gimpel and Smith, 2009), Cube summing is based on an analysis of the approximate search technique known as cube pruning (see section 2.3.5).

$$
\begin{aligned}
\forall N \in \mathcal{N}, 1 \leq i \leq n, \quad \mathsf{c}(N, i-1, i) &= \{N \to x_i\}_{\mathcal{K}} \\
\forall N \in \mathcal{N}, 0 \leq i < k \leq n, \quad \mathsf{c}(N, i, k) &= \bigoplus_{N', N'' \in \mathcal{N}, j : i < j < k} \mathsf{c}(N', i, j) \otimes \mathsf{c}(N'', j, k) \otimes \left\{N \to N' N''\right\}_{\mathcal{K}} \\
\mathsf{goal} &= \mathsf{c}(S, 0, n) \\
\forall N \in \mathcal{N}, x \in \Sigma, \quad \{N \to x\}'_{\mathcal{K}} &= \sum_{i \in \{1, \ldots, n\} : x_i = x} \mathsf{c}'(N, i-1, i) \\
\forall N \in \mathcal{N}, 0 \leq j < k \leq n, \quad \mathsf{c}'(N, j, k) &= \left(\bigoplus_{N', N'' \in \mathcal{N}, i : i < j} \mathsf{c}'(N', i, k) \otimes \mathsf{c}(N'', i, j) \otimes \left\{N' \to N'' N\right\}_{\mathcal{K}} \right) \\
&\oplus \left(\bigoplus_{N', N'' \in \mathcal{N}, \ell : k < \ell} \mathsf{c}'(N', j, \ell) \otimes \mathsf{c}(N'', k, \ell) \otimes \left\{N' \to N N''\right\}_{\mathcal{K}} \right) \\
\forall N, N', N'' \in \mathcal{N}, \quad \left\{N \to N' N''\right\}'_{\mathcal{K}} &= \bigoplus_{i, j, k \in \{0, \ldots, n\} : i < j < k} \mathsf{c}'(N, i, k) \otimes \mathsf{c}(N', i, j) \otimes \mathsf{c}(N'', j, k) \\
\mathsf{c}'(S, 0, n) &= \mathsf{goal}' = \mathbf{1}
\end{aligned}
$$

Figure 5.6: The reverse DP for figure 2.18. In the REAL or LOG-REAL semiring, this is known as the outside algorithm. Note that the original equations are included since the reverse values depend on the original theorems' values.

There are special cases where exact expectations may be calculated for specialized structures. The matrix-tree theorem may be used in calculating feature expectations in arc-factored dependency tree models (Koo et al., 2007, Smith and Smith, 2007).

Loopy belief propagation is a set of general techniques for inference in graphical models that has recently been applied to the structured case (Smith and Eisner, 2008, Sutton and McCallum, 2004, *inter alia*). It is an example of a variational approximation; other variational techniques are discussed in chapter 4.

When dynamic programming is not available, one may use random techniques for generating samples of the complete random variable $\boldsymbol{Y}$, under the desired distribution. Given $\boldsymbol{x}$, let $\langle \hat{\boldsymbol{y}}_1, \ldots, \hat{\boldsymbol{y}}_n \rangle$ be such a random sample, drawn from the posterior $p_{\mathbf{w}}(\boldsymbol{Y} \mid \boldsymbol{X} = \boldsymbol{x})$. As n increases, we know by the law of large numbers that

$$\mathbb{E}_{p_{\mathbf{w}}(\boldsymbol{Y}|\boldsymbol{X}=\tilde{\boldsymbol{x}}_i)}[g_j(\boldsymbol{x}, \boldsymbol{Y})] \approx \frac{1}{n} \sum_{i=1}^{n} g_j(\boldsymbol{x}, \hat{\boldsymbol{y}}_i) \tag{5.46}$$

Markov chain Monte Carlo techniques, such as **Gibbs sampling**, are often straightforward to implement for structured problems (DeNero et al., 2008). We discussed Gibbs sampling in chapter 4, in the context of Bayesian learning.

Here we briefly consider how to sample $\boldsymbol{Y}$ from $\mathcal{Y}_{\boldsymbol{x}}$, given $\boldsymbol{x}$ and weights $\mathbf{w}$. This can be understood as a step within a Gibbs sampler in which structures $\boldsymbol{Y}$ and some other random variables (perhaps the weights $\mathbf{W}$) are unobserved. Consider first the case where features are local. After running the REAL DP to sum over all structures in $\mathcal{Y}_{\boldsymbol{x}}$, we can use the theorem values to sample from the posterior distribution over $\boldsymbol{Y}$.

1. Place goal on a queue.
2. While the queue is not empty:
    (a) Take an item t off the queue, and consult the DP equations for all of the possible products that were summed together to calculate t's value. Equivalently, in a path problem, consider each arc leading to t, or in a hyperpath problem, consider each hyperarc leading to t. (We use the hyperarc terminology from here, as it is general and intuitive.)
    (b) Score each of the hyperarc by its contribution to the value of t, divided by the value of t. The sum of these values will be 1; they define a multinomial distribution $\boldsymbol{\pi}$ over the hyperarc leading to t.
    (c) Randomly sample one of those hyperarcs according to $\boldsymbol{\pi}$. Place all theorems or axioms that correspond to source vertices for the selected hyperarc into the queue.
3. On completion, a hyperpath will have been traversed backwards from goal to a set of axioms. That hyperpath corresponds to a single value of $\mathcal{Y}_{\boldsymbol{x}}$.

For HMMs and PCFGs, the above algorithm can be understood as randomly generating from a HMM or PCFG constrained to yield $\boldsymbol{x}$ and to have probabilities over derivations exactly equal to $p_{\mathbf{w}}(\boldsymbol{Y} \mid \boldsymbol{x})$. This technique was originally described by Goodman (1998) and has been used by Finkel et al. (2006) and Johnson et al. (2007a). It can be understood as a kind of block sampling over many random variables, though our notation has tended to treat $\boldsymbol{Y}$ as a single random variable (Mochihashi et al., 2009).

In the scenario where non-local features influence $p_{\mathbf{w}}(\boldsymbol{Y} \mid \boldsymbol{x})$, the above technique can be used as a proposal distribution within a Metropolis-Hastings sampler (see section 4.2.4).

5.3 MINIMUM BAYES RISK DECODING

For a given cost function, **minimum Bayes risk** decoding is an alternative to choosing the single highest scoring $\boldsymbol{y} \in \mathcal{Y}_{\boldsymbol{x}}$ given $\boldsymbol{x} \in \mathcal{X}$. The decoding rule is:

$$\begin{aligned} h(\boldsymbol{x}) &= \operatorname*{argmin}_{\boldsymbol{y} \in \mathcal{Y}} \mathbb{E}_{p_{\mathbf{w}}(\boldsymbol{Y} \mid \boldsymbol{X}=\boldsymbol{x})}[\mathit{cost}(\boldsymbol{x}, \boldsymbol{y}, \boldsymbol{Y})] \\ &= \operatorname*{argmin}_{\boldsymbol{y} \in \mathcal{Y}} \sum_{\boldsymbol{y}' \in \mathcal{Y}} p_{\mathbf{w}}(\boldsymbol{Y} = \boldsymbol{y}' \mid \boldsymbol{X} = \boldsymbol{x}) \mathit{cost}(\boldsymbol{x}, \boldsymbol{y}, \boldsymbol{y}') \end{aligned} \tag{5.47}$$

Imagine that the true value of $\boldsymbol{Y}$ is random and is distributed according to our model distribution, and we seek to choose the $\boldsymbol{y}$ that, on average, will be the least offensive under that distribution—the $\boldsymbol{y}$ with the lowest *expected* cost. The expectation of cost is sometimes called **risk**. If we believe that our model $p_{\mathbf{w}}$ is a good estimate of the true distribution over $\boldsymbol{Y}$ on the whole, but perhaps not especially well at estimating the mode of that distribution, then this rule is well-motivated.

Equation 5.47 can be simplified if the probability distribution and the cost function decompose in a similar way. In the specific case of the HMM, the Hamming cost is often used in evaluating the quality of a sequence labeling hypothesis $h(\boldsymbol{x})$ against a gold standard $\boldsymbol{y}$ (n is the length of the input $\boldsymbol{x}$):

$$\mathit{cost}_{\text{Hamming}}(\boldsymbol{x}, h(\boldsymbol{x}), \boldsymbol{y}^*) = \sum_{i=1}^{n} \mathbf{1}\{h(\boldsymbol{x})_i \neq y_i\} = \sum_{i=1}^{n} \begin{cases} 0 & \text{if } h(\boldsymbol{x})_i = y_i \\ 1 & \text{otherwise} \end{cases} \tag{5.48}$$

This permits us to break equation 5.47 into n terms, since by linearity of expectation

$$\mathbb{E}_{p(\boldsymbol{Y} \mid \boldsymbol{X}=\boldsymbol{x})}\left[\sum_{i=1}^{n} \mathbf{1}\{h(\boldsymbol{x})_i \neq Y_i\}\right] = \sum_{i=1}^{n} \mathbb{E}_{p(Y_i \mid \boldsymbol{X}=\boldsymbol{x})}[\mathbf{1}\{h(\boldsymbol{x})_i \neq Y_i\}] \tag{5.49}$$

The "most probable $\boldsymbol{y}$" decoder we have used until now is actually a special case of minimum Bayes risk decoding. If the cost function is the **zero-one loss**, defined as

$$\mathit{cost}(\boldsymbol{x}, h(\boldsymbol{x}), \boldsymbol{y}) = \mathbf{1}\{h(\boldsymbol{x}) \neq \boldsymbol{y}\} \tag{5.50}$$

then minimum Bayes risk reduces to choosing $\text{argmax}_{\boldsymbol{y} \in \mathcal{Y}_{\boldsymbol{x}}} p_{\mathbf{w}}(\boldsymbol{Y} = \boldsymbol{y} \mid \boldsymbol{X} = \boldsymbol{x})$ (the derivation is left as an exercise).

Under the assumption that the cost function factors in a way similar to the features, minimum Bayes risk decoding becomes straightforward using two passes. More formally, assume that *cost* factors into $\langle c_1, c_2, \ldots, c_{\#parts(\boldsymbol{x})} \rangle$:

$$cost(\boldsymbol{x}, \boldsymbol{y}, \boldsymbol{y}') = \sum_{j=1}^{\#parts(\boldsymbol{x})} c_j \left(\Pi_j(\boldsymbol{x}, \boldsymbol{y}), \Pi_j(\boldsymbol{x}, \boldsymbol{y}') \right) \tag{5.51}$$

By the linearity of the expectation operator,

$$\mathbb{E}_{p_{\mathbf{w}}(\boldsymbol{Y} \mid \boldsymbol{X}=\boldsymbol{x})}[cost(\boldsymbol{x}, \boldsymbol{y}, \boldsymbol{Y})] = \sum_{j=1}^{\#parts(\boldsymbol{x})} \mathbb{E}_{p_{\mathbf{w}}(\boldsymbol{Y} \mid \boldsymbol{X}=\boldsymbol{x})} \left[c_j \left(\Pi_j(\boldsymbol{x}, \boldsymbol{y}), \Pi_j(\boldsymbol{x}, \boldsymbol{Y}) \right) \right] \tag{5.52}$$

The above is a sum of feature expectations no different from those in section 5.2, except that these "features" are not actually in the model. We can nonetheless use the same "part posteriors" to calculate each cost expectation term, since for any $\boldsymbol{y} \in \mathcal{Y}_{\boldsymbol{x}}$:

$$\mathbb{E}_{p_{\mathbf{w}}(\boldsymbol{Y} \mid \boldsymbol{X}=\boldsymbol{x})} \left[c_j \left(\Pi_j(\boldsymbol{x}, \boldsymbol{y}), \Pi_j(\boldsymbol{x}, \boldsymbol{Y}) \right) \right] = \sum_{\boldsymbol{\pi} \in \mathcal{R}_j(\boldsymbol{x})} p(\Pi_j = \boldsymbol{\pi} \mid \boldsymbol{X} = \boldsymbol{x}) c_j \left(\Pi_j(\boldsymbol{x}, \boldsymbol{y}), \boldsymbol{\pi} \right) \tag{5.53}$$

The central quantity here is actually the *posterior* probability that a particular part $\boldsymbol{\pi}$ will be present in the random variable $\boldsymbol{Y}$; refer to equation 5.27. For many models, dynamic programming with the LOG-REAL or REAL semiring and a reverse algorithm can accomplish this, just as for standard feature expectations.

In the second stage, using the above, we now define local feature functions, which we denote $\mathbf{f}'$. For the jth part, index the features by the possible values $\boldsymbol{\pi} \in \mathcal{R}_j(\boldsymbol{x})$, and let:

$$\bar{f}_{j,\boldsymbol{\pi}}(\boldsymbol{\pi}') = -c(\boldsymbol{\pi}', \boldsymbol{\pi}) \tag{5.54}$$

$$\bar{w}_{j,\boldsymbol{\pi}} = p_{\mathbf{w}}(\Pi_j = \boldsymbol{\pi} \mid \boldsymbol{X} = \boldsymbol{x}) \tag{5.55}$$

This defines a locally factored linear scoring function:

$$score(\boldsymbol{x}, \boldsymbol{y}) = \sum_{j=1}^{\#parts(\boldsymbol{x})} \bar{\mathbf{w}}^\top \bar{\mathbf{f}}(\Pi_j(\boldsymbol{x}, \boldsymbol{y})) \tag{5.56}$$

Decoding in the standard way with this scoring function accomplishes minimum Bayes risk decoding. The second stage algorithm will be as efficient as maximum-score decoding with the original model (since they have the same local factoring assumptions).

Minimum Bayes risk decoding has been proposed in many specific instances, notably by Goodman (1996) for maximizing expected labeled constituent recall in phrase-structure parsing, by Goel and Byrne (2000) in speech recognition, and by Kumar and Byrne (2004) in machine translation.

5.4 COST-AUGMENTED DECODING

We encountered cost-augmented decoding in section 3.6.5, in the context of training a structural SVM, whose objective function included terms of the form

$$\operatorname*{argmax}_{\boldsymbol{y} \in \mathcal{Y}} \mathbf{w}^\top \mathbf{g}(\tilde{\boldsymbol{x}}_i, \boldsymbol{y}) + cost(\tilde{\boldsymbol{x}}_i, \boldsymbol{y}, \tilde{\boldsymbol{y}}_i) \tag{5.57}$$

For arbitrary cost functions, equation 5.57 can be very expensive. In many cases, however, the cost function factors in the same way as the feature vector function $\mathbf{g}$ (equation 5.51). Under these circumstances, cost-augmented decoding can be accomplished by treating the cost function as just another locally factored feature, with weight 1, and applying standard decoding methods to find the maximizer. For example, Lacoste-Julien et al. (2006) formulated cost-augmented inference in an alignment problem as a linear programming problem very similar to the standard decoding problem. The relationship to standard decoding follows for other decoding algorithms that exploit the same locality properties of the features. For cost functions that do not factor, or loss functions that involve constraints not linear in the cost function (e.g., equation 3.104), approximate inference techniques are required, and these sometimes interact very directly with the learning algorithm (see, e.g., Finley and Joachims, 2008).

5.5 DECODING WITH HIDDEN VARIABLES

Hidden variables introduce some challenges to decoding. An obvious solution that is frequently used is to find

$$\operatorname*{argmax}_{\boldsymbol{y} \in \mathcal{Y}_{\boldsymbol{x}}, \boldsymbol{z} \in \mathcal{Z}} \log p(\boldsymbol{y}, \boldsymbol{z}, \mid \boldsymbol{x}) \tag{5.58}$$

This returns both $\boldsymbol{y}$ and $\boldsymbol{z}$, the latter of which can be ignored. This is often tractable using methods like those presented in chapter 2. This kind of inference is called the "most probable explanation."

If we take the probabilistic view (which the majority of hidden variable learning methods do), then the above fails to account for the many different $\boldsymbol{z} \in \mathcal{Z}$ that may contribute to a particular $\boldsymbol{y}$'s score. Generalizing the probabilistic decoding rule (section 3.3.1), we can derive:

$$h(\boldsymbol{x}) = \operatorname*{argmax}_{\boldsymbol{y} \in \mathcal{Y}} \log p_{\mathbf{w}}(\boldsymbol{y} \mid \boldsymbol{x}) = \operatorname*{argmax}_{\boldsymbol{y} \in \mathcal{Y}} \log \sum_{\boldsymbol{z} \in \mathcal{Z}} p_{\mathbf{w}}(\boldsymbol{y}, \boldsymbol{z} \mid \boldsymbol{x}) \tag{5.59}$$

Unlike equation 5.58, this approach takes into account all of the $\boldsymbol{z}$ that contribute to a candidate output's probabilistic score, not just the "best" $\boldsymbol{z} \in \mathcal{Z}$. Now, if $\mathcal{Z}$ is a small, finite set, then equation 5.59 may be solved tractably, but in general, for structured spaces $\mathcal{Y}$ and $\mathcal{Z}$, this problem becomes NP-hard. It corresponds (in the graphical models view) to maximum *a posteriori* inference in the general case, and (in the parsing view) to finding the most likely parse given a sentence, where many derivations may lead to the same parse (Sima'an, 2002).

Matsuzaki et al. (2005) proposed an approximate approach to decoding based on a **variational** approximation to the objective function. (Recall that variational inference was also useful in the

Bayesian setting; see section 4.2.4.) Consider that our goal is equation 5.59, but the form of $p_{\mathbf{w}}(\boldsymbol{Y} \mid \boldsymbol{X})$ does not permit efficient maximization. Let $\mathcal{Q}$ denote a family of models of the form $q(\boldsymbol{Y} \mid \boldsymbol{X})$ that *does* permit efficient maximization.

For example, for Matsuzaki et al. (2005), $p_{\mathbf{w}}$ was a probabilistic context-free grammar augmented with a latent "annotation" on each nonterminal, splitting the grammar's original categories into more fine-grained, specialized categories; they sought to recover the best original tree, taking into account its many fine-grained variants. PCFGs, of course, admit efficient decoding (parsing), in their classical annotation-free form. So for Matsuzaki et al. (2005), $\mathcal{Q}$ was the family of PCFGs using the original nonterminal set.

For this approximation, the key step is to choose a model specific to the $\boldsymbol{x}$ to be decoded that approximates $p_{\mathbf{w}}(\boldsymbol{Y} \mid \boldsymbol{X} = \boldsymbol{x})$, but that is within $\mathcal{Q}$. We want the construction of the approximate model to be efficient, and, by choosing a model in $\mathcal{Q}$, we know that decoding with that model will be efficient. This is accomplished by choosing $q \in \mathcal{Q}$ that minimizes KL divergence to $p_{\mathbf{w}}$, *for only this particular input* $\boldsymbol{x}$:

$$\begin{aligned}
&\min_{q \in \mathcal{Q}} D_{KL}\left(q(\boldsymbol{Y} \mid \boldsymbol{X} = \boldsymbol{x}) \| p_{\mathbf{w}}(\boldsymbol{Y} \mid \boldsymbol{X} = \boldsymbol{x})\right) \\
&\quad = \max_{q \in \mathcal{Q}} \sum_{\boldsymbol{y} \in \mathcal{Y}_{\boldsymbol{x}}} q(\boldsymbol{Y} = \boldsymbol{y} \mid \boldsymbol{X} = \boldsymbol{x}) \log p_{\mathbf{w}}(\boldsymbol{Y} = \boldsymbol{y} \mid \boldsymbol{X} = \boldsymbol{x}) \\
&\quad = \max_{q \in \mathcal{Q}} \sum_{\boldsymbol{y} \in \mathcal{Y}_{\boldsymbol{x}}} q(\boldsymbol{Y} = \boldsymbol{y} \mid \boldsymbol{X} = \boldsymbol{x}) \log \sum_{\boldsymbol{z} \in \mathcal{Z}} p_{\mathbf{w}}(\boldsymbol{Y} = \boldsymbol{y}, \boldsymbol{Z} = \boldsymbol{z} \mid \boldsymbol{X} = \boldsymbol{x})
\end{aligned} \tag{5.60}$$

After solving for q, it can be used to decode:

$$\operatorname*{argmax}_{\boldsymbol{y} \in \mathcal{Y}_{\boldsymbol{x}}} q(\boldsymbol{Y} = \boldsymbol{y} \mid \boldsymbol{X} = \boldsymbol{x}) \tag{5.61}$$

It is most desirable for q to take a linear form in features of $\boldsymbol{x}$ and $\boldsymbol{y}$, i.e.,

$$q(\boldsymbol{Y} = \boldsymbol{y} \mid \boldsymbol{X} = \boldsymbol{x}) \propto \exp \overline{w}^\top \overline{g}(\boldsymbol{x}, \boldsymbol{y}) \tag{5.62}$$

so that the variational decoder in equation 5.61 can be implemented using one of the standard methods for linear model decoding (chapter 2). This means q should not model hidden structure (like $\boldsymbol{Z}$). Matsuzaki et al. (2005) used a variational model $q(\boldsymbol{X}, \boldsymbol{Y})$ that takes a generative, factored form (a PCFG) that can be computed using dynamic programming for feature expectations that are then locally normalized. Petrov et al. (2006) proposed an alternative in which marginal probabilities of different parts were calculated independently (these can also be understood as local feature expectations of features with value one when a part is present, zero when it is not), and they showed that this technique achieved better performance on a parsing task. See Petrov (2009) for more details; we conjecture that this approach equates to a variational approximation in which the variational model makes stronger independence assumptions.

Variational approaches like those above can be understood, in general, as maximizing a product of marginals from the enriched hidden variable model. Recall that minimum Bayes risk decoding (section 5.3) is similar, but maximizes a *sum* of marginals. Minimum Bayes risk decoding is available for hidden variable models as well, with the hidden variable being summed out in the marginal. This technique was used in parsing with a tree substitution grammar by Cohn et al. (2009), among others.

5.6 CONCLUSION

This chapter has presented some inference problems that arise in algorithms for learning linguistic structure predictors. Most of the algorithms relate closely to algorithms already presented in chapter 2, but the problems they solve are distinct from the original decoding problem of equation 2.3, and they are often less intuitive.

APPENDIX A

Numerical Optimization

The aim of this appendix is to provide background and concrete advice about solving numerical optimization problems in NLP. Throughout the text, we have taken a declarative approach to defining prediction and learning problems: state clearly what it is we aim to do, then use the best available techniques to accomplish the goal, approximating if necessary. Here we go into more detail about how to solve a certain class of commonly recurring problems, making frequent references to examples used in NLP.

Many learning problems boil down to **numerical optimization** problems:

$$\min_{\mathbf{w} \in \mathcal{W}} \Phi(\mathbf{w}) \tag{A.1}$$

where $\mathcal{W} \subseteq \mathbb{R}^d$ is called the **feasible set** and $\Phi : \mathcal{W} \to \mathbb{R}$ is called the **objective function**. Maximization problems are not fundamentally different, as $\max_{\mathbf{w} \in \mathcal{W}} \Phi(\mathbf{w})$ is equivalent to $\min_{\mathbf{w} \in \mathcal{W}} -\Phi(\mathbf{w})$.

Depending on the properties of the feasible set $\mathcal{W}$ and the objective function Φ, there are different ways to categorize optimization problems. It is important to point out that the term *programming* is sometimes used in the mathematics and operations research communities to refer to optimization; in the context of optimization, a "program" is an optimization problem, not a computer program or an algorithm for solving the problem.

If $\mathcal{W} = \mathbb{R}^d$, then we say the problem is **unconstrained**. If $\mathcal{W}$ is defined only by upper and/or lower bounds on some or all coordinates, then the problem is **box-constrained**. If $\mathcal{W}$ is defined by a set of linear equalities or inequalities, the problem is **linearly constrained**. Whether the constraints define a convex set is a key property. A convex set $\mathcal{W}$ is one in which, if $\mathbf{w} \in \mathcal{W}$ and $\mathbf{w}' \in \mathcal{W}$, then $\forall \alpha \in (0, 1)$, $\alpha\mathbf{w} + (1 - \alpha)\mathbf{w}' \in \mathcal{W}$. **Constrained optimization** problems are those where $\mathcal{W}$ is a strict subset of $\mathbb{R}^d$.

When the constraints include only integer points or in some other way define a discrete set (e.g., $\mathcal{W} \subseteq \{0, 1\}^k$), the problem is often called **discrete** or **combinatorial optimization** (e.g., the decoding problems in chapter 2) and the solutions are often quite different. This appendix focuses on problems where $\mathcal{W}$ is continuous, a scenario that arises in learning.

Various properties of Φ that may be exploited include its convexity,[1] its continuity,[2] its differentiability,[3] and whether it is linear or quadratic in its arguments.

Developing algorithms for optimization is, of course, a field unto itself. Here we cover some of the key techniques that are most widely used to solve the numerical optimization problems that arise in current NLP research, though new ones are developed all the time. We propose that there are three levels at which an NLP researcher might understand this topic:

1. turning a learning or prediction problem into a well-formed optimization problem, and knowing which of a set of algorithms can be called to solve the probem;

2. understanding intuitively how each algorithm works and being able to implement it; or

3. when faced with a new optimization problem that does not fit existing algorithms, developing a new optimization algorithm that is suitable, or directly improving on runtime or memory efficiency requirements of existing algorithms.

We aim to help the reader attain at least the first level of proficiency, and possibly the second.

A.1 THE HILL-CLIMBING ANALOGY

Consider a numerical optimization problem where $\mathcal{W}$ is continuous and either convex or unconstrained, and where Φ is continuous. We can envision optimization as locating a point in the region $\mathcal{W}$ where Φ reaches its lowest (or highest value). Adopting briefly the maximization version (where we seek the $\mathbf{w} \in \mathcal{W}$ that maximizes $\Phi(\mathbf{w})$), then it is often helpful to imagine the function as defining a geographical landscape. Maximizing the function equates to finding the top of the largest hill.

Many numerical optimization algorithms work in this way, by keeping in memory one value for $\mathbf{w}$ at a time and iteratively finding a better value to replace it, like a hiker taking steps toward the top of a hill. Typically hill-climbing algorithms do not remember where they have been before, only the current $\mathbf{w}$, so it is important to make sure that some guarantees are offered that the algorithm will find improved values as they proceed.

For functions that are concave at all points (or, when minimizing, convex at all points), this approach makes a lot of sense, for we can believe that each iteration that finds a better value for $\mathbf{w}$ is leading us (in some sense) toward a global optimum. For functions that are not concave everywhere, we may still hope to attain a *local* maximum. Each method we consider here can be understood in terms of this analogy. Pseudocode for hill-climbing can be found in algorithm 6.

[1] A function $\Phi : \mathcal{W} \rightarrow \mathbb{R}$ is convex if for $\mathbf{w} \in \mathcal{W}$ and $\mathbf{w}' \in \mathcal{W}$ and $\alpha \in (0, 1)$, $\Phi(\alpha\mathbf{w} + (1-\alpha)\mathbf{w}') \leq \alpha\Phi(\mathbf{w}) + (1-\alpha)\Phi(\mathbf{w}')$.

[2] A function $\Phi : \mathcal{W} \rightarrow \mathbb{R}$ is continuous at a point $\mathbf{w} \in \mathcal{W}$ if, $\forall\epsilon > 0, \exists\delta > 0$ such that if $\mathbf{w} - \delta < \mathbf{w}' < \mathbf{w} + \delta$, then $\Phi(\mathbf{w}') - \epsilon < \Phi(\mathbf{w}) < \Phi(\mathbf{w}') + \epsilon$. Saying a function is "continuous" is an informal way of saying that it is continuous at all points in its domain. Intuitively, small changes in the function's input result in small changes in its output.

[3] A function $\Phi : \mathcal{W} \rightarrow \mathbb{R}$ is differentiable at a point $\mathbf{w} \in \mathcal{W}$ if the derivative of Φ exists at $\mathbf{w}$. Saying a function is "differentiable" is an informal way of saying that it is differentiable at all points in its domain.

Algorithm 6 A generic hill-climbing algorithm. *ascend* : $\mathcal{W} \times (\mathcal{W} \to \mathbb{R}) \to \mathcal{W}$ is a subroutine that, when given $\mathbf{w}^{(t-1)}$ and Φ, is assumed to return $\mathbf{w}$ such that $\Phi(\mathbf{w}) \geq \Phi(\mathbf{w}^{(t-1)})$.

Input: objective function $\Phi : \mathcal{W} \to \mathbb{R}$, initial vector $\mathbf{w}^{(0)}$, maximum iterations t'
Output: final vector $\mathbf{w}$

$t \leftarrow 0$
repeat
  $t \leftarrow t + 1$
  $\mathbf{w}^{(t)} \leftarrow ascend(\mathbf{w}^{(t-1)}, \Phi)$
until convergence, defined as $\mathbf{w}^{(t)} \approx \mathbf{w}^{(t-1)}$, $\Phi(\mathbf{w}^{(t)}) \approx \Phi(\mathbf{w}^{(t-1)})$, and/or $t \geq t'$
$\mathbf{w} \leftarrow \mathbf{w}^{(t)}$
return w

A.2 COORDINATE ASCENT

The basic idea of **coordinate ascent** (for minimization problems, **coordinate descent**) is to iteratively improve on one coordinate per iteration, leaving the others fixed. The choice of which coordinate to optimize on a given round may be predetermined (e.g., by cycling through) or randomized. Each coordinate will likely need multiple updates, so the number of iterations will probably be much larger than d, the length of $\mathbf{w}$. Given the original problem in equation A.1, on iteration t the *ascend* function returns

$$ascend(\mathbf{w}^{(t-1)}, \Phi) = \operatorname*{argmax}_{\mathbf{w} \in \mathcal{W} : \forall i \neq j, w_i = w_i^{(t-1)}} \Phi(\mathbf{w}) \tag{A.2}$$

for some selected coordinate j. Note that this transforms a d-dimensional maximization problem into a one-dimensional optimization problem, exploiting the fact that optimization problems in a single dimension are often very easy to solve. For some functions Φ, the solution may have a closed form, making an iteration very fast, or may simply have more desirable properties (e.g., convexity with respect to each w_j on its own). Note further that the selection of w_j need not be the minimizer of the above expression; the new value needs merely to improve Φ compared to the previous value of w_j.

A variation on coordinate ascent is to consider *subsets* of the coordinates at each round, rather than just one. One view of the Expectation Maximization algorithm (section 4.1.1), suggested by Neal and Hinton (1998), considers that the original maximum likelihood problem

$$\max_{\mathbf{w}} \sum_{i=1}^{\tilde{N}} \log \sum_{\boldsymbol{y} \in \mathcal{Y}_{\tilde{\boldsymbol{x}}_i}} p_{\mathbf{w}}(\tilde{\boldsymbol{x}}_i, \boldsymbol{y}) \tag{A.3}$$

can be rewritten as a function that depends not just on the arguments we ultimately care about ($\mathbf{w}$), but on another set of arguments ($\boldsymbol{q} = \langle q_i(\boldsymbol{y}) \rangle_{i \in \{1,\ldots,\tilde{N}\}, \boldsymbol{y} \in \mathcal{Y}_{\tilde{\boldsymbol{x}}_i}}$), introduced for the purpose of reformulating the problem to be more manageable. These arguments equate to the "q" in the EM algorithm as presented in algorithm 4. The new function has the form:

$$\max_{\boldsymbol{q},\mathbf{w}} \overbrace{-\sum_{i=1}^{\tilde{N}} \sum_{\boldsymbol{y}\in\mathcal{Y}_{\tilde{\boldsymbol{x}}_i}} q_i(\boldsymbol{y}) \log q_i(\boldsymbol{y})}^{\Phi_1(\boldsymbol{q})} + \overbrace{\sum_{i=1}^{\tilde{N}} \sum_{\boldsymbol{y}\in\mathcal{Y}_{\tilde{\boldsymbol{x}}_i}} q_i(\boldsymbol{y}) \log p_{\mathbf{w}}(\boldsymbol{y} \mid \tilde{\boldsymbol{x}}_i)}^{\Phi_2(\boldsymbol{q},\mathbf{w})} + \overbrace{\sum_{i=1}^{\tilde{N}} \log p_{\mathbf{w}}(\tilde{\boldsymbol{x}}_i)}^{\Phi_3(\mathbf{w})} \tag{A.4}$$

To see how optimizing this function using coordinate ascent equates to EM, consider that the E step, given current values $\mathbf{w}$, can be seen as

$$\max_{\boldsymbol{q}} \Phi_1(\boldsymbol{q}) + \Phi_2(\boldsymbol{q}, \mathbf{w}) = \min_{\boldsymbol{q}} \sum_{i=1}^{\tilde{N}} D_{KL}(q_i(\boldsymbol{Y}) \| p_{\mathbf{w}}(\boldsymbol{Y} \mid \tilde{\boldsymbol{x}}_i)) \tag{A.5}$$

Of course, making $q_i(\boldsymbol{Y})$ as close as possible to $p_{\mathbf{w}}(\boldsymbol{Y} \mid \tilde{\boldsymbol{x}}_i)$ can be accomplished by setting $q_i(\boldsymbol{y}) = p_{\mathbf{w}}(\boldsymbol{y} \mid \tilde{\boldsymbol{x}}_i)$, for all $\boldsymbol{y} \in \mathcal{Y}_{\tilde{\boldsymbol{x}}_i}$.

The M step can be seen as fixing $\boldsymbol{q}$ and solving

$$\max_{\mathbf{w}} \Phi_2(\boldsymbol{q}, \mathbf{w}) + \Phi_3(\mathbf{w}) = \max_{\mathbf{w}} \sum_{i=1}^{\tilde{N}} \sum_{\boldsymbol{y}\in\mathcal{Y}_{\tilde{\boldsymbol{x}}_i}} q(\boldsymbol{y}) \log p_{\mathbf{w}}(\boldsymbol{y} \mid \tilde{\boldsymbol{x}}_i) + \log p_{\mathbf{w}}(\tilde{\boldsymbol{x}}_i) \tag{A.6}$$

$$= \max_{\mathbf{w}} \sum_{i=1}^{\tilde{N}} \sum_{\boldsymbol{y}\in\mathcal{Y}_{\tilde{\boldsymbol{x}}_i}} q(\boldsymbol{y}) \log p_{\mathbf{w}}(\tilde{\boldsymbol{x}}_i, \boldsymbol{y}) \tag{A.7}$$

This problem is more attractive than the original likelihood formulation; it is convex in $\mathbf{w}$, and in some cases (e.g., multinomial-based models), there is a closed-form solution.

The E and M steps of EM can therefore be seen as coordinate ascent steps for the objective function in equation A.4.

A.3 GRADIENT ASCENT

In the case where the objective function Φ is differentiable, there is a natural way to define an update for the full vector $\mathbf{w}$ all at once: the vector of first derivatives of Φ with respect to each w_j. This vector is known as the **gradient** with respect to $\mathbf{w}$. We can think of it as a function $\nabla\Phi$ defined by:[4]

$$\begin{aligned} \nabla\Phi(\mathbf{w}) &= \langle \nabla\Phi(\mathbf{w})_1, \nabla\Phi(\mathbf{w})_2, \ldots, \nabla\Phi(\mathbf{w})_d \rangle \\ &= \left\langle \frac{\partial\Phi}{\partial w_1}(\mathbf{w}), \frac{\partial\Phi}{\partial w_2}(\mathbf{w}), \ldots \frac{\partial\Phi}{\partial w_d}(\mathbf{w}) \right\rangle \end{aligned}$$

[4]Think of "$\nabla\Phi$" as a function, $\nabla\Phi : \mathcal{W} \to \mathbb{R}^d$. Evaluating this function at value $\mathbf{w}_0 \in \mathcal{W}$ gives a real vector, denoted $\nabla\Phi(\mathbf{w}_0)$. Note that each coordinate of the function's output vector, in general, depends on the entire input vector $\mathbf{w}_0$.

The gradient at $\mathbf{w}$ can be understood geometrically as defining the angle of a $(d+1)$-dimensional hyperplane passing through $\langle \mathbf{w}, \Phi(\mathbf{w}) \rangle$. The angle is such that the plane is tangent to the surface the function defines (i.e., all points of the plane are on the same side of the surface). See figure A.1.

The direction of steepest ascent from $\mathbf{w}^{(t-1)}$ is $\nabla \Phi(\mathbf{w}^{(t-1)})$. In terms of our generic algorithm 6, **gradient ascent** defines:

$$ascend(\mathbf{w}^{(t-1)}, \Phi) = \mathbf{w}^{(t-1)} + \alpha \nabla \Phi(\mathbf{w}^{(t-1)}) \tag{A.8}$$

The step size α is important. If α is too small, the algorithm will proceed up the hill too slowly; if α is too large, the algorithm may over-shoot and pass the optimal point. From the perspective of a single iteration, the ideal α is

$$\operatorname*{argmax}_{\alpha} \Phi(\mathbf{w}^{(t-1)} + \alpha \nabla \Phi(\mathbf{w}^{(t-1)})) \tag{A.9}$$

This is a one-dimensional optimization problem, the expense of which depends on the expense of calculating Φ repeatedly during hill-climbing on α. In practice, α is chosen using a line search method that approximates the ideal α, or simply chosen according to a predefined schedule. Bertsekas (1999) provides more detail about various ways of setting the step size α and their implications for theoretical convergence rates.

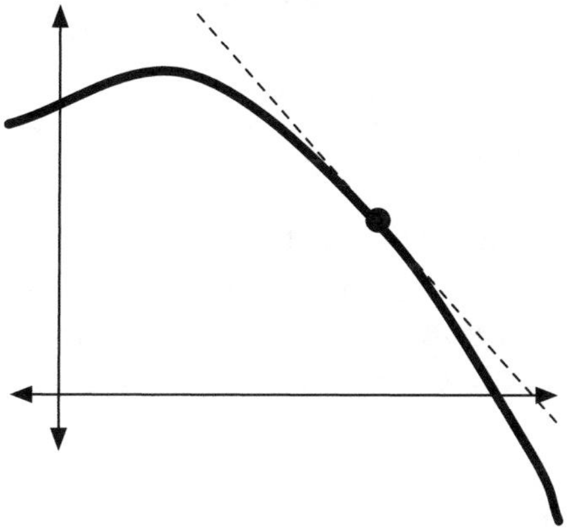

Figure A.1: An example of a function from $\mathbb{R} \rightarrow \mathbb{R}$. The dashed line is tangent to the curve at a single point; the slope of the line is the first derivative of the function. A gradient ascent method would update the value of x proportional to the slope of the line, here resulting in a decrease in x (a move to the left).

Gradient ascent is called a first-order method because it aims to meet the first-order necessary condition for a local optimum of Φ, namely that the first derivatives of Φ with respect to each w_j are 0 (i.e., $\nabla \Phi(\mathbf{w}) = \mathbf{0}$).

In practice, gradient ascent is rarely used. However, it is important to understand because it is the starting point for more effective hill-climbing methods.

Consider briefly the example of optimizing the likelihood of a globally-normalized conditional log-linear model (section 3.5). The objective (repeated from equation 3.74, including an L_2 regularization term) is:

$$\operatorname*{argmax}_{\mathbf{w}\in\mathbb{R}^d} \bar{\Phi}_{\mathrm{LL}}(\mathbf{w}) = \operatorname*{argmax}_{\mathbf{w}\in\mathbb{R}^d} \frac{1}{\tilde{N}} \left(\sum_{i=1}^{\tilde{N}} \mathbf{w}^\top \mathbf{g}(\tilde{\boldsymbol{x}}_i, \tilde{\boldsymbol{y}}_i) - \log z_{\mathbf{w}}(\tilde{\boldsymbol{x}}_i) \right) - \frac{C}{2}\|\mathbf{w}\|_2^2 \tag{A.10}$$

Note that this is an unconstrained problem where $\mathcal{W} = \mathbb{R}^d$. The gradient is defined by the vector of first derivatives with respect to each w_j (see equation 3.77):

$$\nabla \bar{\Phi}_{\mathrm{LL}}(\mathbf{w})_j = \frac{1}{\tilde{N}} \left(\sum_{i=1}^{\tilde{N}} g_j(\tilde{\boldsymbol{x}}_i, \tilde{\boldsymbol{y}}_i) - \mathbb{E}_{p_{\mathbf{w}}(\boldsymbol{Y} \mid \boldsymbol{X}=\tilde{\boldsymbol{x}}_i)}[g_j(\tilde{\boldsymbol{x}}_i, \boldsymbol{Y})] \right) - C w_j \tag{A.11}$$

A.3.1 SUBGRADIENT METHODS

An important generalization of gradient ascent is **subgradient ascent** (or descent), which exploits a generalization of the idea of a gradient for functions that are not everywhere differentiable (Shor, 1985). At a point $\mathbf{w}'$, a subgradient is any vector $\mathbf{u}$ such that, for all $\mathbf{w} \in \mathcal{W}$,

$$\Phi(\mathbf{w}) - \Phi(\mathbf{w}') \geq \sum_{j=1}^{d} u_j (w_j - w'_j) \tag{A.12}$$

If Φ is differentiable at $\mathbf{w}'$, then there is only one subgradient vector: the gradient.

Ratliff et al. (2006) applied the subgradient method to a broad class of structured large margin problems where cost-augmented decoding can be efficiently solved using combinatorial optimization. There, the regularized objective function can be written as (see section 3.6.4):

$$\begin{aligned} &\operatorname*{argmax}_{\mathbf{w}\in\mathbb{R}^d} \bar{\Phi}_{\mathrm{MM}}(\mathbf{w}) \\ &= \operatorname*{argmax}_{\mathbf{w}\in\mathbb{R}^d} \frac{1}{\tilde{N}} \sum_{i=1}^{\tilde{N}} \left(\mathbf{w}^\top \mathbf{g}(\tilde{\boldsymbol{x}}_i, \tilde{\boldsymbol{y}}_i) - \max_{\boldsymbol{y}\in\mathcal{Y}} \left(\mathbf{w}^\top \mathbf{g}(\tilde{\boldsymbol{x}}_i, \boldsymbol{y}) + \ell(\tilde{\boldsymbol{x}}_i, \boldsymbol{y}, \tilde{\boldsymbol{y}}_i) \right) \right) - \frac{C}{2}\|\mathbf{w}\|_2^2 \end{aligned} \tag{A.13}$$

While not everywhere differentiable (because of the max operator), this function does have a subgradient vector, the jth coordinate of which is given by

$$\nabla \bar{\Phi}_{\mathrm{MM}}(\mathbf{w})_j = g_j(\tilde{\boldsymbol{x}}_i, \tilde{\boldsymbol{y}}_i) - g_j \left(\tilde{\boldsymbol{x}}_i, \operatorname*{argmax}_{\boldsymbol{y}\in\mathcal{Y}_{\boldsymbol{x}}} \mathbf{w}^\top \mathbf{g}(\tilde{\boldsymbol{x}}_i, \boldsymbol{y}) + \mathit{cost}(\tilde{\boldsymbol{x}}_i, \boldsymbol{y}, \tilde{\boldsymbol{y}}_i) \right) - C w_j \tag{A.14}$$

A.3.2 STOCHASTIC GRADIENT ASCENT

When learning from a training sample in the generic framework described in section 3.2, the objective function breaks down mostly into addends, e.g., one per training example:

$$\Phi(\mathbf{w}) = \left(\sum_{i=1}^{\tilde{N}} \Phi_i(\mathbf{w}) \right) + \Phi_{\tilde{N}+1}(\mathbf{w}) \tag{A.15}$$

$\Phi_{\tilde{N}+1}$ handles additional terms in the objective, such as regularization terms. Rewriting slightly,

$$\Phi(\mathbf{w}) = \sum_{i=1}^{\tilde{N}} \left(\Phi_i(\mathbf{w}) + \frac{1}{\tilde{N}} \Phi_{\tilde{N}+1}(\mathbf{w}) \right) = \tilde{N} \mathbb{E}_{\mathrm{unif}_{\tilde{N}}(I)} \left[\Phi_I(\mathbf{w}) + \frac{1}{\tilde{N}} \Phi_{\tilde{N}+1}(\mathbf{w}) \right] \tag{A.16}$$

where $\mathrm{unif}_{\tilde{N}}(I)$ is the uniform distribution over $\{1, 2, \ldots, \tilde{N}\}$, set to $\frac{1}{\tilde{N}}$. This suggests a randomized optimization routine where, on each iteration, we draw a training example index i uniformly at random and let

$$\mathit{ascend}(\mathbf{w}^{(t-1)}, \Phi) = \mathbf{w}^{(t-1)} + \alpha \nabla \left[\Phi_i(\mathbf{w}) + \frac{1}{\tilde{N}} \Phi_{\tilde{N}+1}(\mathbf{w}) \right] \tag{A.17}$$

This is called **stochastic gradient ascent** (or descent; LeCun et al., 1998). A detailed discussion from a machine learning perspective can be found in Bottou (2004). This algorithm is often observed to converge very quickly and to be somewhat robust to the choice of the step size α (Finkel et al., 2008, for example).

Stochastic gradient ascent bears a strong resemblance to "online" or "incremental" learning methods that update $\mathbf{w}$ based on consideration of a single training example at a time, and it may be applied in a deterministic version where i cycles through training examples in a fixed order. Online versions of subgradient methods (discussed in section A.3.1) can be derived in the same fashion, using a subgradient vector for one of the Φ_i at a time, as well. The perceptron (section 3.6.2) can be understood as a stochastic subgradient ascent method if the order of the training examples is randomized.

The term "batch" is used to refer to algorithms like (sub)gradient ascent as presented in sections A.3 and A.3.1, in contrast to "online" or "incremental" methods. "Mini-batch" algorithms consider small subsets of the training data on each iteration, and provide a middle ground that, in some cases, works better than either extreme (Gimpel et al., 2010, Liang and Klein, 2009).

A.4 CONJUGATE GRADIENT AND QUASI-NEWTON METHODS

A collection of useful and easily-implemented algorithms have been developed that are much faster to converge in practice than gradient ascent. We consider these next. Because open-source implementations of these methods are now available in many programming languages, and because a full derivation and analysis of these general-purpose optimization algorithms is beyond the scope of this book, we direct the interested reader to Bertsekas (1999) and Nocedal and Wright (2006).

A.4.1 CONJUGATE GRADIENT

The central idea of **conjugate gradient** methods is to design the *ascend* update function in such a way that each successive step is "conjugate" (informally, orthogonal with respect to the objective function Φ) to previous steps. The goal on the tth iteration is to choose a vector $\mathbf{u}^{(t)}$ and update:

$$ascend(\mathbf{w}^{(t-1)}, \Phi) = \mathbf{w}^{(t-1)} + \alpha\mathbf{u}^{(t)} \tag{A.18}$$

with α chosen according to a line search as in gradient ascent (equation A.9). We index $\mathbf{u}$ by the time step t because previous iterations' $\mathbf{u}$ values are required for calculating $\mathbf{u}$, so the *ascend* function must save some state.

There are several variations on calculating $\mathbf{u}$, but most notably, there is an exact method that converges in d iterations when Φ is a quadratic function of the form $\frac{1}{2}\mathbf{w}^\top\mathbf{Q}\mathbf{w} + \boldsymbol{b}^\top\mathbf{w}$ with $\mathbf{Q}$ positive definite. For other functions, the conjugacy property is not guaranteed, and restarts are required from time to time.

The attraction of conjugate gradient methods is that the calculations required are nearly the same as for gradient ascent: the function Φ and its gradient, at different iterates $\mathbf{w}^{(t)}$. The additional calculations (finding $\mathbf{u}$) are generic and do not depend on anything other than the basic calculations Φ and its gradient.

Interested readers are referred to chapter 5 of Nocedal and Wright (2006) for more detail.

A.4.2 NEWTON'S METHOD

Newton's method is a *second*-order method that makes use of the matrix of second derivatives of Φ to take smarter steps toward an optimum. Letting $\mathbf{H}\Phi : \mathbb{R}^d \to \mathbb{R}^{d\times d}$ denote the matrix function that calculates second derivatives of Φ at a given point,[5] Newton's method defines:

$$ascend(\mathbf{w}^{(t-1)}, \Phi) = \mathbf{w}^{(t-1)} + \left[\mathbf{H}\Phi(\mathbf{w}^{(t-1)})\right]^{-1} \nabla\Phi(\mathbf{w}^{(t-1)}) \tag{A.19}$$

Newton's method is not used often for NLP problems because d can be on the scale of $10^{4\sim7}$, making the calculation and storage of $\mathbf{H_w}\Phi$ infeasible. Instead, approximations to the inverse of $\mathbf{H_w}\Phi(\mathbf{w}^{(t-1)})$ are used; these are known as **quasi-Newton** methods.

A.4.3 LIMITED MEMORY BFGS

The Broyden-Fletcher-Goldfarb-Shanno (BFGS) method is the most successful quasi-Newton optimization algorithm. At the tth iteration, the *ascend* function chooses a $d \times d$ matrix $\mathbf{M}^{(t)}$ that approximates the inverse Hessian (equation A.19):

$$ascend(\mathbf{w}^{(t-1)}, \Phi) = \mathbf{w}^{(t-1)} + \alpha\mathbf{M}^{(t)}\nabla\Phi(\mathbf{w}^{(t-1)}) \tag{A.20}$$

[5]"H" is used because this matrix is sometimes called the Hessian.

The L-BFGS method (Liu and Nocedal, 1989) approximates the update vector using a fixed number of vectors in $\mathbb{R}^d$ and is widely used in NLP for unconstrained optimization problems relating to log-linear models (Malouf, 2002). Like conjugate gradient methods, only Φ and its gradient need to be provided; all other calculations depend only on these. Versions dealing with constrained problems involving lower and/or upper bounds on some or all variables (Benson and Moré, 2001, Byrd et al., 1995) and dealing with non-differentiability arising from L_1 regularization (Andrew and Gao, 2007) have been developed. Implementations of these algorithms are widely available.

The BFGS family of algorithms is, at this writing, the most commonly used batch approach for unconstrained optimization of differentiable functions arising in NLP research. Online methods, however, are increasing in popularity.

A.5 "AGGRESSIVE" ONLINE LEARNERS

Recently a technique called the **margin-infused relaxation algorithm** (MIRA; Crammer and Singer, 2003, Crammer et al., 2006) has become popular in NLP, starting with McDonald et al. (2005a). MIRA is an online algorithm that closely resembles the perceptron (section 3.6.2, algorithm 3), but rather than using a fixed learning rate α, a fixed schedule for decreasing α, averaging, or voting, it introduces an alternative way to think about regularization. MIRA can be understood in a larger framework of "aggressive" learning algorithms; see Shalev-Schwartz and Singer (2006).

The central idea in MIRA, on a single iteration, is to update the weights $\mathbf{w}$ in a way that conservatively does not move far from the current solution, while still correctly solving the current example. On an iteration where example i is considered, the *ascend* function for MIRA defines:

$$\begin{aligned} \mathit{ascend}(\mathbf{w}^{(t-1)}, \Phi) &= \min_{\mathbf{w} \in \mathbb{R}^d} \left\| \mathbf{w} - \mathbf{w}^{(t-1)} \right\|_2 \\ &\text{such that } \mathbf{w}^\top \mathbf{g}(\tilde{\boldsymbol{x}}_i, \tilde{\boldsymbol{y}}_i) - \left(\max_{\boldsymbol{y} \in \mathcal{Y}_{\boldsymbol{x}}} \mathbf{w}^\top \mathbf{g}(\tilde{\boldsymbol{x}}_i, \boldsymbol{y}) \right) \geq \mathit{cost}(\tilde{\boldsymbol{x}}_i, \boldsymbol{y}, \tilde{\boldsymbol{y}}_i) \end{aligned} \tag{A.21}$$

The constraint corresponds closely to the constraints in equation 3.103. The above is technically known as "one-best" MIRA; a "k-best" variant is also available, in which k constraints are included for the k highest-scoring $\boldsymbol{y} \in \mathcal{Y}_{\tilde{\boldsymbol{x}}_i}$.

For many problems, the optimization problem in equation A.21 has a closed form. The absence of a line search is, in particular, appealing.

Interestingly, MIRA was not derived starting with any particular objective function Φ. The structural SVM objective can be demonstrated to underlie MIRA. Martins et al. (2010) give a derivation of a class of online training algorithms, of which one-best and k-best MIRA are special cases, starting from objective functions like conditional likelihood (equations 3.74 and A.10) and margin (equations 3.103 and A.13). These algorithms ultimately show a strong resemblence to stochastic (sub)gradient ascent, but with a simple rule for calculating the step size α. The general technique is applicable for training structured models when L_2 regularization is used, and it is known as **dual coordinate ascent**.[6]

A dual coordinate ascent update for maximizing the margin (equation A.13) on an iteration considering training example i is:

$$\begin{aligned}
& \mathit{ascend}(\mathbf{w}^{(t-1)}, \Phi) \\
= \; & \mathbf{w}^{(t-1)} + \min\left(\frac{1}{C}, \frac{\mathbf{w}^{(t-1)\top}\mathbf{g}(\tilde{\boldsymbol{x}}_i, \hat{\boldsymbol{y}}) - \mathbf{w}^{(t-1)\top}\mathbf{g}(\tilde{\boldsymbol{x}}_i, \tilde{\boldsymbol{y}}_i) + \mathit{cost}(\hat{\boldsymbol{y}}, \tilde{\boldsymbol{x}}_i, \tilde{\boldsymbol{y}}_i)}{\left\|\mathbf{g}(\tilde{\boldsymbol{x}}_i, \hat{\boldsymbol{y}}) - \mathbf{g}(\tilde{\boldsymbol{x}}_i, \tilde{\boldsymbol{y}}_i)\right\|_2^2}\right) \\
& \times \left(\mathbf{g}(\tilde{\boldsymbol{x}}_i, \tilde{\boldsymbol{y}}_i) - \mathbf{g}(\tilde{\boldsymbol{x}}_i, \hat{\boldsymbol{y}})\right)
\end{aligned} \tag{A.22}$$

where

$$\hat{\boldsymbol{y}} = \operatorname*{argmax}_{\boldsymbol{y} \in \mathcal{Y}_{\tilde{\boldsymbol{x}}_i}} \mathbf{w}^{(t-1)\top}\mathbf{g}(\tilde{\boldsymbol{x}}_i, \boldsymbol{y}) + \mathit{cost}(\boldsymbol{y}, \tilde{\boldsymbol{x}}_i, \tilde{\boldsymbol{y}}_i) \tag{A.23}$$

The update in equation A.22 is equivalent to the update used by one-best MIRA.

The dual coordinate update for maximizing conditional likelihood (equation A.10) on an iteration considering training example i is:

$$\begin{aligned}
& \mathit{ascend}(\mathbf{w}^{(t-1)}, \Phi_{\mathrm{LL}}) \\
= \; & \mathbf{w}^{(t-1)} + \min\left(\frac{1}{C}, \frac{-\log p_{\mathbf{w}^{(t-1)}}(\tilde{\boldsymbol{y}}_i \mid \tilde{\boldsymbol{x}}_i)}{\left\|\mathbf{g}(\tilde{\boldsymbol{x}}_i, \tilde{\boldsymbol{y}}_i) - \mathbb{E}_{p_{\mathbf{w}^{(t-1)}}(\boldsymbol{Y} \mid \boldsymbol{X} = \tilde{\boldsymbol{x}}_i)}[\mathbf{g}(\tilde{\boldsymbol{x}}_i, \boldsymbol{Y})]\right\|_2^2}\right) \\
& \times \left(\mathbf{g}(\tilde{\boldsymbol{x}}_i, \tilde{\boldsymbol{y}}_i) - \mathbb{E}_{p_{\mathbf{w}^{(t-1)}}(\boldsymbol{Y} \mid \boldsymbol{X} = \tilde{\boldsymbol{x}}_i)}[g(\tilde{\boldsymbol{x}}_i, \boldsymbol{Y})]\right)
\end{aligned} \tag{A.24}$$

We finally give a general form of the dual coordinate ascent update. Let the optimization problem take the form:

$$\max_{\mathbf{w} \in \mathbb{R}^d} \Phi(\mathbf{w}) = \max_{\mathbf{w} \in \mathbb{R}^d} \sum_{i=1}^{\tilde{N}} \Phi_i(\mathbf{w}) - \frac{C}{2}\|\mathbf{w}\|_2^2 \tag{A.25}$$

Then the dual coordinate ascent update on iteration t with selected example i is:

$$\mathit{ascend}(\mathbf{w}^{(t-1)}, \Phi) = \mathbf{w}^{(t-1)} + \min\left(\frac{1}{C}, \frac{-\Phi_i(\mathbf{w}^{(t-1)})}{\|\nabla\Phi_i(\mathbf{w}^{(t-1)})\|_2^2}\right) \nabla\Phi_i(\mathbf{w}^{(t-1)}) \tag{A.26}$$

A.6 IMPROVED ITERATIVE SCALING

Consider the problem of maximizing conditional likelihood for a globally normalized conditional log-linear model with fully observed inputs and outputs (section 3.5):

$$\Phi(\mathbf{w}) = \sum_{i=1}^{\tilde{N}} \left(\mathbf{w}^\top \mathbf{g}(\tilde{\boldsymbol{x}}_i, \tilde{\boldsymbol{y}}_i) - \log \sum_{\boldsymbol{y} \in \mathcal{Y}_{\tilde{\boldsymbol{x}}_i}} \exp \mathbf{w}^\top \mathbf{g}(\tilde{\boldsymbol{x}}_i, \boldsymbol{y})\right) \tag{A.27}$$

[6] Like many names, this one is potentially confusing; it does not work in the dual explicitly. It equates to performing coordinate ascent in the dual. The connection is clarified by Martins et al. (2010).

In most recent implementations, it is common to use quasi-Newton methods or stochastic gradient ascent to optimize equation A.27. Improved iterative scaling is an older technique that is slower in most cases and makes some assumptions about the form of the model. Generalized iterative scaling was derived by Darroch and Ratcliff (1972) and adapted as described here by Rosenfeld (1994) for the conditional modeling case.[7] We follow Berger (1997) in deriving the improved iterative scaling algorithm for learning the weights of this model.[8] We include this derivation as an example of a once widely used algorithm, showing how it can be understood in the more general framework of optimization algorithms.

We seek an update vector $\mathbf{u} \in \mathbb{R}^d$ in order to define

$$ascend(\mathbf{w}^{(t-1)}, \Phi) = \mathbf{w}^{(t-1)} + \mathbf{u} \tag{A.28}$$

We seek $\mathbf{u}$ such that $\Phi(\mathbf{w} + \mathbf{u}) - \Phi(\mathbf{w})$ is as large as possible, so that on iteration t, we might seek to solve the optimization problem

$$\begin{aligned} \max_{\mathbf{u} \in \mathbb{R}^d} \quad & \Phi(\mathbf{w} + \mathbf{u}) - \Phi(\mathbf{w}) \\ &= \sum_{i=1}^{\tilde{N}} \left(\mathbf{u}^\top \mathbf{g}(\tilde{\boldsymbol{x}}_i, \tilde{\boldsymbol{y}}_i) - \log \frac{\sum_{\boldsymbol{y} \in \mathcal{Y}} \exp(\mathbf{w} + \mathbf{u})^\top \mathbf{g}(\tilde{\boldsymbol{x}}_i, \boldsymbol{y})}{\sum_{\boldsymbol{y} \in \mathcal{Y}} \exp \mathbf{w}^\top \mathbf{g}(\tilde{\boldsymbol{x}}_i, \boldsymbol{y})} \right) \end{aligned} \tag{A.29}$$

Optimizing equation A.29 would give us the best possible update; it would lead us to the maximum of Φ. It should be clear, then, that equation A.29 is not realistic, but it does suggest that any step we take such that $\Phi(\mathbf{w} + \mathbf{u}) - \Phi(\mathbf{w}) > 0$ will be an improvement. Our approach will be to produce a lower bound on this function, then optimize the lower bound.

We do so in three steps. The first uses the fact that, for all $a > 0$,

$$-\log a \geq 1 - a \tag{A.30}$$

The second step will make an assumption that all feature values are nonnegative, i.e., that $\mathbf{g} : \mathcal{X} \times \mathcal{Y} \to \mathbb{R}^d_{\geq 0}$. The third step uses Jensen's inequality, if $\mathbf{p}, \mathbf{q} \in \mathbb{R}^d_{\geq 0}$ such that $\sum_{j=1}^d p_j = 1$, then

$$-\exp \mathbf{p}^\top \mathbf{q} \geq -\sum_j p_j \exp q_j \tag{A.31}$$

[7] Rosenfeld attributes the technique to Peter Brown, Stephen Della Pietra, Vincent Della Pietra, Robert Mercer, Arthur Nadas, and Salim Roukos, though the report was cited as "forthcoming" at the time and appears not to be public.

[8] One reviewer notes anecdotally that generalized iterative scaling may be faster than improved iterative scaling in some cases.

The derivation is as follows:[9]

$$\sum_{i=1}^{\tilde{N}} \left(\mathbf{u}^\top \mathbf{g}(\tilde{\boldsymbol{x}}_i, \tilde{\boldsymbol{y}}_i) - \log \frac{\sum_{\boldsymbol{y} \in \mathcal{Y}} \exp(\mathbf{w} + \mathbf{u})^\top \mathbf{g}(\tilde{\boldsymbol{x}}_i, \boldsymbol{y})}{\sum_{\boldsymbol{y} \in \mathcal{Y}} \exp \mathbf{w}^\top \mathbf{g}(\tilde{\boldsymbol{x}}_i, \boldsymbol{y})} \right)$$

$$\overset{\text{eq. A.30}}{\geq} \sum_{i=1}^{\tilde{N}} \left(\mathbf{u}^\top \mathbf{g}(\tilde{\boldsymbol{x}}_i, \tilde{\boldsymbol{y}}_i) + 1 - \frac{\sum_{\boldsymbol{y} \in \mathcal{Y}} \exp(\mathbf{w} + \mathbf{u})^\top \mathbf{g}(\tilde{\boldsymbol{x}}_i, \boldsymbol{y})}{\sum_{\boldsymbol{y} \in \mathcal{Y}} \exp \mathbf{w}^\top \mathbf{g}(\tilde{\boldsymbol{x}}_i, \boldsymbol{y})} \right) \tag{A.32}$$

$$= \sum_{i=1}^{\tilde{N}} \left(\mathbf{u}^\top \mathbf{g}(\tilde{\boldsymbol{x}}_i, \tilde{\boldsymbol{y}}_i) + 1 - \sum_{\boldsymbol{y} \in \mathcal{Y}} p_{\mathbf{w}}(\boldsymbol{y} \mid \tilde{\boldsymbol{x}}_i) \exp \mathbf{u}^\top \mathbf{g}(\tilde{\boldsymbol{x}}_i, \boldsymbol{y}) \right) \tag{A.33}$$

$$= \sum_{i=1}^{\tilde{N}} \left(\mathbf{u}^\top \mathbf{g}(\tilde{\boldsymbol{x}}_i, \tilde{\boldsymbol{y}}_i) + 1 - \sum_{\boldsymbol{y} \in \mathcal{Y}} p_{\mathbf{w}}(\boldsymbol{y} \mid \tilde{\boldsymbol{x}}_i) \exp \sum_{j=1}^{d} u_j g_j(\tilde{\boldsymbol{x}}_i, \boldsymbol{y}) \right) \tag{A.34}$$

$$= \sum_{i=1}^{\tilde{N}} \left(\mathbf{u}^\top \mathbf{g}(\tilde{\boldsymbol{x}}_i, \tilde{\boldsymbol{y}}_i) + 1 - \sum_{\boldsymbol{y} \in \mathcal{Y}} p_{\mathbf{w}}(\boldsymbol{y} \mid \tilde{\boldsymbol{x}}_i) \exp \left(\|\mathbf{g}(\tilde{\boldsymbol{x}}_i, \boldsymbol{y})\|_1 \sum_{j=1}^{d} \frac{u_j g_j(\tilde{\boldsymbol{x}}_i, \boldsymbol{y})}{\|\mathbf{g}(\tilde{\boldsymbol{x}}_i, \boldsymbol{y})\|_1} \right) \right)$$

$$\overset{\text{eq. A.31}}{\geq} \sum_{i=1}^{\tilde{N}} \left(\mathbf{u}^\top \mathbf{g}(\tilde{\boldsymbol{x}}_i, \tilde{\boldsymbol{y}}_i) + 1 - \sum_{\boldsymbol{y} \in \mathcal{Y}} p_{\mathbf{w}}(\boldsymbol{y} \mid \tilde{\boldsymbol{x}}_i) \sum_{j=1}^{d} \frac{g_j(\tilde{\boldsymbol{x}}_i, \boldsymbol{y})}{\|\mathbf{g}(\tilde{\boldsymbol{x}}_i, \boldsymbol{y})\|_1} \exp(\|\mathbf{g}(\tilde{\boldsymbol{x}}_i, \boldsymbol{y})\|_1 u_j) \right) \tag{A.35}$$

The first derivative of equation A.35 with respect to any u_j is:

$$\sum_{i=1}^{\tilde{N}} \left(g_j(\tilde{\boldsymbol{x}}_i, \tilde{\boldsymbol{y}}_i) - \sum_{\boldsymbol{y} \in \mathcal{Y}} p_{\mathbf{w}}(\boldsymbol{y} \mid \tilde{\boldsymbol{x}}_i) g_j(\tilde{\boldsymbol{x}}_i, \boldsymbol{y}) \exp(\|\mathbf{g}(\tilde{\boldsymbol{x}}_i, \boldsymbol{y})\|_1 u_j) \right) \tag{A.36}$$

This gives the following closed form for u_j:

$$\log \frac{\sum_{i=1}^{\tilde{N}} g_j(\tilde{\boldsymbol{x}}_i, \tilde{\boldsymbol{y}}_i)}{\sum_{i=1}^{\tilde{N}} \sum_{\boldsymbol{y} \in \mathcal{Y}} p_{\mathbf{w}}(\boldsymbol{y} \mid \tilde{\boldsymbol{x}}_i) g_j(\tilde{\boldsymbol{x}}_i, \boldsymbol{y}) \exp \|\mathbf{g}(\tilde{\boldsymbol{x}}_i, \boldsymbol{y})\|_1} \tag{A.37}$$

Notice that the denominator corresponds to a sum of expected feature values, scaled by example: $\mathbb{E}_{p_{\mathbf{w}}(\boldsymbol{Y} \mid \tilde{\boldsymbol{x}}_i)}[g_j(\tilde{\boldsymbol{x}}_i, \boldsymbol{Y}) \exp \|\mathbf{g}(\tilde{\boldsymbol{x}}_i, \boldsymbol{Y})\|_1]$. This differs from the expectations we calculated in service of the gradient of Φ in section 3.5. If $\mathbf{g}$ is designed to always sum to a known, fixed value for any $\boldsymbol{y}$ given $\boldsymbol{x}$, then the update is much simpler.

More discussion and extensions relating to improved iterative scaling can be found in Goodman (2002).

[9]Corresponding to equation A.31 let, for each i and $\boldsymbol{y}$ in turn,

$$\begin{aligned} p_j &= \frac{g_j(\tilde{\boldsymbol{x}}_i, \boldsymbol{y})}{\|\mathbf{g}(\tilde{\boldsymbol{x}}_i, \boldsymbol{y})\|_1} \\ q_j &= \|\mathbf{g}(\tilde{\boldsymbol{x}}_i, \boldsymbol{y})\|_1 u_j \end{aligned}$$

APPENDIX B

Experimentation

The aim of this appendix is to provide concrete advice about conducting experiments in NLP.

B.1 METHODOLOGY

At a bare minimum, an experiment involves two predictors, h and h' that differ in a well-defined, experimenter-controled way. This difference is the "independent variable" in the language of experimental design. Some examples of such a difference include:

- the data used to train them (e.g., amount, domain, preprocessing, annotation presence/absence or quality);
- the algorithm used to train them;
- the training criterion or loss function;
- the family, features, or independence assumptions of the underlying model;
- the kinds of approximate inference methods used during training or decoding;
- the model complexity term; or
- the use of prior knowledge and linguistic resources or databases in defining the model.

There may, of course, be more than two predictors.

We assume h and h' are each to be applied to a test dataset, $\langle \dot{\boldsymbol{x}}_1, \ldots, \dot{\boldsymbol{x}}_{\dot{N}} \rangle$, and their predictions compared. Most commonly, the test set includes gold-standard annotations, $\langle \dot{\boldsymbol{y}}_1, \ldots, \dot{\boldsymbol{y}}_{\dot{N}} \rangle$, and our comparison involves determining, for some cost function of interest, whether

$$\frac{1}{\dot{N}} \sum_{i=1}^{\dot{N}} cost(\dot{\boldsymbol{x}}_i, h(\dot{\boldsymbol{x}}_i), \dot{\boldsymbol{y}}_i) \quad < \quad \frac{1}{\dot{N}} \sum_{i=1}^{\dot{N}} cost(\dot{\boldsymbol{x}}_i, h'(\dot{\boldsymbol{x}}_i), \dot{\boldsymbol{y}}_i) \tag{B.1}$$

in which case, we conclude that h is preferable to h'. Note that this is really a proxy for a deeper question, whether:

$$\mathbb{E}[cost(\boldsymbol{X}, h(\boldsymbol{X}), \boldsymbol{Y})] \quad < \quad \mathbb{E}[cost(\boldsymbol{X}, h'(\boldsymbol{X}), \boldsymbol{Y})] \tag{B.2}$$

with the expectations taken under the "true" distribution over $\boldsymbol{X}$ and $\boldsymbol{Y}$.

This is not the only kind of test we might perform, and in a given study, we might be interested in more than one cost function. For example, many linguistic structure predictors involve a tradeoff between precision (i.e., of the predicted target elements, what fraction are correct?) and recall (i.e., what fraction of correct elements were predicted?). Further, it is often the case that more than two predictors are compared at a time. The simple comparison described above serves as an illustrative example.

B.1.1 TRAINING, DEVELOPMENT, AND TESTING

The most important rule of experimentation with empirical methods is to keep the test data out of the training process. If the learning algorithm has been permitted to gather information from the test data, then the test dataset cannot provide a reasonable estimate of the learned predictor's performance on unseen data.

While this may seem simple, it is easy to violate this rule. For example, often learning algorithms include some "hyperparameters" whose settings can affect performance. (An example is the scalar on a regularization term, denoted C throughout this text.) Learning several instances of a predictor h with essentially the same method but different hyperparameter settings can lead to wide variations in measured performance on the test dataset. If one chooses to report the results only under the best-performing hyperparameter setting, then one has permitted the test dataset to influence the choice of the final model. Such a result may be reported, but it should be described as an oracle (see below). The conventional way to avoid this kind of violation is to reserve a development dataset, distinct from the test dataset, for tuning hyperparameters.

Even being careful about hyperparameters is not quite enough since the development of NLP models is not fully automatic. Indeed, any data that the researcher has perused manually is arguably "compromised," in the sense that it could have an influence on the implemented model. This could happen, for example, in the researcher's design of $\mathcal{Y}$ or choice of features. While looking at data is generally a wise practice in empirical research, it is best to evaluate models on test data that one has *not* looked at.

When available, it is wise to conduct experiments on the "standard" splits of a dataset into training, development, and test, ensuring that comparisons to earlier results are valid. There is some danger in standard dataset splits because over time research conclusions may tend to favor techniques that happen, by chance, to perform well on the standard test dataset, a kind of community-wide overfitting. In our opinion, this is a risk run when standard datasets do not change over decades (e.g., in parsing experiments, the Penn Treebank is usually split into §02–21 for training, §22 for development, and §23 for test), but is easily avoided by the regular introduction of new test datasets (e.g., as done in the series of textual entailment challenges, Bar-Haim et al., 2006, Dagan et al., 2005, etc.).

B.1.2 CROSS-VALIDATION

In any experiment, there is always concern that the random choice of the test set leads to an anomalous set of examples and a faulty conclusion. One way to strengthen our conclusions is to test on multiple test datasets. Because the same concern applies to *training* datasets (when we use empirical methods that involve learning from data), we may wish to split our full dataset more than one way and consider a collection of training/testing trials.

At its simplest, cross-validation involves taking the dataset, $\langle\langle \boldsymbol{x}_1, \boldsymbol{y}_1\rangle, \ldots, \langle \boldsymbol{x}_N, \boldsymbol{y}_N\rangle\rangle$, and dividing it into K "folds" or disjoint partitions of equal size (we assume K evenly divides N):

$$\Big\langle \langle \boldsymbol{x}_{i_{1,1}}, \boldsymbol{y}_{i_{1,1}}\rangle, \ldots, \langle \boldsymbol{x}_{i_{1,\frac{N}{K}}}, \boldsymbol{y}_{i_{1,\frac{N}{K}}}\rangle, \langle \boldsymbol{x}_{i_{2,1}}, \boldsymbol{y}_{i_{2,1}}\rangle, \ldots, \langle \boldsymbol{x}_{i_{2,\frac{N}{K}}}, \boldsymbol{y}_{i_{2,\frac{N}{K}}}\rangle,$$
$$\ldots, \quad \langle \boldsymbol{x}_{i_{K,1}}, \boldsymbol{y}_{i_{K,1}}\rangle, \ldots, \langle \boldsymbol{x}_{i_{K,\frac{N}{K}}}, \boldsymbol{y}_{i_{K,\frac{N}{K}}}\rangle \Big\rangle$$

K iterations are performed, each using a different fold k, referring to $\langle\langle \boldsymbol{x}_{i_{k,j}}, \boldsymbol{y}_{i_{k,j}}\rangle\rangle_{j=1}^{\frac{N}{K}}$, as the test dataset and the others for training. Experimental results are typically averaged across the trials, and if K is suitably large, standard error estimates[1] may be included to help understand how much the split of the data affects performance. In this setting, it is crucial to heed the advice above about looking at testing data, yet it is also nearly impossible to do so since all of the data is test data on some iteration.

Therefore, cross-validation is perhaps better used as a technique for tuning hyperparameters and making high-level decisions. After gathering information on K splits of the data, hyperparameters can be set and all of the training set used to train—then a separate unseen test dataset should be used for testing. Another option is to evaluate the K different models each on the single separate test set, then report average performance across the K runs.

When the data are believed to be independently and identically distributed, the division into folds can be a random permutation. In NLP, we often wish to stratify the data to control for effects within documents or temporal/topical effects across text collections. To accomplish this, the folds may be designed to keep the examples in their original order or to keep examples from the same document or source together.

Cross-validation is not widespread in NLP, in part because it is expensive, requiring K times as many runs of training algorithms.

B.1.3 COMPARISON WITHOUT REPLICATION

Not infrequently, an implementation of one (or more) of the predictors h is not readily available to the researcher. In a perfect world, research implementations would be shared openly (Pedersen, 2008), but this is not currently the situation. Reimplementing a predictor h is time-consuming, and it can be avoided if earlier experiments provide sufficient detail to identify the exact training dataset

[1]Discussed in section B.2.2.

used to build h and the exact test dataset upon which h has been evaluated; indeed, this is a key advantage of conventionalizing training/test dataset splits. If the same conditions are provided for the newer approach h' as for earlier experiments with h, it is acceptable to perform the comparison this way. It is helpful if the predictions from the earlier experiment are provided by the authors of the earlier study, permitting more detailed analysis. When citing earlier results that have not been replicated, it is appropriate to make this fact clear.

B.1.4 ORACLES AND UPPER BOUNDS

An **oracle** is a predictor that is given access to certain information about the test data, in order to simulate a kind of "best possible world." For example, consider the matter of tuning model hyperparameters on development data. We may wish to know how much the performance of a predictor suffers due to imperfect tuning methods. We might therefore tune hyperparameters on the *test* data, giving an idea of how much further improvement might be expected from improved tuning. Another example, often appropriate when the prediction is conducted in multiple stages, assumes that a particular stage (or stages) of prediction is correct, to see how much performance is affected by errors at that stage. For example, a parser's performance can be compared given sentences that are automatically part of speech tagged versus sentences with gold-standard part of speech tags (the oracle), to measure the effects of part of speech tagging errors on parser performance. Reporting oracles is good practice, as long as the details are laid bare and the oracle is compared to a realistic predictor that does not have the benefit of oracle information.

B.2 HYPOTHESIS TESTING AND RELATED TOPICS

Because empirical methods for building predictors rely heavily on statistics, there is some danger that the statistical methods we use for *building* predictors and the statistical methods we use for *evaluating* predictors will become confused. It is helpful to remember that statistical hypothesis tests have nothing to do with how we acquired h and h'; the same experimental methodology described here should be used even if h and h' are constructed manually and without the use of training data or automatic learning methods at all.

We turn to statistical analyses like hypothesis testing when we want to know whether we can claim predictor h actually outperforms h' in general, on different test sets. The argument is essentially a response to a skeptic who notes that observed differences in predictor quality might be due to good luck rather than real differences.

Hypothesis testing involves the statement of a **null hypothesis**, or a default theory adopted by our imaginary skeptic. Given our results, we ask the question: is there enough evidence to *reject* the null hypothesis? If the answer is "no," we cannot reject the null hypothesis (though we need not accept it). If the answer is "yes," we may reject the null hypothesis, fully cognizant that there is some possibility that we have been misled by anomalous results (e.g., resulting from anomalous data). Because we will never obtain experimental results where such a mistake is impossible, hypothesis testing typically revolves around the question, "How likely are these results to have occurred by chance, i.e., if the null hypothesis is correct?" The more surprisingly unlikely the results are (conditioned on the null hypothesis), the more easily we may reject the null hypothesis.

Hypothesis testing is one tool for drawing conclusions from experimental data, but it is not the only one. We therefore cover standard errors and confidence intervals first, and introduce the bootstrap, a randomized method that can simplify standard errors, confidence intervals, and hypothesis tests. We then turn to a discussion of hypothesis tests found in NLP.

B.2.1 TERMINOLOGY

We begin with a sample of N events, denoted $\langle u_1, \ldots, u_N \rangle$, each u_i the observed value of a random variable U_i ranging over the event space $\mathcal{U}$, drawn according to an unknown distribution ϕ.[2] We will use V to denote a numerical measurement taken on the sample of events (i.e., V is a function of the random variable U, and hence also a random variable) and $\langle v_1, \ldots, v_N \rangle$ to denote the measurements taken on the sample $\langle u_1, \ldots, u_N \rangle$; we will overload notation and let $v_i = v(u_i)$.

We must now differentiate between two different types of numerical values.

- A **parameter** is a characteristic of the underlying distribution ϕ. In some cases, it may be part of the *definition* of that distribution (e.g., if the sample events U_i were drawn according to a Gaussian and v is the identity function, then the mean and variance define ϕ). A parameter need not be part of the *generative* story for our data, however; the mean value of a fairly-weighted, six-sided die is 3.5, but the uniform multinomial distribution that characterizes ϕ is defined without recourse to that mean. Similarly, if each u_i is a sentence and $v(u_i)$ is the number of words in u_i, most theories of the distribution from which the u_i are drawn do not hinge on the mean sentence length directly (it is an emergent property), but it is nonetheless a parameter of the distribution. We will use μ_V to denote the true mean of some measurement $v : \mathcal{U} \to \mathbb{R}$ under the distribution ϕ:

$$\mu_V = \mathbb{E}_{\phi(U)}[v(U)] = \sum_{u \in \mathcal{U}} \phi(U)v(U) \tag{B.3}$$

  Note that μ_V uses capital "V" since it is really a statement about the random variable V (which is a function of the random variable U). The parameter μ_V is *not* a random variable.

- A **statistic** is a function of a dataset (in our experiments, a test dataset) that serves a descriptive summary of that dataset. For example, the **sample mean**, a statistic, is defined for a random variable V by

$$m_V = \frac{1}{N} \sum_{i=1}^{N} v_i \tag{B.4}$$

[2]In statistics, the "events" are often described as "individuals" sampled from a "population." When dealing with language data, these terms are counter-intuitive as there is not clearly a finite population of sentences or documents from which our sample is drawn.

(The subscript V reminds us which random variable we are referring to.) In the die example, it is easy to imagine m_V being different from the true mean $\mu_V = 3.5$, especially if N is small.[3] It is helpful to remember that a statistic is a random variable, because it depends on a randomly sampled dataset. To be perfectly rigorous in notation, we should write "$m_V(\langle v_1, \ldots, v_N \rangle)$" to indicate that the statistic is a function of the dataset, though we will follow convention in refraining from doing so.

B.2.2 STANDARD ERROR

Of course, the sample mean m_V is often used as an estimate of the true mean μ_V. It is natural to ask how accurate this estimate is, and the field of statistics provides a first answer: for any statistic (which is a random variable), the **standard error** is the standard deviation of the statistic's value, under the sampling distribution ϕ. A small standard error is desirable; it means that the statistic is likely a close proxy for the parameter value. See figure B.1.

Just as there are two means (the true mean, a parameter, which is a property of ϕ, and the sample mean statistic, which is a random variable hinging on the sample), there are two standard errors for any statistic:

1. The *true* standard error, defined as the standard deviation of the distribution over values of the statistic—a parameter. For statistic t_V, we denote the true standard error σ_{t_V}.
2. An estimate of the true standard error—a statistic. We use $\mathfrak{se}_{t_V}$ to denote this estimate.

To take the sample mean statistic m_V as an example, it follows from the Central Limit Theorem[4] that the standard error of the sample mean is

$$\sigma_{m_V} = \frac{\sigma_V}{\sqrt{N}} \tag{B.5}$$

where σ_V denotes the standard deviation of the random variable V under ϕ. σ_V is a parameter, as is σ_{m_V}. Notice that as the size of the sample, N, grows, the standard error diminishes.

We can *estimate* the standard error of the sample mean using the so-called "plug-in principle." If we can estimate σ_V (the true standard deviation), then we can plug that estimate into equation B.5 and obtain an estimate of σ_{m_V} (the true standard error of the sample mean). The sample standard deviation is defined by

$$s_V = \sqrt{\frac{1}{N-1} \sum_{i=1}^{N} (v_i - m_V)^2} \tag{B.6}$$

[3]If $N = 1$ or $N = 3$, it is not possible that $m_V = \mu_V$.

[4]I.e., the sampling distribution of the sample mean m_V approaches a normal distribution with mean μ_V and variance σ_V^2/N as the sample size N increases, where μ_V is the *true* mean of the measurement V under the distribution ϕ, and σ_V^2 is the *true* variance of the measurement V under ϕ.

parameter	μ_V		σ_V		θ_V
sample statistic	m_V	eq. B.4	s_V	eq. B.6	t_V
true standard error (parameter)	σ_{m_V}		σ_{s_V}		σ_{t_V}
estimated standard error (statistic)	$\mathfrak{se}_{m_V}$	eq. B.5	$\mathfrak{se}_{s_V}$		$\mathfrak{se}_{t_V}$

Figure B.1: Notation for parameters, estimates, (true) standard errors, and estimates of standard errors, for the mean μ, standard deviation σ, and arbitrary parameter θ. V denotes the original random variable, samples of which are observed. Note that we could move the bottom two rows up as additional columns and the table would still be correct.

This gives the following estimate of the true standard error for m_V, σ_{m_V}:

$$\mathfrak{se}_{m_V} = \frac{s_V}{\sqrt{N}} \tag{B.7}$$

The plug-in principle boils down to substituting the sample distribution f for the true distribution ϕ. We will write the sample distribution as f; for all $u \in \mathcal{U}$:

$$f(u) = \frac{1}{N}\sum_{i=1}^{N} \delta(u, u_i) = \frac{\mathit{freq}(u)}{N} \tag{B.8}$$

It is by using f as a proxy for ϕ that we obtain the sample mean statistic as an estimate of the true mean parameter, and this technique, we will see, can be exploited much more creatively.

B.2.3 BEYOND STANDARD ERROR FOR SAMPLE MEANS

So far, when our statistic of interest is a sample mean—for example, equation B.1—we have an easy way of quantifying how much error we might expect in our estimate of the true mean parameter. But this does not get us very far. Unfortunately, there is no general closed form for standard errors of other statistics, like medians, variances, correlations, or (more common in NLP research) precisions, recalls, Bleu scores, and so on.

A randomized technique called the **bootstrap** is quite useful in solving this problem. It is applicable to solving several other problems as well, like hypothesis testing, that are of potentially greater interest in NLP, but we introduce it first for estimating standard errors.

The bootstrap was proposed by Efron (1979). The idea can be understood as another instance of the plug-in principle. In more traditional statistics, we have a sample and "plug in" sample statistics for parameter values whose values are unknown. In the bootstrap approach, we have an empirical distribution (equation B.8), and we use it to generate *samples*, effectively plugging in f for ϕ. First, we generate a sequence of B samples

$$\left\langle \begin{array}{ccc} \langle u^*_{1,1}, u^*_{1,2}, \ldots, u^*_{1,N}\rangle, & \langle u^*_{2,1}, u^*_{2,2}, \ldots, u^*_{2,N}\rangle, & \ldots, \\ \ldots, & \ldots, & \langle u^*_{B,1}, u^*_{B,2}, \ldots, u^*_{B,N}\rangle \end{array} \right\rangle \tag{B.9}$$

each of the same size as the original sample, with each $u^*_{b,i}$ drawn according to the empirical distribution f. For each bootstrap iterate, $b \in \{1, \ldots, B\}$, we estimate the statistic of interest, denoted here t_V, giving a sequence of estimates $\langle t_{V,1}, \ldots, t_{V,B}\rangle$. The standard deviation of the statistic t_V is estimated by the sample standard deviation (now across bootstrap iterates),

$$\mathrm{se}^{\text{boot}}_{t_V} = \sqrt{\sum_{b=1}^{B} \frac{\left(t_{V,b} - \frac{1}{N}\sum_{b'=1}^{B} t_{V,b'}\right)^2}{B-1}} \tag{B.10}$$

As $B \to \infty$, this converges on the "ideal" bootstrap estimate, which is the standard error of t_V when the data are drawn according to f. The bootstrap should be understood as two approximations (we borrow the following expression from Wasserman (2004), adapting to our notation):

$$\sigma_{t_V} \approx \mathrm{se}_{t_V} \approx \mathrm{se}^{\text{boot}}_{t_V} \tag{B.11}$$

σ_{t_V} is the *true* standard error for statistic t_V; se_{t_V} is the standard error estimate under the empirical distribution f (which has no closed form in general; when t_V is the sample mean m_V, the closed form is $s_V/\sqrt{N}$), and $\mathrm{se}^{\text{boot}}_{t_V}$ approximates that estimate using the bootstrap.

B.2.4 CONFIDENCE INTERVALS

Another use of the bootstrap is to calculate **confidence intervals**. Consider a parameter θ of the distribution ϕ. (Given ϕ, θ is fixed.) Given a value $\alpha \in (0, 1)$, l and u are statistics (functions of the data, and hence, random variables) such that

$$P(l < \theta < u) \geq 1 - \alpha \tag{B.12}$$

There is often confusion about how to interpret the idea of a confidence interval. It is not a statement about the probability distribution over values for θ; θ is fixed. One interpretation is that, if we repeatedly sampled from ϕ M times and re-calculated l and u each time, then in fewer than αM cases, the confidence interval would fail to include θ.[5,6]

Suppose we have a statistic of interest, t_V whose sampling distribution is known to be normally distributed with mean θ_V (e.g., the sample mean m_V is known to follow a normal distribution with

[5] Wasserman (2004) questions the usefulness of this interpretation since "we rarely repeat the same experiment over and over," a dubious claim in NLP, though typically our repetitions involve using the same sample repeatedly. He suggests a broader interpretation: if you generated M samples and each time produced l and u for a different, unrelated parameter, then αM of your intervals would "trap" their respective true parameter values.

[6] The discussion of confidence intervals is one place where the frequentist and Bayesian views, the major division in statistics, becomes most apparent. In this discussion, we have adopted a frequentist analysis: we estimate parameters assumed to have a true, albeit unknown, value. The Bayesian approach would instead assume that the parameters have no "true" values, and we can only say that some possible values are more believable than others, based on a prior and the evidence (data). Hence the parameters are actually random variables, and Bayesian analysis defines *credible* intervals, based on the posterior distribution for θ. At this writing, frequentist analyses dominate in NLP experiments and indeed most scientific experiments with similarly simple designs.

mean μ_V). The standard error can be used to produce a confidence interval by letting

$$\begin{aligned} l_{t_V} &= t_V - z_{\alpha/2} \times \mathfrak{se}_{t_V} \\ u_{t_V} &= t_V + z_{\alpha/2} \times \mathfrak{se}_{t_V} \end{aligned} \tag{B.13}$$

where $z_{\alpha/2}$ is the value such that $p(Z > z_{\alpha/2}) = \alpha/2$ and, equivalently, $p(-z_{\alpha/2} < Z < z_{\alpha/2}) = 1 - \alpha$ when $Z \sim \text{Normal}(0, 1)$. $z_{0.025} \approx 1.96$. Note that we could use the bootstrap estimate $\mathfrak{se}_{t_V}^{\text{boot}}$ in place of $\mathfrak{se}_{t_V}$. Under our assumptions, we are confident that 95% of the time, performing this operation will yield l_{t_V} and u_{t_V} such that $l_{t_V} < \theta_V < u_{t_V}$.

A more general approach, which does not depend on an assumption about the sampling distribution for t_V, is the **bootstrap percentile interval**. In its simplest form, this involves calculating a sequence of bootstrap iterate estimates $\langle t_{V,1}, \ldots, t_{V,B}\rangle$, then finding the $\alpha/2$ and $1 - \alpha/2$ quantiles. This is accomplished by sorting the values from least to greatest, denoted $\langle \bar{t}_{V,1}, \ldots, \bar{t}_{V,B}\rangle$, and then letting:

$$\begin{array}{cccccccc} \langle \bar{t}_{V,1}, & \bar{t}_{V,2}, & \ldots, & \bar{t}_{V,\frac{B\alpha}{2}}, & \ldots, & \bar{t}_{V,1-\frac{B\alpha}{2}}, & \ldots, & \bar{t}_{V,B}\rangle \\ & & & \| & & \| & & \\ & & & l_{t_V} & & u_{t_V} & & \end{array} \tag{B.14}$$

In practice, various corrections for bias and skewness in the bootstrap distribution are usually applied; see Efron and Tibshirani (1994) or Davison and Hinkley (1997) for details.

B.2.5 HYPOTHESIS TESTS

We return finally to hypothesis tests. Recall that a hypothesis test asks whether, given the observed results, we can reject the null hypothesis. This is done as follows:

1. State an acceptably high probability of falsely rejecting the null hypothesis, called the significance level, and here denoted α. Usually this hypothesis is about the value of an unknown parameter θ. Commonly we set $\alpha = 0.05$.

2. Calculate the statistic of interest t on the observed data. t is an estimate of θ.

3. Calculate some range of "unsurprising" values for t, under the assumption that the null hypothesis about θ holds. In some settings, to perform the test, we explicitly calculate the probability of the observed result, or the total probability of any value more extreme than the observed result, under the assumption of the null hypothesis; this probability is known as the p-value.[7] In some cases, we explicitly calculate a confidence interval for θ under the null hypothesis.

4. Reject the null hypothesis if t is "surprising." (Equivalently, reject the null hypothesis if the p-value is smaller than α or if t falls outside the confidence interval for θ under the null hypothesis.) This is often described as a statistically significant result.

[7]The p-value is *not* the same as the probability that the null hypothesis is true. It is the probability of our observation, given the null hypothesis.

There are two important dangers to be aware of in using statistical hypothesis testing. The first is the use of multiple tests. If we perform a large number H of hypothesis tests at significance level α, then αH, the number of times we incorrectly reject the null hypothesis (known as a "type I error"), will be large. There are techniques for correcting for this problem, most notably the Dunn-Bonferroni correction (Dunn, 1961).[8] The second danger involves confusion between a failure to find statistical significance (e.g., in a difference between two conditions) and a finding that there *is no difference* between two conditions. These are not equivalent, and statistical "insignificance" does not confirm the null hypothesis. A failure to find a difference does not mean one does not exist. With a larger sample size and a different test, a difference might be detected. For these reasons, NLP researchers are encouraged not to rely solely on tests of statistical significance to judge the strength of experimental outcomes.

In the following discussion, we will consider paired tests, where the statistic of interest involves pairs of measurements on the sample of events $\langle u_1, \ldots, u_N \rangle$:

$$\langle \langle v_1, v'_1 \rangle, \langle v_2, v'_2 \rangle, \ldots, \langle v_N, v'_N \rangle \rangle \tag{B.15}$$

where $v_i = v(u_i)$ and $v'_i = v'(u_i)$. In NLP, v_i and v'_i are most commonly measurements of the error or cost of two different systems (in the notation of section B.1, h and h'), on the test data. While there exist other kinds of hypothesis tests (one-sample and two-sample, unpaired tests, for instance) that may be simpler to describe, NLP most commonly involves paired comparisons since we run each system on the same test set. This equates to a "within-subjects" experimental design, which is more sensitive to fine-grained differences than a two-sample, unpaired test. Often, a paired test equates to a one-sample test on differences between measurements under the two conditions (or functions of those differences).

Before computing power was sufficiently advanced or widespread, published tables of threshold values for test statistics, at different thresholds α, were used to determine significance and estimate p-values. Today, software packages and libraries are available for performing tests given the raw data. Rather than the low-level calculations, we focus on the reasoning underlying each of the tests. They are summarized in figure B.2.

We refrain from making one-size-fits-all recommendations about which test to use, rather giving a description of the tests most commonly used in NLP with a common notation. A similar contribution was made by Yeh (2000).

Student t-Test and Wald Test

A common hypothesis to test is whether the means of our two random variables, μ_V and $\mu_{V'}$, are equal, or equivalently whether $\mu_V - \mu_{V'} = 0$. The null hypothesis, of course, is that are equal.[9] For each event u_i, we let the random variable D_i be defined as the difference:

$$d_i = v_i - v'_i \tag{B.16}$$

[8]To wit: if we perform T hypothesis tests, we replace α by $\frac{\alpha}{T}$ to ensure that our chance of at least one false positive stays below α.
[9]The test for equality versus inequality is known as a *two-sided* test. A one-sided test might check whether $\mu_V - \mu_{V'} > 0$, for example.

test	assumptions	null hypothesis
Student t-test	D_i are independent and normally distributed	$\mu_D = 0$
Wald test	independent samples, $T_{V,V'}$ has a normal sampling distribution	$\theta_{V,V'} =$ some value θ
sign test	independent samples, D_i is continuous	sign of D is Bernoulli, $p = \frac{1}{2}$
Wilcoxon signed-rank test	independent samples, D_i is continuous and symmetric about its median	median of $D = 0$
McNemar test	independent samples, binary measurements	marginals for V and V' are identical
permutation test	independent samples	V and V' are identically distributed
bootstrap test	independent samples	$\theta_{V,V'} =$ some value θ

Figure B.2: Paired hypothesis tests commonly used in NLP, summarized. V_i and V_i' are the paired measurements for instance i. D_i refers to the random variable $V_i - V_i'$. $T_{V,V'}$ is a statistic on the paired data.

Rephrased, our hypothesis test is whether $\mu_D \neq 0$ (i.e., whether we can reject the null hypothesis that $\mu_D = 0$). This is equivalent to a one-sample test on the measurements $\langle d_1, d_2, \ldots, d_N \rangle$.

The t-**test** is a simple and widely used test appropriate in cases where the data (here, the D_i) can be assumed to be independent and normally distributed (Gosset, 1908). The t-test proceeds by calculating the statistic:

$$t_D = \frac{m_D}{\text{se}_{m_D}} = \frac{\sqrt{N} \times m_D}{s_D} \tag{B.17}$$

and determining how surprising this value is, under the assumption that $\mu_D = 0$. Intuitively, if t_D is far from zero, the null hypothesis becomes harder to defend.

Under the null hypothesis (i.e., $\mu_D = 0$) and the normality assumption, the random variable T_D will be distributed according to a t-distribution with $N - 1$ degrees of freedom. A t-distribution has a single parameter ν (the number of degrees of freedom) and assigns density:

$$p_\nu(T = t) = \frac{\Gamma(\frac{\nu+1}{2})}{\sqrt{\nu\pi}\Gamma(\frac{\nu}{2})} \left(1 + \frac{t^2}{\nu}\right)^{-\frac{\nu+1}{2}} \tag{B.18}$$

The t-test asks whether the statistic t_D's absolute value is sufficiently large—larger than a value $t_{N-1,\alpha/2}$ defined so that

$$p_{\nu=N-1}(-t_{N-1,\alpha/2} < T < t_{N-1,\alpha/2}) = 1 - \alpha \tag{B.19}$$

where α is the pre-selected significance level. (This is a two-tailed test; the α probability of a false positive is divided evenly between the chance of a large positive value for T_D and the chance of a large negative value for T_D, under the null hypothesis.) If $|t_D| \geq t^*_{N-1,\alpha/2}$, then we reject the null hypothesis.

When the sample is large ($N > 30$ or so), the t-distribution approaches a standard normal distribution, Normal(0, 1), so we can use the latter to calculate the threshold for rejection of the null hypothesis. This is called the **Wald test** (Wald, 1943). The same statistic, t_D in equation B.17, is calculated based on the differences, only now the threshold is $z_{\alpha/2}$, or the value such that

$$p(-z_{\alpha/2} < Z < z_{\alpha/2}) = 1 - \alpha \tag{B.20}$$

where Z is distributed according to Normal(0, 1).

Recall from section B.2.4 that we use the same quantity $z_{\alpha/2}$ to calculate confidence intervals. Indeed, the Wald test rejects the null hypothesis exactly when the parameter θ's value under the null hypothesis (here, μ_D's null hypothesis value is zero) falls outside the estimated confidence interval for the statistic (equation B.13). If the null hypothesis is true, then fewer than 100α% of our experiments will lead to confidence intervals around t_D that do not include the true value of the statistic.

The Wald test is actually a much more generally applicable test. It can be used for any statistic $t_{V,V'}$ that is normally distributed across samples and for which a standard error, $\text{se}_{t_{V,V'}}$, can be estimated. The Wald test, unlike the t-test, does not require an assumption that the *data* (V, V', or

D) are normally distributed, only the test statistic. Note that closed forms for standard errors are not available for all test statistics, but the bootstrap can be used (section B.2.3).

In both the Student t-test and the Wald test, the p-value can be calculated by solving for the smallest α' such that the null hypothesis would be rejected.

The remaining tests are all **nonparametric**, meaning that they do not rely on assumptions that the data follow a particular parametric distribution. For example, the Wald test requires us to assume that the sample statistic is normally distributed (across different, randomly drawn samples). Nonparametric hypothesis tests should not be confused with nonparametric probabilistic *models* (section 4.2.5).

Sign Test and Wilcoxon Signed-Rank Test

Applied to differences, the paired t-test and Wald test involve the null hypothesis that the mean μ_D is equal to zero. The sign test (Arbuthnott, 1710) and Wilcoxon signed-rank test (Wilcoxon, 1945) involve different null hypotheses:

- The sign test tests for whether the number of cases where $v_i > v'_i$ is different from the number of cases where $v_i < v'_i$.
- The Wilcoxon signed-rank test tests for whether the *median* (rather than the mean) of the differences is zero.

These tests depend only on the sign of the differences $D_i = V_i - V'_i$, not the magnitude. They assume the samples are independent and that the difference variable D is continuous. The Wilcoxon signed-rank test assumes further that D is distributed symmetrically about its median.

If there are any observations where $d_i = 0$, these are omitted for both the sign test and the Wilcoxon signed-rank test; let $\bar{\mathbf{d}} = \langle \bar{d}_1, \ldots, \bar{d}_M \rangle$ be the $M \leq N$ nonzero differences.

The sign test's null hypothesis is that the sign of each d_i is determined by a draw from a Bernoulli distribution

$$\begin{aligned} p(d_i > 0) &= 0.5 \\ p(d_i < 0) &= 0.5 \end{aligned}$$

Equivalently, the signs of the observations $\langle \bar{d}_1, \ldots, \bar{d}_M \rangle$ were drawn from a binomial distribution with parameters $n = M$ and $p = 0.5$. This distribution is defined for a discrete random variable K taking values in $\{0, 1, 2, \ldots\}$:

$$p_{n,p}(K = k) = \binom{n}{k} p^k (1 - p)^{n-k} \tag{B.21}$$

(For large values of n, the binomial distribution approaches $\text{Normal}(np, np(1 - p))$.) The random variable K here is the number of observations such that $\bar{d}_i > 0$. The test statistic is

$$k_D = \min \left\{ \left| \{ i \mid \bar{d}_i < 0 \} \right|, \left| \{ i \mid \bar{d}_i > 0 \} \right| \right\} \tag{B.22}$$

For significance level α, we reject the null hypothesis if

$$\begin{aligned} 2\sum_{k=0}^{k_D} p_{M,0.5}(K=k) &= \frac{1}{2^{M-1}}\sum_{k=0}^{k_D}\binom{M}{k} \\ &< \alpha \end{aligned} \tag{B.23}$$

(for a two-tailed test). The quantity on the left is the p-value.

The procedure for the Wilcoxon signed-rank test is similar but a bit more involved.

1. As before, remove all observations where $v_i = v'_i$.
2. For each $i \in \{1, \ldots, M\}$, let $m_i = |\bar{d}_i|$. These are the magnitudes of the nonzero differences.
3. Sort $\langle m_1, \ldots, m_M \rangle$ in increasing order, giving $\bar{\mathbf{m}} = \langle \bar{m}_1, \ldots, \bar{m}_M \rangle$.
4. For $i \in \{1, \ldots, M\}$, let r_i be equal to

   $$\left|\{i' : \bar{m}_{i'} \leq m_i\}\right|$$

   This is the the rank of the value m_i in the sorted list $\bar{\mathbf{m}}$. If there are ties, the ranks are averaged (e.g., if there is a four-way tie among m_9, m_{46}, m_{60}, and m_{93} at ranks 5–8, then $r_9 = r_{46} = r_{60} = r_{93} = \frac{5+6+7+8}{4} = 6.5$).
5. Let the test statistic

   $$w_D = \min\left\{\sum_{i:v_i>v'_i} r_i, \sum_{i:v_i<v'_i} r_i\right\} \tag{B.24}$$

Under the null hypothesis, smaller values of w_D will be less surprising. Let K_D^+ denote the number of d_i that are positive. Under the null hypothesis, K_D^+ should be distributed according to a binomial distribution with $n = M$ and $p = \frac{1}{2}$, as in the sign test. Of course, we have actually observed some number of positive valued d_i, $k_D^+ = |\{i : v_i > v'_i\}|$. But this observed k_D^+ is *not* the test statistic for the Wilcoxon signed-rank test; it is merely the observed value of a random variable with some relationship to the statistic of interest, w_D.

Instead, K_D^+ gets marginalized out in the calculation of the distribution over W_D under the null hypothesis for this test. What we seek to calculate is the probability, under the null hypothesis, that

$$\begin{aligned} p(W_D = w_D) &= \sum_{k=0}^{M} p(K_D^+ = k)p(W_D = w_D \mid K_D^+ = k) \\ &= \sum_{k=0}^{M}\binom{M}{k}\frac{1}{2^M}p(W_D = w_D \mid K_D^+ = k) \end{aligned} \tag{B.25}$$

The values $p(W \mid K^+)$ can be calculated by brute force, assuming that the ranks (all r_i) are chosen uniformly with replacement from $\{1, \ldots, M\}$, and it is not hard to find tables for relatively small values of M. For large values of M, a normal distribution can be used. This calculation gives the p-value, and we reject the null hypothesis if the p-value is smaller than α.

McNemar Test

Here we assume that all V and V' measurements are binary, with values in $\{0, 1\}$. In NLP, for example, V_i and V_i might be indicators for whether h and h', respectively, correctly predict the output on the ith test-set example. Such a representation of the experimental data can be understood as a 2×2 contingency table:

	$V_i = 0$	$V_i = 1$	marginal
$V_i' = 0$	$\mathit{freq}(0, 0)$	$\mathit{freq}(1, 0)$	$\mathit{freq}(\cdot, 0)$
$V_i' = 1$	$\mathit{freq}(0, 1)$	$\mathit{freq}(1, 1)$	$\mathit{freq}(\cdot, 1)$
marginal	$\mathit{freq}(0, \cdot)$	$\mathit{freq}(1, \cdot)$	N

The null hypothesis for the McNemar test (McNemar, 1947) is that the marginal probabilities for the distributions over V and V' are the same:

$$\begin{aligned} p(V = 1) &= p(V' = 1) \\ p(V = 1, V' = 0) + p(V = 1, V' = 1) &= p(V = 0, V' = 1) + p(V = 1, V' = 1) \\ p(V = 1, V' = 0) &= p(V = 0, V' = 1) \end{aligned} \tag{B.26}$$

Under this assumption, we expect that $\mathit{freq}(0, 1)$ and $\mathit{freq}(1, 0)$ will be close. More specifically, $\mathit{freq}(0, 1)$ and $\mathit{freq}(1, 0)$ will each be distributed according to a binominal distribution with $n = \mathit{freq}(0, 1) + \mathit{freq}(1, 0)$ and $p = \frac{1}{2}$. Let the test statistic

$$k_{V,V'} = \min\{\mathit{freq}(0, 1), \mathit{freq}(1, 0)\} \tag{B.27}$$

For significance level α, we reject the null hypothesis if

$$\begin{aligned} 2 \sum_{k=0}^{k_{V,V'}} p_{\mathit{freq}(0,1)+\mathit{freq}(1,0),0.5}(K = k) &= \frac{1}{2^{\mathit{freq}(0,1)+\mathit{freq}(1,0)-1}} \sum_{k=0}^{k_{V,V'}} \binom{\mathit{freq}(0, 1) + \mathit{freq}(1, 0)}{k} \\ &< \alpha \end{aligned} \tag{B.28}$$

(for a two-tailed test). The quantity on the left is the p-value. When we have a very large amount of data, we can use normal approximation.

McNemar's test is similar to the sign test, except that rather than working with signed differences between two continuous scores, we consider binary outcomes for each condition on each example.

Permutation Test

Permutation tests were developed based on ideas exposed by Fisher (1935). The paired permutation test is a test for rejection of the null hypothesis that V and V' are identically distributed. We consider here a paired permutation test, which assumes only that the examples $\langle u_1, u_2, \ldots, u_N \rangle$ are independent of each other. Let $t_{V,V'}$ be the statistic of interest calculated over the paired measurements. The permutation test is particularly appealing when $t_{V,V'}$ is not a mean (e.g., $t_{V,V'}$ is not a mean of the difference $V - V'$).

Under the null hypothesis, the probability that for example i we would have observed

$$V_i = v_i \wedge V_i' = v_i'$$

(as we did) as compared to

$$V_i = v_i' \wedge V_i' = v_i$$

should be identical. In other words, the assignment of $\{v_i, v_i'\}$ to the two random variables ought to be the same. Considering that we have N pairs in the data, there are 2^N possible permutations of these pairs, only one of which we observed. Under the null hypothesis, each of those 2^N different permutations would be equally likely, and so we might calculate the statistic of interest under each one, giving 2^N different values of t: $\langle \bar{t}_{V,V',1}, \bar{t}_{V,V',2}, \ldots, \bar{t}_{V,V',2^N} \rangle$. If the null hypothesis holds, then our value $t_{V,V'}$ should "look like" most of those alternative $\bar{t}_{V,V',j}$.

In practice, we usually cannot calculate all 2^N values, but we can easily sample a large number of them from a binomial distribution with $p = \frac{1}{2}, n = N$. If we generate P such values for the statistic,

$$\bar{\mathbf{t}}_{V,V'} = \langle \bar{t}_{V,V',1}, \bar{t}_{V,V',2}, \ldots, \bar{t}_{V,V',P} \rangle$$

we can then calculate what fraction of the P sampled permutations lead to a value that is at least as extreme (surprising) as $t_{V,V'}$. We can calculate the p-value as this fraction, and we reject the null hypothesis if the p-value is smaller than α. Confidence intervals can also be calculated by looking at the $\frac{P\alpha}{2}$th and $\frac{P(1-\alpha)}{2}$th sorted values in $\bar{\mathbf{t}}_{V,V'}$ (for a two-tailed test).

A widely used tool for testing significance in phrase-structure parsing, provided by Dan Bikel,[10] is essentially a paired permutation test. Methods like the paired permutation test are sometimes called "approximate randomization."

The resampling in the permutation test strongly resembles the bootstrap. The main difference is that permutation tests involve sampling without replacement (an analogous bootstrap might require sampling two values uniformly from $\{v_i, v_i'\}$, with probability $\frac{1}{4}$ of choosing $\langle v_i, v_i \rangle$ and probability $\frac{1}{4}$ of choosing $\langle v_i', v_i' \rangle$). We turn next to paired tests based on the bootstrap.

Bootstrap Hypothesis Tests

It should be clear that hypothesis tests are closely related to the problem of measuring uncertainty about a test statistic due to the randomness in sampling. They often correspond to finding a range

[10] `http://www.cis.upenn.edu/~dbikel/software.html#comparator`

of values for the statistic that would be unsurprising if the null hypothesis were true—a confidence interval under the null hypothesis—and rejecting the null hypothesis if the observed value is outside that range.

The bootstrap approach to hypothesis testing is straightforward: generate bootstrap replicate samples, as in section B.2.3, using the data $\langle u_1, \ldots, u_N \rangle$, then calculate bootstrap confidence intervals for $t_{V,V'}$ as in section B.2.4 for the desired significance level α. If the null hypothesis sets the parameter θ to be some value outside $(l_{t_{V,V'}}, u_{t_{V,V'}})$, then we reject the null hypothesis.

Koehn (2004) considered confidence intervals and significance testing for Bleu scores, an automatically calculated score for evaluating machine translation systems (Papineni et al., 2002), using the bootstrap. He gave empirical support for the accuracy of the bootstrap in drawing conclusions about machine translation performance.

B.2.6 CLOSING NOTES

We have discussed various topics on the quantitative side of experimentation: general methodology used in NLP, and statistics topics of standard errors, confidence intervals, and hypothesis testing. A favorable hypothesis test (i.e., one demonstrating statistical significance) is neither a necessary nor sufficient condition for an interesting, publishable result. It is one tool among many in understanding a method or idea, and it cannot be a substitute for careful analysis of system output. We have explicitly opted not to make recommendations about which tests to use, instead encouraging NLP researchers to use tests alongside standard errors and confidence intervals to make clear arguments about their techniques.

Ideally, a fine-grained analysis, both qualitative and quantitative, is performed when exploring approaches to linguistic structure prediction, to give an understanding of both the errors a new approach helps to correct and the errors it introduces. Because there will always be contention about the value of any particular qualitative judgments on linguistic data by researchers, quantitative analysis is expected to continue to play a major role in building arguments around methods for linguistic structure prediction, but the most compelling arguments will have both elements.

APPENDIX C

Maximum Entropy

Log-linear models are often called "maximum entropy" or "maxent" models. This is because they can be derived from an alternative starting point: the idea of maximizing *entropy* subject to some empirical constraints. This is often the way log-linear models are motivated, and it is helpful to see the historical connection.

Entropy (more precisely, *Shannon* entropy) is a measure of the amount of randomness in a probability distribution. For distribution $p \in \mathbb{P}_{\mathcal{Y}}$ over values of discrete random variable $\boldsymbol{Y}$ over $\mathcal{Y}$, entropy is defined as

$$\boldsymbol{H}(p) = -\sum_{\boldsymbol{y} \in \mathcal{Y}} p(\boldsymbol{Y} = \boldsymbol{y}) \log p(\boldsymbol{Y} = \boldsymbol{y}) = \mathbb{E}_{p(\boldsymbol{Y})}[-\log p(\boldsymbol{Y})] \tag{C.1}$$

The base of the logarithm determines the unit in which entropy is reported: base 2 gives "bits" and base e gives "nats." Entropy can be interpreted as the average number of bits, nats, etc., that it takes to encode the value of Y under repeated independent trials, assuming an ideal coding scheme. If p is a point distribution, placing probability one on a single outcome $\boldsymbol{y}^* \in \mathcal{Y}$, then entropy tends toward zero.[1] $\boldsymbol{H}$ reaches its maximum for the uniform distribution over $\mathcal{Y}$; that maximum is $\log |\mathcal{Y}|$.

The principle of maximum entropy states that when estimating a distribution from data, we should choose the distribution with the greatest entropy that fits the data. This is often understood as a mathematical encoding of Occam's razor, paraphrased as "assume no more than necessary when explaining the phenomenon." Maximizing entropy spreads the probability mass as much as possible, while respecting the data. If we were to drop the clause "respecting the data," then maximizing entropy would simply mean choosing the uniform distribution:[2]

$$\operatorname*{argmax}_{p \in \mathbb{P}_{\mathcal{Y}}} \boldsymbol{H}(p) = \left\{ p \mid \forall \boldsymbol{y} \in \mathcal{Y}, p(\boldsymbol{Y} = \boldsymbol{y}) = \frac{1}{|\mathcal{Y}|} \right\} \tag{C.2}$$

Entropy, it should be noted, is concave in the probability distribution p.

Let the training data be denoted $\langle \tilde{\boldsymbol{y}}_1, \ldots, \tilde{\boldsymbol{y}}_{\tilde{N}} \rangle$; we assume a single discrete random variable $\boldsymbol{Y}$ for clarity of notation. Formally, "respecting the data" is often defined using feature functions. For feature functions $\langle g_1, \ldots, g_d \rangle$, each $g_j : \mathcal{Y} \rightarrow \mathbb{R}$, we define a moment or expectation constraint:

$$\mathbb{E}_{p(\boldsymbol{Y})}[g_j(\boldsymbol{Y})] = \frac{1}{\tilde{N}} \sum_{i=1}^{\tilde{N}} g_j(\tilde{\boldsymbol{y}}_i) \tag{C.3}$$

[1] This is not obvious unless we take a limit, so that $0 \log 0$ is understood to have value 0, as commonly done in information theory.
[2] Of course, this fails if $|\mathcal{Y}|$ is not finite.

The constraints say that the expected feature value under the model distribution p must match the sample mean of the feature value, as calculated from the training data. This gives the following *constrained* optimization problem, which is the maximum entropy problem as understood in learning:

$$\max_{p \in \mathbb{P}_{\mathcal{Y}}} \boldsymbol{H}(p) \tag{C.4}$$

$$\text{such that } \forall j \in \{1, \ldots, d\}, \qquad \mathbb{E}_{p(\boldsymbol{Y})}[g_j(\boldsymbol{Y})] = \frac{1}{\tilde{N}} \sum_{i=1}^{\tilde{N}} g_j(\tilde{\boldsymbol{y}}_i)$$

Importantly, up to this point, we have said nothing about the form of p other than that it should meet the constraints in equation C.3. The connection between maximum entropy and log-linear models is summed up in the following theorem:

Theorem C.1 Given training data $\langle \tilde{\boldsymbol{y}}_1, \ldots, \tilde{\boldsymbol{y}}_{\tilde{N}} \rangle$ and a set of features $\langle g_1, \ldots, g_d \rangle$, there is a unique solution to the constrained maximum entropy problem (equation C.4), which we denote p^*. Further, p^* is the log-linear model with features $\langle g_1, \ldots, g_d \rangle$ that maximizes likelihood on the training data $\langle \tilde{\boldsymbol{y}}_1, \ldots, \tilde{\boldsymbol{y}}_{\tilde{N}} \rangle$. That is, $p^* = p_{\operatorname{argmax}_{\mathbf{w}} \Phi_{\mathrm{LL}}(\mathbf{w})}$.

To prove this theorem, we begin with equation C.4. The first step is to introduce one Lagrangian multiplier for each of the d constraints. Let ω_j denote the multiplier for the jth constraint, and $\boldsymbol{\omega} = \langle \omega_1, \ldots, \omega_d \rangle$. The "primal" form of the problem is as follows:

$$\max_{p \in \mathbb{P}_{\mathcal{Y}}} \boldsymbol{H}(p) + \underbrace{\min_{\boldsymbol{\omega}} \sum_{j=1}^{d} \omega_j \left(\mathbb{E}_{p(\boldsymbol{Y})}[g_j(\boldsymbol{Y})] - \frac{1}{\tilde{N}} \sum_{i=1}^{\tilde{N}} g_j(\tilde{\boldsymbol{y}}_i) \right)}_{penalty(p)} \tag{C.5}$$

An informal way to understand this transformed problem is that if the constraints are all met, then the parenthesized differences inside the summation are all zero. When that is the case, no matter what value $\boldsymbol{\omega}$ takes, the objective function is $\boldsymbol{H}$, which is what we aim for. If, however, the constraints are not met, then the summation term can ruin our chances of optimizing $\boldsymbol{H}(p)$, since there exists a value of $\boldsymbol{\omega}$ that punishes the total quite severely. By including the min operator, we are saying that the $\boldsymbol{\omega}$ will always be chosen so as to hurt the total objective as much as possible, through the *penalty* function.

It is next convenient to represent p as a vector $\mathbf{p} \in \mathbb{R}_{\geq 0}^{|\mathcal{Y}|}$, with dimensions indexed by possible values of the random variable $\boldsymbol{Y}$. We add another Lagrangian multiplier, ν, to force the sum of all elements of $\mathbf{p}$ to be equal to one.

$$\max_{\mathbf{p} \in \mathbb{R}_{\geq 0}^{|\mathcal{Y}|}} - \sum_{\boldsymbol{y} \in \mathcal{Y}} p_{\boldsymbol{y}} \log p_{\boldsymbol{y}} + \sum_{j=1}^{d} \omega_j \left(\min_{\boldsymbol{\omega}} \sum_{\boldsymbol{y} \in \mathcal{Y}} p_{\boldsymbol{y}} g_j(\boldsymbol{y}) - \frac{1}{\tilde{N}} \sum_{i=1}^{\tilde{N}} g_j(\tilde{\boldsymbol{y}}_i) \right) + \min_{\nu} \nu \left(1 - \sum_{\boldsymbol{y} \in \mathcal{Y}} p_{\boldsymbol{y}} \right) \tag{C.6}$$

The next step relies on the theory of Lagrangian duality that allows us to move the min operators *outside* the original max operator, giving a different formulation whose solution is provably equivalent:

$$\min_{\boldsymbol{\omega},\nu} \max_{\mathbf{p}\in\mathbb{R}^{|\mathcal{Y}|}_{\geq 0}} -\sum_{y\in\mathcal{Y}} p_y \log p_y + \sum_{j=1}^{d} \omega_j \left(\sum_{y\in\mathcal{Y}} p_y g_j(y) - \frac{1}{\tilde{N}} \sum_{i=1}^{\tilde{N}} g_j(\tilde{y}_i) \right) + \nu \left(1 - \sum_{y\in\mathcal{Y}} p_y \right) \tag{C.7}$$

Now, when we think about choosing the value of $\mathbf{p}$ (the distribution we seek to estimate), we can think of $\boldsymbol{\omega}$ and ν as fixed rather than free variables, and solve in terms of their values. To do this, we differentiate with respect to an arbitrary p_y.

$$\frac{\partial}{\partial p_y} = -1 - \log p_y + \sum_{j=1}^{d} \omega_j g_j(y) - \nu \tag{C.8}$$

Setting equal to zero gives

$$p_y = \exp(\boldsymbol{\omega}^\top \mathbf{g}(y) - \nu - 1) = \frac{\exp \boldsymbol{\omega}^\top \mathbf{g}(y)}{\exp(\nu + 1)} \tag{C.9}$$

This is nearly a log-linear model over $\boldsymbol{Y}$, with feature vector function $\mathbf{g}$ and weights $\boldsymbol{\omega}$. We can further solve for ν.

$$\begin{aligned} \frac{\partial}{\partial \nu} &= 1 - \sum_{y\in\mathcal{Y}} p_y \\ &= 1 - \sum_{y\in\mathcal{Y}} \frac{\exp \boldsymbol{\omega}^\top \mathbf{g}(y)}{\exp(\nu + 1)} \end{aligned} \tag{C.10}$$

Setting equal to zero, we have

$$\nu = -1 + \log \sum_{y\in\mathcal{Y}} \exp \boldsymbol{\omega}^\top \mathbf{g}(y) \tag{C.11}$$

Plugging this in to equation C.9, we have:

$$p_y = \frac{\exp \boldsymbol{\omega}^\top \mathbf{g}(y)}{\sum_{y\in\mathcal{Y}} \exp \boldsymbol{\omega}^\top \mathbf{g}(y)} = \frac{1}{z_{\boldsymbol{\omega}}} \exp \boldsymbol{\omega}^\top \mathbf{g}(y) \tag{C.12}$$

This is precisely a log-linear model with features $\mathbf{g}$ and weights $\boldsymbol{\omega}$.

We now need to show that the log-linear model that maximizes the constrained entropy problem (equation C.4) is the same one that maximizes likelihood. To do this, we use the closed-form solution for $\mathbf{p}$ and ν in terms of $\boldsymbol{\omega}$ (equations C.9 and C.11) to rewrite the problem in equation C.7:

$$\begin{aligned}
\min_{\boldsymbol{\omega}} & - \sum_{y \in \mathcal{Y}} \frac{\exp \boldsymbol{\omega}^\top \mathbf{g}(y)}{z_{\boldsymbol{\omega}}} \log \frac{\exp \boldsymbol{\omega}^\top \mathbf{g}(y)}{z_{\boldsymbol{\omega}}} \\
& + \sum_{j=1}^{d} \omega_j \left(\sum_{y \in \mathcal{Y}} \frac{\exp \boldsymbol{\omega}^\top \mathbf{g}(y)}{z_{\boldsymbol{\omega}}} g_j(y) - \frac{1}{\tilde{N}} \sum_{i=1}^{\tilde{N}} g_j(\tilde{y}_i) \right) \\
& + (\log z_{\boldsymbol{\omega}} - 1) \left(1 - \sum_{y \in \mathcal{Y}} \frac{\exp \boldsymbol{\omega}^\top \mathbf{g}(y)}{z_{\boldsymbol{\omega}}} \right) \qquad \text{(C.13)}
\end{aligned}$$

The last term disappears since the definition of $z_{\boldsymbol{\omega}}$ forces it to zero. Some algebraic manipulation gives us:

$$\begin{aligned}
\boldsymbol{\omega}^* &= \operatorname*{argmin}_{\boldsymbol{\omega}} - \sum_{y \in \mathcal{Y}} \frac{\exp \boldsymbol{\omega}^\top \mathbf{g}(y)}{z_{\boldsymbol{\omega}}} \log \frac{\exp \boldsymbol{\omega}^\top \mathbf{g}(y)}{z_{\boldsymbol{\omega}}} \qquad \text{(C.14)} \\
& \quad + \sum_{y \in \mathcal{Y}} \frac{\exp \boldsymbol{\omega}^\top \mathbf{g}(y)}{z_{\boldsymbol{\omega}}} \boldsymbol{\omega}^\top \mathbf{g}(y) - \frac{1}{\tilde{N}} \sum_{i=1}^{\tilde{N}} \boldsymbol{\omega}^\top \mathbf{g}(\tilde{y}_i) \\
&= \operatorname*{argmin}_{\boldsymbol{\omega}} - \sum_{y \in \mathcal{Y}} \frac{\exp \boldsymbol{\omega}^\top \mathbf{g}(y)}{z_{\boldsymbol{\omega}}} \boldsymbol{\omega}^\top \mathbf{g}(y) + \sum_{y \in \mathcal{Y}} \frac{\exp \boldsymbol{\omega}^\top \mathbf{g}(y)}{z_{\boldsymbol{\omega}}} \log z_{\boldsymbol{\omega}} \\
& \quad + \sum_{y \in \mathcal{Y}} \frac{\exp \boldsymbol{\omega}^\top \mathbf{g}(y)}{z_{\boldsymbol{\omega}}} \boldsymbol{\omega}^\top \mathbf{g}(y) - \frac{1}{\tilde{N}} \sum_{i=1}^{\tilde{N}} \boldsymbol{\omega}^\top \mathbf{g}(\tilde{y}_i)
\end{aligned}$$

The first and third terms cancel.

$$\begin{aligned}
\boldsymbol{\omega}^* &= \operatorname*{argmin}_{\boldsymbol{\omega}} \sum_{y \in \mathcal{Y}} \frac{\exp \boldsymbol{\omega}^\top \mathbf{g}(y)}{z_{\boldsymbol{\omega}}} \log z_{\boldsymbol{\omega}} - \frac{1}{\tilde{N}} \sum_{i=1}^{\tilde{N}} \boldsymbol{\omega}^\top \mathbf{g}(\tilde{y}_i) \qquad \text{(C.15)} \\
&= \operatorname*{argmin}_{\boldsymbol{\omega}} \log z_{\boldsymbol{\omega}} - \frac{1}{\tilde{N}} \sum_{i=1}^{\tilde{N}} \boldsymbol{\omega}^\top \mathbf{g}(\tilde{y}_i) \qquad \text{(C.16)} \\
&= \operatorname*{argmin}_{\boldsymbol{\omega}} - \frac{1}{\tilde{N}} \Phi_{\mathrm{LL}}(\boldsymbol{\omega}) \qquad \text{(C.17)} \\
&= \operatorname*{argmax}_{\mathbf{w}} \Phi_{\mathrm{LL}}(\mathbf{w}) \qquad \text{(C.18)}
\end{aligned}$$

The Lagrangian multipliers $\boldsymbol{\omega}^*$ that solve the problem take on the role of feature weights in a log-linear model. Hence the maximum likelihood estimate for a log-linear model with features $\mathbf{g}$ is equivalent to the empirically-constrained (for features $\mathbf{g}$) maximum entropy model.

In this discussion, we have kept things simple by ignoring the input variable $\boldsymbol{X}$. It is left as an exercise to show the relationship between maximizing conditional likelihood and maximizing an entropy function. For more details, see Ratnaparkhi (1997) and Berger (date unknown).

APPENDIX D

Locally Normalized Conditional Models

In this appendix, we discuss an alternative approach to probabilistic conditional models (section 3.4), which we call **locally normalized conditional models**.

A conditional model defines $p(\boldsymbol{Y} \mid \boldsymbol{X})$, as discussed in section 3.4. Locally normalized conditional models break the probability that $\boldsymbol{Y} = \boldsymbol{y}$ into steps, much like generative models (section 3.3). We consider two examples.

D.1 PROBABILISTIC FINITE-STATE AUTOMATA

Finite-state automata (FSAs) are a useful formalism for modeling strings with effects that are mostly local. FSAs are the recognition mechanism for regular grammars, discussed in section 2.2.3. Much like other automata and grammars, they can be made probabilistic by adding real-valued weights to the derivation steps. We consider two ways of making an FSA probabilistic, one corresponding to a fully generative model that provides $p(\boldsymbol{X}, \boldsymbol{Y})$, and the other corresponding to a conditional model $p(\boldsymbol{Y} \mid \boldsymbol{X})$.

Let $\mathcal{Q} = \{q_1, \ldots, q_S\}$ be a finite set of S states. We use ➾ to denote a special initial state and ◉ to denote a special final state; neither is included in $\mathcal{Q}$. Let $\Sigma = \{\sigma_1, \ldots, \sigma_V\}$ be a finite vocabulary. In addition to $\mathcal{Q}$ and Σ, an FSA includes a set of *transitions* of the form $\langle q, \sigma, q' \rangle$, meaning that it is possible to move from state $q \in \mathcal{Q} \cup \{➾\}$ to state $q' \in \mathcal{Q} \cup \{◉\}$ while reading $\sigma \in \Sigma \cup \{\epsilon\}$ from the input tape. Note that σ could be the empty string (denoted ϵ). We will let $\mathcal{T}$ denote the set of transitions.

The first way to make an FSA probabilistic is to define a joint distribution over all paths in $\mathcal{T}^*$ through the FSA. Let $\boldsymbol{T}$ denote this random variable. If we know the value of $\boldsymbol{T}$ (the transition sequence taken by the FSA), then we also know the sequence of input symbols (sequence random variable $\boldsymbol{X}$ ranging over Σ^*) and the sequence of states visited (sequence random variable $\boldsymbol{Y}$ ranging over $\mathcal{Q}^*$). However, because there could be more than one path corresponding to the same symbol sequence, the input, the output, and the two together may not fully determine the FSA path. The generative form of the distribution assigns, to each $\langle q, \sigma, \ell, q' \rangle$, a probability:

$$\gamma_{q,\sigma,q'} = p(T_{i+1} = \langle q, \sigma, q' \rangle \mid Y_i = q) = p(Y_{i+1} = q', X_{\tau(i)} = \sigma \mid Y_i = q) \tag{D.1}$$

Note that the length of $\boldsymbol{X}$ may not be the same as the length of $\boldsymbol{Y}$ and $\boldsymbol{T}$; by $X_{\tau(i)}$, we mean the element of the sequence $\boldsymbol{X}$ that is generated on exit from the ith *state*, Y_i, not the ith element of

$\boldsymbol{X}$. By multiplying together the probabilities of all transitions followed in a path, we obtain the distribution $p(\boldsymbol{T} = \boldsymbol{t})$.

(Hidden Markov models can be understood as a special case of the above probabilistic FSA in which the set of HMM states $\Lambda = \mathcal{Q}$ and $\gamma_{q,\sigma,q'}$ factors as $\gamma_{q,q'} \times \eta_{q,\sigma}$. Probabilistic FSAs are more general than HMMs as traditionally defined, allowing direct dependency between a state at time i and the previous symbol. The DP in figure 2.16 can be used for this decoding with the probablistic FSA model with very little adaptation.)

The *conditional* form simply assumes that the sequence $\boldsymbol{X}$ is observed and defines $p(\boldsymbol{T} = \boldsymbol{t} \mid \boldsymbol{X} = \boldsymbol{x})$ or, equivalently, $p(\boldsymbol{Y} = \boldsymbol{y} \mid \boldsymbol{X} = \boldsymbol{x})$. The model parameters are very similar, but condition against each symbol read in from the input tape:

$$\gamma_{q,\sigma,q'} = p(Y_{i+1} = q' \mid X_{\tau(i)} = \sigma, Y_i = q) \tag{D.2}$$

For more discussion of probabilistic finite-state automata, including their generalization to *two* observable strings, finite-state transducers (FSTs), see Roche and Schabes (1997) and Mohri (1997). For a discussion of the use of FSTs in modeling morphology, see Beesley and Kartunnen (2003). Normally probabilistic FSAs and FSTs are based on multinomial distributions, as we have presented them; Eisner (2002) provides an alternative formulation for both the joint and conditional variants based on log-linear models.

D.2 MAXIMUM ENTROPY MARKOV MODELS

Maximum entropy Markov models (MEMMs)[1] are conditional models not unlike the conditional probabilistic FSA discussed in section D.1. They were introduced by McCallum et al. (2000). The model is defined by:

$$p_{\mathbf{w}}(\boldsymbol{Y} = \boldsymbol{y} \mid \boldsymbol{X} = \boldsymbol{x}) = \prod_{i=1}^{n+1} p_{\mathbf{w}}(Y_i = y_i \mid \boldsymbol{X} = \boldsymbol{x}, Y_{i-1} = y_{i-1}) \tag{D.3}$$

$$= \prod_{i=1}^{n+1} \frac{\exp \mathbf{w}^\top \mathbf{f}(\boldsymbol{x}, y_{i-1}, y_i, i)}{\sum_{y' \in \Lambda} \exp \mathbf{w}^\top \mathbf{f}(\boldsymbol{x}, y_{i-1}, y', i)} \tag{D.4}$$

Note that the feature vector is *local*, considering two adjacent labels at a time. The global feature vector "$\mathbf{g}(\boldsymbol{x}, \boldsymbol{y})$" used in decoding (equation 2.3) is not present explicitly in this model.

Indeed, this model is not a global linear model without slight modification. Specifically, when decoding, in general

$$\operatorname*{argmax}_{\boldsymbol{y} \in \mathcal{Y}_x} p_{\mathbf{w}}(\boldsymbol{Y} = \boldsymbol{y} \mid \boldsymbol{X} = \boldsymbol{x}) \neq \operatorname*{argmax}_{\boldsymbol{y} \in \mathcal{Y}_{\boldsymbol{x}}} \sum_{i=1}^{n+1} \mathbf{w}^\top \mathbf{f}(\boldsymbol{x}, y_{i-1}, y_i, i) \tag{D.5}$$

[1]The name is confusing. Nearly every sequence model has some Markovian properties, and "maximum entropy" is a term often used for log-linear models; see appendix C. The name "maximum entropy Markov model" could have been used to describe many models now in use, but the one it refers to happens to have been one of the first invented.

since the latter expression ignores the local normalizing factors (denominators in equation D.4). We return to the decoder in section D.5.

D.3 DIRECTIONAL EFFECTS

The conditional version of the probablistic FSA introduced in section D.1 and the MEMM in section D.2 are examples of conditional models in the sense that they only model $p(\boldsymbol{Y} \mid \boldsymbol{X})$. In section 3.4, we argued that such models, which avoid explaining the distribution of the observed variable $\boldsymbol{X}$, are advantageous when the prediction task is known.

There is, however, an inherent problem with models like the conditional probablistic FSA and the MEMM that break the conditional generative process into derivation steps. Consider a POS-tagging model based on a conditional version of an HMM, in which:[2]

$$p(\boldsymbol{Y} = \boldsymbol{y} \mid \boldsymbol{X} = \boldsymbol{x}) = \prod_{i=1}^{n} p(Y_i = y_i \mid X_i = x_i, Y_{i-1} = y_{i-1}) \tag{D.6}$$

The local factors might be parameterized using multinomial models (as in the probabilistic FSA) or log-linear models (as in the MEMM).

If this model encounters a sentence $\boldsymbol{x}$ whose first word x_1 is out of the vocabulary, we would hope that it would consider the context of that word—the sequence of words following and their possible POS tags—in deciding how to tag it. That behavior is what a traditional HMM would provide. Consider the posterior distribution $p(Y_1 \mid \boldsymbol{X} = \boldsymbol{x})$, as calculated by the HMM. For each value y:

$$p(Y_1 = y \mid \boldsymbol{X} = \boldsymbol{x}) = \frac{\sum_{\boldsymbol{y} \in \mathcal{Y}_{\boldsymbol{x}} : y_1 = y} p(\boldsymbol{Y} = \boldsymbol{y}, \boldsymbol{X} = \boldsymbol{x})}{\sum_{\boldsymbol{y} \in \mathcal{Y}_{\boldsymbol{x}}} p(\boldsymbol{Y} = \boldsymbol{y}, \boldsymbol{X} = \boldsymbol{x})} \tag{D.7}$$

There is no way to simplify the above calculation; the entire sequence must be taken into account to determine the probability of each label for the unknown first word. The same will hold during decoding, where the Viterbi algorithm does not actually label any word until it has performed calculations for all of the words.

Now consider the conditional version based on the model in equation D.6:

$$\begin{aligned} p(Y_1 = y \mid \boldsymbol{X} = \boldsymbol{x}) &= \sum_{\boldsymbol{y} \in \mathcal{Y}_{\boldsymbol{x}} : y_1 = y} p(\boldsymbol{Y} = \boldsymbol{y} \mid \boldsymbol{X} = \boldsymbol{x}) \\ &= p(Y_1 = y \mid X_1 = x_1, Y_0 = ◈) & \text{(D.8)} \\ &\quad \times \sum_{\langle y_2, \ldots, y_n \rangle} p(\langle Y_2, \ldots, Y_n \rangle = \langle y_2, \ldots, y_n \rangle \mid Y_1 = y_1, \boldsymbol{X} = \boldsymbol{x}) \\ &= p(Y_1 = y \mid X_1 = x_1, Y_0 = ◈) \times 1 & \text{(D.9)} \end{aligned}$$

[2]This model is sometimes called a "conditional Markov model."

This means that the model's distribution over x_1's label is not influenced by any of the following words or their labels. More generally, this model is asymmetrical in that Y_i is influenced by the labels to its left, but not to its right. If a label y at position i fits its left context well, it need not explain the word x_i or attain a high score with the label that follows it.

A more general form of this problem has been described as the "label bias" effect (Lafferty et al., 2001), in which the model has a tendency to prefer labels that give low entropy distributions over following states while ignoring the observations of those labels. This is an effect of the local conditional structure of the model, not of the fact that the model *is* conditional.

Klein and Manning (2002a) sought to separate "conditional structure" from "conditional estimation." Our terminology is somewhat different; we have defined conditional models as those that define conditional distributions, regardless of their parameterizations, and described a theoretical weakness of locally-normalized parameterizations. In some experiments, Klein and Manning observe conditional FSA-like models over-attending to the *observations*, contrary to the label bias effect. Johnson (2001) also reported some problems with locally-normalized conditional models.

Label bias and observation bias, to the extent that each occurs, are problems with the locally normalized form of conditional models, not with the general ideas of conditional modeling or log-linear models.

D.4 COMPARISON TO GLOBALLY NORMALIZED MODELS

Consider again the globally normalized models of section 3.5, exemplified by the CRF, in comparison to locally normalized models. Both define $p(\boldsymbol{Y} \mid \boldsymbol{X})$ (i.e., they are conditional models), and both rely on the use of locally factored feature functions, $\mathbf{g}(\boldsymbol{x}, \boldsymbol{y}) = \sum_{j=1}^{\#parts(\boldsymbol{x})} \mathbf{f}(\Pi_j(\boldsymbol{x}, \boldsymbol{y}))$ for efficiency. We discuss here some important differences.

The first has to do with the asymmetry discussed in section D.3. Globally normalized models do not have such directional biases, and in most comparisons, they appear to perform better than local models.

Another difference has to do with the expressive power of the model. Given the same set of features, there are distributions that can be modeled by a globally normalized model, but not a locally normalized one; an example due to Michael Collins is presented by Smith and Johnson (2007).

Arguments in favor of locally normalized models hinge on training efficiency. Neither type of model has a closed-form solution for maximum likelihood estimation (or maximum *a priori* estimation). Both require numerical optimization for training the parameters $\mathbf{w}$. As noted, the gradient for the globally normalized model depends on feature value expectations under the model (equation 3.77), $\mathbb{E}_{\mathbf{p_w}(\boldsymbol{Y} \mid \tilde{\boldsymbol{x}}_i)}[g_j(\tilde{\boldsymbol{x}}_i, \boldsymbol{Y})]$. These expectations require inference routines, often based on dynamic programming (see chapter 5). Locally normalized models have the advantage that only local expectations are required. Here is the log-likelihood function for an MEMM for sequence labeling (section D.2):

$$\Phi_{\text{LL}}(\mathbf{w}) = \sum_{i=1}^{\tilde{N}} \sum_{k=1}^{|\tilde{\boldsymbol{x}}_i|+1} \left(\mathbf{w}^\top \mathbf{f}(\tilde{\boldsymbol{x}}_i, \tilde{y}_{i,k-1}, \tilde{y}_{i,k}, k) - \log \sum_{y' \in \Lambda} \exp \mathbf{w}^\top \mathbf{f}(\boldsymbol{x}, \tilde{y}_{i,k-1}, y', k) \right) \tag{D.10}$$

The first derivative with respect to w_j is:

$$\frac{\partial \Phi_{\text{LL}}}{\partial w_j}(\mathbf{w}) = \sum_{i=1}^{\tilde{N}} \sum_{k=1}^{|\tilde{\boldsymbol{x}}_i|+1} \left(f_j(\tilde{\boldsymbol{x}}_i, \tilde{y}_{i,k-1}, \tilde{y}_{i,k}, k) - \underbrace{\sum_{y' \in \Lambda} p_{\mathbf{w}}(y' \mid \tilde{\boldsymbol{x}}_i, \tilde{y}_{i,k-1}) f_j(\tilde{\boldsymbol{x}}_i, \tilde{y}_{i,k-1}, y', k)}_{\mathbb{E}_{p_{\mathbf{w}}(Y_k \mid \tilde{\boldsymbol{x}}_i, \tilde{y}_{i,k-1})}[f_j(\tilde{\boldsymbol{x}}_i, \tilde{y}_{i,k-1}, Y_k, k)]} \right) \tag{D.11}$$

Compared to the expectations for globally normalized models like CRFs, this is incredibly simple; instead of summing over all sequence labelings, we only need to sum over Λ for each symbol in the data. Because the MEMM is really just a sequence of local classifiers, training it is essentially the same as training a multinomial logistic regression model (section 3.5.1). For the feature function factoring above, the dynamic programming algorithm used by the globally normalized model, a variant of figure 2.16, has runtime $O(n|\Lambda|^2)$ where n is the total length of the training data, while the MEMM's algorithm is only $O(n|\Lambda|)$.

Noting the approximate training method for CRFs discussed in section 3.5.6, pseudolikelihood, it is interesting to compare the locally normalized model to the pseudolikelihood approximation for the corresponding globally normalized model, since both turn the structured problem of predicting $\boldsymbol{Y}$ into a collection of locally modeled predictions. Consider again sequence labeling. The locally normalized model (e.g., the MEMM) factors $p(\boldsymbol{Y} \mid \boldsymbol{X})$ into local factors of the form $p(Y_k \mid \boldsymbol{X}, \{Y_j\}_{j<k})$, while pseudolikelihood has factors of the form $p(Y_k \mid \boldsymbol{X}, \{Y_j\}_{j \neq k})$. Pseudolikelihood is not directional; it conditions Y_k on its entire context. The locally normalized model, while more understandable as a generative process, ignores the right context when learning to predict each label. If we take pseudolikelihood to be a reasonable approximate learning technique, then the asymmetry in the MEMM is striking and appears to be missing something.

D.5 DECODING

As noted in section D.2, if we wish to apply standard linear decoding techniques with the MEMM (and similar models), we must take into account the normalizing terms (denominators in equation D.4). We define a new local feature vector function $\mathbf{f}'$. Let the first d components of $\mathbf{f}'$ be the same as in $\mathbf{f}$, with the same weights as in the MEMM.

We next add $|\Lambda|(n+1)$ more features of the following form:

$$f'_{\ell,i}(\boldsymbol{x}, \ell, \ell', i) = \begin{cases} 1 & \text{if } y_i = \ell \\ 0 & \text{otherwise} \end{cases} \tag{D.12}$$

The weight of feature $f'_{\ell,i}$ is the log of the local normalizer and is fully defined by the rest of the model:

$$w_{\ell,i} = -\log \sum_{y' \in \Lambda} \exp \mathbf{w}^\top \mathbf{f}(x_i, y_{i-1}, y', i) \tag{D.13}$$

Using the $(d + |\Lambda|(n + 1))$-featured model, decoding can proceed using the standard approach of dynamic programming with the extended local feature vector $\mathbf{f}'$ (see figure 2.16).

While training a locally normalized model avoids the need for inference by dynamic programming (or some other global reasoning technique), such inference is required at decoding time. The mismatch between the inference required for training (separate local sums over labels) and the inference required for exact decoding (global maximization via dynamic programming) warrants some discussion. Note that when learning to predict the label for a given word x_i in context, it is assumed that the preceding word's label, y_{i-1}, is known. Of course, when carrying out prediction of Y_i, the value of Y_{i-1} is *not* known. The classification task solved by equation D.4 does not accurately represent the prediction problem that must be performed at decoding time. Indeed, the Viterbi algorithm calculates the best possible score for any label *sequence* leading up to position i with each label, but no commitment as to which label to choose at position i is made until the dynamic programming equations are solved.

D.6 THEORY VS. PRACTICE

Despite the concerns discussed above, locally normalized models are widely used. Examples include history-based structure models (Ratnaparkhi, 1996), maximum entropy Markov models for information extraction (McCallum et al., 2000), and transition-based parsing models (Henderson, 2003, Nivre et al., 2004). Such models often obtain state-of-the-art performance, suggesting that the dangers discussed here can be overcome by some combination of wise feature design and engineering, sufficiently large amounts of training data, and/or the use of non-probabilistic models (e.g., large margin training).

Bibliography

Steven Abney. *Semisupervised Learning for Computational Linguistics*. Number 8 in Chapman and Hall/CRC Computer Science and Data Analysis Series. CRC Press, 2007. Cited on page(s) 109

Hirotugu Akaike. A new look at the statistical model identification. *IEEE Transactions on Automatic Control*, 19(6), 1974. DOI: 10.1109/TAC.1974.1100705 Cited on page(s) 134

Galen Andrew and Jianfeng Gao. Scalable training of l_1-regularized log-linear models. In *Proceedings of the 24th International Conference on Machine Learning*, pages 33–40, Corvalis, Oregon, USA, 2007. DOI: 10.1145/1273496.1273501 Cited on page(s) 96, 177

John Arbuthnott. An argument for divine providence, taken from the constant regularity observed in the births of both sexes. *Philosophical Transactions of the Royal Society of London*, 27:186–190, 1710. DOI: 10.1098/rstl.1710.0011 Cited on page(s) 193

Amit Bagga and Breck Baldwin. Entity-based cross-document coreferencing using the vector space model. In *Proceedings of the 36th Annual Meeting of the Association for Computational Linguistics and 17th International Conference on Computational Linguistics*, pages 79–85, Montréal, Québec, Canada, August 1998. DOI: 10.3115/980845.980859 Cited on page(s) 14

Collin F. Baker, Charles J. Fillmore, and John B. Lowe. The Berkeley FrameNet project. In *Proceedings of the 36th Annual Meeting of the Association for Computational Linguistics and 17th International Conference on Computational Linguistics*, pages 86–90, Montréal, Québec, Canada, August 1998. DOI: 10.3115/980845.980860 Cited on page(s) 14

James K. Baker. The Dragon system—an overview. *Transactions on Acoustic Speech Signal Processing*, ASSP-23(1):24–29, 1975. DOI: 10.1109/TASSP.1975.1162650 Cited on page(s) 74

James K. Baker. Trainable grammars for speech recognition. In *Proceedings of the Acoustical Society of America*, pages 547–550, Boston, Massachusetts, USA, June 1979. DOI: 10.1121/1.2017061 Cited on page(s) 54, 117

Gökhan Bakır, Thomas Hofmann, Bernhard Schölkopf, Alexander J. Smola, Ben Taskar, and S. V. N. Vishwanathan, editors. *Predicting Structured Data*. MIT Press, 2007. Cited on page(s) 106

Srinivas Bangalore and Aravind K. Joshi. Supertagging: An approach to almost parsing. *Computational Linguistics*, 25(2):237–265, 1999. Cited on page(s) 6

Mohit Bansal, Claire Cardie, and Lillian Lee. The power of negative thinking: Exploiting label disagreement in the min-cut classification framework. In *Companion Volume to the Proceedings of the 22nd International Conference on Computational Linguistics*, pages 15–18, Manchester, UK, August 2008. Cited on page(s) 67

Roy Bar-Haim, Ido Dagan, Bill Dolan, Lisa Ferro, Danilo Giampiccolo, Bernardo Magnini, and Idan Szpektor. The second PASCAL recognising textual entailment challenge. In *Proceedings of the Second PASCAL Challenges Workshop on Recognising Textual Entailment*, pages 1–9, Venice, Italy, 2006. Cited on page(s) 182

Regina Barzilay and Lillian Lee. Learning to paraphrase: An unsupervised approach using multiple-sequence alignment. In *Proceedings of the Human Language Technology Conference of the North American Chapter of the Association for Computational Linguistics*, pages 16–23, Edmonton, Alberta, Canada, May–June 2003. DOI: 10.3115/1073445.1073448 Cited on page(s) 18

L. E. Baum and T. Petrie. Statistical inference for probabilistic functions of finite state Markov chains. *Annals of Mathematical Statistics*, 37:1554–1563, 1966. DOI: 10.1214/aoms/1177699147 Cited on page(s) 74

L. E. Baum, T. Petrie, G. Soules, and N. Weiss. A maximization technique occurring in the statistical analysis of probabilistic functions of Markov chains. *Annals of Mathematical Statistics*, 41:164–171, 1970. DOI: 10.1214/aoms/1177697196 Cited on page(s) 117

Matthew J. Beal, Zoubin Ghahramani, and Carl Edward Rasmussen. The infinite hidden Markov model. In Thomas G. Dietterich, Suzanna Becker, and Zoubin Ghahramani, editors, *Advances in Neural Information Processing Systems 14*. MIT Press, 2002. Cited on page(s) 134

Kenneth R. Beesley and Lauri Kartunnen. *Finite State Morphology*. CSLI Publications, 2003. Cited on page(s) 7, 204

Steven J. Benson and Jorge J. Moré. A limited memory variable metric method for bound constraint minimization. Technical Report ANL/ACSP909-0901, Argonne National Labs, 2001. Cited on page(s) 177

Taylor Berg-Kirkpatrick, Alexandre Bouchard-Coté, John DeNero, and Dan Klein. Painless unsupervised learning with features. In *Proceedings of the Human Language Technologies Conference of the North American Chapter of the Association for Computational Linguistics*, Los Angeles, California, USA, June 2010. Cited on page(s) 123

Adam Berger. The improved iterative scaling algorithm: A gentle introduction, 1997. URL `http://www.cs.cmu.edu/~aberger/ps/scaling.ps`. Cited on page(s) 179

Adam Berger. MaxEnt and exponential models, date unknown. URL `http://www.cs.cmu.edu/~aberger/maxent.html`. Cited on page(s) 202

Dimitri P. Bertsekas. *Nonlinear Programming*. Athena Scientific, second edition, 1999. Cited on page(s) 173, 176

Dimitris Bertsimas and John N. Tsitsiklis. *Introduction to Linear Optimization*. Athena Scientific, 1997. Cited on page(s) 31

Julian Besag. Statistical analysis of non-lattice data. *Journal of the Royal Statistical Society, Series D (The Statistician)*, 24(3):179–195, 1975. DOI: 10.2307/2987782 Cited on page(s) 98

Christopher M. Bishop. *Pattern Recognition and Machine Learning*. Springer, 2006. Cited on page(s) xv, 122

David M. Blei, Andrew Y. Ng, and Michael I. Jordan. Latent Dirichlet allocation. *Journal of Machine Learning Research*, 3:993–1022, 2003. DOI: 10.1162/jmlr.2003.3.4-5.993 Cited on page(s) 127, 129

John Blitzer, Ryan McDonald, and Fernando Pereira. Domain adaptation with structural correspondence learning. In *Proceedings of the Conference on Empirical Methods in Natural Language Processing*, pages 120–128, Sydney, Australia, 2006. DOI: 10.3115/1610075.1610094 Cited on page(s) 6

Phil Blunsom, Trevor Cohn, and Miles Osborne. A discriminative latent variable model for statistical machine translation. In *Proceedings of the 46th Annual Meeting of the Association for Computational Linguistics: Human Language Technologies*, pages 200–208, Columbus, Ohio, USA, June 2008. Cited on page(s) 143

Phil Blunsom, Trevor Cohn, and Miles Osborne. Bayesian synchronous grammar induction. In Daphne Koller, Dale Schuurmans, Yoshua Bengio, and Léon Bottou, editors, *Advances in Neural Information Processing Systems 21*. MIT Press, 2009. Cited on page(s) 139

Alena Böhmová, Jan Hajič, Eva Haijičová, and Barbora Hladká. The Prague Dependency Treebank: A three-level annotation scenario. In Anne Abeillé, editor, *Treebanks: Building and Using Parsed Corpora*, volume 20 of *Text, Speech, and Language Technology*, chapter 7. Kluwer, 2003. Cited on page(s) 6

Léon Bottou. Stochastic learning. In Olivier Bousquet and Ulrike von Luxburg, editors, *Advanced Lectures on Machine Learning*, number 3176 in Lecture Notes in Artificial Intelligence, pages 146–168. Springer, 2004. Cited on page(s) 175

Alexandre Bouchard-Côté, Percy Liang, Thomas Griffiths, and Dan Klein. A probabilistic approach to diachronic phonology. In *Proceedings of the Joint Conference on Empirical Methods in Natural Language Processing and Computational Natural Language Learning*, pages 887–896, Prague, Czech Republic, June 2007. Cited on page(s) 18

Stephen Boyd and Lieven Vandenberghe. *Convex Optimization*. Cambridge University Press, 2004. Cited on page(s) 143

Thorsten Brants, Ashok C. Popat, Peng Xu, Franz J. Och, and Jeffrey Dean. Large language models in machine translation. In *Proceedings of the Joint Conference on Empirical Methods in Natural Language Processing and Computational Natural Language Learning*, pages 858–867, Prague, Czech Republic, June 2007. Cited on page(s) 20

Peter F. Brown, John Cocke, Stephen A. Della Pietra, Vincent J. Della Pietra, Frederick Jelinek, John D. Lafferty, Robert L. Mercer, and Paul S. Roossin. A statistical approach to machine translation. *Computational Linguistics*, 16(2):79–85, 1990. Cited on page(s) 17, 79, 115

Sabine Buchholz and Erwin Marsi. CoNLL-X shared task on multilingual dependency parsing. In *Proceedings of the Tenth Conference on Computational Natural Language Learning*, pages 149–164, New York City, USA, June 2006. DOI: 10.3115/1596276.1596305 Cited on page(s) 19

David Burkett and Dan Klein. Two languages are better than one (for syntactic parsing). In *Proceedings of the Conference on Empirical Methods in Natural Language Processing*, pages 877–886, Honolulu, Hawaii, USA, October 2008. DOI: 10.3115/1613715.1613828 Cited on page(s) 18

Richard H. Byrd, Peihuang Lu, Jorge Nocedal, and Ciyou Zhu. A limited memory algorithm for bound constrained optimization. *SIAM Journal on Scientific and Statistical Computing*, 16(5): 1190–1208, 1995. DOI: 10.1137/0916069 Cited on page(s) 177

Paolo M. Camerini, Luigi Fratta, and Francesco Maffioli. The *k* best spanning arborescences of a network. *Networks*, 10(2):91–110, 1980. DOI: 10.1002/net.3230100202 Cited on page(s) 66

Sharon A. Caraballo and Eugene Charniak. New figures of merit for best-first probabilistic chart parsing. *Computational Linguistics*, 24(2):275–298, 1998. Cited on page(s) 61

Lynn Carlson, Daniel Marcu, and Mary Ellen Okurowski. Building a discourse-tagged corpus in the framework of rhetorical structure theory. In Jan van Kuppevelt and Ronnie W. Smith, editors, *Current and New Directions in Discourse and Dialogue*. Springer, 2003. Cited on page(s) 16

Bob Carpenter. *Type-Logical Semantics*. MIT Press, 1998. Cited on page(s) 13

Xavier Carreras and Lluís Màrquez. Introduction to the CoNLL-2004 shared task: Semantic role labeling. In *Proceedings of the Eighth Conference on Computational Natural Language Learning*, pages 89–97, Boston, Massachusetts, USA, May 2004. Cited on page(s) 14

Xavier Carreras and Lluís Màrquez. Introduction to the CoNLL-2005 shared task: Semantic role labeling. In *Proceedings of the 9th Conference on Computational Natural Language Learning*, pages 152–164, Ann Arbor, Michigan, USA, June 2005. DOI: 10.3115/1706543.1706571 Cited on page(s) 14

Xavier Carreras, Michael Collins, and Terry Koo. TAG, dynamic programming and the perceptron for efficient, feature-rich parsing. In *Proceedings of the 12th Conference on Computational Natural Language Learning*, pages 9–16, Manchester, UK, August 2008. DOI: 10.3115/1596324.1596327 Cited on page(s) 11, 92

Glen Carroll and Eugene Charniak. Two experiments on learning probabilistic dependency grammars from corpora, 1992. AAAI Technical Report WS-92-01. Cited on page(s) 122

Ming-Wei Chang, Dan Goldwasser, Dan Roth, and Vivek Srikumar. Discriminative learning over constrained latent representations. In *Proceedings of the Human Language Technologies Conference of the North American Chapter of the Association for Computational Linguistics*, Los Angeles, California, USA, June 2010. Cited on page(s) 140

Eugene Charniak. A maximum-entropy-inspired parser. In *Proceedings of the First Conference on North American Chapter of the Association for Computational Linguistics*, pages 132–139, Seattle, Washington, USA, May 2000. Cited on page(s) 11

Eugene Charniak. *Statistical Language Learning*. MIT Press, 1993. Cited on page(s) xix

Eugene Charniak and Mark Johnson. Coarse-to-fine n-best parsing and maxent discriminative reranking. In *Proceedings of the 43rd Annual Meeting of the Association of Computational Linguistics*, pages 173–180, Ann Arbor, Michigan, USA, June 2005. DOI: 10.3115/1219840.1219862 Cited on page(s) 64

Eugene Charniak, Sharon Goldwater, and Mark Johnson. Edge-based best-first chart parsing. In *Proceedings of the Sixth Workshop on Very Large Corpora*, pages 127–133, Montréal, Québec, Canada, August 1998. Cited on page(s) 61

Eugene Charniak, Mark Johnson, Micha Elsner, Joseph Austerweil, David Ellis, Isaac Haxton, Catherine Hill, R. Shrivaths, Jeremy Moore, Michael Pozar, and Theresa Vu. Multilevel coarse-to-fine pcfg parsing. In *Proceedings of the Human Language Technology Conference of the North American Chapter of the Association for Computational Linguistics*, pages 168–175, New York City, USA, June 2006. DOI: 10.3115/1220835.1220857 Cited on page(s) 64

Ciprian Chelba and Alex Acero. Adaptation of maximum entropy capitalizer: Little data can help a lot. *Computer Speech and Language*, 20(4), 2006. DOI: 10.1016/j.csl.2005.05.005 Cited on page(s) 95

Stanley F. Chen and Joshua Goodman. An empirical study of smoothing techniques for language modeling. Technical Report TR-10-98, Center for Research in Computing Technology, Harvard University, 1998. DOI: 10.3115/981863.981904 Cited on page(s) 83

Stanley F. Chen and Roni Rosenfeld. A survey of smoothing techniques for maximum entropy models. *IEEE Transactions on Speech and Audio Processing*, 8(1):37–50, 2000. DOI: 10.1109/89.817452 Cited on page(s) 95

David Chiang. A hierarchical phrase-based model for statistical machine translation. In *Proceedings of the 43rd Annual Meeting of the Association of Computational Linguistics*, pages 263–270, Ann Arbor, Michigan, USA, June 2005. DOI: 10.3115/1219840.1219873 Cited on page(s) 18

David Chiang. Hierarchical phrase-based translation. *Computational Linguistics*, 33(2):201–228, 2007. DOI: 10.1162/coli.2007.33.2.201 Cited on page(s) 62, 63

David Chiang and Daniel M. Bikel. Recovering latent information in treebanks. In *Proceedings of the 19th International Conference on Computational Linguistics*, pages 183–189, Taipei, Taiwan, August–September 2002. DOI: 10.3115/1072228.1072354 Cited on page(s) 142

Yejin Choi and Claire Cardie. Learning with compositional semantics as structural inference for subsentential sentiment analysis. In *Proceedings of the Conference on Empirical Methods in Natural Language Processing*, pages 793–801, Honolulu, Hawaii, USA, October 2008. DOI: 10.3115/1613715.1613816 Cited on page(s) 16

Yejin Choi, Claire Cardie, Ellen Riloff, and Siddharth Patwardhan. Identifying sources of opinions with conditional random fields and extraction patterns. In *Proceedings of Human Language Technology Conference and Conference on Empirical Methods in Natural Language Processing*, pages 355–362, Vancouver, British Columbia, Canada, October 2005. DOI: 10.3115/1220575.1220620 Cited on page(s) 16

Noam Chomsky. *Aspects of the Theory of Syntax*. MIT Press, 1965. Cited on page(s) 70

Y. J. Chu and T. H. Liu. On the shortest arborescence of a directed graph. *Science Sinica*, 14: 1396–1400, 1965. Cited on page(s) 66

Massimiliano Ciaramita and Yasemin Altun. Broad-coverage sense disambiguation and information extraction with a supersense sequence tagger. In *Proceedings of the Conference on Empirical Methods in Natural Language Processing*, pages 594–602, Sydney, Australia, 2006. DOI: 10.3115/1610075.1610158 Cited on page(s) 14

Alexander Clark and Shalom Lappin. *Linguistic Nativism and the Poverty of the Stimulus*. Wiley-Blackwell, 2011. Cited on page(s) 70

Stephen Clark and James R. Curran. Parsing the WSJ using CCG and log-linear models. In *Proceedings of the 42nd Meeting of the Association for Computational Linguistics*, pages 103–110, Barcelona, Spain, July 2004. DOI: 10.3115/1218955.1218969 Cited on page(s) 11, 143

James Clarke and Mirella Lapata. Constraint-based sentence compression: An integer programming approach. In *Proceedings of the 21st International Conference on Computational Linguistics and 44th Annual Meeting of the Association for Computational Linguistics*, pages 144–151, Sydney, Australia, July 2006. DOI: 10.3115/1273073.1273092 Cited on page(s) 37

James Clarke, Dan Goldwasser, Ming-Wei Chang, and Dan Roth. Driving semantic parsing from the world's response. In *Proceedings of the Fourteenth Conference on Computational Natural Language Learning*, pages 18–27, Uppsala, Sweden, July 2010. Cited on page(s) 13

John Cocke and Jacob T. Schwartz. Programming languages and their compilers: Preliminary notes. Technical report, Courant Institute of Mathematical Sciences, New York University, 1970. Cited on page(s) 54

Shay B. Cohen and Noah A. Smith. Joint morphological and syntactic disambiguation. In *Proceedings of the Joint Conference on Empirical Methods in Natural Language Processing and Computational Natural Language Learning*, pages 208–217, Prague, Czech Republic, June 2007. Cited on page(s) 5

Shay B. Cohen and Noah A. Smith. Viterbi training for PCFGs: Hardness results and competitiveness of uniform initialization. In *Proceedings of the 48th Annual Meeting of the Association for Computational Linguistics*, pages 1502–1511, Uppsala, Sweden, July 2010. Cited on page(s) 111

Shay B. Cohen, Kevin Gimpel, and Noah A. Smith. Logistic normal priors for unsupervised probabilistic grammar induction. In Daphne Koller, Dale Schuurmans, Yoshua Bengio, and Léon Bottou, editors, *Advances in Neural Information Processing Systems 21*, pages 321–328. MIT Press, 2009. Cited on page(s) 129

Shay B. Cohen, David M. Blei, and Noah A. Smith. Variational inference for adaptor grammars. In *Proceedings of the Human Language Technologies Conference of the North American Chapter of the Association for Computational Linguistics*, pages 564–572, Los Angeles, California, USA, June 2010. Cited on page(s) 139

William W. Cohen. Information extraction and integration: An overview, 2004. Tutorial available at `http://www.cs.cmu.edu/~wcohen/ie-survey.ppt`. Cited on page(s) 9

Trevor Cohn, Sharon Goldwater, and Phil Blunsom. Inducing compact but accurate tree-substitution grammars. In *Proceedings of the Human Language Technologies Conference of the North American Chapter of the Association for Computational Linguistics*, pages 548–556, Boulder, Colorado, USA, June 2009. Cited on page(s) 139, 167

Michael Collins. Discriminative reranking for natural language parsing. In *Proceedings of the 17th International Conference on Machine Learning*, pages 175–182, Stanford, California, USA, June–July 2000. DOI: 10.1162/0891201053630273 Cited on page(s) 64

Michael Collins. Discriminative training methods for hidden Markov models: Theory and experiments with perceptron algorithms. In *Proceedings of the Conference on Empirical Methods in Natural Language Processing*, pages 1–8, Philadelphia, Pennsylvania, USA, July 2002. DOI: 10.3115/1118693.1118694 Cited on page(s) 101, 102

Michael Collins. Head-driven statistical models for natural language parsing. *Computational Linguistics*, 29(4):589–637, 2003. DOI: 10.1162/089120103322753356 Cited on page(s) 11

Michael Collins. The EM algorithm, 1997. URL `http://people.csail.mit.edu/mcollins/papers/wpeII.4.ps`. DOI: 10.1007/978-3-642-05258-3_48 Cited on page(s) 122

Michael Collins. *Head-Driven Statistical Models for Natural Language Parsing*. PhD thesis, University of Pennsylvania, 1999. DOI: 10.1162/089120103322753356 Cited on page(s) 12

Michael Collins and Nigel Duffy. New ranking algorithms for parsing and tagging: Kernels over discrete structures, and the voted perceptron. In *Proceedings of 40th Annual Meeting of the Association for Computational Linguistics*, pages 263–270, Philadelphia, Pennsylvania, USA, July 2002. DOI: 10.3115/1073083.1073128 Cited on page(s) 99

George Corliss, Christele Faure, Andreas Griewank, Laurent Hascoet, and Uwe Naumann, editors. *Automatic Differentiation of Algorithms: From Simulation to Optimization*. Springer, 2002. Cited on page(s) 159

Corinna Cortes and Vladimir Vapnik. Support-vector networks. *Machine Learning*, 20:273–297, 1995. DOI: 10.1023/A:1022627411411 Cited on page(s) 99

Koby Crammer and Yoram Singer. On the algorithmic implementation of multiclass kernel-based vector machines. *Journal of Machine Learning Research*, 2(5):265âŁ"–292, 2001. Cited on page(s) 103

Koby Crammer and Yoram Singer. Ultraconservative online algorithms for multiclass problems. *Journal of Machine Learning Research*, 3:951–991, 2003. DOI: 10.1162/jmlr.2003.3.4-5.951 Cited on page(s) 105, 177

Koby Crammer, Ofer Dekel, Joseph Keshet, Shai Shalev-Shwartz, and Yoram Singer. Online passive-aggressive algorithms. *Journal of Machine Learning Research*, 7:551–585, 2006. Cited on page(s) 105, 177

Aron Culotta, Michael Wick, and Andrew McCallum. First-order probabilistic models for coreference resolution. In *Proceedings of the Human Language Technologies Conference of the North American Chapter of the Association for Computational Linguistics*, pages 81–88, Rochester, New York, USA, April 2007. Cited on page(s) 16

Ido Dagan, Oren Glickman, and Bernardo Magnini. The PASCAL recognising textual entailment challenge. In Joaquin Quiñonero Candela, Ido Dagan, Bernardo Magnini, and Florence d'Alché Buc, editors, *Machine Learning Challenges, Evaluating Predictive Uncertainty, Visual Object Classification and Recognizing Textual Entailment, First PASCAL Machine Learning Challenges Workshop*, volume 3944 of *Lecture Notes in Computer Science*, pages 177–190. Springer, 2005. Cited on page(s) 182

Deborah A. Dahl, Madeleine Bates, Michael Brown, William Fisher, Kate Hunicke-Smith, David Pallett, Christine Pao, Alexander Rudnicky, and Elizabeth Shriberg. Expanding the scope of the ATIS task: The ATIS-3 corpus. In *Proceedings of the ARPA Human Language Technology Workshop*, pages 43–48, Plainsboro, New Jersey, USA, March 1994. DOI: 10.3115/1075812.1075823 Cited on page(s) 13

J. N. Darroch and D. Ratcliff. Generalized iterative scaling for log-linear models. *Annals of Mathematical Statistics*, 43(5):1470–1480, 1972. DOI: 10.1214/aoms/1177692379 Cited on page(s) 179

Dipanjan Das and Noah A. Smith. Paraphrase identification as probabilistic quasi-synchronous recognition. In *Proceedings of the Joint Conference of the 47th Annual Meeting of the Association for Computational Linguistics and the 4th International Joint Conference on Natural Language Processing of the Asian Federation of Natural Language Processing*, pages 468–476, Singapore, August 2009. Cited on page(s) 140

Dipanjan Das, Nathan Schneider, Desai Chen, and Noah A. Smith. Probabilistic frame-semantic parsing. In *Proceedings of the Human Language Technologies Conference of the North American Chapter of the Association for Computational Linguistics*, pages 948–956, Los Angeles, California, USA, June 2010. Cited on page(s) 14

Hal Daumé and Daniel Marcu. A Bayesian model for supervised clustering with the Dirichlet process prior. *Journal of Machine Learning Research*, 6:1551–1577, September 2005. Cited on page(s) 139

Hal Daumé, John Langford, and Daniel Marcu. Search-based structured prediction. *Machine Learning*, 75(3):297–325, 2009. DOI: 10.1007/s10994-009-5106-x Cited on page(s) 106

Anthony C. Davison and David V. Hinkley. *Bootstrap Methods and their Application*. Cambridge University Press, 1997. Cited on page(s) 189

William H. E. Day. Computationally difficult parsimony problems in phylogenetic systematics. *Journal of Theoretical Biology*, 103(3):429–438, 1983. DOI: 10.1016/0022-5193(83)90296-5 Cited on page(s) 111

Marie-Catherine de Marneffe and Christopher D. Manning. The Stanford typed dependencies representation. In *Proceedings of the COLING Workshop on Cross-Framework and Cross-Domain Parser Evaluation*, pages 1–8, Manchester, UK, August 2008. DOI: 10.3115/1608858.1608859 Cited on page(s) 11

Jeffrey Dean and Sanjay Ghemawat. MapReduce: Simplified data processing on large clusters. *Communications of the ACM*, 51(1):107–114, 2008. DOI: 10.1145/1327452.1327492 Cited on page(s) 20

Scott Deerwester, Susan T. Dumais, George W. Furnas, Thomas K. Landauer, and Richard Harshman. Indexing by latent semantic analysis. *Journal of the American Society for Information Science*, 41(6):391–407, 1990.
DOI: 10.1002/(SICI)1097-4571(199009)41:6%3C391::AID-ASI1%3E3.0.CO;2-9 Cited on page(s) 128

Stephen Della Pietra, Vincent Della Pietra, and John Lafferty. Inducing features of random fields. *IEEE Transactions on Pattern Analysis and Machine Intelligence*, 19(4):380–393, 1997.
DOI: 10.1109/34.588021 Cited on page(s) 92

A. P. Dempster, N. M. Laird, and D. B. Rubin. Maximum likelihood from incomplete data via the EM algorithm. *Journal of the Royal Statistical Society, Series B (Methodological)*, 39(1):1–38, 1977. Cited on page(s) 111

John DeNero and Dan Klein. The complexity of phrase alignment problems. In *Companion Volume to the Proceedings of the 46th Annual Meeting of the Association for Computational Linguistics: Human Language Technologies*, pages 25–28, Columbus, Ohio, USA, June 2008. Cited on page(s) 65, 152

John DeNero, Alexandre Bouchard-Côté, and Dan Klein. Sampling alignment structure under a Bayesian translation model. In *Proceedings of the Conference on Empirical Methods in Natural Language Processing*, pages 314–323, Honolulu, Hawaii, USA, October 2008. Cited on page(s) 162

Pascal Denis and Jason Baldridge. Joint determination of anaphoricity and coreference resolution using integer programming. In *Proceedings of the Human Language Technologies Conference of the North American Chapter of the Association for Computational Linguistics*, pages 236–243, Rochester, New York, USA, April 2007. Cited on page(s) 37

E. W. Dijkstra. A note on two problems in connexion with graphs. *Numerische Mathematik*, 1: 269–271, 1959. DOI: 10.1007/BF01386390 Cited on page(s) 40

Pedro Domingos and Daniel Lowd. *Markov Logic: An Interface Layer for Artificial Intelligence.* Morgan and Claypool, 2009. Cited on page(s) 31

Markus Dreyer and Jason Eisner. Better informed training of latent syntactic features. In *Proceedings of the Conference on Empirical Methods in Natural Language Processing*, pages 317–326, Sydney, Australia, 2006. DOI: 10.3115/1610075.1610120 Cited on page(s) 142

Markus Dreyer and Jason Eisner. Graphical models over multiple strings. In *Proceedings of the Conference on Empirical Methods in Natural Language Processing*, pages 101–110, Singapore, August 2009. Cited on page(s) 18

Olive Jean Dunn. Multiple comparisons among means. *Journal of the American Statistical Association*, 56(294):52–64, 1961. DOI: 10.2307/2282330 Cited on page(s) 190

Richard Durbin, Sean R. Eddy, Anders Krogh, and Graeme Mitchison. *Biological Sequence Analysis: Probabilistic Models of Proteins and Nucleic Acids.* Cambridge University Press, 1998. Cited on page(s) 74

Jay Earley. An efficient context-free parsing algorithm. *Communications of the ACM*, 13(2):94–102, 1970. DOI: 10.1145/362007.362035 Cited on page(s) 55

Jack Edmonds. Optimum branchings. *Journal of Research of the National Bureau of Standards*, 71B: 233–240, 1967. Cited on page(s) 66

Jack Edmonds and Richard M. Karp. Theoretical improvements in algorithmic efficiency for network flow problems. *Journal of the ACM*, 19(2):248–264, 1972. DOI: 10.1145/321694.321699 Cited on page(s) 67

Bradley Efron. Bootstrap methods: another look at the jackknife. *Annals of Statistics*, 7:1–26, 1979. DOI: 10.1214/aos/1176344552 Cited on page(s) 187

Bradley Efron and Robert J. Tibshirani. *An Introduction to the Bootstrap.* Chapman and Hall, 1994. Cited on page(s) 189

Jacob Eisenstein and Regina Barzilay. Bayesian unsupervised topic segmentation. In *Proceedings of the Conference on Empirical Methods in Natural Language Processing*, pages 334–343, Honolulu, Hawaii, USA, October 2008. DOI: 10.3115/1613715.1613760 Cited on page(s) 4

Jason Eisner. Parameter estimation for probabilistic finite-state transducers. In *Proceedings of 40th Annual Meeting of the Association for Computational Linguistics*, pages 1–8, Philadelphia, Pennsylvania, USA, July 2002. Cited on page(s) 204

Jason Eisner, Eric Goldlust, and Noah A. Smith. Dyna: A declarative language for implementing dynamic programs. In *Companion Volume to the Proceedings of 42nd Annual Meeting of the Association for Computational Linguistics*, pages 218–221, Barcelona, Spain, July 2004. Cited on page(s) 52

Jason Eisner, Eric Goldlust, and Noah A. Smith. Compiling Comp Ling: Practical weighted dynamic programming and the Dyna language. In *Proceedings of Human Language Technology Conference and Conference on Empirical Methods in Natural Language Processing*, pages 281–290, Vancouver, British Columbia, Canada, October 2005. DOI: 10.3115/1220575.1220611 Cited on page(s) 52, 59, 60, 150, 160

P. Elias, A. Feinstein, and C. E. Shannon. Note on maximal flow through a network. *Transactions on Information Theory*, 2:117–199, 1956. DOI: 10.1109/TIT.1956.1056816 Cited on page(s) 67

Micha Elsner, Eugene Charniak, and Mark Johnson. Structured generative models for unsupervised named-entity clustering. In *Proceedings of the Human Language Technologies Conference of the North American Chapter of the Association for Computational Linguistics*, pages 164–172, Boulder, Colorado, USA, June 2009. Cited on page(s) 139

David Elworthy. Does Baum-Welch re-estimation help taggers? In *Proceedings of the 4th Applied Natural Language Processing Conference*, pages 53–58, Stuttgart, Germany, October 1994. DOI: 10.3115/974358.974371 Cited on page(s) 120

Gülşen Eryiğit, Joakim Nivre, and Kemal Oflazer. Dependency parsing of Turkish. *Computational Linguistics*, 34(3):357–389, 2008. DOI: 10.1162/coli.2008.07-017-R1-06-83 Cited on page(s) 7, 8

Christiane Fellbaum, editor. *WordNet: An Electronic Lexical Database*. MIT Press, 1998. Cited on page(s) 13, 14

Thomas S. Ferguson. A Bayesian analysis of some nonparametric problems. *Annals of Statistics*, 1 (2):209–230, 1973. DOI: 10.1214/aos/1176342360 Cited on page(s) 136

Jenny Rose Finkel and Christopher D. Manning. Hierarchical Bayesian domain adaptation. In *Proceedings of the Human Language Technologies Conference of the North American Chapter of the Association for Computational Linguistics*, pages 602–610, Boulder, Colorado, USA, June 2009. Cited on page(s) 5

Jenny Rose Finkel, Trond Grenager, and Christopher Manning. Incorporating non-local information into information extraction systems by Gibbs sampling. In *Proceedings of the 43rd Annual Meeting of the Association of Computational Linguistics*, pages 363–370, Ann Arbor, Michigan, USA, June 2005. DOI: 10.3115/1219840.1219885 Cited on page(s) 20, 134

Jenny Rose Finkel, Christopher D. Manning, and Andrew Ng. Solving the problem of cascading errors: Approximate Bayesian inference for linguistic annotation pipelines. In *Proceedings of the Conference on Empirical Methods in Natural Language Processing*, pages 618–626, Sydney, Australia, 2006. DOI: 10.3115/1610075.1610162 Cited on page(s) 5, 163

Jenny Rose Finkel, Trond Grenager, and Christopher D. Manning. The infinite tree. In *Proceedings of the 45th Annual Meeting of the Association of Computational Linguistics*, pages 272–279, Prague, Czech Republic, June 2007. Cited on page(s) 139

Jenny Rose Finkel, Alex Kleeman, and Christopher D. Manning. Efficient, feature-based, conditional random field parsing. In *Proceedings of the 46th Annual Meeting of the Association for Computational Linguistics: Human Language Technologies*, pages 959–967, Columbus, Ohio, USA, June 2008. Cited on page(s) 175

Thomas Finley and Thorsten Joachims. Training structural SVMs when exact inference is intractable. In *Proceedings of the 25th International Conference on Machine Learning*, pages 304–311, Helsinki, Finland, July 2008. DOI: 10.1145/1390156.1390195 Cited on page(s) 165

Ronald A. Fisher. *The Design of Experiments*. Oliver and Boyd, 1935. Cited on page(s) 196

L. R. Ford and D. R. Fulkerson. Maximal flow through a network. *Canadian Journal of Mathematics*, 8:399–404, 1956. DOI: 10.4153/CJM-1956-045-5 Cited on page(s) 67

Jerome Friedman, Trevor Hastie, and Robert Tibshirani. Regularized paths for generalized linear models via coordinate descent. Technical report, Stanford University, 2008. Cited on page(s) 95

William A. Gale and Kenneth W. Church. A program for aligning sentences in bilingual corpora. *Computational Linguistics*, 19(1):75–102, 1993. DOI: 10.3115/981344.981367 Cited on page(s) 17

Ruifang Ge and Raymond Mooney. A statistical semantic parser that integrates syntax and semantics. In *Proceedings of the 9th Conference on Computational Natural Language Learning*, pages 9–16, Ann Arbor, Michigan, USA, June 2005. DOI: 10.3115/1706543.1706546 Cited on page(s) 13

Ulrich Germann, Mike Jahr, Kevin Knight, Daniel Marcu, and Kenji Yamada. Fast decoding and optimal decoding for machine translation. In *Proceedings of 39th Annual Meeting of the Association for Computational Linguistics*, pages 228–235, Toulouse, France, July 2001. DOI: 10.3115/1073012.1073042 Cited on page(s) 37

Daniel Gildea and Daniel Jurafsky. Automatic labeling of semantic roles. *Computational Linguistics*, 24(3):245–288, 2002. DOI: 10.1162/089120102760275983 Cited on page(s) 14, 19

Kevin Gimpel and Noah A. Smith. Feature-rich translation by quasi-synchronous lattice parsing. In *Proceedings of the Conference on Empirical Methods in Natural Language Processing*, pages 219–228, Singapore, August 2009. Cited on page(s) 18, 62, 63, 160

Kevin Gimpel and Noah A. Smith. Softmax-margin CRFs: Training log-linear models with loss functions. In *Proceedings of the Human Language Technologies Conference of the North American Chapter of the Association for Computational Linguistics*, pages 733–736, Los Angeles, California, USA, June 2010. Cited on page(s) 106

Kevin Gimpel, Dipanjan Das, and Noah A. Smith. Distributed asynchronous online learning for natural language processing. In *Proceedings of the Fourteenth Conference on Computational Natural Language Learning*, pages 213–222, Uppsala, Sweden, July 2010. Cited on page(s) 175

Kevin Gimpel, Nathan Schneider, Brendan O'Connor, Dipanjan Das, Daniel Mills, Jacob Eisenstein, Michael Heilman, Dani Yogatama, Jeffrey Flanigan, and Noah A. Smith. Part-of-speech tagging for Twitter: Annotation, features, and experiments. In *Proceedings of the 49th Annual Meeting of the Association for Computational Linguistics*, Portland, Oregon, USA, June 2011. To appear. Cited on page(s) 6

Vaibhava Goel and William J. Byrne. Minimum Bayes risk automatic speech recognition. *Computer Speech and Language*, 14(2):115–135, 2000. DOI: 10.1006/csla.2000.0138 Cited on page(s) 164

E. Mark Gold. Language identification in the limit. *Information and Control*, 10(5):447–474, 1967. DOI: 10.1016/S0019-9958(67)91165-5 Cited on page(s) 70

Sharon Goldwater and Thomas L. Griffiths. A fully Bayesian approach to unsupervised part-of-speech tagging. In *Proceedings of the 45th Annual Meeting of the Association of Computational Linguistics*, pages 744–751, Prague, Czech Republic, June 2007. Cited on page(s) 129, 139

Sharon Goldwater, Thomas L. Griffiths, and Mark Johnson. Interpolating between types and tokens by estimating power-law generators. In Yair Weiss, Bernhard Schölkopf, and John Platt, editors, *Advances in Neural Information Processing Systems 18*. MIT Press, 2006a. Cited on page(s) 4, 139

Sharon Goldwater, Thomas L. Griffiths, and Mark Johnson. Contextual dependencies in unsupervised word segmentation. In *Proceedings of the 21st International Conference on Computational Linguistics and 44th Annual Meeting of the Association for Computational Linguistics*, pages 673–680, Sydney, Australia, July 2006b. DOI: 10.3115/1220175.1220260 Cited on page(s) 139

Joshua Goodman. Sequential conditional generalized iterative scaling. In *Proceedings of 40th Annual Meeting of the Association for Computational Linguistics*, pages 9–16, Philadelphia, Pennsylvania, USA, July 2002. DOI: 10.3115/1073083.1073086 Cited on page(s) 180

Joshua Goodman. Exponential priors for maximum entropy models. In *Proceedings of the Human Language Technology Conference of the North American Chapter of the Association for Computational Linguistics*, pages 305–312, Boston, Massachusetts, USA, May 2004. Cited on page(s) 96

Joshua Goodman. Parsing algorithms and metrics. In *Proceedings of the 34th Annual Meeting of the Association for Computational Linguistics*, pages 177–183, Santa Cruz, California, USA, June 1996. DOI: 10.3115/981863.981887 Cited on page(s) 164

Joshua Goodman. Global thresholding and multiple-pass parsing. In *Proceedings of the Second Conference on Empirical Methods in Natural Language Processing*, pages 11–25, Providence, Rhode Island, USA, August 1997. Cited on page(s) 64

Joshua Goodman. *Parsing Inside-Out*. PhD thesis, Harvard University, 1998. Cited on page(s) 163

Joshua Goodman. Semiring parsing. *Computational Linguistics*, 25(3):573–605, 1999. Cited on page(s) 48, 50, 52, 56, 57, 63, 149

Joshua Goodman, Gina Venolia, Keith Steury, and Chauncey Parker. Language modeling for soft keyboards. In *Proceedings of the 18th National Conference on Artificial Intelligence*, pages 419–424, July–August 2002. DOI: 10.1145/502716.502753 Cited on page(s) 2

William Sealy Gosset. The probable error of a mean. *Biometrika*, 6(1):1–25, 1908. Published under pseudonym *Student*. DOI: 10.1093/biomet/6.1.1 Cited on page(s) 192

João Graça, Kuzman Ganchev, and Ben Taskar. Expectation maximization and posterior constraints. In John C. Platt, Daphne Koller, Yoram Singer, and Sam Roweis, editors, *Advances in Neural Information Processing Systems 20*. MIT Press, 2008. Cited on page(s) 123

Isabelle Guyon and André Elisseeff. An introduction to variable and feature selection. *Journal of Machine Learning Research*, 3:1157–1182, 2003. DOI: 10.1162/153244303322753616 Cited on page(s) 92

Aria Haghighi and Dan Klein. Unsupervised coreference resolution in a nonparametric Bayesian model. In *Proceedings of the 45th Annual Meeting of the Association of Computational Linguistics*, pages 848–855, Prague, Czech Republic, June 2007. Cited on page(s) 139

Aria Haghighi and Dan Klein. Simple coreference resolution with rich syntactic and semantic features. In *Proceedings of the Conference on Empirical Methods in Natural Language Processing*, pages 1152–1161, Singapore, August 2009. Cited on page(s) 16

Aria Haghighi, Percy Liang, Taylor Berg-Kirkpatrick, and Dan Klein. Learning bilingual lexicons from monolingual corpora. In *Proceedings of the 46th Annual Meeting of the Association for Computational Linguistics: Human Language Technologies*, pages 771–779, Columbus, Ohio, USA, June 2008. Cited on page(s) 18

Eric Hardisty, Jordan Boyd-Graber, and Philip Resnik. Modeling perspective using adaptor grammars. In *Proceedings of the Conference on Empirical Methods in Natural Language Processing*, pages 284–292, Cambridge, MA, USA, October 2010. Cited on page(s) 19

Peter E. Hart, Nils J. Nilsson, and Bertram Raphael. A formal basis for the heuristic determination of minimum cost paths. *IEEE Transactions on Systems Science and Cybernetics*, 4(2):100–107, 1968. DOI: 10.1109/TSSC.1968.300136 Cited on page(s) 61

W. Keith Hastings. Monte Carlo sampling methods using Markov chains and their applications. *Biometrika*, 57(1):97–109, 1970. DOI: 10.1093/biomet/57.1.97 Cited on page(s) 131

Marti A. Hearst. Multi-paragraph segmentation of expository text. In *Proceedings of the 32nd Annual Meeting of the Association for Computational Linguistics*, pages 9–16, Las Cruces, New Mexico, USA, June 1994. DOI: 10.3115/981732.981734 Cited on page(s) 4

Michael Heilman and Noah A. Smith. Good question! statistical ranking for question generation. In *Proceedings of the Human Language Technologies Conference of the North American Chapter of the Association for Computational Linguistics*, Los Angeles, California, USA, June 2010. Cited on page(s) 18

Gregor Heinrich. Parameter estimation for text analysis. Technical report, University of Leipzig, 2008. URL `http://www.arbylon.net/publications/text-est.pdf`. Cited on page(s) 132

James Henderson. Inducing history representations for broad coverage statistical parsing. In *Proceedings of the Human Language Technology Conference of the North American Chapter of the Association for Computational Linguistics*, pages 24–31, Edmonton, Alberta, Canada, May–June 2003. DOI: 10.3115/1073445.1073459 Cited on page(s) 208

Geoffrey E. Hinton. Training products of experts by minimizing contrastive divergence. *Neural Computation*, 14(8):1771–1800, 2002. DOI: 10.1162/089976602760128018 Cited on page(s) 124

Thomas Hofmann. Probabilistic latent semantic analysis. In *Proceedings of the 15th Conference on Uncertainty in Artificial Intelligence*, pages 289–296, Stockholm, Sweden, July–August 1999. Cited on page(s) 128

Mark Hopkins and Greg Langmead. Cube pruning as heuristic search. In *Proceedings of the Conference on Empirical Methods in Natural Language Processing*, pages 62–71, Singapore, August 2009. Cited on page(s) 62

Liang Huang. Advanced dynamic programming in semiring and hypergraph frameworks, 2008. Tutorial available at `http://www.cis.upenn.edu/~lhuang3/coling.pdf`. Cited on page(s) 45

Liang Huang and David Chiang. Better k-best parsing. In *Proceedings of the Ninth International Workshop on Parsing Technology*, pages 53–64, Vancouver, British Columbia, Canada, October 2005. DOI: 10.3115/1654494.1654500 Cited on page(s) 64

Liang Huang and David Chiang. Forest rescoring: Faster decoding with integrated language models. In *Proceedings of the 45th Annual Meeting of the Association of Computational Linguistics*, pages 144–151, Prague, Czech Republic, June 2007. Cited on page(s) 64

Rebecca Hwa, Philip Resnik, Amy Weinberg, Clara Cabezas, and Okan Kolak. Bootstrapping parsers via syntactic projection across parallel texts. *Journal of Natural Language Engineering*, 11 (3):311–325, 2005. DOI: 10.1017/S1351324905003840 Cited on page(s) 18

Frederick Jelinek. A fast sequential decoding algorithm using a stack. *IBM Journal of Research and Development*, 13:675–685, 1969. DOI: 10.1147/rd.136.0675 Cited on page(s) 74

Frederick Jelinek. *Statistical Methods for Speech Recognition*. MIT Press, 1997. Cited on page(s) 3

Yongho Jeon and Yi Lin. An effective method for high-dimensional log-density ANOVA estimation, with application to nonparametric graphical model building. *Statistica Sinica*, 16(2):353–374, 2006. Cited on page(s) 85

Richard Johansson and Pierre Nugues. LTH: Semantic structure extraction using nonprojective dependency trees. In *Proceedings of the Fourth International Workshop on Semantic Evaluations*, pages 227–230, Prague, Czech Republic, June 2007. DOI: 10.3115/1621474.1621522 Cited on page(s) 14

Mark Johnson. Joint and conditional estimation of tagging and parsing models. In *Proceedings of 39th Annual Meeting of the Association for Computational Linguistics*, pages 322–329, Toulouse, France, July 2001. DOI: 10.3115/1073012.1073054 Cited on page(s) 206

Mark Johnson. Parsing with discontinuous constituents. In *Proceedings of the 23rd Annual Meeting of the Association for Computational Linguistics*, pages 127–132, Chicago, Illinois, USA, July 1985. DOI: 10.3115/981210.981225 Cited on page(s) 11

Mark Johnson. PCFG models of linguistic tree representations. *Computational Linguistics*, 24(4): 613–32, 1998. Cited on page(s) 141

Mark Johnson, Thomas L. Griffiths, and Sharon Goldwater. Adaptor grammars: A framework for specifying compositional nonparametric Bayesian models. In John Platt Bernhard Schölkopf and Thomas Hofmann, editors, *Advances in Neural Information Processing Systems 19*. MIT Press, 2007a. Cited on page(s) 139, 163

Mark Johnson, Thomas L. Griffiths, and Sharon Goldwater. Bayesian inference for PCFGs via Markov chain Monte Carlo. In *Proceedings of the Human Language Technologies Conference of the North American Chapter of the Association for Computational Linguistics*, pages 139–146, Rochester, New York, USA, April 2007b. Cited on page(s) 83

Daniel Jurafsky and James H. Martin. *Speech and Language Processing: An Introduction to Natural Language Processing, Computational Linguistics, and Speech Recognition*. Prentice Hall, second edition, 2008. Cited on page(s) xv

Narendra Karmarkar. A new polynomial time algorithm for linear programming. *Combinatorica*, 4 (4):373–395, 1984. DOI: 10.1007/BF02579150 Cited on page(s) 35

Richard M. Karp. Reducibility among combinatorial problems. In Raymond E. Miller and James W. Thatcher, editors, *Complexity of Computer Computations*, pages 85–103. Plenum Press, 1972. Cited on page(s) 47

T. Kasami, H. Seki, and M. Fujii. Generalized context-free grammars, multiple context-free grammars, and head grammars. Technical report, Osaka University, 1987. DOI: 10.1002/scj.4690200705 Cited on page(s) 37

Tadao Kasami. An efficient recognition and syntax-analysis algorithm for context-free languages. Technical Report AFCRL-65-758, Air Force Cambridge Research Lab, 1965. Cited on page(s) 54

Jun'ichi Kazama and Jun'ichi Tsujii. Evaluation and extension of maximum entropy models with inequality constraints. In *Proceedings of the Conference on Empirical Methods in Natural Language Processing*, pages 137–144, Sapporo, Japan, July 2003. DOI: 10.3115/1119355.1119373 Cited on page(s) 96

Dan Klein and Christopher D. Manning. Parsing and hypergraphs. In *Proceedings of the Seventh International Workshop on Parsing Technologies*, pages 123–134, Beijing, China, October 2001. Cited on page(s) 41, 54

Dan Klein and Christopher D. Manning. Conditional structure versus conditional estimation in NLP models. In *Proceedings of the Conference on Empirical Methods in Natural Language Processing*, pages 9–16, Philadelphia, Pennsylvania, USA, July 2002a. DOI: 10.3115/1118693.1118695 Cited on page(s) 206

Dan Klein and Christopher D. Manning. A generative constituent-context model for improved grammar induction. In *Proceedings of 40th Annual Meeting of the Association for Computational Linguistics*, pages 128–135, Philadelphia, Pennsylvania, USA, July 2002b. DOI: 10.3115/1073083.1073106 Cited on page(s) 115

Dan Klein and Christopher D. Manning. Accurate unlexicalized parsing. In *Proceedings of the 41st Annual Meeting of the Association for Computational Linguistics*, pages 423–430, Sapporo, Japan, July 2003. DOI: 10.3115/1075096.1075150 Cited on page(s) 11, 61, 142

Kevin Knight and Jonathan Graehl. Machine transliteration. *Computational Linguistics*, 24(4): 599–612, 1998. Cited on page(s) 18

Kevin Knight and Daniel Marcu. Summarization beyond sentence extraction: A probabilistic approach to sentence compression. *Artificial Intelligence*, 139(1):91–107, 2002. DOI: 10.1016/S0004-3702(02)00222-9 Cited on page(s) 18

Donald E. Knuth. A generalization of Dijkstra's algorithm. *Information Processing Letters*, 6(1):1–5, 1977. DOI: 10.1016/0020-0190(77)90002-3 Cited on page(s) 59

Philipp Koehn. Statistical significance tests for machine translation evaluation. In *Proceedings of the Conference on Empirical Methods in Natural Language Processing*, pages 388–395, Barcelona, Spain, July 2004. Cited on page(s) 197

Philipp Koehn. *Statistical Machine Translation*. Cambridge University Press, 2009. Cited on page(s) 18

Daphne Koller and Nir Friedman. *Probabilistic Graphical Models: Principles and Techniques*. MIT Press, 2009. Cited on page(s) 31

Grzegorz Kondrak. A new algorithm for the alignment of phonetic sequences. In *Proceedings of the First Conference on North American Chapter of the Association for Computational Linguistics*, pages 288–295, Seattle, Washington, USA, May 2000. Cited on page(s) 19

Terry Koo and Michael Collins. Hidden-variable models for discriminative reranking. In *Proceedings of Human Language Technology Conference and Conference on Empirical Methods in Natural Language Processing*, pages 507–514, Vancouver, British Columbia, Canada, October 2005. DOI: 10.3115/1220575.1220639 Cited on page(s) 143

Terry Koo and Michael Collins. Efficient third-order dependency parsers. In *Proceedings of the 48th Annual Meeting of the Association for Computational Linguistics*, pages 1–11, Uppsala, Sweden, July 2010. Cited on page(s) 92

Terry Koo, Amir Globerson, Xavier Carreras, and Michael Collins. Structured prediction models via the matrix-tree theorem. In *Proceedings of the Joint Conference on Empirical Methods in Natural Language Processing and Computational Natural Language Learning*, pages 141–150, Prague, Czech Republic, June 2007. Cited on page(s) 150, 162

Terry Koo, Xavier Carreras, and Michael Collins. Simple semi-supervised dependency parsing. In *Proceedings of the 46th Annual Meeting of the Association for Computational Linguistics: Human Language Technologies*, pages 595–603, Columbus, Ohio, USA, June 2008. Cited on page(s) 92

Robert A. Kowalski. The early years of logic programming. *Communications of the ACM*, 31(1): 38–43, January 1988. DOI: 10.1145/35043.35046 Cited on page(s) 41

Sandra Kübler, Ryan McDonald, and Joakim Nivre. *Dependency Parsing*. Morgan and Claypool, 2009. Cited on page(s) 66

Harold W. Kuhn. The Hungarian method for the assignment problem. *Naval Research Logistic Quarterly*, 2:83–97, 1955. DOI: 10.1002/nav.3800020109 Cited on page(s) 65

Shankar Kumar and William Byrne. Minimum Bayes-risk decoding for statistical machine translation. In *Proceedings of the Human Language Technology Conference of the North American Chapter of the Association for Computational Linguistics*, pages 169–176, Boston, Massachusetts, USA, May 2004. Cited on page(s) 164

Simon Lacoste-Julien, Ben Taskar, Dan Klein, and Michael I. Jordan. Word alignment via quadratic assignment. In *Proceedings of the Human Language Technology Conference of the North American Chapter of the Association for Computational Linguistics*, pages 112–119, New York City, USA, June 2006. DOI: 10.3115/1220835.1220850 Cited on page(s) 67, 165

John D. Lafferty, Andrew McCallum, and Fernando C. N. Pereira. Conditional random fields: Probabilistic models for segmenting and labeling sequence data. In *Proceedings of the 18th International Conference on Machine Learning*, pages 282–289, Williamstown, Massachusetts, USA, June–July 2001. Cited on page(s) 89, 90, 206

Yan LeCun, Léon Bottou, Yoshua Bengio, and Patrick Haffner. Gradient-based learning applied to document recognition. *Proceedings of the IEEE*, 86(11):2278–2324, 1998. DOI: 10.1109/5.726791 Cited on page(s) 175

V. I. Levenshtein. Binary codes capable of correcting spurious insertions and deletions of ones. *Problems of Information Transmission*, 1:8–17, 1965. Cited on page(s) 49, 50

Percy Liang and Michael I. Jordan. An asymptotic analysis of generative, discriminative, and pseudolikelihood estimators. In *Proceedings of the 25th International Conference on Machine Learning*, pages 584–591, Helsinki, Finland, July 2008. DOI: 10.1145/1390156.1390230 Cited on page(s) 99

Percy Liang and Dan Klein. Online EM for unsupervised models. In *Proceedings of the Human Language Technologies Conference of the North American Chapter of the Association for Computational Linguistics*, pages 611–619, Boulder, Colorado, USA, June 2009. Cited on page(s) 123, 175

Percy Liang, Alexandre Bouchard-Côté, Dan Klein, and Ben Taskar. An end-to-end discriminative approach to machine translation. In *Proceedings of the 21st International Conference on Computational Linguistics and 44th Annual Meeting of the Association for Computational Linguistics*, pages 761–768, Sydney, Australia, July 2006. DOI: 10.3115/1220175.1220271 Cited on page(s) 18

Percy Liang, Slav Petrov, Michael Jordan, and Dan Klein. The infinite PCFG using hierarchical Dirichlet processes. In *Proceedings of the Joint Conference on Empirical Methods in Natural Language Processing and Computational Natural Language Learning*, pages 688–697, Prague, Czech Republic, June 2007. Cited on page(s) 139

Percy Liang, Hal Daumé, and Dan Klein. Structure compilation: Trading structure for features. In *Proceedings of the 25th International Conference on Machine Learning*, pages 592–599, Helsinki, Finland, July 2008. DOI: 10.1145/1390156.1390231 Cited on page(s) 92

Percy Liang, Michael I. Jordan, and Dan Klein. Learning dependency-based compositional semantics. In *Proceedings of the 49th Annual Meeting of the Association for Computational Linguistics*, Portland, Oregon, USA, June 2011. To appear. Cited on page(s) 13

Jimmy Lin and Chris Dyer. *Data-Intensive Text Processing with MapReduce*. Morgan and Claypool, 2010. Cited on page(s) 20

Dong C. Liu and Jorge Nocedal. On the limited memory method for large scale optimization. *Mathematical Programming B*, 45(3):503–528, 1989. DOI: 10.1007/BF01589116 Cited on page(s) 177

John Wylie Lloyd. *Foundations of Logic Programming*. Springer-Verlag, second edition, 1987. Cited on page(s) 41

Bruce T. Lowerre. *The Harpy Speech Recognition System*. PhD thesis, Carnegie Mellon University, 1976. Cited on page(s) 62

Robert Malouf. A comparison of algorithms for maximum entropy parameter estimation. In *Proceedings of the 6th Workshop on Computational Natural Language Learning*, Taipei, Taiwan, August–September 2002. DOI: 10.3115/1118853.1118871 Cited on page(s) 177

Christopher D. Manning and Hinrich Schütze. *Foundations of Statistical Natural Language Processing*. MIT Press, 1999. Cited on page(s) xv

Christopher D. Manning, Prabhakar Raghavan, and Hinrich Schütze. *Introduction to Information Retrieval*. Cambridge University Press, 2008. Cited on page(s) 1

Yi Mao and Guy Lebanon. Generalized isotonic conditional random fields. *Machine Learning*, 77: 225–248, 2009. DOI: 10.1007/s10994-009-5139-1 Cited on page(s) 16

Mitchell P. Marcus, Beatrice Santorini, and Mary Ann Marcinkiewicz. Building a large annotated corpus of English: the Penn treebank. *Computational Linguistics*, 19(2):313–330, 1993. Cited on page(s) 9, 10

André F. T. Martins, Noah A. Smith, and Eric P. Xing. Concise integer linear programming formulations for dependency parsing. In *Proceedings of the Joint Conference of the 47th Annual Meeting of the Association for Computational Linguistics and the 4th International Joint Conference on Natural Language Processing of the Asian Federation of Natural Language Processing*, pages 342–350, Singapore, August 2009. DOI: 10.3115/1687878.1687928 Cited on page(s) 37, 92

André F. T. Martins, Kevin Gimpel, Noah A. Smith, Eric P. Xing, Pedro M. Q. Aguiar, and Mário A. T. Figueiredo. Learning structured classifiers with dual coordinate descent. Technical report, Carnegie Mellon University, 2010. Cited on page(s) 134, 177, 178

Takuya Matsuzaki, Yusuke Miyao, and Jun'ichi Tsujii. Probabilistic CFG with latent annotations. In *Proceedings of the 43rd Annual Meeting of the Association of Computational Linguistics*, pages 75–82, Ann Arbor, Michigan, USA, June 2005. DOI: 10.3115/1219840.1219850 Cited on page(s) 142, 165, 166

David McAllester. On the complexity analysis of static analyses. *Journal of the ACM*, 49(4):512–537, 2002. DOI: 10.1145/581771.581774 Cited on page(s) 52

David McAllester, Michael Collins, and Fernando C. N. Pereira. Case-factor diagrams for structured probabilistic modeling. In *Proceedings of the 20th Conference on Uncertainty in Artificial Intelligence*, pages 382–391, Banff, Alberta, Canada, July 2004. DOI: 10.1016/j.jcss.2007.04.015 Cited on page(s) 41

Andrew McCallum. Efficiently inducing features of conditional random fields. In *Proceedings of the 19th Conference in Uncertainty in Artificial Intelligence*, pages 403–410, Acapulco, Mexico, August 2003. Cited on page(s) 92

Andrew McCallum, Dayne Freitag, and Fernando Pereira. Maximum entropy Markov models for information extraction and segmentation. In *Proceedings of the 17th International Conference on Machine Learning*, pages 591–598, Stanford, California, USA, June–July 2000. Cited on page(s) 204, 208

Ryan McDonald. Discriminative sentence compression with soft syntactic evidence. In *Proceedings of the Eleventh Conference of the European Chapter of the Association for Computational Linguistics*, pages 297–304, Trento, Italy, April 2006. Cited on page(s) 18

Ryan McDonald and Fernando Pereira. Online learning of approximate dependency parsing algorithms. In *Proceedings of the Eleventh Conference of the European Chapter of the Association for Computational Linguistics*, pages 81–88, Trento, Italy, April 2006. Cited on page(s) 92

Ryan McDonald and Giorgio Satta. On the complexity of non-projective data-driven dependency parsing. In *Proceedings of the Tenth International Conference on Parsing Technologies*, pages 121–132, Prague, Czech Republic, June 2007. DOI: 10.3115/1621410.1621426 Cited on page(s) 66, 150

Ryan McDonald, Koby Crammer, and Fernando Pereira. Online large-margin training of dependency parsers. In *Proceedings of the 43rd Annual Meeting of the Association of Computational Linguistics*, pages 91–98, Ann Arbor, Michigan, USA, June 2005a. DOI: 10.3115/1219840.1219852 Cited on page(s) 177

Ryan McDonald, Fernando Pereira, Kiril Ribarov, and Jan Hajič. Non-projective dependency parsing using spanning tree algorithms. In *Proceedings of Human Language Technology Conference and Conference on Empirical Methods in Natural Language Processing*, pages 523–530, Vancouver, British Columbia, Canada, October 2005b. DOI: 10.3115/1220575.1220641 Cited on page(s) 66

Ryan McDonald, Kerry Hannan, Tyler Neylon, Mike Wells, and Jeff Reynar. Structured models for fine-to-coarse sentiment analysis. In *Proceedings of the 45th Annual Meeting of the Association of Computational Linguistics*, pages 432–439, Prague, Czech Republic, June 2007. Cited on page(s) 16

Quinn McNemar. Note on the sampling error of the difference between correlated proportions or percentages. *Psychometrika*, 12(2):153–157, 1947. DOI: 10.1007/BF02295996 Cited on page(s) 195

I. Dan Melamed. Models of translational equivalence among words. *Computational Linguistics*, 26 (2):221–249, 2000. DOI: 10.1162/089120100561683 Cited on page(s) 65

Bernardo Merialdo. Tagging English text with a probabilistic model. *Computational Linguistics*, 20 (2):155–72, 1994. Cited on page(s) 120

Daichi Mochihashi, Takeshi Yamada, and Naonori Ueda. Bayesian unsupervised word segmentation with nested Pitman-Yor language modeling. In *Proceedings of the Joint Conference of the 47th Annual*

Meeting of the Association for Computational Linguistics and the 4th International Joint Conference on Natural Language Processing of the Asian Federation of Natural Language Processing, pages 100–108, Singapore, August 2009. Cited on page(s) 163

Mehryar Mohri. Semiring frameworks and algorithms for shortest-distance problems. *Journal of Automata, Languages and Combinatorics*, 7(3):321–350, 2002. Cited on page(s) 48

Mehryar Mohri. Finite-state transducers in language and speech processing. *Computational Linguistics*, 23(2):269–311, 1997. Cited on page(s) 204

Richard Montague. The proper treatment of quantification in ordinary English. In Jaakko Hintikka, Julius Moravcsik, and Patrick Suppes, editors, *Approaches to Natural Language*, pages 221–242. Dordrecht, 1973. Cited on page(s) 13

Raymond J. Mooney. Inductive logic programming for natural language processing. In Stephen Muggleton, editor, *Inductive Logic Programming: Selected Papers from the 6th International Workshop*, pages 3–22. Springer, 1997. Cited on page(s) 13

Radford M. Neal and Geoffrey E. Hinton. A view of the EM algorithm that justifies incremental, sparse, and other variants. In Michael I. Jordan, editor, *Learning in Graphical Models*. MIT Press, 1998. Cited on page(s) 123, 171

Mark-Jan Nederhof. Weighted deductive parsing and Knuth's algorithm. *Computational Linguistics*, 29(1):135–143, 2003. DOI: 10.1162/089120103321337467 Cited on page(s) 43, 59

Andrew Y. Ng and Michael I. Jordan. On discriminative vs. generative classifiers: A comparison of logistic regression and naïve Bayes. In Thomas G. Dietterich, Suzanna Becker, and Zoubin Ghahramani, editors, *Advances in Neural Information Processing Systems 14*, pages 841–848. MIT Press, 2002. Cited on page(s) 99

Vincent Ng and Claire Cardie. Identifying anaphoric and non-anaphoric noun phrases to improve coreference resolution. In *Proceedings of the 19th International Conference on Computational Linguistics*, Taipei, Taiwan, August–September 2002. DOI: 10.3115/1072228.1072367 Cited on page(s) 14

Joakim Nivre, Johan Hall, and Jens Nilsson. Memory-based dependency parsing. In *Proceedings of the Eighth Conference on Computational Natural Language Learning*, pages 49–56, Boston, Massachusetts, USA, May 2004. Cited on page(s) 208

Joakim Nivre, Johan Hall, Sandra Kübler, Ryan McDonald, Jens Nilsson, Sebastian Riedel, and Deniz Yuret. The CoNLL 2007 shared task on dependency parsing. In *Proceedings of the Joint Conference on Empirical Methods in Natural Language Processing and Computational Natural Language Learning*, pages 915–932, Prague, Czech Republic, June 2007. Cited on page(s) 20

Jorge Nocedal and Stephen J. Wright. *Numerical Optimization.* Springer, second edition, 2006. Cited on page(s) 176

Martha Palmer, Daniel Gildea, and Paul Kingsbury. The Proposition Bank: An annotated corpus of semantic roles. *Computational Linguistics*, 31(1):71–105, 2005. DOI: 10.1162/0891201053630264 Cited on page(s) 14, 15

Bo Pang and Lillian Lee. A sentimental education: Sentiment analysis using subjectivity summarization based on minimum cuts. In *Proceedings of the 42nd Meeting of the Association for Computational Linguistics*, pages 271–278, Barcelona, Spain, July 2004. DOI: 10.3115/1218955.1218990 Cited on page(s) 4, 16, 67

Bo Pang and Lillian Lee. Opinion mining and sentiment analysis. *Foundations and Trends in Information Retrieval*, 2(1–2):1–135, 2008. DOI: 10.1561/1500000011 Cited on page(s) 16

Bo Pang, Lillian Lee, and Shivakumar Vaithyanathan. Thumbs up? sentiment classification using machine learning techniques. In *Proceedings of the Conference on Empirical Methods in Natural Language Processing*, pages 79–86, Philadelphia, Pennsylvania, USA, July 2002. Cited on page(s) 16

Kishore Papineni, Salim Roukos, Todd Ward, and Wei-Jing Zhu. Bleu: a method for automatic evaluation of machine translation. In *Proceedings of 40th Annual Meeting of the Association for Computational Linguistics*, pages 311–318, Philadelphia, Pennsylvania, USA, July 2002. DOI: 10.3115/1073083.1073135 Cited on page(s) 20, 197

Karl Pearson. On lines and planes of closest fit to systems of points in space. *Philosophical Magazine*, 2(6):559–572, 1901. Cited on page(s) 128

Ted Pedersen. Empiricism is not a matter of faith. *Computational Linguistics*, 34(3):465–470, 2008. DOI: 10.1162/coli.2008.34.3.465 Cited on page(s) 183

Fernando C. N. Pereira and Stuart M. Shieber. *Prolog and Natural Language Analysis.* Center for the Study of Language and Information, 1987. Cited on page(s) 52

Fernando C. N. Pereira and David H. D. Warren. Parsing as deduction. In *Proceedings of the 21st Annual Meeting of the Association for Computational Linguistics*, pages 137–144, Cambridge, Massachusetts, USA, June 1983. DOI: 10.3115/981311.981338 Cited on page(s) 52

Slav Petrov. *Coarse-to-Fine Natural Language Processing.* PhD thesis, University of California at Berkeley, 2009. Cited on page(s) 166

Slav Petrov and Dan Klein. Sparse multi-scale grammars for discriminative latent variable parsing. In *Proceedings of the Conference on Empirical Methods in Natural Language Processing*, pages 868–876, Honolulu, Hawaii, USA, October 2008. Cited on page(s) 11

Slav Petrov, Leon Barrett, Romain Thibaux, and Dan Klein. Learning accurate, compact, and interpretable tree annotation. In *Proceedings of the 21st International Conference on Computational Linguistics and 44th Annual Meeting of the Association for Computational Linguistics*, pages 433–440, Sydney, Australia, July 2006. DOI: 10.3115/1220175.1220230 Cited on page(s) 64, 142, 166

Hoifung Poon and Pedro Domingos. Joint unsupervised coreference resolution with Markov logic. In *Proceedings of the Conference on Empirical Methods in Natural Language Processing*, pages 650–659, Honolulu, Hawaii, USA, October 2008. DOI: 10.3115/1613715.1613796 Cited on page(s) 16

Martin F. Porter. An algorithm for suffix stripping. *Program*, 14(3):130–137, 1980. DOI: 10.1108/eb046814 Cited on page(s) 5

Rashmi Prasad, Nikhil Dinesh, Alan Lee, Eleni Miltsakaki, Livio Robaldo, Aravind Joshi, and Bonnie Webber. The Penn discourse treebank 2.0. In *Proceedings of the Sixth International Language Resources and Evaluation*, pages 2961–2968, Marrakech, Morocco, May 2008. Cited on page(s) 17

Detlef Prescher. Head-driven PCFGs with latent-head statistics. In *Proceedings of the Ninth International Workshop on Parsing Technology*, pages 115–124, Vancouver, British Columbia, Canada, October 2005. DOI: 10.3115/1654494.1654506 Cited on page(s) 142

Vasin Punyakanok, Dan Roth, Wen-tau Yih, and Dav Zimak. Semantic role labeling via integer linear programming inference. In *Proceedings of the 20th International Conference on Computational Linguistics*, pages 1346–1352, Geneva, Switzerland, August 2004. DOI: 10.3115/1220355.1220552 Cited on page(s) 37

Ariadna Quattoni, Sybor Wang, Louis-Phillipe Morency, Michael Collins, and Trevor Darrell. Hidden-state conditional random fields. *IEEE Transactions on Pattern Analysis and Machine Intelligence*, 29(10):1848–1852, 2007. DOI: 10.1109/TPAMI.2007.1124 Cited on page(s) 143

Daniel R. Rashid and Noah A. Smith. Relative keyboard input system. In *Proceedings of the International Conference on Intelligent User Interfaces*, pages 397–400, Canary Islands, Spain, January 2008. DOI: 10.1145/1378773.1378839 Cited on page(s) 2

Nathan Ratliff, J. Andrew Bagnell, and Martin Zinkevich. Subgradient methods for maximum margin structured learning. In *Proceedings of the International Conference on Machine Learning Workshop on Learning in Structured Output Spaces*, Pittsburgh, Pennsylvania, USA, 2006. Cited on page(s) 105, 174

Adwait Ratnaparkhi. A maximum entropy model for part-of-speech tagging. In *Proceedings of the Conference on Empirical Methods in Natural Language Processing*, pages 133–142, Philadelphia, Pennsylvania, USA, May 1996. Cited on page(s) 208

Adwait Ratnaparkhi. A simple introduction to maximum entropy models for natural language processing. Technical Report IRCS-97-08, University of Pennsylvania Institute for Research in Cognitive Science, 1997. Cited on page(s) 202

Philip Resnik and Eric Hardisty. Gibbs sampling for the uninitiated. Technical Report CS-TR-4956, University of Maryland Computer Science Department, 2010. URL `http://hdl.handle.net/1903/10058`. Cited on page(s) 132

Jeffrey C. Reynar and Adwait Ratnaparkhi. A maximum entropy approach to identifying sentence boundaries. In *Proceedings of the Fifth Conference on Applied Natural Language Processing*, Washington, DC, USA, March–April 1997. DOI: 10.3115/974557.974561 Cited on page(s) 4

Sebastian Riedel and James Clarke. Incremental integer linear programming for non-projective dependency parsing. In *Proceedings of the Conference on Empirical Methods in Natural Language Processing*, pages 129–137, Sydney, Australia, 2006. DOI: 10.3115/1610075.1610095 Cited on page(s) 37

Stefan Riezler, Detlef Prescher, Jonas Kuhn, and Mark Johnson. Lexicalized stochastic modeling of constraint-based grammars using log-linear measures and EM training. In *Proceedings of the 38th Annual Meeting of the Association for Computational Linguistics*, Hong Kong, October 2000. DOI: 10.3115/1075218.1075279 Cited on page(s) 11

Ellen Riloff and Janyce Wiebe. Learning extraction patterns for subjective expressions. In *Proceedings of the Conference on Empirical Methods in Natural Language Processing*, pages 105–112, Sapporo, Japan, July 2003. DOI: 10.3115/1119355.1119369 Cited on page(s) 19

Jorma Rissanen. Modeling by shortest data description. *Automatica*, 14(5):465–471, 1978. DOI: 10.1016/0005-1098(78)90005-5 Cited on page(s) 81, 134

Christian P. Robert and George Casella. *Monte Carlo Statistical Methods*. Springer, second edition, 2004. Cited on page(s) 132

Emmanuel Roche and Yves Schabes, editors. *Finite-State Language Processing*. MIT Press, 1997. Cited on page(s) 204

Kenneth Rose, Eitan Gurewitz, and Geoffrey C. Fox. Statistical mechanics and phase transitions in clustering. *Physical Review Letters*, 65(8):945–948, 1990. DOI: 10.1103/PhysRevLett.65.945 Cited on page(s) 123

Azriel Rosenfeld. *An Introduction to Algebraic Structures*. Holden-Day, 1968. Cited on page(s) 49

Roni Rosenfeld. *Adaptive Statistical Language Modeling: A Maximum Entropy Approach*. PhD thesis, Carnegie Mellon University, 1994. Cited on page(s) 179

Roni Rosenfeld, Stanley F. Chen, and Xiaojin Zhu. Whole-sentence exponential language models: A vehicle for linguistic-statistical integration. *Computer Speech and Language*, 15(1):55–73, 2001. DOI: 10.1006/csla.2000.0159 Cited on page(s) 85

Dan Roth and Wen-tau Yih. A linear programming formulation for global inference in natural language tasks. In *Proceedings of the Eighth Conference on Computational Natural Language Learning*, pages 1–8, Boston, Massachusetts, USA, May 2004. Cited on page(s) 37

Alexander M. Rush, David Sontag, Michael Collins, and Tommi Jaakkola. On dual decomposition and linear programming relaxations for natural language processing. In *Proceedings of the Conference on Empirical Methods in Natural Language Processing*, pages 1–11, Cambridge, MA, USA, October 2010. Cited on page(s) 67

Lawrence Saul and Fernando Pereira. Aggregate and mixed-order Markov models for statistical language processing. In *Proceedings of the Second Conference on Empirical Methods in Natural Language Processing*, pages 81–89, Providence, Rhode Island, USA, August 1997. Cited on page(s) 112

Bernhard Schölkopf and Alexander J. Smola. *Learning with Kernels: Support Vector Machines, Regularization, Optimization, and Beyond.* MIT Press, 2001. Cited on page(s) 99

Gideon E. Schwarz. Estimating the dimension of a model. *Annals of Statistics*, 6(2):461–464, 1978. DOI: 10.1214/aos/1176344136 Cited on page(s) 134

Shai Shalev-Schwartz and Yoram Singer. Online learning meets optimization in the dual. In Gabor Lugosi and Hans Ulrich Simon, editors, *Proceedings of the Nineteenth Annual Conference on Learning Theory*, number 4005 in Lecture Notes in Artificial Intelligence, pages 423–427, Pittsburgh, Pennsylvania, USA, 2006. Cited on page(s) 177

Stuart M. Shieber, Yves Schabes, and Fernando C. N. Pereira. Principles and implementation of deductive parsing. *Journal of Logic Programming*, 24(1–2):3–36, 1995. DOI: 10.1016/0743-1066(95)00035-I Cited on page(s) 52, 59

Solomon Eyal Shimony. Finding MAPs for belief networks is NP-hard. *Artificial Intelligence*, 68 (2):399–410, 1994. DOI: 10.1016/0004-3702(94)90072-8 Cited on page(s) 31

Naum Zuselevich Shor. *Minimization Methods for Non-Differentiable Functions.* Springer, 1985. Cited on page(s) 174

Klaas Sikkel. *Parsing Schemata.* PhD thesis, University of Twente, 1993. Cited on page(s) 52

Khalil Sima'an. Computatoinal complexity of probabilistic disambiguation. *Grammars*, 5(2):125–151, 2002. DOI: 10.1023/A:1016340700671 Cited on page(s) 165

David A. Smith and Jason Eisner. Dependency parsing by belief propagation. In *Proceedings of the Conference on Empirical Methods in Natural Language Processing*, pages 145–156, Honolulu, Hawaii, USA, October 2008. DOI: 10.3115/1613715.1613737 Cited on page(s) 162

David A. Smith and Noah A. Smith. Bilingual parsing with factored estimation: Using English to parse Korean. In *Proceedings of the Conference on Empirical Methods in Natural Language Processing*, pages 49–56, Barcelona, Spain, July 2004. Cited on page(s) 18

David A. Smith and Noah A. Smith. Probabilistic models of nonprojective dependency trees. In *Proceedings of the Joint Conference on Empirical Methods in Natural Language Processing and Computational Natural Language Learning*, pages 132–140, Prague, Czech Republic, June 2007. Cited on page(s) 150, 162

Noah A. Smith. *Novel Estimation Methods for Unsupervised Discovery of Latent Structure in Natural Language Text*. PhD thesis, Johns Hopkins University, 2006. Cited on page(s) 124

Noah A. Smith and Jason Eisner. Annealing techniques for unsupervised statistical language learning. In *Proceedings of the 42nd Meeting of the Association for Computational Linguistics*, pages 487–494, Barcelona, Spain, July 2004. DOI: 10.3115/1218955.1219017 Cited on page(s) 123

Noah A. Smith and Jason Eisner. Contrastive estimation: Training log-linear models on unlabeled data. In *Proceedings of the 43rd Annual Meeting of the Association of Computational Linguistics*, pages 354–362, Ann Arbor, Michigan, USA, June 2005. DOI: 10.3115/1219840.1219884 Cited on page(s) 124

Noah A. Smith and Jason Eisner. Annealing structural bias in multilingual weighted grammar induction. In *Proceedings of the 21st International Conference on Computational Linguistics and 44th Annual Meeting of the Association for Computational Linguistics*, pages 569–576, Sydney, Australia, July 2006. DOI: 10.3115/1220175.1220247 Cited on page(s) 123

Noah A. Smith and Mark Johnson. Weighted and probabilistic context-free grammars are equally expressive. *Computational Linguistics*, 33(4):577–491, 2007. DOI: 10.1162/coli.2007.33.4.477 Cited on page(s) 206

Noah A. Smith, Douglas L. Vail, and John D. Lafferty. Computationally efficient M-estimation of log-linear structure models. In *Proceedings of the 45th Annual Meeting of the Association of Computational Linguistics*, pages 752–759, Prague, Czech Republic, June 2007. Cited on page(s) 85

Rion Snow, Daniel Jurafsky, and Andrew Y. Ng. Semantic taxonomy induction from heterogenous evidence. In *Proceedings of the 21st International Conference on Computational Linguistics and 44th Annual Meeting of the Association for Computational Linguistics*, pages 801–808, Sydney, Australia, July 2006. DOI: 10.3115/1220175.1220276 Cited on page(s) 19

Benjamin Snyder, Tahira Naseem, Jacob Eisenstein, and Regina Barzilay. Unsupervised multilingual learning for POS tagging. In *Proceedings of the Conference on Empirical Methods in Natural Language Processing*, pages 1041–1050, Honolulu, Hawaii, USA, October 2008. DOI: 10.3115/1613715.1613851 Cited on page(s) 18

Richard Sproat and Thomas Emerson. The first international Chinese word segmentation bakeoff. In *The Second SIGHAN Workshop on Chinese Language Processing*, Sapporo, Japan, July 2003. DOI: 10.3115/1119250.1119269 Cited on page(s) 4

Andreas Stolcke. An efficient probabilistic context-free parsing algorithm that computes prefix probabilities. *Computational Linguistics*, 21(2):165–201, 1995. Cited on page(s) 58

Charles Sutton and Andrew McCallum. Collective segmentation and labeling of distant entities in information extraction. In *Proceedings of the International Conference on Machine Learning Workshop on Statistical Relational Learning and its Connections to Other Fields*, Banff, Alberta, Canada, July 2004. Cited on page(s) 162

Charles Sutton and Andrew McCallum. Piecewise pseudolikelihood for efficient CRF training. In *Proceedings of the 24th International Conference on Machine Learning*, pages 863–870, Corvalis, Oregon, USA, 2007. DOI: 10.1145/1273496.1273605 Cited on page(s) 98

Charles Sutton, Andrew McCallum, and Khashayar Rohanimanesh. Dynamic conditional random fields: Factorized probabilistic models for labeling and segmenting sequence data. *Journal of Machine Learning Research*, 8:693–723, 2007. Cited on page(s) 143

Robert E. Tarjan. Finding optimum branchings. *Networks*, 7:25–35, 1977. DOI: 10.1002/net.3230070103 Cited on page(s) 66

Ben Taskar, Vassil Chatalbashev, and Daphne Koller. Learning associative Markov networks. In *Proceedings of the 21st International Conference on Machine Learning*, pages 102–109, Banff, Alberta, Canada, July 2004a. DOI: 10.1145/1015330.1015444 Cited on page(s) 34

Ben Taskar, Carlos Guestrin, and Daphne Koller. Max-margin Markov networks. In Sebastian Thrun, Lawrence Saul, and Bernhard Schölkopf, editors, *Advances in Neural Information Processing Systems 16*. MIT Press, 2004b. Cited on page(s) 103, 105

Yee Whye Teh. A hierarchical Bayesian language model based on Pitman-Yor processes. In *Proceedings of the 21st International Conference on Computational Linguistics and 44th Annual Meeting of the Association for Computational Linguistics*, pages 985–992, Sydney, Australia, July 2006. DOI: 10.3115/1220175.1220299 Cited on page(s) 137, 139

Yee Whye Teh, Michael Jordan, Matthew Beal, and David Blei. Hierarchical Dirichlet processes. In Lawrence K. Saul, Yair Weiss, and Léon Bottou, editors, *Advances in Neural Information Processing Systems 17*. MIT Press, 2005. Cited on page(s) 138

Kristina Toutanova, Dan Klein, Christopher D. Manning, and Yoram Singer. Feature-rich part-of-speech tagging with a cyclic dependency network. In *Proceedings of the Human Language Technology Conference of the North American Chapter of the Association for Computational Linguistics*, pages 252–259, Edmonton, Alberta, Canada, May–June 2003. Cited on page(s) 6, 98

Ioannis Tsochantaridis, Thomas Hofmann, Thorsten Joachims, and Yasemin Altun. Support vector machine learning for interdependent and structured output spaces. In *Proceedings of the 21st International Conference on Machine Learning*, pages 104–111, Banff, Alberta, Canada, July 2004. DOI: 10.1145/1015330.1015341 Cited on page(s) 104, 105

Peter Turney. Thumbs up or thumbs down? semantic orientation applied to unsupervised classification of reviews. In *Proceedings of 40th Annual Meeting of the Association for Computational Linguistics*, pages 417–424, Philadelphia, Pennsylvania, USA, July 2002. DOI: 10.3115/1073083.1073153 Cited on page(s) 16

W. T. Tutte. *Graph Theory*. Addison-Wesley, 1984. Cited on page(s) 150

Naonori Ueda and Ryohei Nakano. Deterministic annealing EM algorithm. *Neural Networks*, 11 (2):271–282, 1998. DOI: 10.1016/S0893-6080(97)00133-0 Cited on page(s) 123

Leslie G. Valiant. The complexity of computing the permanent. *Theoretical Computer Science*, 8: 189–201, 1979. DOI: 10.1016/0304-3975(79)90044-6 Cited on page(s) 150

K. Vijay-Shanker, David J. Weir, and Aravind K. Joshi. Characterizing structural descriptions produced by various grammatical formalisms. In *Proceedings of the 25th Annual Meeting of the Association for Computational Linguistics*, pages 104–111, Stanford, California, USA, July 1987. DOI: 10.3115/981175.981190 Cited on page(s) 37

Andrew J. Viterbi. Error bounds for convolutional codes and an asymptotically optimum decoding algorithm. *IEEE Transactions on Information Theory*, 13(2):260–269, 1967. DOI: 10.1109/TIT.1967.1054010 Cited on page(s) 52

Martin J. Wainwright and Michael I. Jordan. *Graphical Models, Exponential Families, and Variational InferencE*. Number 1 in Foundations and Trends in Machine Learning. Now Publishers, 2008. Cited on page(s) 134

Martin J. Wainwright, Tommi S. Jaakkola, and Alan S. Willsky. MAP estimation via agreement on (hyper)trees: Message-passing and linear programming approaches. Technical Report UCB/CSD-03-1269, EECS Department, University of California, Berkeley, 2003. Cited on page(s) 34

Abraham Wald. Tests of statistical hypotheses concerning several parameters when the number of observations is large. *Transactions of the American Mathematical Society*, 54:426–482, 1943. DOI: 10.1090/S0002-9947-1943-0012401-3 Cited on page(s) 192

Mengqiu Wang, Noah A. Smith, and Teruko Mitamura. What is the Jeopardy model? a quasi-synchronous grammar for QA. In *Proceedings of the Joint Conference on Empirical Methods in Natural Language Processing and Computational Natural Language Learning*, pages 22–32, Prague, Czech Republic, June 2007. Cited on page(s) 143

Larry Wasserman. *All of Statistics: A Concise Course in Statistical Inference*. Springer, 2004. Cited on page(s) 188

Warren Weaver. Translation. In William N. Locke and A. Donald Booth, editors, *Machine Translation of Languages: Fourteen Essays*, pages 15–23. Technology Press of the Massachusetts Institute of Technology, John Wiley and Sons, and Chapman and Hall, 1949. Collection published in 1955. Cited on page(s) xiv

Bonnie Webber, Markus Egg, and Valia Kordoni. Discourse structure: Theory, practice and use, 2010. Tutorial available at `http://www.coli.uni-saarland.de/~kordoni/ACL10Tutorial-T6-DiscourseStructure.pdf`. Cited on page(s) 17

David Weiss and Ben Taskar. Structured prediction cascades. In *Proceedings of the 13th International Conference on Artificial Intelligence and Statistics*, pages 916–923, Sardinia, Italy, May 2010. Cited on page(s) 64

Frank Wilcoxon. Individual comparisons by ranking methods. *Biometrics Bulletin*, 1(6):80–83, 1945. DOI: 10.2307/3001968 Cited on page(s) 193

Theresa Wilson, Janyce Wiebe, and Paul Hoffmann. Recognizing contextual polarity in phrase-level sentiment analysis. In *Proceedings of Human Language Technology Conference and Conference on Empirical Methods in Natural Language Processing*, pages 347–354, Vancouver, British Columbia, Canada, October 2005. DOI: 10.3115/1220575.1220619 Cited on page(s) 16

Florian Wolf and Edward Gibson. Representing discourse coherence: A corpus-based study. *Computational Linguistics*, 31(2):249–287, 2005. DOI: 10.1162/0891201054223977 Cited on page(s) 16

Yuk Wah Wong and Raymond Mooney. Learning synchronous grammars for semantic parsing with lambda calculus. In *Proceedings of the 45th Annual Meeting of the Association of Computational Linguistics*, pages 960–967, Prague, Czech Republic, June 2007. Cited on page(s) 13

C. F. Jeff Wu. On the convergence properties of the EM algorithm. *Annals of Statistics*, 11(1): 95–103, 1983. DOI: 10.1214/aos/1176346060 Cited on page(s) 122

Dekai Wu. Stochastic inversion transduction grammars and bilingual parsing of parallel corpora. *Computational Linguistics*, 23(3):377–404, 1997. Cited on page(s) 18

Kenji Yamada and Kevin Knight. A syntax-based statistical translation model. In *Proceedings of 39th Annual Meeting of the Association for Computational Linguistics*, pages 523–530, Toulouse, France, July 2001. DOI: 10.3115/1073012.1073079 Cited on page(s) 18

David Yarowsky. Word-sense disambiguation using statistical models of Roget's categories trained on large corpora. In *Proceedings of the 14th International Conference On Computational Linguistics*, pages 454–460, Nantes, France, 1992. DOI: 10.3115/992133.992140 Cited on page(s) 14

David Yarowsky and Grace Ngai. Inducing multilingual POS taggers and NP bracketers via robust projection across aligned corpora. In *Second Meeting of the North American Chapter of the Association for Computational Linguistics*, pages 200–207, Pittsburgh, Pennsylvania, USA, June 2001. DOI: 10.3115/1073336.1073362 Cited on page(s) 18

Alexander Yeh. More accurate tests for the statistical significance of result differences. In *Proceedings of the 18th International Conference on Computational Linguistics*, pages 947–953, Saarbrücken, Germany, July–August 2000. DOI: 10.3115/992730.992783 Cited on page(s) 190

Daniel H. Younger. Recognition and parsing of context-free languages in time n^3. *Information and Control*, 10(2), 1967. DOI: 10.1016/S0019-9958(67)80007-X Cited on page(s) 54

Chun-Nam John Yu and Thorsten Joachims. Learning structural SVMs with latent variables. In *Proceedings of the 26th International Conference on Machine Learning*, Montréal, Québec, Canada, 2009. DOI: 10.1145/1553374.1553523 Cited on page(s) 143

John M. Zelle and Raymond J. Mooney. Learning to parse database queries using inductive logic programming. In *Proceedings of the 13th National Conference on Artificial Intelligence*, pages 1050–1055, Portland, Oregon, USA, August 1996. Cited on page(s) 13

Luke S. Zettlemoyer and Michael Collins. Learning to map sentences to logical form: Structured classification with probabilistic categorial grammars. In *Proceedings of the 21st Conference in Uncertainty in Artificial Intelligence*, pages 658–666, Edinburgh, UK, July 2005. Cited on page(s) 13

Xiaojin Zhu and Andrew B. Goldberg. *Introduction to Semi-Supervised Learning*. Morgan and Claypool, 2009. Cited on page(s) 109

George K. Zipf. *The Psychobiology of Language*. Houghton-Mifflin, 1935. Cited on page(s) 138

Author's Biography

NOAH A. SMITH

Noah A. Smith is an assistant professor in the Language Technologies Institute and Machine Learning Department at the School of Computer Science at Carnegie Mellon University. He received his Ph.D. in Computer Science from Johns Hopkins University (2006) and his B.S. in Computer Science and B.A. in Linguistics from the University of Maryland (2001). He was awarded a Hertz Foundation fellowship (2001–2006), served on the DARPA Computer Science Study Panel (2007) and the editorial board of the journal *Computational Linguistics*, and received a best paper award from the Association for Computational Linguistics (2009) and an NSF CAREER grant (2011). His research interests include statistical natural language processing, especially unsupervised methods, machine learning for structured data, and applications of natural language processing.

Index

Printed in the United States
by Baker & Taylor Publisher Services